THE

MONUMENTS

OF

EGYPT

THE NAPOLEONIC EDITION

THE COMPLETE ARCHAEOLOGICAL PLATES

FROM

LA DESCRIPTION DE L'EGYPTE

Edited with an Introduction
by
Charles Coulston Gillespie
Princeton University
and
Michel Dewachter
Collège de France

KONECKY&KONECKY

Konecky & Konecky
72 Ayers Point Rd.
Old Saybrook, CT 06475

This book was made possible by a generous grant from the J. Paul Getty Trust.

Professor Gillespie's research was supported by a National Endowment for the
Humanities Grant number RH-20741-86.

ISBN: 1-56852-265-7

Printed and bound in South Korea.

HISTORICAL INTRODUCTION

C. C. GILLISPIE

THE WORK

The *Description de l'Egypte* is itself a monument. Ten folio volumes and two atlases contain 837 copper engravings, many of them comprising multiple illustrations that number over 3,000 in all. Volumes I through V are devoted to antiquity. They gave a modern reading public the first comprehensive view of the architectural and artistic legacy of ancient Egypt. Two further volumes exhibit the artifacts and life of the country from the time of the Arab conquest in the seventh century until the French occupation of 1798–1801, and three more illustrate the natural history of the Nile Valley and the Red Sea coastal area.

The regular plates measure 20 by 26 old French inches, which were five percent longer than the English counterpart. An historical preface by the mathematician Joseph Fourier was bound separately and printed on paper of the same size, called *Jésus* in the trade. A hundred plates are of still more heroic dimensions, seventy-three of them 40 by 26, twenty-six 50 by 26, and one (the circular zodiac of Dendara, Volume IV, Plate 21) 42 by 30. No paper-maker had ever before been called on to produce these *Grand-Jésus* sheets, which were bound separately in the two supple-mentary atlases. A third atlas contains a topographical chart of Egypt and the Holy Land (then part of Syria) in forty-seven leaves drawn at a scale of 1:100,000, toge-ther with an overall map in three leaves at 1:1,000,000. In addition, nine volumes of memoirs, description, and commentary, averaging 800 pages each, may be con-sidered the point of departure of Egyptol-ogy as a field of study. Their format was in-folio *Grand-aigle*, dwarfing an ordinary book, easy to read but not to hold.

Subscribers might order a cabinet of mahogany veneer to accommodate the set. It was designed by the principal editor, Edme Jomard, executed by a leading cabi-netmaker, one Morel, rue Gaillon, and decorated by a sculptor, Dantan, rue du faubourg Saint-Denis. Its pilasters were carved in motifs of temples, lotus flowers,

and busts from Thebes and Dendara. Two basilisks framed a winged globe set in a cornice of lotus leaves. There were four-teen narrow shelves to hold the albums horizontally and a vertical slot for each volume of text. The top could be raised to form a reading rack. A model of this piece of furniture, which cost a thousand francs, went on display in a gallery of the Louvre in August 1827, the year before publication ended with the topographical atlas. The first installment bore the dateline 1809, the year when Napoleonic magnificence was at its zenith.

This colossal work was the creation not of archaeologists, nor of antiquarians, nor even, with a few exceptions, of artists, but for the most part of engineers together with several architects. They were fledgling engineers when they landed in Egypt, students and recent graduates of the Ecole polytechnique, the military engineering school founded in 1794, and of the Ecole des Ponts et Chaussées, the civil engineering school reorganized and revitalized at the same time. Drafting and surveying were major subjects in both cur-riculums. A graduate could be expected to sit down in front of a structure with draw-ing board, pencil, ruled paper, compass, and straight edge and produce a sketch from which to develop exact architectural plans, elevations, and sections. He would also measure off the site and the dimen-

1

sions with surveying instruments. Not that Napoleon Bonaparte had included these youngsters in the Expedition in order to produce the *Description de l'Egypte*; his staff recruited them with a view to their building roads, bridges, canals, and other public works, and to their collaborating on topography and cartography with the slightly older colleagues who already held military commissions in the Corps of Engineers.

They did do those things. What enthralled them, however, was Egypt, its sand-choked monuments, its stilled enigma, its petrified humanity. Egypt was their great adventure, and their engagement with it left a more lasting legacy than did the presence there of the famous scientists of Bonaparte's immediate entourage, Gaspard Monge, Claude-Louis Berthollet, and Fourier himself.

NAPOLEON
BONAPARTE

THE EGYPTIAN EXPEDITION

Bonaparte's expedition in Egypt, like his campaign in Italy in 1796–97, had, one will not say a cultural justification, but a cultural or, perhaps better, a constitutive component. Later conquests, after Bonaparte became Napoleon I in 1804, were by contrast merely imperial. But in that early part of his historical trajectory, his army was the bearer of the French Revolution, and his occupation of conquered territories turned them toward modernity. Italy was the making of his military reputation, legendary from the outset, and Egypt the interlude before seizing power, proconsular and as it turned out pre-Consular.

From the beginning, Bonaparte manifested an affinity for men of science, making courtiers and retainers of them and dispensing patronage even as Italian despots of the Renaissance had done with artists, creators of the culture characteristic of their time. "The Emperor," wrote Bourrienne years later, "liked only men who occupied themselves with positive, exact subjects...." In the first fine flush of Italian optimism, and hopes never entirely soured, the French came on as liberators and harbingers of national dignity. Enlightened civic sentiment rallied to their cause. Bonaparte flattered its representatives in Milan and other cities of northern Italy. He visited universities, sought out scientists, and took a hand in framing laws and constitutions for the Cispadane and the Cisalpine Republics, with which he replaced the crazy quilt of Austrian-ruled duchies.

Attached to his general staff was a civilian Commission of Science and Arts. Only later did its chief mission become the selection of works of art for removal from Italian collections to France. In the intervals of the campaign, Bonaparte preferred the conversation of its leading members, Monge and Berthollet, to the company of others of his entourage. When, exceeding his powers, he negotiated the treaty of Campo-Formio with the defeated Austrians, he chose two messengers, Monge and his chief of staff, General Alexandre Berthier, to carry the text to the Executive Directory, the governing body in Paris from 1795 to 1799. "We must," he charged the rulers of France, "esteem scientists and support science. Pray extend an equally honorable welcome to the distinguished general and the learned scientist. Both are a credit to the country and contribute to the reputation of France."

Following the trauma of the Terror, which ended with the overthrow of Robespierre in July 1794, the Directory failed to redeem the political credit of the French Revolution from impending bankruptcy. It offers a classic instance of an unstable regime increasingly at the mercy of military commanders upon whom it depended for victories abroad and protection against disorder and constitutional disintegration at home. Still, the time was not quite ripe for receivership when, on 5 December 1797, the 28-year-old Bonaparte returned from Italy to a triumph in Paris. The standard and too obvious explanation of the ensuing maneuvers is twofold. It is said that Bonaparte needed further stature beyond the fame acquired in one campaign, however brilliant, while the apprehensive Directory wished to remove so formidable a Praetorian from the political arena. The remaining opponent was England. After Campo-Formio, and while Bonaparte was still in Italy, the Directory gave him command of the army that would form to assault and destroy this first, last, and most implacable enemy of the Republic. An intensive reconnaissance of channel ports in January 1798 convinced him that an invasion could not succeed in the absence of naval superiority, which was unattainable. The alternative was Egypt.

History tends to be written according to the lights of the eventual victor, and historians have either ignored the rationale of the Egyptian expedition or else taken it for a piece of special pleading. Let us try to enter into the minds of the participants, however, if only that the campaign may seem less a strategic aberration than it otherwise might. For the choices that Bonaparte and his contemporaries made become comprehensible in the perspective of the history, not of Britain, but of classical antiquity. Awareness of such precedents informed the whole French Revolution. Think of Caesar winning consular and eventually imperial power in consequence of victories in distant regions. Think of Alexander conquering the very birthplace of civilization, to which now Bonaparte would restore science and the arts exiled during millenia of barbarism (see the Frontispiece). The memoir of 13 February 1798, in which Talleyrand, then foreign minister, commends the prospect to the Directory, opens with this language: "Egypt was a province of the Roman Republic; she must become a province of the French Republic. Roman rule saw the decadence of this beautiful country; French rule will bring it prosperity. The Romans wrested Egypt from kings distinguished in arts and science; the French will lift it from the hands of the most appalling tyrants who have ever existed."

Talleyrand meant the Mamelukes. An account of their regime appears in Volney's *Voyage en Syrie et en Egypte,* an early geopolitical work, perhaps the earliest, which enjoyed a fine success on its publication in 1787. And indeed, the natural history of human society exhibits few examples of adaptive hybridization more surprising than that of this colony of gorgeous but sterile Caucasian parasites, rulers of Egypt from the thirteenth through the eighteenth centuries. They had originated as a militia composed of slaves taken in infancy from Georgia and Turkestan by the Ayyubite dynasty in Cairo. Eventually they gathered their masters' power into their own hands, as their successors did that of the Ottoman Porte,

nominally suzerain in the centuries following the conquest of Egypt by Selim I in 1517. Horsemen, swordsmen, equally skilled with sabre and musket, they lived a sybaritic existence at the expense of the laboring population, upon whom they levied taxes and with whom they had nothing in common ethnically. The Egyptian *fellahin* suffered these exactions, mediated by the spiritual and moral authority of their own *ulemas,* as they did the raids of nomadic Arabs, the swirlings of sandstorms, and the depredations of locusts.

Mameluke feudalism was military but not hereditary. The elite kept harems in splendid palaces but established no families. Those born into Islam could not be slaves, and only slaves could be brought up to be warriors. Thus, until late in the eighteenth century they replenished their ranks by the purchase of Circassian boys in their homeland. By the time of the French occupation, the Mamelukes numbered some 9,000 men of arms commanded by twenty-four *beys* ever embroiled in factious and regional rivalries while holding the Pasha, hapless representative of the Turkish Sultan, a virtual prisoner in the citadel of Cairo. Their commercial oversight was corrupt and the tribute extorted from French merchants onerous. Though not, perhaps, the greatest of Mameluke barbarities in the eyes of Europeans, these practices did offer Talleyrand and the Directory a concrete pretext for Bonaparte's intervention.

Military intervention, then, was not merely an impulse imparted by Bonaparte's ambition. In a recent thesis on the intellectual origins of the Expedition, Henry Laurens argues that Bonaparte was simply the accident precipitating an eventuality that had been gathering for the better part of a century. French commercial interests in Egypt and the Near East were greater than those of any European power, and the area was the most important overseas sector for French trade after the Caribbean colonies. France maintained a general consulate in Cairo. There were thirty or forty French merchants and traders resident in Egypt. The foreign ministry trained and kept up a small corps of orientalists versed in Arabic and Turkish. Provision for the teaching of Oriental languages in Paris went back to the foun-

MONGE

dation of the Collège de France in the sixteenth century.

Statesmen had never reconciled themselves to the loss of the French position in India in the Seven Years War. For a moment in 1768, Choiseul, minister for foreign affairs, considered the prospect for seizing Egypt from the faltering hands of the Turks by way of compensation. The ancient access to Asia across the Isthmus of Suez would thus have been reopened. Officials in the ministry put similar projects before his successors on several occasions during the 1770s and 1780s. They were undoubtedly known to Talleyrand, already in the diplomatic service. Attitudes that would produce applause for such a venture in the name of a "civilizing mission" were fully formed at this, the culminating stage of the Enlightenment, which largely coincided with the descent of the Ottoman Empire into decadence.

The article on Egypt in the *Encyclopédie* of Diderot and d'Alembert contains this sentence: "It was once a country to be admired; nowadays it is one to be studied." Condorcet appears to have been the first leader of opinion to use the term "Occident," the West, in its modern sense, connoting the combination of cultural family with civilized norm. In Volney's account, despotism was the besetting vice of the Orient and liberty its greatest need, the precondition of prosperity and civic virtue. Already, the French distinguished between two colonial strategies. That of the British in India replaced native despotism by foreign oppression. The alternative, their own, would in principle constitute a liberating operation to the mutual benefit of both parties.

Such were the suppositions on which Fourier could draw in composing the "Préface historique" that commended the *Description de l'Egypte* to the public in 1809. Egypt was to have become, not simply a colony, but a French province. From the Mediterranean to Nubia, the country might "be considered an enormous garden" capable of supporting the most varied and valuable agricultural yields. Sugar cane, flax, and indigo (Talleyrand had already written off the American colonies) might be cultivated along with wheat, rice, and other cereals, which

Egypt produced abundantly. Soda, alkali, and mineral salts might be extracted from rich deposits of natron. Had the French remained, the local population would have devoted themselves to agriculture and enjoyed the fruits of their labor in full security. The introduction of mechanical inventions would have eased that labor and increased productivity. Arab tribes would have been settled on lands newly rendered fertile by rational irrigation, and the nomads would have been exiled to the desert. The Nile Valley above Aswan would have been explored and central Africa opened to trade in iron, gold, and raw materials of all sorts. Most important of all, the canal that had linked the Mediterranean to the Red Sea in antiquity would have been reconstructed. Let us cite the text of the engineering study that Fourier had before his eyes: "Suppose there were a strong and enlightened European government running the affairs of an industrious colony solidly established on the eastern side of the Mediterranean. It would have good harbors, powerful military forces, and ready communications by sea with the home country and overland with India. It is obvious that, no longer obliged like its rivals...to make the enormous detour around Africa, the country with such a colony would soon obtain a monopoly of the trade with India." The site for that colony must evidently be Egypt, and the Mediterranean was not too large a sea to become the maritime preserve of France and her continental allies.

THE COMMISSION OF SCIENCE AND ARTS

Fourier's words about what might have been—except for Nelson and the British fleet—were written in the knowledge that they would be censored by the Emperor. So they were, and modified in important respects at Napoleon's command. All the more do they represent official thinking. For if the notion of westernizing Egypt was not original with Bonaparte, the idea of accomplishing the task through the agency of an elaborate scientific and cultural detachment was certainly his. Apart from the small-scale precedent in Italy, nothing of the sort had ever before accompanied a military task force. On his return from Italy, Bonaparte had himself

BERTHOLLET

4

been elected to the Institute of France in the section of mechanics. In Egypt he styled his signature of civil decrees, "Bonaparte, Membre de l'Institut, Général en Chef."

The Directory reached its decision to authorize the Egyptian expedition in the first days of March 1798. On 19 May 1798, the main flotilla sailed from Toulon. It consisted of 13 ships of the line carrying 1,026 cannon; 42 frigates, brigs, and corsairs; and 130 transport vessels of all sorts. Aboard were 17,000 soldiers, an equal number of sailors and marines, 1,000 artillery pieces, 467 vehicles, and 700 horses. Three smaller convoys sailed from Genoa, Ajaccio, and Civita Vecchia, bringing the total armada to some 400 ships and 36,000 men. At sea, it covered a span of eight to ten kilometers.

Bonaparte had imagined, organized, and assembled that expeditionary force in ten weeks' time and in perfect secrecy. Thus, for example, the young lieutenant of engineers, Etienne Malus, received orders in Frankfurt detaching him from garrison duty and directing him to report to Toulon for service with the Left Wing of the Army of England. That was the code name. No one knew the real destination apart from Bonaparte's senior commanders, Kléber, Desaix, and Caffarelli du Falga, and the three senior members of the future Commission of Science and Arts, Monge, Berthollet, and Fourier.

Monge embarked with the troops under Desaix's command at Civita Vecchia, Bonaparte having commissioned him to requisition the printing press from the Office of Propaganda at the Vatican for the sake of its Arabic, Syriac, and Greek fonts, together with the personnel who could set type in those languages. The convoys joined off Malta. The island fell on 10 June with scarcely a struggle, and with it the feudal regime of the Knights of Saint John of Jerusalem, less brutal though no less anomalous than that of the Mamelukes in Egypt. Only at sea again did the rank and file learn their destination, though rumors had begun to run, the more briskly when several civilians fluent in Arabic were recruited in Malta.

Some 500 civilians of all ranks and vocations accompanied the Expedition. During the weeks of preparation, the names of about a third of that number appeared on varying lists as "scientists and artists attached to the Army of England." For the Commission of Science and Arts was formally constituted only after debarkation at Alexandria. In the opinion of Jean Edouard Goby, whose researches into these matters are the first and last word in precision, its membership at the outset consisted of 151 persons. He classified them as follows (with the number of students in each category in parenthesis):

FOURIER

Mathematicians	4	
Chemist	1	
Astronomers	3	(1)
Writers	3	
Economist	1	
Former Knight of Malta	1	
Archaeologists	2	(1)
Interpreters	8	
Surgeons	7	
Pharmacists	3	
Naturalists	7	(2)
Architects	4	
Artists	8	
Mining engineers	5	(3)
Surveyors	14	(7)
Civil engineers	14	(2)
Powdermakers	3	(2)
Mechanical engineers	3	
Shipbuilders	3	
Polytechnique students	13	(13)
Other students	5	(5)
Mechanics	9	
Printers	27	
Printers' wives	3	
TOTAL	151	(36)

Of that number, five—Monge, Berthollet, Fourier, Etienne Geoffroy Saint-Hilaire, and Déodat de Dolomieu—were established scientists. Monge and Berthollet, men in their fifties, the founders respectively of descriptive geometry and physical chemistry, figured largely as statesmen of science. Fourier, thirty years old, had yet to invent the mathematical analysis that has immortalized his name. But he had made an impression on his elders Lagrange and Monge, and had been engaged to teach mathematics at the Ecole polytechnique. Geoffroy was twenty-six and had been named to the chair of zoology at the Muséum d'Histoire naturelle on its foundation in 1793. Dolomieu, mineralogist and geologist, was included because he had been a Knight of Malta (the one cited in the table above was not he, but André-Louis de Saint-Simon, younger brother of the Saint-Simon of socialist fame). Dolomieu considered that Bonaparte had deceived him into appearing to betray the Order, departed Egypt when he could arrange passage, and was shipwrecked in Calabria and thrown into prison by the Neapolitans while trying to reach France.

Another twenty-two people, diplomats, military engineers, army officers, and administrators, joined in one or another of the projects assigned to the Commission, while not officially part of it, and there were about fifteen minor figures who may or may not have been considered members.

Of the certain membership, then, ninety, or 58%, including the students, were engineers or technicians of the same ilk. The youngest, Antoine Viard, was fifteen, ten others were not yet twenty, and the mean age was twenty-five. They were an adaptable lot.

How were they recruited? Bonaparte himself specified what skills were to be represented and how many people he wanted of each sort. He charged General Caffarelli du Falga, commander of the Corps of Engineers, with administrative and financial oversight and with procurement of technical equipment, maps, and books for a library of 500-odd volumes. Monge was already in Rome, fully occupied with culling art collections for the benefit of the Louvre. Thus, the main professional responsibility fell to Berthollet and Fourier, Berthollet for the scientists and senior people, Fourier for the students.

In approaching his colleagues, Berthollet could say only that they were needed for a mission of vital importance to the Republic, that Bonaparte would be its commander, and that Monge and he would be with them. Those with official posts were promised an increased stipend and protection of their positions and seniority on their return. From the Observatory of Paris came the astronomers Nicolas-Auguste Nouet, François Quesnot, and a student, Jérome Méchain, and from the Jardin des Plantes, besides Geoffroy

MALUS

Saint-Hilaire, the naturalists Jules-César Lelorgne de Savigny, Hippolyte Nectoux (recently returned from Santo Domingo), Alyre Delile (not to be confused with his brother, the engineer Adrian Raffeneau-Delile), and two students, Antoine Coquebert and Alexandre Gérard. The latter institution also furnished the flower painter Henri-Joseph Redouté, younger brother of the more famous Pierre-Joseph, "Raphael of the Roses." Departing from the brigade of military balloonists stationed at Meudon were both its director, Nicolas Conté, a mechanical genius, the inventor of the graphite pencil and the semaphore telegraph, and Joseph Coutelle, pilot of the first balloon to fly in combat, at the battle of Fleurus in June 1794.

Not everyone agreed to go. Georges Cuvier, beginning his study of comparative anatomy, did not, though he encouraged the 21-year-old botanist Savigny to accept a place as zoologist, saying there was always time to learn the science. Dubois Isnard, director of the Printing Press of the Republic, begged off, and was replaced by the Orientalist J.-J. Marcel. Madame Monge was furious with her husband for following his idol of a young general once again to parts unknown. An "old fool," she called him, running around the world at his age.

Fourier drew on the schools. Seven students were required from the Ecole des Ponts et Chaussées. A document in its archives gives the names of those whom the Director, Antoine Chézy, nominated to take part in "the expedition against England"—Pierre Arnollet, Gaspard-Antoine Chabrol, Simon Fèvre, J.-B. Prosper Jollois, Michel-Ange Lancret, Adrian Raffeneau-Delile, and Claude-François Thévenot. The school gave advanced training, to which the strongest students from the Ecole polytechnique might be admitted on graduation. Jollois, for example, had entered Ecole polytechnique with its famous first class in 1794 and been a *chef de brigade*, rather like a prefect, throughout his three years there. He and the others already knew the thirteen polytechnicians whom Fourier selected from the classes immediately behind them, notably Edouard Devilliers and Joseph Dubois-Aymé. In Egypt Jollois and Devilliers worked as a team. Along with Edme

Jomard, they were among the most prolific contributors to the *Description de l'Egypte*, and they were instrumental in its eventual completion. Jomard, for his part, had his training in the school of topography, the Ecole des Ingénieurs-Géographes, subordinate to the Ponts et Chaussées.

Apparently, they might choose whether or not to go. In a letter to his father, Jollois explains why he has agreed to "so crazy an idea." He has always wanted to travel. Here is his chance. He is eager to learn, eager to improve himself, eager for new experiences. Older people, among them the most distinguished of scientists and engineers, are leaving behind their fortunes, wives, children, and brilliant situations. Advisers in whom he has confidence would not propose something likely to be prejudicial to his welfare. The person—he does not name Fourier—who made the proposal knows the purpose of the expedition, at least in large part, but cannot reveal the secret. The Ionian Isles? Constantinople? Italy? Cutting a canal through the Isthmus of Suez? It's all conjecture—at any rate, he's going.

His 18-year-old companions, Dubois-Aymé and Devilliers, rode from Paris to Lyons in a diligence with Berthollet, the senior scientist; Fourier, their professor of mathematics; Louis Costaz, their examiner in mathematics at Ecole polytechnique and professor in another school; and Collet Descostils, of the Corps of Mining Engineers. The two undergraduates faced each other in the middle seats squeezed between their elders in the four outside places. A pair of younger teenagers, Antoine Viard and François Vincent, rode with the coachman up in front. From Lyons to Avignon they traveled on by post-boat, and from Aix to Marseilles and on to Toulon, Dubois and Devilliers walked.

This very first leg was adventure enough. Devilliers had never been away from Paris. He was surprised to note how speech changed as they traveled south, and how beyond Avignon people spoke only Provençal. The two classmates were from good families of the Old Regime. The one was styled de Villiers du Terrage before and after the Revolution; the other was pleased to derive "Dubois" from one Guiffroi de Bouès, who had served

Duguesclin. Devilliers' mother had died when he was a child. His father was in prison during the Terror. He and his sister, who was then sixteen, survived that year in an attic room by peddling their father's library book by book and the family silver piece by piece. An uncle then came to the rescue of his education. The Dubois family, suspected of wishing to emigrate, passed much of the same period prudently in Germany.

The two were of complementary temperaments, Dubois an extrovert, vigorous and muscular, an athlete, of a riotous disposition; Devilliers quiet, reflective, hard-working, the very type of the good student, with a fund of inner strength to overcome self-doubts. In Marseilles, Dubois had an affair with an Italian beauty, a married woman who had followed General Dumas from Milan. What with his amours, he missed the *Franklin*, on which he and Devilliers were to have embarked, and barely caught the *Tonnant* before she weighed anchor.

None of their comrades enjoyed the voyage. Dubois, ever the student rebel, resented the distinctions that assimilated the scientists to the rank of senior officers and the engineers only to that of lieutenants. Thus, the older of the Delile brothers, who had graduated from the Ecole polytechnique, ate with the subalterns, while the younger, the botanist ("and that is certainly not a very difficult science": he could not even have got into Polytechnique) was at the captains' table. As for the old bore Costaz, a mediocre math professor in a high school, he dined with the generals.

Devilliers' billet was a hammock with a broken cord in the hold with eighty others, mostly common soldiers. Inevitably, the civilians on the Expedition were the butt of barracks gibes and ribaldry. Devilliers searched the ship for a corner where he could be alone and found a spot behind a coil of rope in which he curled up with his calculus textbook. He whiled away the tedium teaching mathematics to Ripault, a young archaeologist. Ashore in Malta, Dubois-Aymé and the naturalist Coquebert talked of quitting the Expedition and going back to France. Devilliers dissuaded them, but then at sea again began to worry about what possible use he and his comrades

DOLOMIEU

could be among all these soldiers, now that he knew the destination to be Egypt.

THE OCCUPATION OF EGYPT

The landing at Alexandria on 1 July was confused but largely unopposed, and nothing that happened in the first month or so dispelled the civilians' anxieties. Inevitably, the high command, deploying the army, disembarking materiel, securing the fleet, organizing a civil administration, marching on Cairo, had no attention to spare for the Commission of Science and Arts. With no lodgings, no rations, left to shift for themselves in the teeming alleys of Alexandria, the engineers fell into a mood of juvenile self-pity. The third day ashore, a group gathered around the foot of Pompey's Column to pool their discontents, young men uprooted—they complained—from families, lives, and prospects, to whom marvels had been promised, and who were now abandoned even by their immediate superiors. The latter—as they understood—were to be moved by water from the squalor of Alexandria along the coast and up the Nile to quarters in Rosetta, there to await more permanent dispositions in Cairo. The junior members of the Commission insisted on being included. Dolomieu made himself their spokesman. Costaz was in despair. Fourier—Jollois recounts—managed to get himself aboard a galley, "abandoning the young people for whom he was responsible to their unhappy fate." Thanks to the intercession of Geoffroy, twenty-eight places were found for them on another boat, the *Sans-Quartier*, an evil bark whose captain refused them rations.

In Rosetta the prospect brightened. True, their lodging was uninhabitable at first, a house filthy beyond imagining, but they emptied it out, burned the bedding, scoured the whole place with vinegar against the plague, improvised furniture out of packing crates, and formed a mess, everyone contributing to the costs and sharing the work. The cuisine improved markedly, and within eight or ten days "we were eating very well." Caffarelli received them all, listened to their grievances, jollied them along, and promised that in Cairo the work of the Commission would be effective, important, and

worthy of their talents. Meanwhile Jollois began reading up on botany with the naturalists and busied himself making architectural drawings of Malta and Alexandria from sketches in his notebook.

The Commission was still in Rosetta on 1 August when, a month to the day after the debarkation, Nelson surprised and destroyed the French fleet at anchor in Abukir Bay. Hearing the cannon fire in the evening, Jollois, Devilliers, and others climbed to the roof. They could see great flashes over the horizon and took the spectacle for the sound and light of victory.

This is not the place to retell the military or political history of the Expedition, thus marooned. That has been done many times and very well in readily accessible accounts. Suffice it to indicate the main phases in order to situate the work of the Commission within them.

The first comprises the occupation of Cairo and the consolidation of French rule. Bonaparte had swiftly marched on the capital across the desert from Alexandria, defeated the Mameluke army at Imbaba opposite Cairo (the battle of the Pyramids) on 21 July, and entered the city on the 25th. Of the duumvirate who had shared power, Ibrahim Bey retired with the Turkish Pasha to Syria. Murad Bey, the more warlike of the two, retreated south to upper Egypt with the surviving Mameluke forces. The French substituted their own authority for that of the *beys* and imposed it on the officials who ran the country. The transition appeared smooth until Cairo exploded in rebellion on 21 October 1798, a bloody revolt quickly suppressed. Thereafter, the appearance of a liberation gave way before the reality of a military occupation.

The second phase concerns operations in upper Egypt. On the night of 25 August 1798, Desaix led a task force out of Cairo in pursuit of Murad Bey. For ten months, Desaix sought to bring the Mamelukes to battle, sweeping up the Nile Valley to Philae and the first cataract, sending detachments laterally to the Red Sea at Qoceyr and into the Fayoum. Desaix never lost a battle and never pinned his enemy down. When early in the following July he returned to Cairo briefly, upper Egypt was under French control, but the Mamelukes were still at large.

GEOFFROY
SAINT-HILAIRE

8

The third main set of episodes begins with Bonaparte's invasion of the Holy Land and ends with his departure from Egypt. The advance party left Cairo for the Sinai in late January 1799; Bonaparte followed on 10 February. On 20 February, the fortress of El Arish surrendered to the French. In May, Bonaparte suffered the first strategic reverse of his career. He failed to reduce the crusader town and tower of Acre. Its defenders were supported from the sea by the British fleet under Admiral Sir Sidney Smith. Monge nearly died of dysentery and Malus of the plague. Caffarelli, having long since lost a leg in Germany, lost an arm and did die of the infection. The army riddled with plague, Bonaparte withdrew to Cairo, staging a "triumphal" entry on 14 June. On 25 July, he annihilated a Turkish army that the British fleet had landed at Abukir. Newspapers put ashore by Sir Sidney Smith contained accounts of French reverses in Italy. Thereupon, Bonaparte decided to return to France. He spirited Monge and Berthollet away with him, abandoning his army and departing Alexandria in secret on 22 August. A dismayed Kléber was left in command. Bonaparte arrived in Paris on 16 October and seized power on 9 November (18 brumaire), to be named First Consul the next day.

The fourth stage of the Egyptian expedition is that of Kléber in command. His first purpose was to evacuate his army to France. In November 1799, a Turkish army under the Grand Vizier began advancing through Syria. Though not threatened with defeat, Kléber wished to avoid further bloodshed and opened negotiations with the Ottoman command through the good offices of Sir Sidney Smith. The Convention of El Arish was signed on 28 January 1800. It called for an honorable withdrawal by the French. The terms were disavowed by the British government. Kléber thereupon turned on the Turkish army that had advanced into lower Egypt, defeated it roundly at Heliopolis on 20 March, reoccupied the country, and settled in for an extended presence. He was assassinated in the gardens of the palace that served as General Headquarters on 14 June by a devout young Moslem acting under the direction of higher authority in Syria. Walking with him was

one of the contributors, the architect Jean Constantin Protain, who was injured in the mêlée.

The fifth and final phase transpired under the next in command, General Abdallah Jacques Menou, who had both become a Moslem and married one. His was a holding operation that failed to hold. A British landing west of Alexandria, coordinated with a further Turkish invasion from the east, forced the surrender of Cairo on 18 June and of Alexandria on 3 September 1801, three years and two months after the initial debarkation.

By far the most important phases for the work of the Commission were the second, the campaign in upper Egypt, and the fourth, the period of the Kléber command. Indeed, one of the remarkable features of the whole enterprise is that the enthusiasm of its members survived both the prospect of an indefinite exile after the battle of Abukir Bay and the desertion a year later by Bonaparte. Perhaps it is a measure of his stature that until Waterloo his leadership somehow transcended conduct that would have cost an ordinary man all credit and reputation.

The confidence that Bonaparte inspired in soldiers, to cite the most important example, was proof against his complete indifference to their welfare. When there was no provision for water during the hundred-mile march in Alpine uniforms from Alexandria to Cairo in the heat of an Egyptian July, when afflicted with opthalmia they were sent out, their eyes running with pus, to do battle under the tropical sun, when Bonaparte proposed containing the contagion of the plague by poisoning the sick, when Egypt proved more like hell than the paradise where Bonaparte had promised them booty and fortune, when, in short, things went wrong, the rank and file blamed, not the commander who had brought them there, but some subordinate malevolence, some low-ranking incompetence. Among the targets of their resentment was the Commission of Science and Arts. The surveyors, the bug-collectors, the scribblers, the scavengers in filthy old tombs, in a word the savants— they were the ones who had instigated this fouled-up campaign.

Bonaparte himself reacted to military reverses by increasing the emphasis on

SAVIGNY

9

DESCOSTILS

cultural and technical missions. In August 1798, he had Caffarelli bring the Commission from Rosetta to Cairo. On 13 September, he ordered that students who had not yet graduated from the Ecole polytechnique should sustain their final examination in public. Dubois, Devilliers, and their classmates settled down to review their courses and on 6 October appeared one by one before a committee consisting of Monge, Berthollet, Fourier, Costaz, and Corancez. The date was about the same that it would have been in Paris. Everyone passed, and Bonaparte directed that their commissions be issued. Devilliers urged Dubois-Aymé, who was leaning towards the military engineers, to join him in preferring the Corps des Ponts et Chaussées. It was a fortunate decision. Comrades who made the other choice died of plague or wounds in Syria. Devilliers would have been included in that ill-starred campaign anyway except that he had lost his horse. A few weeks earlier he had fallen asleep in the saddle on a mission in the Delta, rolled off into the sand, and been awakened by a soldier stumbling over him in the dark.

Meanwhile, the senior members of the Commission of Science and Arts, together with leading military and administrative figures, were gathered into the Institut d'Egypte, in form and in spirit a colonial adaptation of the Institut de France. The forty-eight places (only thirty-six of which were filled at the outset) were distributed evenly among four sections—mathematical science, physical science, political economy, and arts and letters. The Institute occupied the palace of Hassan-Bey Kachef and met in the great chamber of the harem. Installed in neighboring properties were a botanical garden, provision for a menagerie and a collection of natural history and mineralogy, the printery, and Conté's machine shop. The opening meeting occurred on 23 August. Monge was elected president for the initial quarter, Fourier permanent secretary, and Bonaparte vice president. The vice president set the problems: to find methods for improving the efficiency of ovens used to bake bread for the army; to devise techniques for clarifying and purifying water from the Nile; to determine whether raw materials for manufacturing gunpowder were to be found in Egypt.

The Commission also received its first formal task at Bonaparte's express initiative. One of the stated goals of the Expedition was to reopen the nautical link between the Mediterranean and the Red Sea that had served commerce in antiquity. Bonaparte started his favorite engineering project himself. On 24 December 1798, he left Cairo with a detachment of 300 men to make his first reconnaissance since securing the capital.

In the party were generals Berthier and Caffarelli du Falga together with Monge, Berthollet, and other members of the Institute, among them Costaz and Jacques-Marie Le Père, a chief civil engineer. They took the pilgrims' road for Mecca, arrived in Suez on the 26th, and visited the nearby springs of Moses. On the 30th, the main party went on northwest toward Ageroud while Bonaparte with Monge and two or three others peeled off in search of traces of the ancient "Canal of the Prince of the Faithful," said to have been filled in by order of the Caliph Abou Jafir Al Mansour between 762 and 767 A.D. Its course had been north through the Bitter Lakes, where it turned west along the Wadi Tumilat to open eventually into the Pelusiac branch of the Nile. From there a further system of waterways had reached Alexandria.

Accounts agree that Bonaparte himself was the first to descry vestiges of the thousand-year-old banks emerging here and there from the shifting sands about two kilometers north of the head of the Gulf of Suez. All excited, he and his companions rode on without armed escort following the trace as far as the Little Bitter Lake and rejoining the caravan that night. Returning to Cairo a few days later, Bonaparte came on another section of the one-time waterway in the Wadi Tumilat. Back at General Headquarters, he ordered Le Père to assemble a team and undertake a topographical survey of the isthmus of Suez, with a view to making recommendations on the construction of a canal.

We have already cited a passage from the eventual report. Le Père departed Cairo on 16 January 1799, accompanied by the other two principals in the project, his brother Gratien (who had been a schoolmate of Bonaparte at Brienne) and Bourges Saint-Genis. In Suez they enlisted the services of Dubois-Aymé, already there on another mission. Working with them at the outset were the astronomer Nouet and his assistant Coraboeuf. Those two determined the geographical coordinates of Suez (as they did appropriate points of reference throughout Egypt, some thirty-six in all).

The first traverse followed the old canal bed. Between 31 January and 4 February they covered forty-six kilometers to a point on the edge of the Bitter Lakes. Their drinking water low, they broke off, left a marker, and made for the Wady Tumilat. A menacing band of Bedouins turned aside when they saw the size of the escort. Flasks were dry and the camels had been without water for six days when they arrived.

Seven months passed. Bonaparte was back in Paris. Not until October could Kléber spare security forces that would allow Le Père to resume. He now had Dubois-Aymé, Fèvre, Favier, and Duchanoy working under him. They began to the west of Lake Timsah at Mouqfâr, near to the present-day Ismailia, and moved south for fifty-one kilometers until with enormous difficulty they located the marker of seven months before. Exhausted and again waterless, they doubled back to Cairo by way of Suez.

Finally, in November, two parties repaired to the reference point at Mouqfâr, the one (Le Père, his brother, Saint-Genis, and Chabrol) extending their line from the Red Sea in a hell-for-leather survey to come out on the shore of the Mediterranean at Pelusium, the other (Fèvre, Devilliers, Alibert, and Duchanoy) backtracking from Mouqfâr 120 kilometers through Bilbeys to the Nilometer on the isle of Roudah just below Cairo.

The data would in principle allow comparison of the level of the Red Sea with that of the Mediterranean and also show the extent of the fall of the Nile between Cairo and the sea. Finally, at the end of December, Gratien Le Père, assisted by Jollois and several others, ran a traverse that tied the whole survey to the northeast corner of the Great Pyramid at Giza (see Vol. V, Pl. 19, fig. 3). Thus, a dozen of the civil engineers were employed at one time or another on the project.

The text of the *Description de l'Egypte* contains Le Père's report on the operations. In subsidiary respects, the monograph is a masterpiece. It deserves to rank high in the genre of desert travel and adventure. Its account of the ancient canal is a fine piece of archaeology, comprising both field work and extensive extracts from the writings of antiquity. Its observations on the port of Suez and on trade and navigation in the Red Sea are models of political economy and political geography.

The memoir is not, however, a masterpiece of accurate topography. Le Père had the misfortune to calculate from his data that at mean tide the level of the Red Sea is some 8.50 meters or 33 feet higher than that of the Mediterranean. Only the barrier of the isthmus of Suez prevented the Red Sea from pouring into the Mediterranean and inundating the Delta. That had also been the opinion of Aristotle. It was dead wrong, of course. Sea level is sea level everywhere in the world. Almost alone among ancient writers, the mathematician Strabo had seized that point, citing the hydrostatics of Archimedes.

Among the experts of Le Père's generation, it was also the mathematicians who were skeptical of his results. Any global variation in mean sea level was entirely inconsistent with Laplace's analysis of tidal action. Fourier quite agreed with Laplace. They only spoke their reservations later on, however, sometimes scornfully, and never wrote them. Engineers and geographers accepted Le Père's findings, which were taken as axiomatic by the General Council of the Corps des Ponts et Chaussées. Only in 1847 did a survey directed by Adrien-Paul Bourdaloë determine the facts correctly. Such was the commitment of members of the Expedition to the great adventure of their youth that Devilliers and Favier, the only survivors among Le Père's subordinates, took personal affront over the uniformity of sea level.

How could these well-trained people have gone so wrong? Theirs had been no ordinary survey. They had to move fast, for they could stay in the field only as long as their water lasted. On several occasions, the high command had to cut short their operations, either because the guards could not be spared or intelligence had brought word of danger. In the year required to complete the survey, actual work in the field occupied only twenty-five

DUBOIS-AYME

11

days. In order to cover ten to twelve kilometers a day, the observers took very long sightings. The distance between stations averaged 530 meters and sometimes stretched to 600, thus magnifying the effect of any error. Their equipment was makeshift. The fine repeating circles shipped from France had been lost with the bulk of the scientific instruments, some of it in the sinking of the *Patriot*, the rest in the sack of Caffarelli's lodgings during the revolt in Cairo. Le Père's people had to make do with crude leveling telescopes, which were graduated in decimal units, while the stakes were marked in the traditional duodecimal system. Mirages and less drastic optical effects in the glare of the desert sun produced further uncertainties. Sand got into everything. Worst of all, except for the first leg, the measurements were never repeated as in any proper survey they are bound to be. Circumstances precluded that elementary precaution.

Nevertheless, Le Père was persuaded that a new canal was entirely feasible. His memoir includes detailed and elaborate estimates of the prospective cost, time, and work force. Not the least prescient feature is the recommendation that private enterprise undertake the task on concession, an association for all the world like the Compagnie Universelle Maritime de Suez floated in 1858.

Le Père did attempt experimental verification of a sort. As it happened, the rising of the Nile in the late summer of 1800 was of flood proportions, the highest in nearly a century. Menou was now in command. Wishing to turn the Expedition into a permanent occupation, he welcomed Le Père's proposal to do a reconnaissance of the flood. In the coursing of the waters through the slopes, ditches, and valleys of the Delta, Le Père found confirmation that he had the contours right and that a new canal could be supplied with water from the Nile at the altitude of Cairo. On 6 December 1800, he addressed a report to that effect to Bonaparte in Paris. He wrote up the full text after the evacuation of Egypt and presented it to the First Consul on 14 August 1803. "It's a great thing, publish...," he reports Bonaparte saying, "and force the Turkish government to see

the combination of profit and glory (*son intérêt et sa gloire*) in the execution of the project." Thus, foremost among the sources of engineering error may well have been the incentive to give the man in power what he so expressly wanted. The irony is that when the Suez Canal opened in 1869, it had been less difficult for Ferdinand de Lesseps to pierce the isthmus at sea level than it would have been to reopen a waterway from the Nile.

So far, the antiquities of Egypt figured only in a desultory way in the occupations of the Commission. Apart from Giza, Memphis, and Saqqara, the impressive sites were in upper Egypt. Bonaparte did take a day for sightseeing at Giza. On 24 September 1798, he convoked the usual courtiers for a visit to the great pyramids and the Sphinx. In the party were Berthier, Caffarelli, Monge, Berthollet, Denon, Fourier, Costaz, Geoffroy Saint-Hilaire, and others of the Institute. Dubois-Aymé and Devilliers were not invited, but they learned of the plans and stowed away in the barges the night before, to be treated with indulgence when their presence was discovered.

Geoffroy left an account of the outing. The voyage up from Cairo, several hours by tortuous canal, was occupied by Bonaparte's leading a spirited discussion of political economy. Ought he to put into effect in Egypt a scheme for regenerating society by giving cultivators title to the value their labor and improvements created in the land they farmed? Everyone knew, and Caffarelli laughingly admitted authorship, that such ruminations were the favorite recreation of this military Saint-Simonian *avant la lettre*. Arabs were camped everywhere around the monuments, which had their inevitable effect of surprising the visitor into the awe he rather expected to have to feign. That did not preclude a festive mood. Bonaparte led the raillery, as he did anything that occurred in his company. Who would be first to reach the top? Not the youngest but the oldest met the challenge—encouraging himself and others from a gourd of eau-de-vie that apparently he always carried, Monge scrambled to the summit and found himself waving down rather from a platform than a point. Bonaparte teased Berthier about his infatuation with his mistress and

KLEBER

shamed him, along with Geoffroy, into following Monge. Watching and sketching all the while was another of the elders of the Expedition, the artist and illustrator Vivant Denon.

EXPLORATION OF UPPER EGYPT

Denon it was who in the months that followed discovered ancient Egypt to the members of the Expedition and, immediately upon his return to France with Bonaparte, to the French public. His *Voyage dans la Basse et la Haute Egypte* appeared in 1802, only a few months after the French capitulation in Egypt and the repatriation of those, the great majority of the Expedition, who had perforce remained until the bitter end. That book contributed more than any other item to the vogue for things Egyptian that swept the decorative arts and the world of fashion. The publisher Firmin Didot printed it in the same lavish format in which the *Description* later appeared. The age was a gilded one. Collectors demanded luxurious editions and seldom read them.

All this magnificence was misplaced in the case of Denon's book, and its popularity has survived the splendor in which it was entombed. It has gone through at least forty readable editions, for it is very readable indeed, and the drawings are charming. But they are on a human scale and a little lost surrounded by the immense margins in which Didot framed them. Denon was not a great artist. He was an illustrator who could see even better than he could draw and who never stopped looking. Consider, for example, his appreciation of the colossi of Memnon (the wording is that of a contemporary English translation):

These two pieces of art, which are without grace, expression, or action, have nothing which seduces the judgment; but their proportions are faultless, and this simplicity of attitude, and want of decided expression, has something of majesty and seriousness, which cannot fail to strike the beholder. If the limbs of these figures had been distorted in order to express some violent passion, the harmony of their outline would have been lost, and they would be less conspicuous at the distance at which they begin to strike the eye, and produce their effect on the mind of the spectator, for

they may be distinguished as far as four leagues off.

The story of Denon's travels keeps his book alive. Not a young man—like Monge he was over fifty—he chose, and was allowed, to join Desaix's command for the lethal game of tag with Murad Bey in upper Egypt. His frustrations were those incident to any military operation. When the army was finally on the move after weeks and months of idleness in places like Beni Suef and Girga, where there was nothing much to draw, General Belliard could allow him only half an hour to sketch the temple at Hermopolis, the first monument that gave him an idea of what lay ahead. The gratifications, on the other hand, are the stuff of legends: Rounding a bend in the river and coming upon the temples of Karnak and Luxor amid the ruins of Thebes,

PROTAIN

the whole army, suddenly and with one accord, stood in amazement . . . and clapped their hands with delight, as if the end and object of their glorious toils, and the complete conquest of Egypt, were accomplished and secured by taking possession of the splendid remains of this ancient metropolis . . . . The knees of the enthusiastic soldiers served me as a table, their bodies as a shade, whilst the dazzling rays of the burning sun enlightened this magnificent spectacle, and exhibited the electric emotion of a whole army of soldiers, whose delicate sensibility made me feel proud of being their companion and glory in calling myself a Frenchman.

The few hours at Dendara on the march south had already awakened the enthusiasm of the military. At first impatient when Denon asked for a little time, Desaix rallied and entered into the spirit of the opportunity. General Belliard, second-in-command, shared cramped quarters with the artist. Having sketched his way from the propylon through the hypostyle into the interior of the temple, Denon climbed out on the roof towards the end of the afternoon and came upon the circular zodiac, wonder of wonders. Totally absorbed, he worked until dark to capture what detail he could. Others drifted back to camp while Belliard remained quietly at his side in order that he not be alone amid the Arabs doubtless watching from the shadows.

Rumors of these finds reached Cairo. After nine months sharing the life of the task force, Denon returned in early July 1799. His portfolio of drawings excited the admiration of his colleagues of the Institute, where he reported on what he had seen and learned of Egypt ancient and modern. Bonaparte himself was newly back from the Syrian fiasco and secretly preparing his departure after the second battle of Abukir. With him went Denon and the portfolio. In 1802, the year the *Voyage* appeared, Bonaparte named Denon director of museums, in effect of the Louvre, which post he occupied throughout the Napoleonic regime.

LE PERE AINE

Among the last decisions Bonaparte made in Egypt was to instruct the Commission of Science and Arts to undertake systematically the inventory of antiquity that Denon had begun single-handed and on the run. A decree of 13 August 1799 appointed two ad hoc commissions to carry out the task. The first group, headed by the mathematician Costaz, consisted of fourteen men: an archaeologist, Ripault; two architects, Balzac and J. B. Lepère (not to be confused with the Le Père brothers); two astronomers, Nouet and Méchain; two mechanical engineers, Coutelle and Lenoir; a civil engineer, Saint-Genis, with a student, Viard; a topographical engineer, Coraboeuf; a surgeon, Labate; and two naturalists, Coquebert and Savigny. Its orders were to depart Cairo on 16 August.

The second commission was headed by Fourier and, after certain changes, consisted of twelve others: an artist, Redouté; a musician, Villoteau; a mechanical engineer, Cécile; two civil engineers, Arnollet and Chabrol, with a student, Vincent; a pharmacist, Rouyer, and a student surgeon, Lacipierre; and two naturalists, Delile and Geoffroy Saint-Hilaire. Two of the most valuable members, both then and in the eventual publication of the *Description*, were the topographical engineer Edme Jomard and the civil engineer Michel-Ange Lancret. They contrived to substitute themselves for others after the orders had been drawn. Jomard had somehow incurred the animosity of General Berthier, chief of staff, who threatened him with confinement in the Citadel if his importunities continued. Only eleven days after the departure of this second

commission, on 18 August, did Jomard catch up with it. By then, Berthier himself had left, along with Bonaparte.

Fourier, in the "Préface historique" to the *Description,* makes it sound as if those in charge had all deliberately chosen the late summer out of their deep knowledge of the river and its ways. The Nile was always on the rise in August, covering islets and sand bars that impeded navigation during the months of low water. The prevailing wind was then from the north, strong enough by day to carry river craft upstream. The commissions embarked in the double-masted vessels called *djermes,* or *dahabiahs,* a type still to be seen plying the Nile. They sailed the thousand kilometers to Aswan in four weeks, stopping briefly at Antinoé, Asyut, Antaeopolis, and Sheikh el-Haridy. Otherwise, they had only glimpses of the monuments they were to investigate. The plan called for arriving at the first cataract (actually the fourth as the Nile flows) and conducting their researches step by step on the way back downstream.

News of Bonaparte's departure reached them as they set to work on the isles of Philae and Elephantine. The surprise was less than total. On 7 August, Bonaparte had apprised Monge, Berthollet, and Denon of the plans and told them to be ready. Thereafter, Monge's deportment mingled joy with shiftiness in so unnatural a proportion that his colleagues suspected what might be in the wind. When asked point-blank, Monge would say only that he had Bonaparte's word that the entire Commission would return to France on completion of the mission in upper Egypt, and that he envied them their chance to visit Thebes. Fourier and Costaz refused to believe that their leaders, military and scientific, would abandon them. Geoffroy Saint-Hilaire did believe it. The naturalist proved right, the mathematicians wrong.

Meanwhile, another ad hoc commission was already in the field and well-advanced with archaeology at the initiative, not of the high command, but of its junior members, Devilliers, Jollois, and Dubois-Aymé. The express mission was hydrographical, not antiquarian. Its chief, the civil engineer Pierre-Simon Girard, received orders from Bonaparte to journey up the Nile to the first cataract in order to make a general study of the influence of the river on the fertility of the entire country. Along the way they were to collect comprehensive information on systems of irrigation. As a subsidiary charge, the commission was to assemble as complete a documentation as possible on commerce, agriculture, trades, natural history, geography, and antiquities. Others assigned were the sculptor Castex, the student engineer Duchanoy, and the mining engineers Collet-Descostils, Rozières, and Dupuy, nine in all. Devilliers had orders to report to Giza ready for departure with a military convoy on the morning of 19 March. He was to provide himself with pencils, four reams of paper, and five sticks of paste.

Stopping the first night at El-Saff, they traced a profile of the Nile and calculated the volume of water and rate of flow. Such observations occupied them on the way upstream to Asyut (*Description* Vol. V, Pl. 19, fig. 4–5). The party arrived there on 28 March 1799. With all his marches and countermarches, Desaix had not yet succeeded in pacifying middle and upper Egypt, and he refused to allow these civilians to go further. There they remained for seven weeks until 17 May, insufficiently occupied by the tombs in the mountains behind the town (IV, 43–49) and chafing in near idleness. Devilliers and Jollois made an unauthorized excursion to visit what turned out to be a Coptic ruin some distance west of the Nile; they found it a dejected place. Dubois-Aymé and Descostils also went off on their own. What little cohesion the group had started with then evaporated. Girard was not a leader of men. On an expedition like this, Jollois reports him to have said, ''It's every man for himself.'' For his own part, Girard eventually contributed admirable memoirs to the *Description* on the agriculture, commerce, and industry of Egypt, on the configuration of the Nile Valley, on the Nilometer at Elephantine, and on the Red Sea coast. That, after all, was the Commission's job. He is remembered, however, mainly for the contempt his junior colleagues felt for the philistinism of his sense of duty and for his interference with their liberties.

Finally, on 18 May, Desaix allowed the party to proceed upstream with a detachment under the command of Belliard. Afflicted like most others with the prevalent opthalmia, Devilliers rode blindfolded, his mare following Jollois's horse nose to tail. She stumbled and rolled over on him crossing a dry creek bed. The column advanced southward on the east bank, reached Qena on the 25th, and settled in while Belliard led part of his force over the eastern desert to secure the Red Sea port of Quseir.

Dendara is just a few kilometers from Qena, across the river. Its fame had spread throughout the army since Denon's arrival just a few weeks earlier. Denon was back in Qena briefly and showed Jollois and Devilliers his portfolio. They were particularly struck by the circular zodiac. Denon had had time for no more than a sketch. They resolved to make a copy exact in every detail. Before departing, Belliard authorized them a military escort that they might visit the site for themselves. There began the intensive collaboration to which we owe such plates as those on Esna (I, 72–80), on the topography of Thebes (II, 1; III, 1), on Karnak (III, 5–11), and, to indicate only a sampling, on Dendara, where they started (IV, 8–11, 14–16, 18–22). Engrossed, the two young engineers resolved to devote every spare moment to archaeology, exact and exacting.

No one could prevent them. Girard had accompanied Belliard to Quseir. When he did return, he made one visit to Dendara and slept through three of the four hours he spent there. Belliard had expressly forbidden civilian personnel to go off on their own. Nevertheless, to have asked repeatedly for a security guard would have worn out the tolerance of the military. Devilliers and Jollois ignored orders. Every day at the end of the morning they went to the landing across from the ruins. There a boatman ferried them over and awaited their return at dusk. One day, totally absorbed, they were later than usual and from afar saw him gesturing to hurry. He was in a fever of anxiety lest harm had befallen them at the hands of malevolent Arabs. They doubled his fee and felt that he was even more joyful at their safety. The temple itself was spooky enough. On the way back to Cairo some months later, Devilliers and Jollois with a few others

G. LE PERE

15

returned to gather further detail. The only access to a room under the shrine containing the circular zodiac was through a small hole in the ceiling. They provided the slightest of their companions, the polytechnician Moret Saint-Amand, with a torch and lowered him on a length of rope. As he felt about for a footing in the debris, his feet kicked against something soft, not a mummy but a corpse some three or four years dead. The hands were still tied behind its back; the strangler's noose still looped around the neck.

DENON

The pains Devilliers and Jollois took over the circular zodiac will give an idea of their occupations. The shrine wherein it decorated the ceiling was dark. The bas-relief itself was blackened by the ages. In order to make out the detail, Devilliers and Jollois had to crane their necks to stare up, often for quite an interval, at the ceiling illuminated by flickering torchlight, and then copy what they had discerned into their notepads. At the outset, they divided the scene into eight equal sectors by means of cords stretched like chalk lines across the surface. These served them for coordinates by which to establish the relative positions of the various figures. Their drawing was on a scale of one to five. The work, says Devilliers in his *Journal*, ''was long and arduous.'' The reader who wishes to judge of their success may compare Plate 21, Vol. IV, with the original, now suspended in the Louvre, and imagine what it must have been to draw in such a posture. In fact, their inaccuracies were few and slight.

Devilliers and Jollois also discovered the astronomical scenes on the ceiling of the outer hypostyle at Dendara (IV, 18–20) and conceived the hope that the study of these and similar representations might permit recovering the astronomical science of ancient Egypt. The zodiacs on the ceilings of the temples at Esna (I, 79), Esna North (I, 87), and Armant (I, 96, fig. 2) encouraged that ambition, as did the tableau discovered by Ripault and copied by the military engineer Le Gentil in the tomb of Ramesses VII in the Valley of the Kings (II, 82). It appears from their memoir in the text of the *Description* (*Antiquités* I, app. 2), however, that they felt obliged to defer to the authority of Fourier, who arrived later on the scene

and took the subject for his own. Having thus preempted it, he ultimately wrote only one of the several memoirs he had projected.

The Girard Commission remained at Qena until 25 June, a month in all. Belliard wished them to inspect the maintenance of irrigation ditches, and they took advantage of the mission to explore thoroughly on their way south. The heat was ferocious. They marched by night, still on the east bank, passing through Qift and Qous (Koptos) and reaching Thebes on the 28th for their first sight of Karnak and Luxor. Girard refused to tarry for more than a day, however, and on they went to Esna. There Desaix had established his headquarters, and there the commission settled down again, enjoying the relative comfort of a provincial capital where the magnate, Hassan Bey, was such an enemy of Murad that the local sheikhs gave the French a feast. Neither side could speak the other's language. Nevertheless, gaiety reigned. Seated on the ground and served by waiters who tore the boiled sheep apart with their hands, the guests were surprised by all the flavors that went well with mutton.

There, however, the discords between Girard and his young colleagues broke into the open. With Dubois-Aymé, ever rebellious, hostility had graduated into outright enmity, and Girard had detached him from the commission in Quseir, in effect exiling him for service by the Red Sea. Faults on both sides—so Devilliers had to admit in a letter to their comrade Ripault back in Cairo. Girard for his part went to Belliard complaining that his engineers were ''doing hieroglyphs, and that was not their job.'' They on their side had enlisted the sympathy of Denon, who was still in Esna and who no doubt interceded with the general on their behalf. He had no orders to give them, Belliard told Jollois and Devilliers—they knew what they were supposed to do. And even Girard had to admit that they carried out all the hydrographical missions he assigned them.

In July, the now fragmented commission made an excursion to the limit of occupied Egypt, to Elephantine and to Philae. The sculptor Jean-Jacques Castex there inscribed on the pylon of the Temple of

Isis the famous legend recording the French presence and the names of his colleagues. They had time for three visits to Philae. The Nubian inhabitants resented their interest, let them know that the French were more troublesome than the Mamelukes, and threatened to tear down the remains of the temples which attracted such intrusive visitors. The way downstream gave the group a day at Kom Ombo, where the heat was the fiercest yet, and another at Edfu, both of which sites they had visited briefly on the way south. A few days more at Esna and, on 7 August, the commission departed for Thebes, some by boat, Girard and Devilliers on horseback, for apparently they were not irreconcilable. Alone, without servants or an escort of soldiers, they came upon an Arab encampment. Alarm turned to relief when the hospitality of the desert was extended them and they were given the bread of friendship.

The Turkish invasion of the Delta produced momentary disarray when orders came from the high command in Cairo to evacuate upper Egypt. They were countermanded, however, after Bonaparte's victory at Abukir on 25 July. Our engineers turned archaeologists settled in at Thebes about 9 August. There they received from Conté a shipment of pencils to replenish their original supply, which they had long since run through, making do in the meantime with stubs and stalks of lead improvised out of bullets (for which Desaix had also to keep asking). In the next two months, they and their colleagues of the other two commissions accomplished almost all the work published in Volumes I through IV, some 80% of the *Antiquités* in the *Description de l'Egypte*. The Costaz and Fourier commissions, however, arrived at Esna only on 20 September and had, therefore, not quite a month in upper Egypt.

With all three groups on the scene, the distinctions between them disappeared. Girard made several excursions back to Esna and to Elephantine, where to his joy he identified a monument of hydrographical interest, the remains of the Nilometer described by Strabo (I, 33). He exercised no further direction, and neither did Fourier or Costaz. Fourier did no archaeology himself of which there is any record, preferring to analyze the work of others. It is unclear how long he remained in upper Egypt. Costaz did remain, but participated as one among equals. Collegiality took over from authority, and the participants divided up their enormous task by taste and inclination, and to some degree by chance.

Jollois and Devilliers took primary responsibility for topography, surveying the sites with theodolite, plumb-bob, compass, and T-square, and keeping careful record. The first such people ever in the field, they in effect established the procedures of scientific archaeology, working sometimes by themselves, sometimes with Descostils, Duchanoy, Rozières, and Dupuy, and most often with Dutertre and Nectoux. But they did not limit themselves to the geometry of plans and charts. Many of the architectural sections and elevations are theirs (e.g., III, 5–12), many facades and surfaces (e.g., I, 74; II, 11), and also several tombs (e.g., III, 78–79). They, indeed, discovered the isolated tomb of Amenophis III in the Valley of the Kings (III, 79, fig. 5).

Responsible for a large proportion of the architectural drawings (e.g., I, 50–54; II, 4–7) was another team: Jean-Baptiste Lepère, Bourges Saint-Genis, and Jean-Baptiste Coraboeuf. "Lepère architecte." as he is always called to distinguish him from the Le Père brothers of Suez fame, is perhaps best known for the column in the Place Vendôme in Paris. He was assisted in all the surveys by the two engineers, the former experienced, the latter a student. Saint-Genis and Coraboeuf also helped Devilliers and Jollois with several site plans, for example, Philae (I, 1) and Dendara (IV, 2).

Three among the prolific contributors were rather artists than engineers. André Dutertre was a book illustrator and pioneer in lithography. Along the way, he dashed off the profiles that appear alongside this essay. Many of the panoramic plates are his (e.g., I, 49; II, 25; IV, 3–4; V, 5). Charles-Louis Balzac had done architectural drawings and paintings before ever joining the Expedition. He appears to have preferred general views of a whole ensemble (e.g., I, 48; II, 15; III, 44) to the more technical plans, elevations, and sections executed by the engineers. Occa-

DESAIX

sionally he collaborated with the mechanical engineer Antoine Cécile (III, 18), who became an architect in later life. Redouté, the flower painter, did not limit himself to natural history. He did many of the artifacts, as did the sculptor Castex, and helped with inscriptions and bas-reliefs.

Without some such division of labor, the task would have been insurmountable. But people did not confine themselves to specialties. When it was a question of copying all the bas-reliefs on a certain surface before moving on, everyone on the site pitched in and formed an assembly line. The scenes of battle on the north wall of the temple at Karnak (III, 38–39) are by Jollois and Devilliers, and their continuation (III, 40) is by Cécile, Lancret, Balzac, and Dutertre. To judge from the great variety of his contributions, the civil engineer Antoine Chabrol de Volvic stood ready to leap into any breach. Several military engineers also lent a hand, notably Le Gentil.

GIRARD

The account of Philae that Michel-Ange Lancret composed for the text of the *Description* conveys the spirit shared by everyone. He had ridden to the landing by moonlight along the ancient way taken by Strabo, who had traveled by carriage.

Night rides always have a grave and portentous quality that predisposes the mind to profound impressions. But what other place could produce stronger sensations or leave so many memories? I reflected with a mingling of excitement, pleasure, and apprehensiveness that I was in one of the most extraordinary locations on the earth, amid places that partake of the fabulous, the very names of which, recited since childhood, have assumed gigantic and almost magical significance. I could touch the rocks of the cataracts at the gates of Ethiopia, at the boundary of the Roman Empire. Soon I would cross to that island where the tomb of Osiris had been, an island once sacred and now ignored, the sanctuary of an ancient religion, the mother of so many others. Finally, I was close to one of the immutable divisions of our globe [the Tropic of Cancer] and the step I had just taken might have carried me into the equatorial zone. No doubt the austere beauty of a great river flowing among the rocks was not unique to Egypt. Nowhere else, however, are monuments still surviving of one of the most ancient peoples of the world, inscriptions that it

has carved into the rocks through which it seems to speak to posterity. Such objects, carrying the mind back to the most distant centuries, enrich the panorama with a beauty greater than anything that nature alone can offer in its most imposing sites.

On approaching the pylon, his eye falls on words inscribed in Latin: "I, L. Trebonius Oricula, I lived here" and "I, Numonius Valla, I dwelt here under the Emperor Caesar, consul for the thirteenth time." *Inscriptions of this kind are nothing solemn or monumental. You do not study them for the date of an event or for the dedication of a temple. Another kind of curiosity, another interest, attracts and touches you. Here is a man who has been no more for centuries, and who is speaking to you. Like you, he came to see these very places. Like you, he was a foreigner. He wrote down his name, even as you write yours. Perhaps the same thoughts stirred in him. It is a joy to imagine what they may have been. You have just learned his name. You guess his occupation. You think you see him in his uniform and in the act of writing. I picture to myself a soldier of the Roman garrison, long absent from his country amid incessant wars. Full of the memory of home, he whiles away the boredom of exile, hoping to be able one day to tell family and friends how he carved his name on the most distant temples of mysterious Egypt.*

Perhaps the most pleasing single discovery fell to the lot of Bourges Saint-Genis, who penetrated into the rock tombs of El-Kab (I, 67–71) and opened the first window onto the daily life of ancient Egypt. Until then, everything had been mythical and ceremonial, military and religious— gods, kings, priests, warriors. Here all of a sudden were ordinary people, real people, plowing their fields, sowing their crops, harvesting their wheat, pressing their grapes, fishing and hunting, preparing their meals, practicing their arts and crafts, embalming their dead. At the news, everyone in the commission dropped what he was doing and rushed to see. Half the group were dispersed among the monuments of Eileithyia. The others, having already moved on downstream, hurried back from Esna, some twenty-five kilometers north. Enthusiasm was high and general. Everyone set to work to copy as many scenes as possible.

Saint-Genis himself made rubbings of the rest.

Edme Jomard began coming to the fore in Aswan and Elephantine Island. In the published text, the descriptions of those sites are his, as are those of Edfu and the private tombs or *hypogées* at Thebes. The latter were nearly overwhelming. The first horror of clambering among piles of mummies heaped up pell-mell was soon dissipated. The bituminous odor was not that of death, and the worry was rather that a spark might set the highly inflammable remains afire, turning the cave into an inferno. How, moreover, convey the wonder of the contents, these walls and ceilings covered with paintings and bas-reliefs wrought by artists whose work was destined never to be seen? It would take a modern artist years to copy the contents of a single chamber, even if he could stand working by torchlight in the fetid heat of underground. Worst of all were the bats, their horrid blind flight squeaking past your ears, the stink of their droppings piled in the corners.

Bats nearly proved fatal to Jomard. On 13 October 1799, in the inexperience of an early visit, he and a companion entered a tomb about five o'clock in the afternoon. They had only two candles. After penetrating a considerable distance into the labyrinth and skirting several vertical shafts and side passages, they stood lost in admiration of a wall of carvings in high relief. Suddenly, a great flight of bats swished by, blowing out first one candle and, before it could be relit, the other. Immobile in near panic for a few seconds, they made their way several paces back by the slight glow of the wicks, but were soon in complete darkness. They called out. Total silence. Holding hands, they worked their way by huge slow steps in the direction they hoped they had taken, one of them always touching the wall or the ceiling with his free hand. After about a hundred paces, the walls receded on both sides. They had reached an intersection with another corridor and had no recollection of how they had come. Thereupon, they decided to hug the wall to the right and follow it no matter what. They were near exhaustion. It would be growing dark outside. In the distance, a light—their imagination? An Arab scavenger deep in the cave? A ray of the setting sun? They dropped hands and ran to see. It was only six o'clock. The eternity of the misadventure had lasted exactly an hour.

The only vestige of Costaz's initial leadership is his authorship of the description of the Valley of the Kings in the published text. The tourist today takes the same road through the mountains of the Libyan Chain. Two soldiers had died of sunstroke when Desaix first reconnoitered the oven of that valley. Even so, in company with Saint-Genis and Coraboeuf, Costaz climbed a side path leading to the top of the range. There the air was cool and refreshing, the sky blue and the sun brilliant with a clarity never to be experienced in Europe. The whole sweep of Thebes lay before them on both sides of the Nile, from beyond Karnak to the far side of Medinet Habu, the city of a hundred gates, deserted before anyone had thought of building any cities that now exist. Costaz gave the designations Harps, Metempsychosis, and Astronomical to the tombs now assigned respectively to Ramesses III (II, 79, fig. 6), Ramesses VI (II, 78, fig. 1–2), and Ramesses VII (II, 79, fig. 13–14). He and his colleagues regretted that time had permitted only a sampling of the paintings that adorn the royal tombs. They were leaving their successors a "rich harvest." For himself, Costaz had already traversed both banks of the Nile and studied all the monuments from Philae to Thebes. He had spent twenty-four intense days working without respite amid the ruins of the latter. He had grown jaded. When they struck their tents to move to the Valley of the Kings, he did not imagine himself to be capable of a rebirth of admiration, let alone of wholly new reactions. The first glance undeceived him. Here was something else. "I felt a sort of seizure. My soul was stirred. My curiosity, ready to die out, flared up with all its initial ardor."

The Commission passed its scant month at Thebes almost unguarded. From time to time Desaix sent a detachment from Esna to see whether they were safe. The journey downstream resumed on or about 18 October. Jollois and Devilliers had five days to revisit Dendara, relieved to find that it did not suffer by comparison with all they had seen. Jollois still thought their

JOLLOIS

first temple to be the *chef-d'oeuvre* of Egyptian architecture. The treatment of the remaining sites in upper and middle Egypt—Abydos, Antaeopolis, Asyut, Antinoë, and the sites of the Heptanomide and Fayoum—is more cursory. Jomard was responsible for much of it.

Their portfolios bulging with notes, drawings, and data, our explorers remembered the promise relayed by Monge that they would go home when their mission was accomplished. Bonaparte had in fact left just such orders with Kléber, dictated and signed in Alexandria before taking ship on 22 August. The Commission of Science and Arts was to be returned to France in November, except that Kléber was authorized to retain any of its members for whose services he had special need. Back in Cairo with his colleagues on 6 November, Jollois soon recognized that things had changed and that pining for home was useless.

DEVILLIERS

INCEPTION OF THE
DESCRIPTION DE L'EGYPTE

No one felt resentment toward Kléber. He was a person of sterling character who commanded not only his troops but the admiration and loyalty of all his subordinates. He clearly had the interest of the entire Expedition at heart. When elected to the Institut d'Egypte on 10 November 1799 (along with Desaix and Reynier), he at first demurred, saying that he had no qualification to be among scientists, and finally accepted a place in the section of arts and letters. For all his lack of pretention, Kléber took the initiative that led to eventual publication of the *Description de l'Egypte*, combining the study of ancient and modern Egypt in a single work. There had been no thought of that until the return to Cairo from upper Egypt. Every man for himself, as Girard had said at the outset. Then, on 19 November, Kléber appointed a Commission des Renseignements sur l'Etat moderne de l'Egypte. Fourier was elected president, and the active members were Conté, Desgenettes, Dutertre, Jacotin, Girard, J.-M. Le Père, and Protain. The Institute thereupon distributed its membership among sub-committees on (1) Legislation, (2) Administration, (3) Police, (4) Government and History, (5) Military organization, (6) Commerce and Industry, (7) Agriculture, (8) Natural history of the population, (9) Monuments and Costumes, and (10) Geography and Hydrography. On 22 November, Kléber sent a further message to the Institute in the name of the government, inviting the Commission of Science and Arts to join in assembling all they had collected in upper Egypt. In response, some forty-seven members of the Commission held a meeting under the presidency of Nouet, the senior in age, and resolved to conduct their further affairs on the model of a learned society. At the initiative of a merchant and entrepreneur, Antoine-Romain Hamelin, a joint-stock company was formed among some fourteen members of the Commission to undertake the publication in France. The venture had the blessing of Kléber.

On the very day the Hamelin contract was signed, 29 December 1799, a Turkish army that had been massing in Syria occupied the fortress of El Arish. Negotiations for an armistice culminated in the Convention of El Arish, signed by Desaix and accepted by Kléber on 24 January 1800. By its terms, the French were to fall back on Alexandria, Rosetta, and Abukir. The Army would then be accorded the honors of war and evacuated to France with its equipment. The Commission of Science and Arts would also be assured safe passage. Its members cut short their projects, gathered their materials, and left Cairo for Rosetta in early February. Quarantined with the others on the nearby isle of Farehi, Devilliers took his gun and went bird hunting in the marshes. He was surprised, and Dubois-Aymé amazed, that he proved a good shot. Certified free of plague, the group moved on to Alexandria in March. Two ships were to be assigned them. Half their number were given passports and embarked on the first vessel to be ready for departure, the brig *L'Oiseau*. The engineers and artists had their notebooks, drawings, and souvenirs all carefully packed. The naturalists had their specimens ranged in cases or preserved in bottles of alcohol. For a month they bobbed in the harbor awaiting clearance. It never came. Higher British authority required that the French be treated as prisoners of war. Sir Sidney Smith honorably apprised Kléber of the setback before the evacuation of Cairo had been completed. The French commander responded by routing the Turkish army at Heliopolis on 20 March and reinstating the occupation in full force.

The Institut d'Egypte thereupon resumed its meetings, but the heart had gone out of it and out of the Commission. The remaining fifteen months after the assassination of Kléber on 14 June 1800 were an unhappy time. Menou was a political person, a phrase maker, a desk general rather than a commander, respected neither by the soldiers under his command nor by the civilians under his authority. The Institute's failure to elect him to membership was an affront, and no doubt meant as such. For he was no fool. He might well have been a success had he been a colonial administrator. That is precisely what he meant to be, and there was the root of his trouble with the Commission. They wanted him to end the occupation, as Kléber had wished to do, while his purpose was to consolidate and continue it.

Useful work was, nevertheless, accomplished. Much of the material contained in the *Etat moderne* volumes, both plates and text, was assembled during this period, and also much of the topographical atlas. Menou assigned civil engineers to the provincial capitals, to their great anger, and sent off a mission to explore and map the Sinai. As for archaeology, charting and measuring the pyramids of Giza and excavating in the interiors and the surrounding tombs was the signal mission of the Menou command. Jacotin surveyed the site (V, 6). Jomard and Cécile measured the base of the Great Pyramid, the successive courses of the masonry, the slope of the faces, in short, every feature of the dimensions. Coutelle and the architect Lepère, assisted by Jomard, investigated the interior (V, 13–18), penetrating into a chamber previously unknown. Balzac, Dutertre, and Cécile did the picturesque views (V, 6–10, 12). Conté drew the Sphinx (V, 11), subject of the one important plate we have from him.

The most important single object in the care of the Institute was, of course, the Rosetta Stone (V, 52–54). It had been discovered in July 1799, some days before the second battle of Abukir. Accounts of the circumstances vary, but the most plausible version has it built into an ancient wall that impeded constructing the foundation for an enlargement of the stronghold later called Fort Julien. The engineering officer in charge of the demolition, Lieutenant François-Xavier Bouchard, at once recognized that the trilingual inscriptions might provide the key to deciphering the hieroglyphs at the top and the script in the middle (taken for "Syriac") from the Greek at the bottom. He notified Menou, then in command at Rosetta, who immediately arranged for a translation of the Greek. Lancret, also in Rosetta, took it on himself to write the letter to the Institut d'Egypte that apprised it of the discovery. That message—Monsieur Goby has established—was read out in the meeting of 29 July. The stone itself was brought to Cairo in mid-August, almost simultaneously with Bonaparte's departure. A public announcement appeared in the official *Courier de l'Egypte* in September (No. 37, le 29 fructidor, An VII).

Interest in the Institute was intense. The two senior orientalists, Jean-Joseph Marcel and Remi Raige, set to work studying the inscriptions with the collaboration of a classicist, Jacques-Denis Delaporte. They succeeded in recognizing the middle part for the cursive form of the hieroglyphs at the top. Copyists set to work, but the task was laborious and perfect accuracy unattainable. Marcel was also director of the printery, however, and—anticipating the invention of lithography by about ten years—it occurred to him that the stone itself could serve as a printing form. He had the surface washed meticulously. Brushing removed all the specks and left the grooves moist so that they would not take ink. Printer's ink was then spread upon the dried surface, and a damp sheet was pressed gently into contact with all the raised areas. Marcel made the trial on 24 January 1800. It succeeded perfectly. When he pulled the sheet, he had a reproduction of the text, the letters white on black, which could be read through the back or in a mirror.

The fertile Conté imagined an alternative procedure, treating the stone as a copper plate and taking prints with the letters black on white. Copies of both sorts circulated among the learned. A bit later,

LEPERE
ARCHITECTE

LANCRET

Raffeneau-Delile made a sulfur cast, and fortunately so. Otherwise, the French would have been left with nothing but these proofs, the first of which reached Paris in the baggage of General Dugua, commandant of Cairo at the time. The plates (V, 53–54) showing the cursive and Greek inscriptions were made from Raffeneau's cast. The part containing the hieroglyphs (V, 52) was reproduced from a plaster cast that Jomard traveled to London in 1815 to make in the British Museum.

The Rosetta Stone had remained in Cairo throughout the false departure after the Convention of El Arish. Had it been left there until the final capitulation, it would be in the Louvre today. The sands had run out by the summer of 1801. A British expeditionary force under Sir Ralph Abercromby landed in Abukir Bay on 8 March 1801. Menou's ill-conceived tactics produced bloodbath and disaster in the Battle of Canopus on 21 March. The French survivors fell back on Alexandria, where Menou had his headquarters, leaving Belliard largely cut off in the citadel of Cairo. A Turkish Army was advancing on the capital from the East. Following Kléber's example, Belliard resolved to spend no more lives in a hopeless cause. He was losing thirty or forty men a day to the plague alone, among them the 20-year-old naturalist Coquebert, who died in the arms of his friends on 7 April. Belliard asked for an armistice and on 27 June accepted terms modeled on the Convention of El Arish. A week later, orders came from Menou to fight to the death. Instead, the French withdrew with full honors of war, taking their equipment and all possessions with them. The Rosetta Stone would have accompanied the body of Kléber had it not already been sent to Alexandria. As it was, the Institut d'Egypte held its final meeting on 22 March, and most of its members departed for Alexandria in early April, taking the Rosetta Stone with them.

There it was placed in a warehouse with the baggage of the commander in chief. Menou's inevitable capitulation, consummated on 3 September, compounded incoherence with indignity. The remaining members of the Commission had tried to get away earlier, as those who had

stayed in Cairo with Belliard had succeeded in doing. Menou appeared to accept the argument that their continued presence served no military purpose, but he kept them waiting, again aboard *L'Oiseau*, Captain Murat, from 9 June until 11 July. When clearance finally came, after this second month of tenterhooks on that ill-omened brig, the ship was headed off by the British corvette *Cynthia*. Despite the renewed intervention of Sir Sidney Smith, Fourier and Murat failed to persuade Admiral Keith to let the learned company pass. On their forced return to harbor, Menou at first refused to let them land, threatening to sink *L'Oiseau* if they tried and expressing outrage that Murat had flown the Union Jack in hopes of getting clear.

Once the capitulation was signed, the British commander, General J. H. Hutchinson, claimed that its article 16 required surrender of everything the French had acquired in Egypt, including documents, notes, papers, and all that the Commission had assembled. Had he prevailed, there would be no *Description de l'Egypte,* and the material—or so the Commission darkly suspected—would have been exploited by Sir William Hamilton, who was at Hutchinson's elbow, for his writings on Egypt. Not trusting in Menou to defend their interests, a deputation headed by Geoffroy Saint-Hilaire waited on the British commander, in one breath refusing to be parted from their collections even if that meant accompanying the objects to England, and in another threatening to throw everything into the sea and publish to the world that British vandalism was responsible for this, a destruction of science and culture in Alexandria comparable to the burning of its library in ancient times. In the end, what could be construed as personal property went with the French. Hutchinson rejected Menou's claim that the Rosetta Stone belonged to him. Among other monumental objects that went to London were the black-granite statue from Abydos (IV, 37, fig. 6–11), the colossal wrist from Memphis (V, 4, fig. 1), and the sarcophagus from the mosque of Saint Athanasius in Alexandria (V, 39–41).

Dispersed among all sorts of transports, our people departed Egypt in late September. On the 25th, Jollois, Devilliers,

Dubois-Aymé, Cécile, Fèvre, and others went aboard *Il Amico Sincero*. They debarked in Marseilles in mid-November and after several weeks in quarantine reached their families, Devilliers on 28 December, Jollois on 10 January. By the turn of the year 1802, everyone was home, each with his mementos and materials, except for the military engineers and others who had participated in mapping the terrain. Data for the topographical atlas belonged to the Corps of Engineers. Menou had seen to that, and properly so. The civilians had refused a last-ditch order that they too pool their documentation and deliver it into the keeping of the high command.

PUBLICATION OF THE WORK

It is characteristic of the Bonapartist regime that the authorities should now have seized the opportunity to act in the name of the state while also respecting the rights of private property. They acted fast. Bonaparte would have none of the Hamelin joint-stock company, there agreeing with Menou. The Hamelin contract was quashed. Instead, a Consular decree of February 1802 called for publication "of the memoirs, plans, drawings, and generally all the results relative to science and art obtained during the course of the Expedition." The expense was to be borne by the government. The profits were to go to the authors. On 20 March 1802, Jean-Antoine Chaptal, the industrial chemist who as Minister of the Interior first organized the Bonapartist administration, invited all interested parties to submit an inventory of what they proposed to contribute, drawings, memoirs, or both.

Collaboration thus carried over from the exploration of Egypt to publication of the *Description de l'Egypte*. Remembering their resolution to conduct themselves in the manner of a learned society, the leading people evolved controls that would now be called peer review. The contributors, all those within reach of Paris, met together at frequent intervals in a General Assembly. The model must almost certainly have been the Assembly of the Corps des Ponts et Chaussées, the civil engineering corps in which many of our leading people made their careers. Projects for public works were put before that body, a council composed of the inspectors-general and certain of the chief engineers. It carefully scrutinized every proposed construction, often requiring modifications in detail and sometimes in overall design. Similarly, every drawing, every plan, all the elevations, sections, and panoramic views, and equally all the memoirs for the volumes of text, in a word the entire contents of the *Description de l'Egypte*, had to be submitted to the Assemblée Générale des Collaborateurs. It soon came to work by ad hoc committees, of course. Notes were compared, memories pooled, and decisions reached. Authors were often required to make revisions. Certain contributions were rejected altogether. Others were eliminated for reasons of redundancy. Thus could Fourier assert in the "Préface historique":

JOMARD

The series of plates represents existing objects which can be observed and described in an exact manner and which, for that reason, are to be considered as so many positive elements in the study of Egypt.

Unlike the exploration, the publication of Egypt required direction. Final authority rested with the Minister of the Interior. A commissioner whose functions were those of editor-in-chief reported to him. Conté first held that post. He succumbed of an aneurysm in 1805, to be succeeded by Lancret, who died in 1807. Thereupon, Jomard became commissioner and saw the project through to completion, an unforeseen twenty years later. An executive committee had the responsibility of a board of editors and held its first meeting under the presidency of Berthollet on 7 June 1802. Its secretary, essentially the managing editor, assisted the commissioner. Lancret had that job under Conté, Jomard under Lancret, and Jollois under Jomard. Besides the above, the committee initially consisted of Monge, Fourier, Conté, Costaz, Girard, and Desgenettes. Ten years later, in 1812, Desgenettes and Girard had been replaced by Devilliers and Alyre Raffeneau-Delile. Direction of the edition was a full-time occupation. Members of the committee who did not have other official posts were paid a salary. In 1808, Jomard received 6,000 francs and Jollois 4,600. The remaining contributors received retainers in proportion to the importance of their contributions. As of 1 June 1809, there were 36 people on a payroll that was running at 62,359 francs annually and that had disbursed a total of 503,715 francs out of a global expenditure of 1,454,818 since the inception of the project seven years previously.

Nothing had yet appeared. It is, perhaps, a general law of large editorial projects involving the collaboration of many contributors that what was to have taken days inevitably requires weeks. Weeks turn into months, months into years, and years into decades. So it was throughout the publication of the *Description de l'Egypte*. Quite probably, it was the largest such venture ever undertaken. Certainly, it was one of the most complex. An enormous body of material had had to be organized, as Lancret explained to an impatient Minister late in 1806. It had been collected with no prior ordering and according to no common plan by a large number of people very different from one another in age, standing, profession, and commitment. Thousands of illustrations had to be correlated with thousands of pages of text to ensure that subject and key letters in the one should correspond to the references and explanations in the other.

COSTAZ

The Commission started out with quarters in the Louvre. Then, from 1804 until 1810, it rented inadequate editorial offices in the rue du Doyenné, no. 12. Roomier accommodations were finally assigned in the Institut de France, three adjoining rooms and a guardian's cubicle under the mansard along the rue Mazarine. There, each finished plate had a file drawer to itself capacious enough to hold a thousand copies. The cabinets were six drawers deep, and every Egyptian site had a bank of drawers to itself arranged in the order of the finished work. Contributors who gave problems ran the gamut from those who repeatedly missed deadlines to those who wished to preprint their memoirs separately. The Le Père brothers, for example, clamored to bring out the *Mémoire sur le Canal entre les Deux Mers* in advance. In 1815, six years after the initial publication, it was printed separately. Dutertre at first held aloof with the inten-

tion of publishing his work on his own account, like Denon. After two years of discussion, he did come in, in April 1804, and immediately demanded that his retainer be retroactive. He also wanted to sell the Commission the copper plates he had had engraved, and when they were judged of inferior quality, he asked for reimbursement of the cost. Fourier managed to be both delinquent contributor and stern taskmaster. Nothing could appear until he had completed his "Préface historique." and to increasingly desperate appeals from Jomard he answered blaming the delay on the failure of other authors to finish their memoirs, all of which he must have under his eyes there in Grenoble, where he was Prefect of the Isère and where he had the assistance of Champollion's older brother, J.-J. Champollion-Figeac.

The order of magnitude had become clear by 1807, so that contracts could be let to papermakers and printers. The estimate was that over 3,000 reams of paper would be required. Few papermakers dared bid on a job that would require retooling to form the outsize, *Grand Jésus* sheets. The contract went to Desgranges, a manufacturer in Arches, much to the discomfiture of the better-known firm of Montgolfier in Annonay, who had enlisted the influence of the ministry. Not all the batches were satisfactory, and the Commission had to take Desgranges to task from time to time. With respect to printing the plates, the Commission bypassed the Imperial Printing House, even though the director, J.-J. Marcel, was a contributor. In June 1807, it chose to divide the work among a consortium of four printers, all located in or near the rue Saint-Jacques. Jean-Pierre Langlois had done work both in half-tones and in color and was specially known for the ornithology of Levaillant. Ambroise Sampier d'Arena was printer to the *Dépôt de la Guerre*, the cartographical section of the War Department. He had worked for Conté and given satisfaction. François-Dominique Ramoz was printer to the Louvre and a specialist in half-tones. Jean-Charles Rémond, on the other hand, was known for color printing, notably the flower pictures of Redouté the elder. In October, a fifth printer, Charles-Nicolas Richomme, took a piece of the contract.

Impatience gathered in high places. A report of 20 August 1807 records that in five years' time 442 plates had been completed, or at least started, with 338 still to do. The limiting factor, if we may believe the increasingly defensive explanations of Lancret and Jomard, was that appropriations were insufficient to pay for more than about ninety plates each year. At the outset, the intention had been to publish the entire work at once. All the text could then be coordinated with all the plates in advance. Late in 1806, however, Napoleon himself ordered that sheets be printed off as soon as the copper plates were engraved and issued in batches of ten or twelve at a time. Apparently, he accepted the objection that the work would lose all impact if it dribbled out like that, but required that it appear not later than 1809. Desperately the Commission appealed to contributors to send their material, hoping still to buy time to salvage the original plan. There is a pained letter from Jollois begging Fourier for the preface on 14 September 1808 and telling of his last interview with the Minister of the Interior: "His Excellency manifested much impatience, I might say anger, that no part of the work has yet appeared." He could not again go to the Emperor and ask for more money until something was in print. He would then, and these were the Minister's own words, says Jollois, "be dismissed with loss of credit, and he did not wish to expose himself to that."

Thereupon, the Commission resigned itself to an installment plan, undertaking to produce the first *livraison* in 1809, the second in 1810, and the third in 1811. Even that did not actually happen, of course. Napoleon's orders were respected, formally at least. The title page bears the publication date of 1809, but 1810 was far advanced before the printing was accomplished. For the rest, the simplest course will be to tabulate the entire sequence in which the four divisions did eventually appear.

ANTIQUITES

Planches	Tome I	1809
	Tomes II, III	1812
	Tome IV	1817
	Tome V	1822

Mémoires	Tome I	1809
	Tome II	1818
Description	Tome I	1809
	Tome II	1818

ETAT MODERNE

Planches	Tome I	1809
	Tome II	1817
Texte	Tome I	1809
	Tome II	1812
	Tome II, Pt. 2	1822

HISTOIRE NATURELLE

Planches	Tome I	1809
	Tome II	1817
	Tome II bis	c1824
Texte	Tome I	1809
	Tome II	1813

CARTE TOPOGRAPHIQUE (1828)

Thus, just about half of the entire work, excluding the atlas, reached publication before the fall of Napoleon in 1815—three of the five volumes of plates that we reproduce together with one volume of plates in the modern Egypt division, one of Natural History, and one volume of the text in each of the main categories. Whether the restored monarchy would patronize an enterprise so expressly glorifying the usurper was a question. The government of Louis XVIII took it as a matter of national prestige, however, a thing to be finished with, though not relished, as rapidly as possible. The new Minister of the Interior imposed a cutoff that held. The Commission was forbidden to accept any material submitted later than 31 December 1816. The final volume of memoirs on modern Egypt took another six years to revise and edit, and the Natural History, although it contains many beautiful plates, never was completed.

In one respect, the restored monarchy was more forthcoming than the imperial regime had finally been. It carried through on the original intention of publishing the topographical atlas. At the very outset, on 2 December 1802, the Commission requested that the fifty sheets already being engraved in the Dépôt de la Guerre be incorporated in the work. Bonaparte gave his assent on 3 January following. The Peace of Amiens had been in effect since 3 March 1802. Although the truce with England lasted barely a year,

MENOU

the map of Egypt formed part of the Commission's planning until early in 1808. The paper was on order from Desgranges, and printing was to begin that year. The military had never been happy over the prospect, however, and it was probably Sanson, the chief of engineers, who got Napoleon's ear in time to stop it. Berthollet received a curt refusal of the Commission's request for final clearance: "His Majesty has ordered that this map remain under the seal of a state secret."

Nevertheless, there had to be a map of Egypt, and the first volume of Plates does contain one, issued in 1765! In their extremity, the Commission fell back on the work of an armchair cartographer, the chevalier Bourguignon d'Anville, whose artistically drawn maps were based on the study of other maps and of books. With all Fourier's parade of positive facts, the Commission knew a makeshift when forced to adopt one. Immediately on Napoleon's departure for his first exile in Elba, it requested the ministry for authority to include the Expedition's map of Egypt in the *Description de l'Egypte* and received permission on 14 August 1814. It does not appear that Napoleon got around to undoing that during the hundred days, but even so, the atlas did not actually reach subscribers until 1828, by which time a second edition of the entire work was well advanced.

PREPARATION OF THE PLATES

Tipped in at the end of Part 2 of the second volume of memoirs on modern Egypt is a design that folds out, showing the machine invented by Conté for ruling copper plates. Alongside is a sheet exhibiting samples of what it could do—forty-two patches consisting of patterns of lines, thick and thin, light and heavy; horizontal, vertical, and diagonal; parallel, converging, and diverging; rectilinear and undulating; equidistant with intervals of varying breadth and graduated in varying intervals; produced both by etching and by dry-point. The reader who examines the plates closely will see how the engravers have employed these possibilities in creating the texture of surfaces, skies, and water. Occasional passages in the work allude to the importance of this machine. The papers of the Commission in the

Bibliothèque nationale even contain a memoir (NAF 21,950, vol. 17, no. 58) from the not very literate hand of the artisan who built it, one Gallet, referring to Jomard's account and setting him straight about certain fine points in operating it. All this is tantalizing, since nowhere in the *Description de l'Egypte* itself is any such account to be found nor any explanation of the design thus left to explain itself.

Then, as sometimes happens in historical research, luck intervenes where system has failed, and one comes on Jomard's report dated 26 June 1822 in the *Bulletin de la Société d'Encouragement pour l'Industrie Nationale* (vol. 22, ccxxix, 169–183). It gives the same illustration as the *Description*. (A plate with the patches accompanied the next number, ccxxx.) The Conté machine, it there appears, was a rational, even a mathematical, solution to specific problems posed by preparation of the *Description de l'Egypte*. There was a saying about Conté, attributed sometimes to Bonaparte, sometimes to Monge, to the effect that he had all the sciences in his head and all the arts in his hand. Besides the graphite pencil and the semaphore telegraph, he had also worked on a varnish that would make balloons impermeable, losing an eye in an explosion in the laboratory. In charge of the machine shop in Cairo, he improvised instruments to replace those lost in the rising of October 1798, and thanks to him the army was supplied with ammunition fabricated in Egypt.

No sooner did Conté assume charge of the Commission on the *Description de l'Egypte* early in 1803 than he recognized that engraving the plates would present the greatest of many difficulties. The problems were of several sorts. First of all, the majority of plates contain large expanses of sky, of architectural surfaces, and of background to the figures in bas-reliefs. Producing an undifferentiated texture, called in the trade *teintes plates*, required ruling the plates horizontally. The depth and separation of the grooves determines the relative lightness or darkness of the tone, and the success of an artist working burin in hand depended on how exactly he could maintain the equidistance and equal depth of lines. Conté's machine accomplished that automatically and with a perfection that no artist could

CECILE

achieve. It had further advantages. The copper was never of uniform density, and the carriage was fitted with a device that varied the pressure on the point in proportion to the resistance of the metal. Another attachment, a triangular cam that rotated as the carriage advanced, could also produce the wavy lines required for water.

Picturing the sky presented a second order of difficulty beyond the mere framing of objects in the texture of a background. The problem, called specifically *ciel* in the trade, was perspective. To create a naturalistic setting for objects shown in perspective, the reflection of light by the atmosphere has to be shown increasing from the minimum that makes the zenith appear deep blue to a maximum in the paleness of the horizon. The procedure classically employed in copper engraving achieved that effect by gradually increasing the separation and lessening the depth of lines ruled in the plate. The more uniform the gradient in both dimensions, the more successful the sky. That was the most difficult of the engraver's operations. The artist often, and indeed normally, covered his unavoidable slips of hand and eye by putting in clouds.

But there are no clouds over Egypt, and Conté solved that problem in the spirit of the calculus. Each interval was slightly— Jomard says infinitesimally—greater than the one before it. The machine was so designed that 360 of these differences were equal to one-half the initial interval. If that width is supposed to be one millimeter, and usually it is much less, then each increment would be 1/720 millimeter. But that is only half the solution. Since the depth of the grooves determines the darkness of the lines, it must diminish proportionally to the increasing separation between them. Two arithmetical series with the same difference are thus inverse. Readers interested in the technical detail may consult the Jomard report.

In 1825, the entire *Description de l'Egypte* went on display in the Louvre in an exhibition of the application of technology to the fine arts. Notable were the fabrication of *velin* paper in giant sheets and the advantages just indicated of the Conté machine. In addition, a manuscript that Jomard composed for the occasion

enlarges on the improvements both in economy and quality that mechanical engraving brought to color prints (BN, NAF 21,950, vol. 17, fo. 52). The classical method required engraving multiple plates, one for each of the principal shades, and impressing the sheets upon all the plates in turn. The time and expense were exorbitant, the more so that the tones were likely to be false. Worse, after four or five sheets had been pulled, the colors would no longer be constant, and lines would begin to blur or double. Jomard cited the genre scenes from El-Kab (I, 70) as evidence of these defects. Faced with this disappointment, the Commission experimented with the Conté plates to see whether colors could not be printed from one or at most two of them. In the technique it developed, the fundamental colors were printed, and the proofs were then touched up by hand with watercolors in the workshop. Jomard indicated the restorations at Philae (I, 18) and Medinet Habu (II, 12) as examples of the success. Each of these plates would have cost 150 to 200 francs to produce by the old method, whereas their cost to the Commission was one-tenth of that. Twenty-nine colored plates of birds and minerals, which had been much admired in the Natural History volumes, were also printed by this technique. Wall paintings, on the other hand, required two plates, one carrying the background color, the other the color that outlines the figures (II, 82–87, 89–91).

Mechanical engraving was a technique whose time had come. Commenting on the acquisition of a set of the *Description de l'Egypte* in 1838, the librarian of the London Institution says that one Lowry had been ruling plates with some such device since 1798. Jomard acknowledged that the English had similar machines, though he had never been able to see a model. They had been unknown to Conté, however, whose own invention passed into use in France without ever being patented or written up. Governments discouraged publicizing these techniques because they would ease the practice of counterfeiting currency. At all events, it is clear that the printing of 820,000 sheets, 60,000 of them in color, from the 837 plates—the press run was 1,000—of the *Description de l'Egypte*

COUTELLE

transformed the engraver's trade. The work could not have been completed without the Conté machine. Jomard estimated that it accomplished in two or three days what an artist working by hand would have needed six months to complete, and that the total saving was on the order of 300,000 francs. That was equivalent to approximately 20% of all the sums expended by the end of July 1809, when the first installment was due to appear. Two of the machines were set up in the workshop, one for the normal plates and one for the large size. Eighty to a hundred engravers were employed there during the life of the project. They took the technique with them to other jobs and even to other trades. Textiles as well as paper were printed on adaptations of the Conté machine, which was the point of departure for the nineteenth-century graphic arts in France.

CONTE

Each illustration in the *Description de l'Egypte* gives the engraver's name at the lower right or middle and the author's at the lower left. Lists of contributors were drawn up from time to time in the course of the project. A list of 1812 specifying who were to receive complimentary sets contains seventy names. What may be taken as the definitive roster is dated 23 June 1820 (BN NAF 21,950). The occasion was acceptance by the government of a bid from the publisher Panckoucke to do a second edition. Honoring the initial commitment that royalties should go to the authors, the Commission there gives sixty-two names, each with the amount he is to receive under the new contract. The sums were proportional to the importance of the contribution, both to the text and to the four divisions of the plates. Amounts range from 12,042.90 francs for Jomard and 11,521.60 for Jollois and Devilliers down through 4,821.40 for Lepère the architect, 3,959.50 for Cécile, and 3,286.20 for Balzac to 789.80 for Dubois-Aymé, 24 francs for Malus, and 6 for Regnault. Using these and other indices, Monsieur Goby has calculated a coefficient of participation for each of the contributors. Without aspiring to that nice a precision, we have made a rougher estimate of the distribution of authorship among the plates here reproduced. Of a total of 289 unitary plates and 850 figures in the remaining 137 composite

plates, Jomard and the partnership of Jollois and Devilliers drew 119 plates and 300 figures. A further set of authors, consisting of Balzac, Cécile, Chabrol, Dutertre, Lancret, Lenoir, Redouté, Viard, and the team of Lepère the architect, Coraboeuf, and Saint-Genis, account for 160 plates and 471 figures. In those totals, Lenoir did no plates and 86 figures and Viard 1 and 79, respectively. That leaves only 10 plates and 79 figures that came from occasional contributors. It is to be noted, however, that the distribution would look quite different if the *Etat moderne*, *Histoire naturelle*, and *Atlas topographique* were included.

The plates afford frequent glimpses of the authors at work. One has the feeling that it was as souvenirs, and not only as a means of establishing scale, that they sometimes put themselves into their pictures, for example, at Philae (I, 3), Kom Ombo (I, 40), Medinet Habu (II, 15), and the Great Pyramid of Khufu (V, 13). Moored at Silsila (I, 47) is one of the *djermes* in which they traveled the Nile. Pitched outside the temple of Horus at Edfu is the tent that sheltered the artist. Bearers are busy with his mount, his gun, and the preparation of his meal. On the ceiling at Kom Ombo survived a sketch for a bas-relief that the ancient sculptor had never carved (I, 44, fig. 3). The reproduction shows the copy paper ruled in a grid. Our authors made all their drawings on sheets like this. Those were what they carried back to France together with detailed notes, the record of precise measurements, and their memories. The line drawings that accompany the astronomical plates give a further notion of the unadorned draftsmanship. We reproduce the one of the circular zodiac at Dendara (IV, 21). Comparison of the naked drawing with the finished plate will also bring home what the engraving machine accomplished.

In interpreting what they saw and drew, the contributors had nothing to guide sensibility except accounts of Egypt by writers in classical antiquity, notably Herodotus, Strabo, Diodorus of Sicily, and Pliny. The most elementary facts contained in the most superficial of modern guidebooks were unknown to them. For the deities the only names they had were Isis, Osiris, *some error. Everyone wants to provide a history for this great people, enlightened, powerful, separated from us by a mysterious barrier at a remove of centuries on centuries. Everyone wants to see some premature system applied to these, the first fragments of Egyptian monuments transported to Europe. All impatient, they think to find there this people's explanation of heaven and earth, its principles of government, its manners and morals; the explanation, too, of its religious ceremonies, of its art, of its science, and of its industry. Its hieroglyphs lend themselves to the wildest flights of imagination, and, relying on hypothesis, everyone presses forward with equal authority by different routes, all of them equally obscure and hazardous. To put some system together, to collect those artifacts that offer support and agreement, is not to shed light; it is only to strike the stone from which the spark escapes that produces it. Thus persuaded, I have discovered in myself the willpower required to remain passive while simply drawing hieroglyphs. Mine is an ardent piety, a blind zeal ultimately to be compared only to that of vestals of old who prayed, believed, and adored in a foreign language they did not understand.*

It is, indeed, thanks to the courage and zeal of men like Denon, Jollois, Devilliers, Jomard, Dutertre, Castex, and Redouté that we owe the majority of the engravings of inscriptions in the *Description*. Twenty years after the repatriation of the Army of the Orient, the spark evoked by Denon could fire the genius of Champollion, and thus it was that a new scientific discipline, Egyptology, came to be founded.

LABATE

THE EGYPTIAN COLLECTIONS

FORMED DURING THE EXPEDITION DE L'EGYPTE

MICHEL DEWACHTER

More than a century and a half after the appearance of the *Description de l'Egypte*, sustained consultation of this, in effect the first modern encyclopaedia devoted to a single country, makes evident that there is still much to be learned from the materials assembled and skillfully worked up by the many conscientious contributors.

What is true of the work as a whole is equally so of the five volumes of plates devoted to Antiquity, which we reproduce in the present edition, and especially with respect to the artifacts brought back to Europe by members of the Expedition. That such should be the case may well be found surprising, given the development of Egyptology since 1822.

Why has no one until now thought of making a bibliographical catalogue of everything engraved in the plates? This deficiency in the documentation requires scholars who depend on museums to undertake repeated, tedious, and too often useless or inconclusive searches in which they risk missing what they are looking for. Very recently, for example, the modern history of the little group of Amenope and Tamerout in the Louvre (N 1594) was traced back as far as 1824. Its original provenance escaped that investigation; consulting the *Description* (Volume V, Plate 64) would have revealed that this piece was found in 1798-99 during the exploration of the Theban necropolis.

We had thought to tell readers of the present reprint what has become of the various objects depicted in the plates. In attempting to carry out that perfectly reasonable task, we have discovered, first of all, that finding the information is rarely easy and, secondly, that the *Description* has never yet been used for what it was meant to be, that is, a real Register of Monuments.

A funerary ritual, a series of ushabtis, a fragmented casing, or a dismembered mummy, even if they no longer exist or cannot be located, nevertheless afford evidence of a visit to a tomb, often identifiable today, that still contained some part of its contents at the time of the Expedition. Whenever an anthroponymous relation may be deciphered from these copies, more or less carefully done, of what then survived, it would be best if the information were to be entered directly in files maintained for each necropolis and reported in the master catalogues.

To take a single example, consider the case of the stamped bricks that Jomard drew with—it must be said—extraordinary care (II, 48, fig. 6–8). Their representation makes it possible today to complete and correct types 336 and 346 of the compilation of cones still being used (see N. de Garis Davies and M. F. Laming Macadam, *A Corpus of Inscribed Egyptian Funerary Cones* [Oxford, 1957]). Jomard states that these bricks had been ''collected in one of the tombs in the environs of the Memnonium where there was found a small wall built of bricks that were all alike'' (*Texte*, 2nd ed. [as in all citations in this essay], X, 170). It is thus evident that the cones of types 336 and 346 of the *Corpus* were prepared for the Theban tomb of Djéhoutymès, the great intendant of Amon, a sepulchre (TT32) of the Khôkha for which the beautiful group in the Cairo Museum (CG 549) must doubtless have been executed. This tomb has just been excavated by a team of Hungarians; a study will be published by Professor L. Kákosy.

As it fell out, the sudden arrival in Europe of the whole mass of Egyptian relics had a powerful effect in arousing the curiosity of the public at the beginning of the nineteenth century. The episode has never been studied seriously. It must be appreciated, moreover, that many of the pieces brought back by members of the Expedition were not engraved either in the *Description* or in Denon's *Travels*. Their absence from these works greatly complicates investigation and facilitates the specious and, in the case of certain dealers, improper characterization of every object coming up for sale as having been "brought back at the time of the Expedition."

COQUEBERT

At the same time, false attributions of Egyptian relics to members of the Expedition do not all stem from intrigues of dealers and collectors. Sometimes these factitious connections were made after the object was already in a museum. Examples that I have discussed elsewhere are the papyrus of Néféroubenef and a mummy in the museum in Châteauroux, which have mistakenly been considered to be souvenirs brought back at the time of the Expedition, the former by the botanist Alyre Raffeneau-Delile, the latter by General Bertrand (see M. Dewachter, "L'histoire moderne du papyrus de Néféroubenef [P. Louvre N.3092 and E.25565]," *Chronique d'Egypte* LV [1980]: 37–42; and "L'Egypte dans les collections de l'Indre," *Carobrias* 4 [1981]: 11–27).

Another object about which similar questions may well be raised is the inscription added in ink inside a solar disk that appears prominently on the lid of the coffin of Néhemesmontou in Grenoble (Inv. 1995). It is labeled "Momie des catacombes de Thèbes (Haute Egypte) rapportée par Vivant-Denon, lors de l'Expédition française, en 1799" (see Abbé Paul Tresson, *Catalogue descriptif des antiquités égyptiennes de la Salle Saint-Ferriol* [1933], 72, fig. 112). But should it not be placed in the category of improper ascriptions to the collections formed during the Expedition? Such may well be the case. For one thing, this coffin, which is of very high quality, does not appear, and there is nothing like it, either in the atlas of *Voyage dans la Basse et la Haute Egypte*, which Denon brought out in 1802, or in the plates of the *Description*. For another, it is nowhere mentioned even in the meticulous catalogue of Denon's collection "so readily accessible and so much visited," drawn up by Léon Jean Joseph Dubois at the time of Denon's death (see Dubois, *Description des objets d'art qui composent le Cabinet de Feu M. le Baron V. Denon* [1826], v). Thus, it must certainly have been the success of Denon's *Voyage* and the fame of his collection that were responsible for the ascription to him of a coffin taken from the Theban necropolis, not in 1799, but most probably a good twenty years later.

Similar reservations ought perhaps to attach to other coffins that are absent from the *Description*. One instance is that of Hatshepsut, the singer of Amon, located at Grenoble (Inv. 3572), which Dubois-Aymé is said to have brought back. He did indeed send several pieces to the Commission on the *Description de l'Egypte*, but not this one. Another dubious case is the coffin of Djedmoutioues-ânkh, nurse and singer of Khonsou, now in Avignon (A53), which a certain Cucurini is said to have "found in 1798 during the Egyptian Expedition in a pyramid near Thebes." To the best of my knowledge, however, the modern history of this coffin does not extend beyond 1820.

A further class of improper attributions, harder to detect, includes those objects added to the collections of participants in the Expedition well after their return from Egypt, whether such objects had been acquired from other members of the Army of the Orient or brought to Europe later. It is to be remembered that certain of the new collectors returned to Egypt themselves, for example, Livron and General Marmont, while others sent agents there. Consider the case of General Tarayre's collection. This officer had been governor of Suez. In the sale of the remainder of his collection, the Museum of Fine Arts in Boston recently acquired a superb lid to a small sarcophagus (MFA Inv. 1977.717; see William Kelly Simpson, *Bulletin de l'Institut Français d'Archéologie Orientale, Supplément* [1981], 325–329, pl. XLI). In practice, it is very difficult to know whether items in the Tarayre collection are really objects that the general took away himself or rather things acquired by his son. The former governor sent the young Amans Tarayre to Egypt in 1841–1842 in order to verify certain information that he needed in writing his study, *Importance de l'Egypte et de l'Isthme de Suez.* Certain of these latter acquisitions found their way into the Museum of Rodez in the course of the last century (see M. Dewachter, *Bulletin de l'Institut Français d'Archéologie Orientale, Supplément* [1981], 7–10; and *La collection égyptienne du Musée Champollion* [1986], 13–15).

But of course, the most distinguished putative patronage is that of the chief of the Expedition himself, and a number of works of art have rather hastily been said to have been "brought back by General Bonaparte." Thanks to Dubois (*Catalogue des objets d'art . . . qui composaient les collections de feu M. le Comte de Pourtalès-Gorgier et dont la vente aura lieu le 6 Février 1865*, fig. 4, n. 1), we have an 1841 list of seven objects, several of which graced Josephine's gallery at Malmaison for a time. One of them, the small statue of Senousret-Senebefni is now in the Brooklyn Museum (Inv. 39,602). John D. Cooney has given a masterly account of its recent history ("A Souvenir of Napoleon's Trip to Egypt," *Journal of Egyptian Archaeology* 35 [1949]: 153–157, pl. XVII). What is surprising is that none of these seven pieces was engraved either in the *Description* or in Denon's *Voyage.* Moreover, all that we know about Bonaparte's precipitate return to France makes it very doubtful that there was room for ancient works of art in Bonaparte's baggage (see Georges Douin, "Le retour de Bonaparte en France," *Bulletin de l'Institut d'Egypte* 23 [1941]: 185–216). Nothing is said about them by the Mameluke Roustam, who during the voyage was in charge of the baggage, which was pillaged near Aix-en-Provence (Paul Cottin, *Souvenirs de Roustam, Mamelouck de Napoléon Ier* [n.d.], 82–86).

The greatest skepticism is called for, then, with respect to Egyptian works of art "brought back," let alone "found," by Bonaparte, especially those of any size. Instances include the two statues of the Lady Yinyhay that Bonaparte is supposed to have transported to the Château des Ergalades, not far from Marseilles. It is indirectly owing to Brummer and Samuel

Untermyer that one of them has ended up in Baltimore (Georges Steindorff, "Two Egyptian Statues of the Ramesside Period," *Journal of the Walters Art Gallery* 5 [1942]: 9 et seq.), whereas the other departed recently for Japan following a sale at Christie's on 6 July 1976 (*Archeologia* 99 [Oct. 1976]: 73). In point of fact, there is no basis for tracing the provenance of these two statues further back than the Castellane collection, and the future maréchal de Castellane (1788–1862) was too young to have participated in the Egyptian expedition.

In short, then, any attribution of an object to the Expedition is to be treated with reservations unless there is reference to unimpeachable testimony. Too often, the earliest allusion in the literature was made at the time of a sale long after the return of the Army of the Orient. For example, only on the death of Louis Bonaparte in 1846 was the superb bronze inscribed as representing Osiris said to be a gift received by the aide-de-camp of his brother, Napoleon. The aide was in Egypt for an extremely brief time, reembarking on *Le Vif* on 7 November 1798. After having passed through the hands of the dealers Rollin and Feuardent, whose pieces were often labeled "Expédition d'Egypte," this bronze found its way to Holland in 1880 (J. van Dijk, "Egyptian Antiquities in the Bijbels Museum, Amsterdam," *Göttinger Miszellen* 43 [1981]: 7–8, pl. II, fig. 36).

Actually, a good many of the participants in the Expedition made a point of offering Josephine, Napoleon, or members of his entourage, Egyptian souvenirs that they had themselves obtained on the banks of the Nile. Thus the "head of a mummy of a woman," a feature of Bois-Préaux's natural history collection at Malmaison in 1814, was identical with the one that A. Delile brought back from Qurna and that was reproduced beautifully in the *Description*, without any reference to Malmaison (II, 50; *Texte* X, 172–173; see Serge Grandjean, *Inventaire après décès de l'Impératrice Joséphine à Malmaison* [1964], 256, fig. 2587). According to a handwritten annotation in a catalogue at the British Museum, this piece figured in an anonymous sale of 24 March 1819 in Paris before turning up in the collection of

Vivant Denon (*Notice d'une très belle collection . . . le tout provenant du château et de la galerie de M***[Malmaison]*, BM between nos. 23–24; Dubois, *Description des objets . . . V. Denon*, 55, fig. 246).

The same 1814 inventory of Malmaison designates as fig. 1511 "deux fragments égyptiens en granit noir" (Grandjean, *Inventaire*, 194). They may very well correspond to the head and torso that M. de Chanaleilles had found at Mendès. After his death at Saint-Jean d'Acre, they were offered to Bonaparte, who placed them in Malmaison (Jomard, *Texte* IX, 374, n. 1). The torso may be the one now preserved in the Fitzwilliam Museum in Cambridge, England (E. 31.1973), unless perhaps it corresponds to the fragment of a statue still in the possession of a dealer in Paris (Hermann de Meulenaere and P. Mackay, *Mendès* II [1976], 197, fig. 44b, 45; *Mendès* I [1980], 80).

Besides Josephine's collection, Bonaparte also gave several pieces to the Cabinet des médailles, notably the splendid torso of Nectanebo I (V, 69, fig.7–8). General Vial had found that sculpture at Samanhoud (*Texte* X [1821], 572–573). Today it is in the Louvre (E 25492). The Cabinet des médailles also received the funerary papyrus mentioned by Dubois in 1841 (*Catalogue des objets . . . le comte de Pourtalès-Gorgier*, fig. 4, n. 1). It is now difficult to identify this document, unless it perhaps corresponds to the portion of the Book of the Dead of Ouahibrê, reproduced in the *Description* (II, 66–69), that belonged to General Andréossy in 1802 (see below).

Napoleon's largesse also enriched the small museum that Denon installed on the Quai Voltaire. The Emperor gave him the beautiful manuscript of the Livre des respirations of Nes-paouty-taouy (Denon, *Voyage*, pl. 136, and Cabinet de Denon, no. 230). Certain scholars thought this papyrus had reached the Bibliothèque nationale (Jean-Claude Goyon, *Rituels funéraires de l'ancienne Egypte* [1972], 231). In fact, however, it ended up in The Hague, in the Musée Meermano-Westreenianum (H. de Meulenaere, *Chronique d'Egypte* 57 [1982]: 228, n. 3). It was also at the sale of the Denon collection that comte Turpin de Crissé, onetime lord-in-waiting in Josephine's household, obtained the handsome heart scarab of the

royal scribe Akh(y)-pet. Probably another gift of the Emperor, this object came to the Museum of Angers in 1858 and was afterwards stolen (M. Dewachter, *Bulletin de la Société Française d'Egyptologie* 103 [June 1985]: 32).

Denon also made gifts or exchanges from his Egyptian collection. For example, he gave Alexandre Brongniart the fine funerary cone of Shepenmout now in the ceramics museum at Sèvres (Sèvres Inv. MNC 1250; Jeanne Bulté, *Catalogue des collections égyptiennes du Musée National de Céramiques à Sèvres* [1981], 75–76, pl. XIII and C, fig. 95). From the catalogue of the Denon collection, it appears that he did not have a duplicate.

No sooner, evidently, was the Army of the Orient repatriated than its collections began to be widely dispersed, and by now the consequences complicate museum searches in no small degree. Who knows today, for instance, exactly which sculptures General Dugua gave to the newly-opened museum in Toulouse upon his return from Egypt? The matter is especially difficult in the case of papyrus manuscripts. Highly valued at the time, they were often for that reason divided. Such was the case with the Book of the Dead of Ouahibrê, which has now been reassembled in the Bibliothèque nationale (pBN 112–117). Discovered at Thebes, this ptolemaic papyrus was taken back to France by the geographical engineer Simonel (*Texte* X, iv). Thereafter, it was divided between General Andréossy and Colonel Jacotin (Denon, *Voyage*, xlvii, pl. 141; *Description* II, 70–71, and *Texte* X, iv, 204–205). Since the part that went to the General (II, 66–69) had already been transmitted to the Commission d'Egypte by the Bibliothèque impériale (*Texte* X, iv), it seems reasonable to surmise that it may have corresponded to the papyrus that, according to Dubois, Napoleon had presented to the Bibliothèque. The gift is not mentioned in the *Inventaire* of Egyptian papyruses in the Cabinet des manuscrits orientaux, but a note in the *Magasin encyclopédique* of Millin (Vol. I, 402) states that the bust of Nectanebo was sent to the Bibliothèque nationale together with "the Egyptian manuscript given to Bonaparte by General Andréossy." The same Simonel also took with him another ptole-

DUTERTRE

maic Book of the Dead, that of Padiamon-Nebnessouttaouy. It came into the possession of Cadet de Metz, who published it in 1805, and, thereafter, it belonged to Jean-Jacques Marcel (II, 72–75; *Texte* X, iv, 205–209). Marcel presented it with other pieces to the Bibliothèque impériale (pBN 1–19). This ritual is the first Book of the Dead to have been reproduced in its entirety. Since 1841, Colmar has possessed a facsimile in color executed early in the century (Madeleine Jehl, *La collection égyptienne du Musée d'Histoire naturelle de Colmar* [1967], 3).

The papyruses in the collection of d'Hermand, administrator of the consulates in the Levant, were evidently also divided early on. His anonymous Livre de l'Amdouat, which is now in the Louvre (Inv. 3288), was sent to the Commission d'Egypte by Révil (V, 44, fig. 7; *Texte* X, ix, 540). Moreover, a fragment of the Book of the Dead given in 1858 to the city of Angers, where it still remains, and before that bought by Turpin de Crissé from Révil, had also come from d'Hermand's collection.

That the Livre des respirations of Nespaouty-taouy should, as we have seen, have come to rest in The Hague, shows that the search for traces of particular papyruses is not to be confined to French collections. To cite another example, one must go to the Hermitage in Leningrad to find the funerary ritual of Osorkon, first prophet of Amon. This papyrus was sent to Denon (*Voyage*, pl. 138) by "le citoyen Amelin." Antoine-Romain Hamelin was a businessman who was in charge of the commissary during the Expedition. He it was who formed an association among members of the Expedition in Cairo during the Kléber command, with a view to publishing their discoveries. In addition to his official responsibilities, Hamelin collected a number of works of art. He supplied Dubois-Aymé with a small carved gem (V, 82, fig. 9; *Texte* X, 587). He even had three statues of Sekhmet removed from the Temple of Mut at Karnak. One of them corresponds to a sculpture in the British Museum, No. 88 (III, 48, fig. 1–2; *Texte* X, 312–313; see *Bibliothèque égyptologique* VI [1904]: 243).

It would clearly be impossible to indicate here the location of all the objects traces of

which may gradually come to light. Our notes at the end of the volume will serve that purpose as far as may be for the works depicted in the *Description*. What is important here is to show clearly how difficult the search becomes once it leads beyond the collections in the British Museum, the Bibliothèque nationale, and the Louvre. The difficulty arises as much from the failure of most museums yet to publish catalogues of their Egyptian holdings as from the extreme dispersal of the pieces. The consequence is that any comprehensive survey will for long remain out of the question, and ad hoc results are all that can be hoped for.

It was thus chance, and not a systematic canvass, that led to the discovery in Avallon of a small, unpublished collection formed by two members of the Expedition, the Caristie brothers. One of them discovered the stele of the decree of Canopus in the mosque of the Emir Khour (*Texte* IX, 314–317), which can now be found in the Louvre (C 122). Similarly, certain objects from Jomard's collection, dispersed in 1863, passed into the Berthoud collection and thereby came to the Musée de la Chartreuse at Douai, destroyed by fire during the Second World War. Twenty-three pieces from the former Dutertre collection reached the Bibliothèque in 1838, and other specimens were given to the ceramics museum at Sèvres by Léon Jean Joseph Dubois in 1843. Other objects from the same collection had already been sent to the Commission by the Bibliothèque impériale (V, 69, fig. 11, 23). A propos of this definite attribution to Dutertre, it is legitimate to wonder whether the fragment of a handsome ceramic vase and parts of a necklace (Sèvres MNC 3076-3 and 3077-3) of unknown origin may not have been taken from the tomb of Amenophis III.

Let us now confine ourselves, however, to mentioning certain works of art that have found their way to the United States, such as the little statue from Malmaison, the pretty lid from the former Tarayre collection, and the Lady Yinyhay, already mentioned. It is, to begin with, surprising that the fine granite bust of a queen, or divine consort, in the Joslyn Art Museum in Omaha (1953.80) should not have been engraved for the *Description*, for this piece

RIPAULT

of sculpture belonged to the future General and comte Le Marois (1776–1836), Bonaparte's aide-de-camp and witness at his wedding to Josephine. The bust is a masterpiece of Egyptian art, which Bernard V. Bothmer has attributed to Amenirdis the Elder (*Egyptian Sculpture of the Late Period* [1960], 1–2, pl. I–II). On the other hand, the alabaster head of an ushabti of Amenophis III, drawn by Jollois and Devilliers (II, 80, fig. 3, 7; *Texte X*, 225–226) is certainly the piece that has come to the Metropolitan Museum of Art (66.99.29) as part of the Albert Gallatin Collection (John D. Cooney, *Journal of Near Eastern Studies* 12 [1953]: 1–9, fig. 40; Henry G. Fischer, "The Gallatin Egyptian Collection," *The Metropolitan Museum of Art Bulletin* XXV [March 1967]: 256–258).

BALZAC

Also in the Metropolitan, from the former Pratt collection, is the small statue of Senenmout Sistrophorus (48.149.7). Drawn by Dutertre (V, 69, fig. 12–15), it belonged to Simon de Sucy (1764–1799), chief administrator of the Army of Egypt (see the bibliography in Christine Meyer, *Senenmut, eine prosopographische Untersuchung* [1982], 45; Bernard V. Bothmer, *The Brooklyn Museum Annual* XI [1969–1970]: 135, n. 16).

Here we finish with this enumeration, even though ushabtis, fragments of coffins or casings, amulets, vases, or pieces of walls might still be added to the list. The present reprint of the Plates of the *Description* is easier to handle than the original volumes and can readily be used in the working areas of museums. May its availability lead to further identifications and bring to light others that may already have been proposed but that have escaped us.

To that end, let us call attention to several points about the use of the original *Explications des Planches*. Although the *Description* often omits the name of the collector who owned an object reproduced in the plates, it is sometimes possible to establish his identity. Thus, the piece of decorated fabric of which Dutertre published a drawing (V, 47, fig. 10) is identical with that in the Descostils collection engraved by Denon (*Voyage*, pl. 139, fig. 18). The same is true of the little naos of Amenhotep-Houy discovered at Saqqara, also drawn by Dutertre for the *Description* (V, 47, fig. 6–8) and sent by Descostils to Denon (*Voyage*, pl. 124, fig. 4–6). The wooden mask discovered "in the grottos of Thebes" and reproduced by Dubois-Aymé (V, 73, fig. 9) corresponds without the slightest possible doubt to the object appearing in an old photograph of the Dubois-Aymé collection, a picture taken before the sale of 1907 (Abbé Paul Tresson, "Une petite stèle inédite du Moyen Empire provenant de la collection Dubois-Aymé," *Kêmi* I [1928], pl. VII). This detail suggests, as a first hypothesis, that the author of a drawing was often the owner of the object. There are many exceptions to the rule, however, for example, the drawings of Dutertre just cited and the ushabti of Dubois-Aymé's collection sketched by Jollois and Devilliers (II, 81, fig. 5).

Moreover, the information about the original site is not always to be taken literally. Thus, the legend "found in the tombs of the kings" very often refers to the whole Theban necropolis and not to the Biban el-Molouk, or Valley of the Kings, itself. Instances include the ushabti of the first prophet of Amon, Bakenkhonsou, in Jomard's collection (V, 87, fig. 14; *Texte X*, 598); two other funerary statuettes (V, 69, fig. 1–2, 9–10; *Texte X*, 572–573); and the small group of Amenemope and Tamerout drawn by Castex (V, 64; *Texte X*, 569). On the other hand, places of origin given in the *Description* have sometimes been forgotten even though there is no ground for putting them in doubt. An example is the little make-up spoon from Fayoum (V, 67, fig. 10–11; *Texte X*, 570), which can now be found in the Louvre (AF 6762; see J. Vandier d'Abadie, *Catalogue des objets de toilette égyptiens* [1972], 34–35, OT.88).

Remarks like the following, "All these objects were collected or purchased in various localities in Egypt, *which it is now impossible to identify*" (*Texte X*, 591), show that, generally, any indication of place of origin in the *Description* has to be seriously considered, for the collectors one and all were concerned to specify the source of their acquisitions. Allusions to purchasing may be confirmed by many examples, and it would appear that this was a normal mode of acquisition in all regions from the Delta (V, 82, fig. 15; *Texte X*, 587) to the first cataract (V, 87, fig. 2–4; *Texte X*, 597).

In certain cases, one wonders whether the sellers did not afterward lead the French to the source. Instances are the ushabti of the first prophet of Amon, Bakenkhonsou (II, 80, fig. 8, 11; *Texte* X, 226). Two other statuettes of the same pontiff, to which must certainly be added the ushabti from the Jomard collection already cited, were "found in one of the *hypogées* of the Memnonium," probably the tomb of Bakenkhonsou (TT 35) at Dra' Abu el-Naga" (II, 76, fig. 2–4, 1, 5–6; *Texte* X, 209).

As to specification of the nature of the stone, there is no reason to be skeptical a priori, for several geologists were members of the Commission d'Egypte. Traditional terminology was, of course, employed. Thus, *pierre ollaire* means serpentine while *pierre de touche* corresponds to hard, dark-colored rock, often basalt. Caution is required in using the recent literature, however, for modifications have sometimes been introduced. For example, the beautiful ushabti under the names of Amenophis III and Tiy, from the former Devilliers du Terrage collection (II, 80, fig. 6, 13), is now said to be of alabaster (Aubert, *Statuettes égyptiennes* [1974], 52), whereas the *Description* gives the specification "sandstone grit with a fine grain that takes a high polish" (*Texte* X, 225–226).

That the scale of the drawings is often not given complicates attempts to identify the subjects. At the same time, the size of certain pieces does preclude accepting identifications that have sometimes been proposed. For example, the ushabti of Amenophis III now in the Museum of Ancient Art in Brussels after a detour through an English collection (Jean Capart, "Statuettes funéraires égyptiennes," *Chronique d'Egypte* 16 [1941]: 196–204) measures 40 centimeters high. Aubert must, therefore, be mistaken (Aubert, *Statuettes*, 47) in identifying it with one that apparently belonged to Devilliers (II, 81, fig. 3), for the latter is 67 centimeters in height. It may further be noted that the red granite of this exceptional ushabti should alone have precluded confusing it with the statuette in Brussels, which is of alabaster. There is, indeed, every reason to think that the granite ushabti has reached the Louvre (Roland Tefnin, "A propos d'une tête royale du Musée

d'Aberdeen," *Chronique d'Egypte* 49 [1974]: 13–14, exemple OA III, 2).

In describing the pieces, the *Explications des Planches* necessarily employ the old terminology of eighteenth-century archaeology. Only after hieroglyphs had been deciphered and Champollion and Dubois had begun publishing the *Panthéon égyptien* in 1823, were the traditional designations gradually reformed. Even so, they continued to be widely used in catalogues of sales and inventories of collections. It is thus to be noted that a mention of "Nephthys" in the *Description* refers not to that goddess but to Thouéris (V, 87, fig. 2–4, 23; *Texte* X, 597–598). "Typhon" corresponds to Bès (V, 87, fig. 31–32; *Texte* X, 595). The "Sarcophage d'Osiris" is the pillar *djed* (V, 86, fig. 31; *Texte* X, 595), sometimes also called the Nilometer. Ushabtis are often presented as figures of Isis or as "Divinités égyptiennes" (V, 86, fig. 51, 59–60, 64–65; *Texte* X, 596). The figurines of priests and priestesses are really amulets representing divinities (V, 87, fig. 15–16, 22; *Texte* X, 598). The "Eye of Osiris" obviously is the amulet *oudjat*-eye (V, 86, fig. 37; *Texte* X, 595). There would be no point in reproducing these obsolete designations in the present edition, in which we have restricted the commentary simply to identifying the plates.

Since the time when the collections were assembled, the appearance of many of the objects has been much altered by cleaning, restoration, or mutilation. Some have been destroyed in the course of being examined. The members of the Expedition themselves often recorded the condition of the materials, for example, in the distinctive case of the mask taken from a sarcophagus in Asyut: "The wood of this fragment was in a state of perfect preservation when it was found, but it is noteworthy that it began to rot as soon as it was taken to Europe" (II, 76, fig. 10–11; *Texte* X, 210). Several mummies, human and animal, were dismembered and others dissected by the naturalists in making preparations for the *Description*. Washing has changed or destroyed colors. Sometimes, objects were cleaned the moment they were discovered, as were the contents of the tombs of Ramesses III and Amenophis III.

The following two passages will convey an idea of the conditions in which tombs

REDOUTE

were explored and the finds gathered up as well as energetically cleaned: ''It must be appreciated that, in general, close attention is required in order to recognize the nature of the debris encountered in the tombs. So numberless are the bats that occupy the grottos that the ground and the debris lying thereon are hidden under a thick layer of droppings.'' And further on, ''These ancient artifacts were unrecognizable under the droppings of bats, but once we saw that the debris we were trampling under foot might hold some interest, the realization sufficed for us to undertake a thorough investigation. Still, only after we had taken considerable trouble to wash the interesting fragments in the Nile did we have the great satisfaction of appreciating their value'' (*Texte* X, 215, 220).

VILLOTEAU

The impulse to renovate the works of art and to restore the ruins was fully in the taste of the eighteenth century. An example is the drawing Jollois and Devilliers did of the Temple of Qurna (V, 43). It immediately calls to mind an Egyptian architectural reconstruction by Cassas. Beyond that, the sensibility of the Old Regime makes itself felt in many prints in the *Description*. Such is especially the case in the subjects taken from bas-reliefs, wherein the hieratic attitudes and absence of perspective were clearly disconcerting. Numerous renderings, on the other hand, are quite precise and faithful. The copies of certain inscriptions may still be used. That is true not only of several papyruses but also of various funerary statuettes, notably that of Tanedjmet, governess of the harem of Amon (II, 76, fig. 7), and also of the ushabtis of Bakenkhonsou already cited. Indeed, renderings of this quality made the *Description* the point of departure for systematic surveys of Egyptian antiquity, and it is to be remembered that this, the first of them, was the work of artists who had to invent the entire genre and who could not understand what they were copying. All in all, they acquitted themselves very creditably and produced a collection of such value that it will continue to serve Egyptian studies for a long time to come.

Thus, the acquisitions of some thirty-odd collections of the period have had to be considered in order that we might indicate the full importance of this Register of Monuments, whether with respect to the history of interest in Egypt, which should one day be written, or with regard to a tally of the objects that reached Europe, not all of which were illustrated in the *Description*. Jomard traveled soon afterward to London with the official mission of copying or taking casts of the objects that went to the British Museum in consequence of the French capitulation. Apart from that in the British Museum, the collections were modest in scale and exceptional in content. Still, they furnished the material for more than a thousand drawings of ancient works of art contained in the *Description*. To that considerable set must be added, besides certain newly copied inscriptions (V, 56, fig. 24), the illustrations of objects transported to Europe following the repatriation of the Army of the Orient, such as various medals (V, 58, fig. 10, 47; *Texte* X, 559–560, 563–564). Further to be emphasized is the inclusion of a monument that was not transferred to Europe by a member of the Expedition. The fragmentary Naos of the Decades (V, 48; *Texte* X, 543–544), which is now in the Louvre (D 37), had been discovered at Abukir in November 1777 during the travels of Sonnini de Manoncour. At some time between 1784 and 1792, it came into the collection of Choiseul-Gouffier, the Ambassador of Louis XVI to the Sultan of Turkey.

Such a body of material, it will be agreed, formed the first solid basis for Egyptology as a museum science. Champollion, too, was a founder of that science, and it is to be recalled that the members of the Commission d'Egypte are themselves to be seen as successors of the authors of several remarkable compilations from the preceding century, the Benedictine Bernard de Montfaucon (1655–1741) and the academician comte de Caylus (1692–1765).

To conclude this introduction, and to recapture the spirit that animated the men to whom we owe this magisterial work, let us cite Vivant Denon, who better than any of the others expressed the mingling of amazement and respect that gripped these Frenchmen confronted with the discovery of the civilization of Egypt:

Every ancient artifact that is found supplies a statement in support, often enough, only of

Horus, Apis, Serapis, Typhon, and Nephthys. Their iconography could only be guesswork. They took the crowns of upper and lower Egypt for elaborate coiffures. Large structures they supposed to be palaces; middling ones were temples; small ones were chapels or shrines. The editors have not tried to look over their shoulders or, beyond identifying the principal structures, to bring them up to date. Nothing less than the whole of Egyptology has done that. It started with them. Our purpose is simply to show what they saw and explain how they came to see it. The opportunity to exhibit the subject matter of a science in the absence of the science is perhaps unique in the history of learning.

To think that our young men should have copied these thousands of hieroglyphs in total ignorance of the meaning! The work was being wound up when, in 1822, Champollion found the key and opened the door to philology. What is seldom appreciated, however, is that not until the 1850s could his successors decipher more than the odd cartouche or construe entire texts. All that was possible in the *Description de l'Egypte* was a sampling of the enormous fund of inscriptions. Sometimes, the surfaces would be left blank when there was no time for copying. Other times, the authors would supply hieroglyphs and decoration of the sort found in similar or adjacent locations. They cared about architectural effect, after all. That was one of their motivations. But they were scrupulous in saying whether the rendering was exact or imagined.

Fact and fancy equally inform the strictly architectural drawings and there too are kept distinct. The plans, sections, and elevations of the monuments are based on exact measurements. Having distinguished what they had actually seen and surveyed from what they built around it in imagination, our authors let their imaginations go. Theirs was the first generation of romanticism, after all. The grand march through the south gate at Karnak (III, 51), the festival of the Nile before Dendara (IV, 6), belong in Verdi's *Aida*. Indeed, some stage designer must almost certainly have put them there. Better than anything else, the restorations show how the subject grew upon its first investigators. Occasional remarks escape them in the early stages about a priest-ridden society devoted to some cult of the dead and incapable of perfecting its artistry with the geometry of perspective. In the absorption of the work, these expressions of eighteenth-century impatience with a primitive past soon give way to simple, complete respect for human capacity.

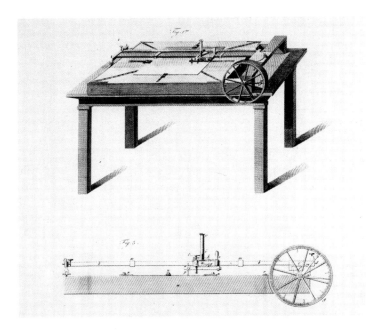

CONTE MACHINE

ORGANIZATION AND BIBLIOGRAPHY

ARRANGEMENT OF THE WORK

The sequence of sites follows the flow of the Nile from south to north, beginning at Philae and ending at Alexandria. Plates are numbered consecutively within each volume. At the top of each plate the division **A** for *Antiquités*, **EM** for *Etat moderne*, or **HN** for *Histoire naturelle*, appears to the left, followed by a Roman numeral indicating the volume. The name of the site appears in the middle, with the Greek or Latin equivalent at the head of each section, and the number of the individual plate at the right. The regular and the outsize plates are numbered in a single sequence. In the case of the sets of highest quality (see below), for which the cabinet was designed, the arrangement can be confusing since the larger plates were bound separately in two atlases in order to avoid folding. Even so, those of the largest dimensions had to be creased near one end. In the less expensive sets, and in all copies of the second edition, the large plates are folded in the middle and tipped in to the binding on a stem, the sequence thus being continuous. In our edition, the large plates are folded and bound in sequences, while those in color are gathered in a separate section.

We reproduce the title page of the first volume only. The wording changed with Volume IV (1817), which was "publié par l'ordre du Gouvernement." Volume I covers the sites of upper Egypt from Philae to Armant, Volume II the west bank at Thebes and Volume III the east bank, Volume IV the remaining monuments from Thebes to Memphis, and Volume V the sites of lower Egypt. Volume V also contains facsimiles of certain papyri and inscriptions, notably the Rosetta Stone, together with reproductions of manuscripts and drawings of various artifacts.

The map of Egypt that we include is one of a pair prepared by Jomard and Jacotin from the larger scale maps destined for the topographical atlas. Its companion, intended to accompany the *Etat moderne* volumes, shows the area of the Nile Delta at twice the scale. The two were folded into the back of the second volume of *Antiquités, Mémoires*, published in 1818.

For each locality, the plates are arranged in a consistent order: (1) General and topographical charts, (2) Views of the monuments in their actual state, (3) Architectural plans, sections, and elevations of whole edifices, (4) Architectural detail, (5) Bas-reliefs, inscriptions, statues, and other ornaments. In many instances, panoramic restorations are added and also line engravings of inscriptions.

Two scales appear on most of the plates, the metric units to the right and the old units to the left. The scale was uniform for all the monuments: 1:400 for the plans and 1:100 for the sections and elevations. It was in order to make this possible that outsize sheets had to be employed for the larger structures. In the representation of architectural detail, the scale was often larger. For the topographical charts, the scales, all in metric units, varied depending on the extent of the area. In the original set, papyri and medals were reproduced in their actual dimensions. Charts and plans are orientated by an arrow indicating magnetic north. The principal monuments and vantage points for the picturesque views are indicated by capital letters on the face of the charts. Capital letters also mark the lines for the sections in the architectural plates, whereas lower case letters and italics identify the location of particular features. These indications are keyed to the *Explications*, which we abridge in the Notes at the end of this volume.

A further convention needs emphasis. The plans show in black the foundations of structures that actually existed, in medium grey the foundations on which nothing remained standing, and in light grey the foundations restored on the basis of analogy or symmetry.

After much discussion between the Minister of the Interior and the Commission concerning price, quantity, and quality, it was decided to print the first edition in a thousand copies of four different qualities. The least expensive, at 750 francs for the first *livraison*, contained only one plate in color and was printed on ordinary stock. The next, also on ordinary paper at 800 francs, contained sixteen plates in color. The third, at 1,200 francs, was printed on *papier fin* with a complete complement of plates in color. Finally, the *de luxe* edition consisted of the 200 first impressions of each plate, on *papier velin* with all the color plates retouched by hand. The price was 1,350 francs. These sets were reserved for Napoleon to present to notable persons, for example, the Tsar Alexander.

The set from which the present edition is reproduced is the *de luxe* printing. Penciled in the margins of several of the astronomical line drawings is the name, comte de Pourtalès. Several noblemen bore that title in the nineteenth century. Comte Albert Alexandre de Pourtalès (1812–1861) was in the Prussian diplomatic service. He was ambassador to Turkey in 1850, and to France in 1854. He had an Egyptian collection that may have been in the family for at least a generation. The inventory of the Berlin Museum records a Pourtalès gift of two Theban coffins (no. 8 and 28) in 1825. The collection was inherited by Albert Alexandre's brother, the comte James-Alexandre de Pourtalès-Gorgier, on whose death in 1865 it was sold.

Together with other works on Egypt and the ancient Near East, the set was presented to Princeton University in 1921 by the sons of Ralph E. Prime, Jr., of the Class of 1888, after the latter's death. He had inherited it from a great-uncle, William Cowper Prime (1824–1905), of the Class of 1843. It was evidently he who acquired the *Description de l'Egypte* at the Pourtalès sale or soon afterward. First a lawyer and then a journalist, William Cowper Prime was also a scholar and an antiquarian who traveled extensively in Europe and the Near East. Among his many writings was a delightful travel book, *Boat Life in Egypt and Nubia* (New York: Harper, 1858), as well as works on numismatics and on pottery and porcelain. In 1875, Princeton conferred on him the honorary degree of LL.D. A widely-known collector, he was a trustee of the Metropolitan Museum in New York in its early years. In 1882, he proposed to the Princeton trustees "the establishment of a department of art instruction in the College of New Jersey," as Princeton was officially known until 1896. He further offered the college the porcelains that he and his wife had collected, on the condition that a fireproof building be constructed to house them as well as other works of art that might be donated. The Prime-Trumbull collection—he wished his wife's maiden name joined to his—thus became the nucleus of the Princeton Art Museum. Prime himself held the nominal and unpaid post of professor of the History of Art in his alma mater during his later years. At all events, the plates presented to the University by his collateral descendants have been dismounted from their bindings, which had fallen into ruinous condition, and are conserved in the Rare Book Room of the Firestone Library.

A second edition was undertaken in 1820, before the first edition was completed, by the firm of C. L. F. Panckoucke, publisher of the *Encyclopédie méthodique*. It was dedicated to Louis XVIII, an appropriate frontispiece was substituted for the original apotheosis of Napoleon, and references to the Hero were removed from the Preface. The text and *Explications* were reprinted in twenty-six manageable octavo volumes. The whole appeared between 1821 and 1829. The quality and definition of the plates are not as good as in the original and none is in color. They were reprinted from the original copper engrav-

LENOIR

ings, most of which are still preserved in the Louvre. The reader may like to know that it is possible to order copies even today from the Département des Arts graphiques, formerly the Département de Chalcographie.

SELECT BIBLIOGRAPHY

(Unless otherwise indicated, all titles in French were published in Paris.)

The starting point is a work that is almost contemporary with the completion of the *Description de l'Egypte*, Louis Reybaud, *Histoire scientifique et militaire de l'expédition française en Egypte*, 10 vol. (1830–36). In the complete set, the history of the Expedition occupies the six middle volumes numbered as a sub-series within the ten volumes of the whole, in which the first two concern the history of Egypt through the eighteenth century and the final two the developments following the French withdrawal. The work was a collaborative one, in which Reybaud had the principal part. Bibliographically it is confusing, for the publisher, A. J. Dénain, also issued the six central volumes separately but simultaneously, in which edition they appear under the name of another of the collaborators, X.-B. Saintine.

The ten-volume edition is illustrated by sketches of members of the Expedition drawn by André Dutertre, from among which we have reproduced those of contributors and of certain other principal figures. The originals, both pencil drawings and etchings made from the drawings after Dutertre had returned to France, are in the Bibliothèque nationale, with the exception of the profile of Bonaparte, which is in the museum at Versailles. There are 184 portraits altogether. Desgenettes tells the story that after the retreat from Syria Dutertre would ask, ''How is so and so?'' ''He's dead.'' ''The devil! Too bad! I haven't done him.'' And of another, ''He's dead, too.'' ''That's all right. I've got him.'' There is a notice on the Dutertre portraits at the end of Devilliers' *Journal et Souvenirs*, cited below.

The most comprehensive and the indispensable bibliography is Henri Munier, *Tables de la Description de l'Egypte, suivies d'une bibliographie sur l'expédition française de Bonaparte* (Cairo, 1943). The first part is a detailed table of contents for the whole work, plates and text, giving the location of every item both in the original and in the Panckoucke edition. Munier largely supersedes Gabriel Guémard, *Essai de bibliographie critique de la Commission des Sciences et Arts et de l'Institut d'Egypte* (Cairo, 1936). Two briefer hand-lists are also useful. One, *A bibliographical account and collation of La Description de l'Egypte* (1838), was printed for the London Institution. A gift of a hundred guineas by Sir Thomas Baring in 1837 went to purchasing the work, which, says the unnamed librarian, ''in its original and perfect state, is rapidly becoming of the greatest rarity and value.'' The second appears in André Monglond, *La France révolutionnaire et impériale* in *Annales de bibliographie méthodique et description des livres illustrés* VIII (années 1809–1810: 1957), 268–343.

The essential contemporary sources are *La Décade égyptienne*, the learned journal published in Cairo in three volumes from 1798 to 1801 and modeled on the Parisian *La Décade philosophique*; the official bulletin *Courier de l'Egypte*, of which 116 numbers appeared in the same interval; and *Mémoires sur l'Egypte*, published in four volumes in Paris from 1799 to 1802. Many members of the Commission sent reports of their researches and observations back to Paris to be published in these volumes before the evacuation. The *Décade égyptienne* and the *Courier de l'Egypte* have been reprinted in a ten-volume set, *The journals of Bonaparte in Egypt, 1798–1801* (Cairo, 1971), edited by Saladin Boustany. Among other things, Boustany also reprints the texts of the official proclamations and (Vol. X) *Lettres de l'armée française...interceptées par l'escadre de Nelson*, published in London and Hamburg in 1799. For printings in French and English, see Munier, par. 144–149. For the first twenty-four pages of what was to have been Vol. IV of *La Décade égyptienne*, see a 21 December 1979 communication presented to the Académie des Sciences.

The most valuable set of sources consists in the journals and correspondence of members of the Expedition (Munier, xxiii), and most signally those of Jollois and Devilliers. Prosper Jollois, *Journal d'un ingénieur attaché à l'expédition d'Egypte*, was published as volume 6 (1904) of the series

CARISTIE

GERARD

Bibliothèque égyptologique, edited by G. Maspero. Appended are fragmentary notes by Fourier, Delile, Balzac, Descostils, Jomard, Saint-Genis, and Coraboeuf. Edouard de Villiers du Terrage, *Journal et souvenirs sur l'expédition d'Egypte* (1899), was edited and published by his grandson. The style is livelier than Jollois', but many of the passages were modified by the author, on the basis of his journals, long after the events. Equally vivid is Etienne Geoffroy Saint-Hilaire, *Lettres écrites d'Egypte,* ed. E. T. Hamy (1901). The disaffection and misfortunes of Dolomieu are recorded in A. Lacroix and G. Daressy, eds., *Dolomieu en Egypte* in *Mémoires de l'Institut d'Egypte* 3 (1922). Also informative, in descending order, are René Nicolas Desgenettes, *Souvenirs d'un médecin de l'expédition d'Egypte* (1893); Etienne Malus, *Agenda: Souvenirs de l'expédition de l'Egypte* (1892); and Charles Norry, *Relation de l'expédition d'Egypte* (1800). Nearly in the contemporary category belong J. J. Champollion-Figeac, *Fourier et Napoléon: l'Egypte et les cent jours* (1844), and Edme Jomard, *Souvenirs sur Gaspard Monge et ses rapports avec Napoléon* (1853). Monge's correspondence, a copy of which remains in manuscript in the Bibliothèque de l'Institut de France (MSS 2151), contains letters to his wife from Egypt. Finally, the letters of the head military tailor, François Bernoyer, have recently been published by Christian Tortel, *Bonaparte en Egypte et en Syrie* (Editions Curandera: 1981). They have nothing to do with the work of the Commission, except for passing expressions of the author's contempt for the *savants,* but they are the liveliest and most amusing item in this literature.

Our account of the publication of the *Description de l'Egypte* is based on the papers of the Commission conserved in the Bibliothèque nationale, the registers in NAF 3577 and supporting documents in NAF 21,950. There is also extensive documentation in the Archives nationales and in the Archives de la Guerre at Vincennes.

All subsequent accounts of the military history of the Expedition depend on Clément de La Jonquière, *L'Expédition de l'Egypte,* 2nd ed., 5 vols. (1899–1907), which publishes official documents in extenso. Unfortunately, it covers only the period down to Bonaparte's return to France. It may be supplemented by M. F. Rousseau, *Kléber et Menou en Egypte depuis le départ de Bonaparte* (1900), and G. Rigault, *Le général Abdallah Menou et la dernière phase de l'expédition de l'Egypte* (1911). Mention should also be made of Jean Thiry, *Bonaparte en Egypte* (1973), which has an extensive bibliography. A more popular account is Christopher Herold, *Bonaparte in Egypt* (New York and London, 1962). Of the many pertinent writings of François Charles-Roux, the most important are *Les origines de l'expédition de l'Egypte* (1910) and *Bonaparte, gouverneur d'Egypte* (1935). Also well worth consulting is the admirable catalogue prepared for the 1969 exhibition *Napoléon,* which appeared in the Grand Palais, Paris, on the 200th anniversary of Napoleon's birth.

Among Egyptian writings on the Expedition, the following have been translated: Nicolas Turc, *Chronique d'Egypte 1798–1804,* ed. and trans. by Gaston Wiet (Cairo, 1950); *Al-Jabarti's Chronicle of the First Seven Months of the French Occupation of Egypt,* ed. and trans. by Shmuel Moreh (Brill: Leiden, 1975); Abd-al-Rahmân al-Jabarti, *Journal d'un notable du Caire durant l'expédition française 1798–1801,* ed. and trans. by Joseph Cuoq (Paris, 1979).

Three contemporary scholars have kindly allowed us to consult their unpublished writings: Monsieur Henry Laurens his Thèse pour le doctorat du 3ème cycle, "Les origines intellectuelles de l'expédition de l'Egypte, 1689–1798"; Madame Hélène Duriot her thesis in progress on "L'Apport de la 'Description de l'Egypte' à la connaissance de Thèbes"; and Monsieur Stéphane Callens his memoir, "Etude sur la *Description de l'Egypte*: Histoire d'une enquête (1798–1830)."

The memoirs of Jean-Edouard Goby are in a class by themselves. A civil engineer formerly with the Suez Canal Co. and longtime resident in Egypt, Monsieur Goby has devoted many years to the study of the history of the Expedition, of the Suez Canal, and of the Isthmus of Suez. His brochure, *Travaux essentiels* (Sèvres, 1982), gives the themes and the bibliographical detail of those writings. It will be convenient to group those on which we have drawn most fully by the journals or collections in which they were published.

Bulletin de l'Institut d'Egypte.

"Composition du premier Institut d'Egypte," XXIX, 1946–47, 343–367; and XXX, 1947–48, 81–99.

"Antoine-François Coquebert de Montbret, bibliothécaire du premier Institut d'Egypte," XXXI, 1948–49, 77–87.

"Contribution à l'inventaire des sources manuscrits et à l'étude bibliographique de l'histoire de l'Expédition française en Egypte," XXXIII, 1950–51, 303–322.

"Les carnets d'Henri-Joseph Redouté," XXXV, 1952–53, 77–91.

"Composition de la Commission des Sciences et Arts d'Egypte," XXXVII, fasc. 1, 1955–56, 315–342.

Bulletin de la Société française d'Egyptologie.

"Travaux du premier Institut d'Egypte," No. 66, March 1973, 15–35.

Bulletin de la Société d'Etudes Historiques et Géographiques de l'Isthme de Suez.

"La participation de l'ingénieur Jean-Baptiste-Simon Fèvre au nivellement de l'Isthme de Suez en 1799," III, 1949–50, 99–108.

"Histoire des nivellements de l'Isthme de Suez," IV, 1951–52, 99–177.

"Modification des rivages de la mer Rouge et de la Méditerranée à l'époque historique," V, 1953–54, 23–44.

Cahiers d'Histoire égyptéenne.

"Un compagnon de Bonaparte en Egypte: Dubois-Aymé," 3ème série, fasc. 3, March 1951, 221–254.

"Etienne Geoffroy Saint-Hilaire en Egypte," 5ème série, fasc. 2–3, June 1953, 139–160.

"L'oeuvre scientifique et culturelle du général Menou en Egypte," 7ème série, fasc. 1, February 1955, 43–60.

Revue de l'Institut Napoléon.

"Les travaux d'un siècle en Egypte sur l'Expédition française de 1798–1801," 54, 1955, 4–16.

"Principaux 'témoins utiles' de l'Expédition d'Egypte dans la Mouvance française," 135, 1979, 67–85.

"Nouvelles contributions à la bibliographie de l'Expédition d'Egypte," 132, 1976, 207–213.

Congrès national des Sociétés Savantes. Proceedings of annual meetings.

"Ingénieurs, 'témoins utiles,' de l'Expédition d'Egypte," *Actes du 101ème Congrès* (Lille, 1976), Section d'histoire moderne et contemporaine, tome II, 255–268.

"Le *Courier de l'Egypte,* source de l'histoire de l'Expédition française...," *Actes du 102ème Congrès* (Limoges, 1977), Section d'histoire moderne et contemporaine, tome II, 171–185.

"Bonaparte, Kléber, Menou et les coopérateurs de la *Description de l'Egypte,*" *Actes du 103ème Congrès* (Nancy-Metz, 1978), Section d'histoire moderne et contemporaine, tome II, 333–347.

Finally, there are valuable articles by other authors on several members of the Expedition: In the *Bulletin de l'Institut d'Egypte,* Georges Legrain, "Guillaume-André Villoteau, Musicographe de l'Expédition française en Egypte," 5ème série, XI (1917), 1–30; Georges Daressy, "L'ingénieur Girard et l'Institut d'Egypte," 5ème série, XII (1918), 13–32; Edouard Driault and Emile Houth, "Alyre Raffeneau-Delile," XVI (1934), 86–92; and in the *Mémoires présentés à l'Institut d'Egypte,* the three-part monograph by Paul Pallary, *Marie Jules-César Savigny, sa Vie et son Oeuvre,* tomes 17 (1931), 20 (1932), and 23 (1934). Pallary has also published *Les rapports originaux de Larrey à l'armée de l'Orient,* in *Mémoires de l'Institut d'Egypte* 30 (1936).

NOUET

ACKNOWLEDGEMENTS

First and foremost, the editors express their appreciation to Monsieur Jean Leclant, Professor of Egyptology in the Collège de France and Permanent Secretary of the Académie des Inscriptions et Belles Lettres. It was he who introduced them to each other, and their collaboration has benefited from his counsel and support. Professor Gillispie also wishes to express his particular gratitude to two other friends and colleagues, Dr. Robert Bianchi, associate curator of Egyptology at the Brooklyn Museum, for his expert advice, and Madame Magdeleine Hours, Inspecteur-Général des Muséums de France, for her enthusiasm and wisdom in the ways of the world of the Louvre and its sister institutions. Michel Dewachter wishes to express his special gratitude to Professor John D. Cooney, former curator of the Cleveland Museum of Art, who strongly encouraged him to continue the research that Professor Cooney himself had begun on the collections formed during the Expedition. M. Dewachter is grateful also to the curators of the many museums that replied to his inquiries and notably to Mme Florence Callu, *Conservateur en Chef du Cabinet des Manuscrits de la Bibliothèque nationale.*

This edition originated in a conversation about the set at Princeton between Professor Gillispie and the publisher, Kevin Lippert, president of Princeton Architectural Press. Without his enterprise and experience of photographic publishing, it would not exist. All concerned are grateful to the staffs of the Department of Rare Books in Firestone Library at Princeton and of the library in the Cabinet d'Egyptologie at the Collège de France, in the case of the former to Professor Richard M. Ludwig, its director until recently, and his associates Charles Greene and Karl Buchberg, and of the latter to M. Jean-Claude Degardin, Librarian of the Salle Champollion. None of these kind people is responsible for whatever errors or infelicities the editors may have committed in preparing the material for this book.

DESCRIPTION DE L'ÉGYPTE,

OU

RECUEIL

DES OBSERVATIONS ET DES RECHERCHES

QUI ONT ÉTÉ FAITES EN ÉGYPTE

PENDANT L'EXPÉDITION DE L'ARMÉE FRANÇAISE,

PUBLIÉ

PAR LES ORDRES DE SA MAJESTÉ L'EMPEREUR

NAPOLÉON LE GRAND.

———

ANTIQUITÉS, PLANCHES.

TOME PREMIER.

A PARIS,

DE L'IMPRIMERIE IMPÉRIALE.

M. DCCC. IX.

ÎLE DE PHILÆ.

Pl. 1.

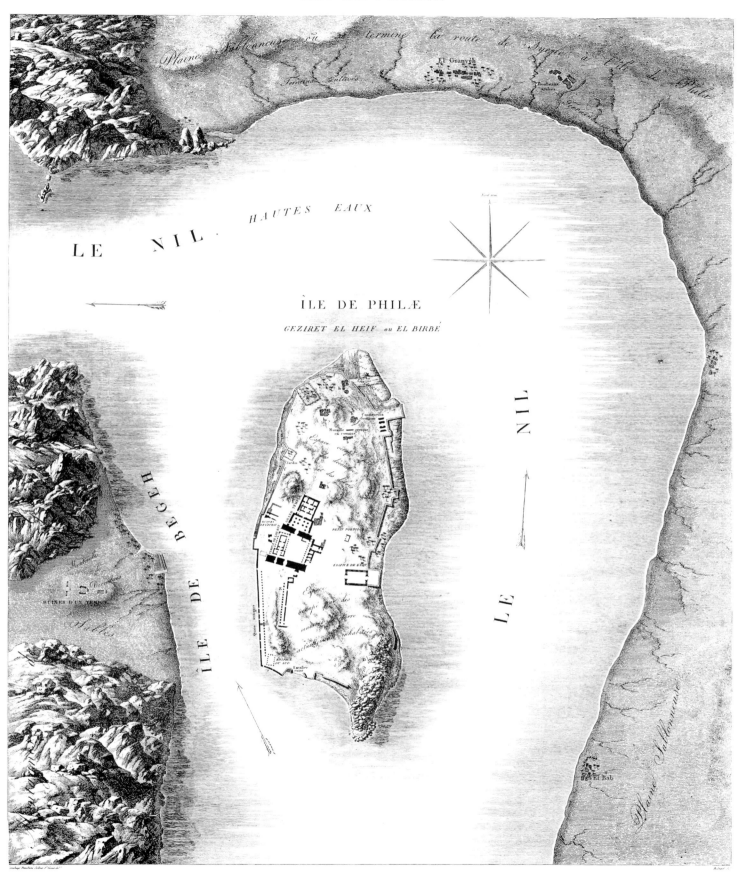

HAUTES EAUX

LE NIL.

ÎLE DE PHILÆ

GEZIRET EL HEIF ou EL BIRBÉ

LE NIL

ÎLE DE BEGEH

PLAN GÉNÉRAL DE L'ÎLE ET DE SES ENVIRONS.

VUE GÉNÉRALE PRISE

Duhamel et Lorieux Sc.

DU NORD-OUEST.

NES DE GRANIT QUI L'ENVIRONNENT.

ÎLE DE PHILÆ.

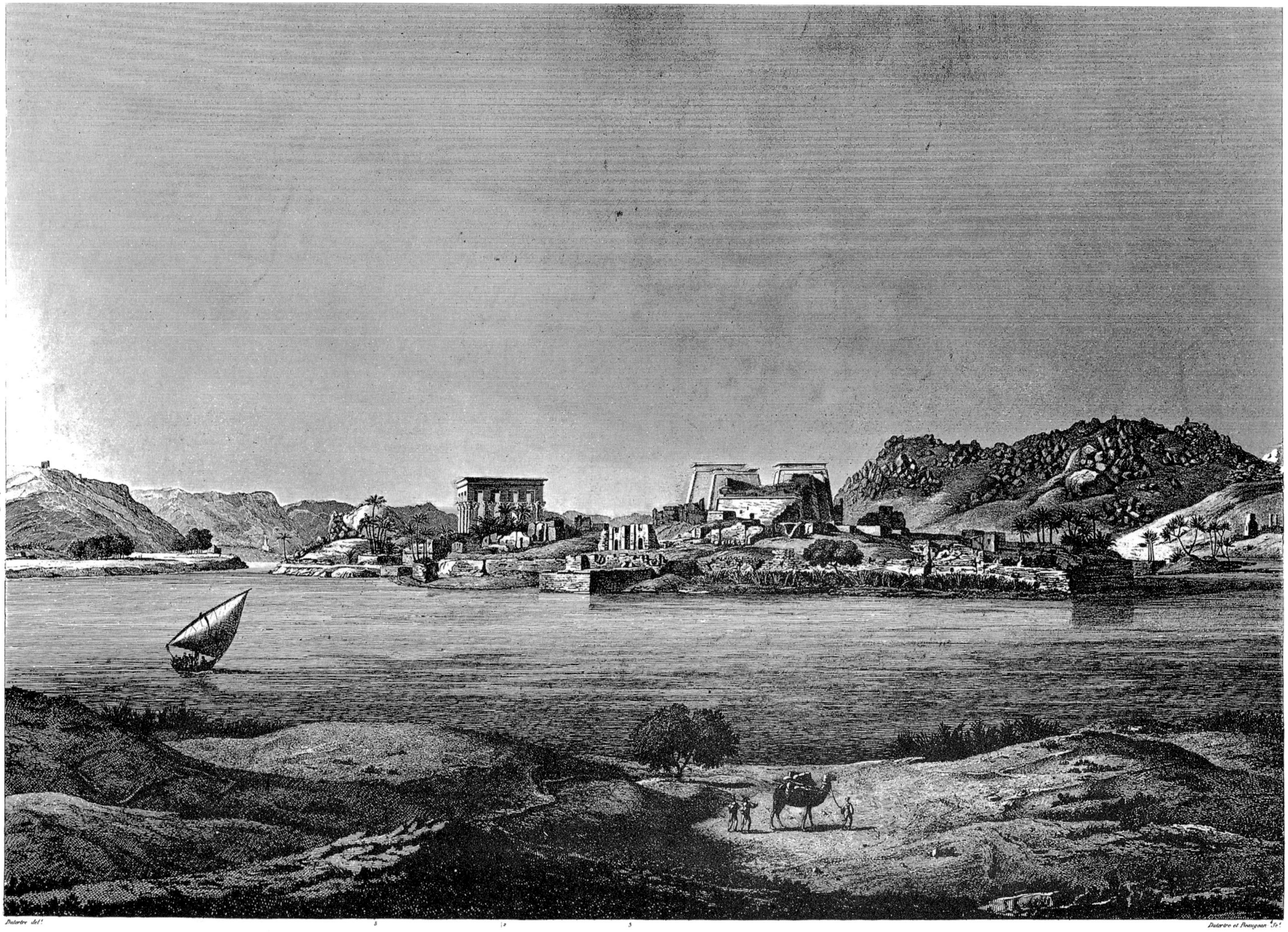

Dutertre del.

Dutertre et Beaugean Sc.

VUE GÉNÉRALE PRISE DU COTÉ DU NORD EST.

Pl. 5.

ILE DE PHILÆ.

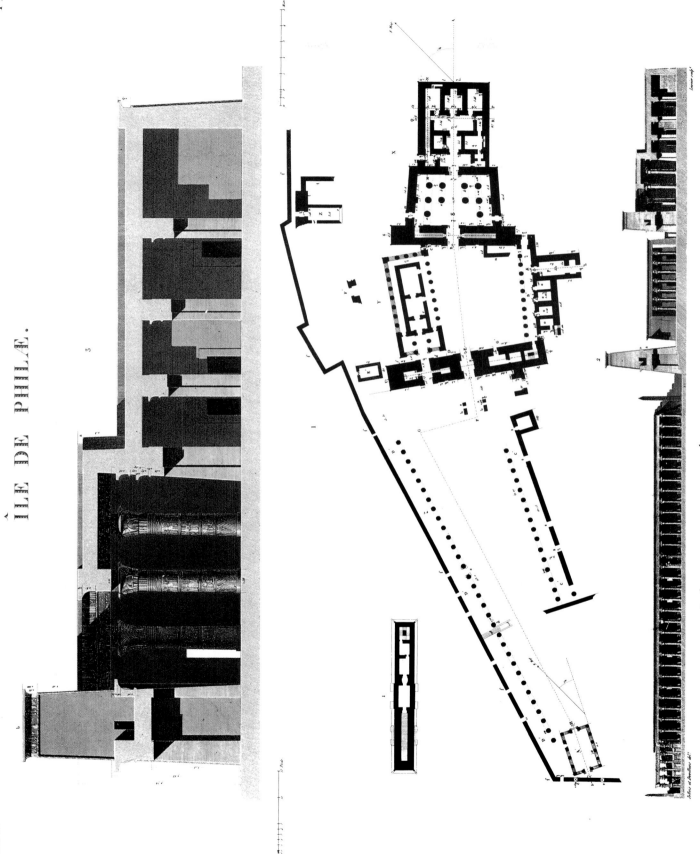

PLAN ET COUPE GÉNÉRALE DES PRINCIPAUX ÉDIFICES. 3 COUPE LONGITUDINALE DU GRAND TEMPLE.

1

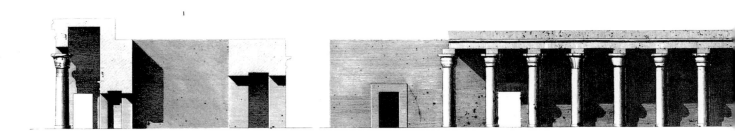

6

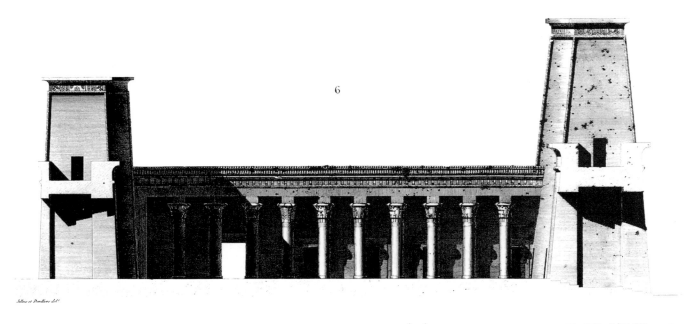

Sellier et Devilliers del.t

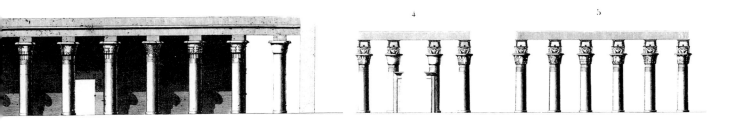

NS DES DEUX COLONNADES ET DE L'ÉDIFICE DU SUD.

IER PYLÔNE.

Pl.7.

ÎLE DE PHILÆ.

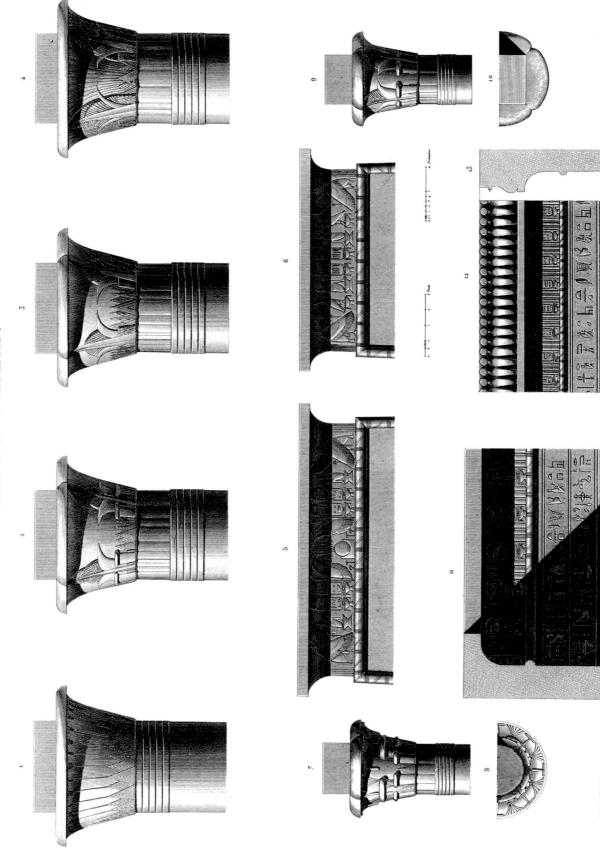

1.2.3.4.11 **CHAPITEAUX ET CORNICHE DU PORTIQUE DU GRAND TEMPLE.** 5.6 **CORNICHES DES DEUX PYLÔNES.**

7.8.9.10.12.13 **CHAPITEAUX ET CORNICHE DE LA GALERIE DE L'EST.**

Pl. 8.

ÎLE DE PHILÆ.

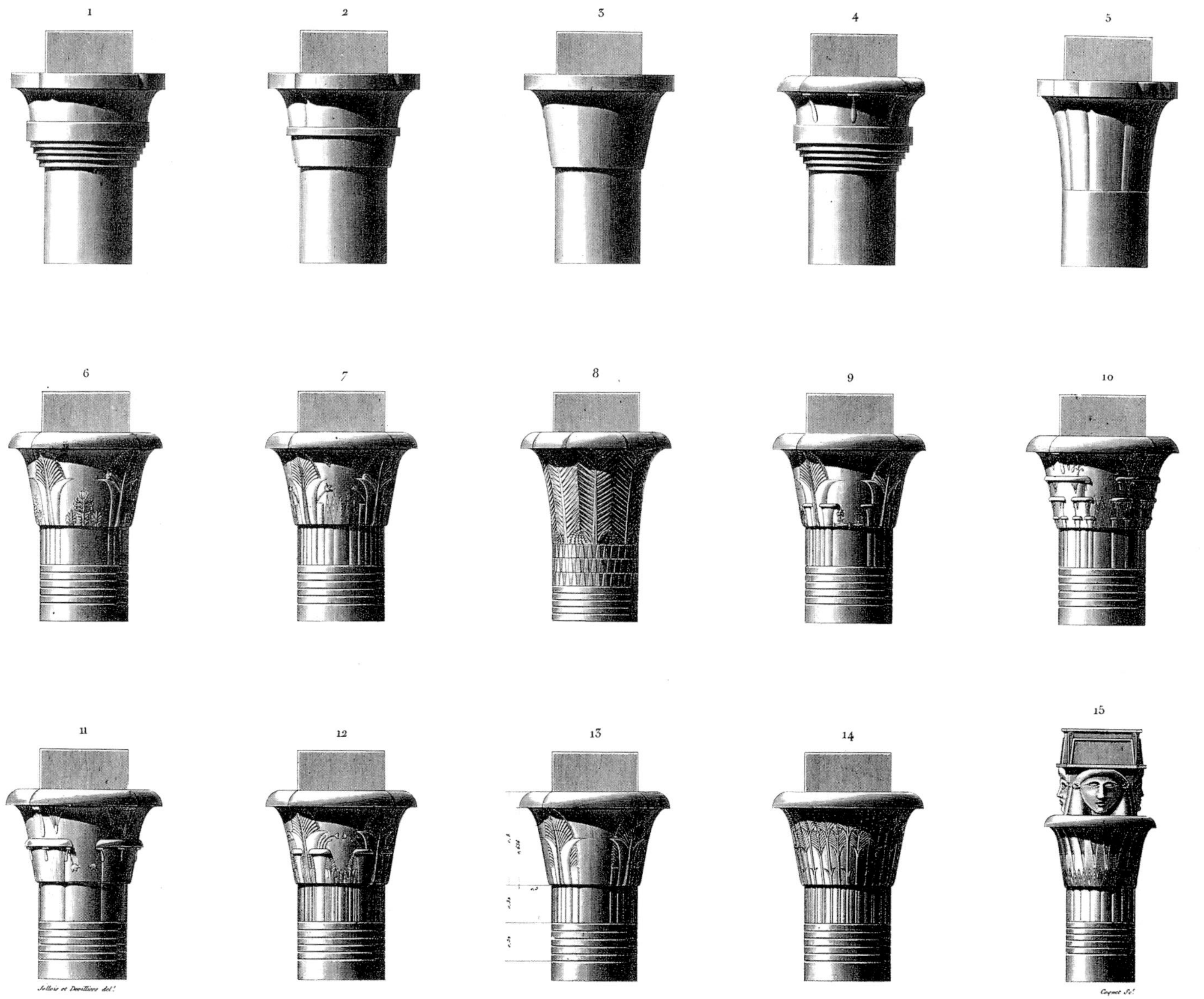

DÉTAILS DE QUATORZE CHAPITEAUX DES DEUX COLONNADES. 1. 2. 3. 4. 5. CHAPITEAUX ÉBAUCHÉS.

15. CHAPITEAU DE L'ÉDIFICE DU MIDI.

Pl. 9.

ÎLE DE PHILÆ.

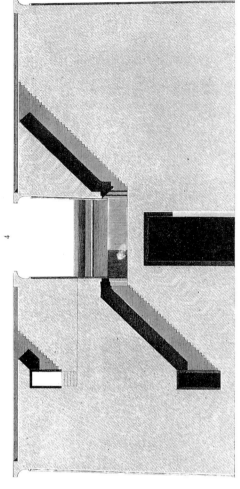

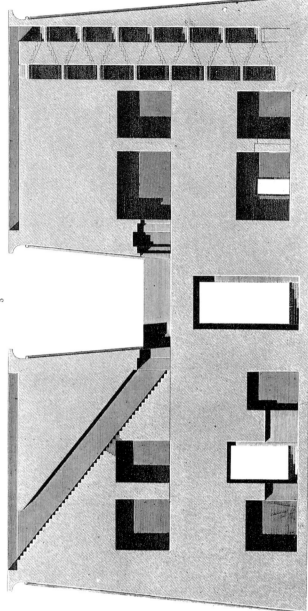

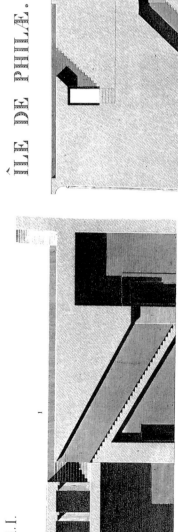

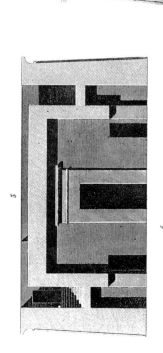

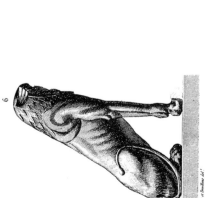

1. 2. 3. 4. 5. DIVERSES COUPES DU GRAND TEMPLE ET DES DEUX PYLÔNES, 6. 7. DÉTAILS DES LIONS PLACÉS DEVANT LE PREMIER PYLÔNE.

ÎLE DE PHILÆ.

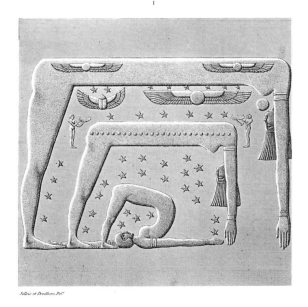

1.2.3.4 SCULPTURES DU PORTIQUE DU GRAND TEMPLE. 5.6.7 ÉLÉVATION, COUPE

ET PLANS D'UN MONOLITHE DU MÊME TEMPLE.

ÎLE DE PHILÆ.

Pl. 11.

1

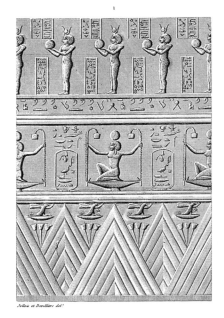

2

3

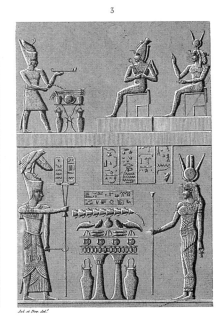

4

1.2.4 SCULPTURES DU PORTIQUE DU GRAND TEMPLE ET DU PREMIER PYLÔNE.

3 BAS-RELIEF DE L'ÉDIFICE RUINÉ DE L'OUEST.

ÎLE DE PHILÆ.

Pl. 12.

1.3 SCULPTURES DES DEUX PYLÔNES. 2 BAS-RELIEF DU TEMPLE DE L'OUEST.
4.5 BAS-RELIEFS DU GRAND TEMPLE. 6....11 INSCRIPTIONS HIÉROGLYPHIQUES.

ÎLE DE PHILÆ.

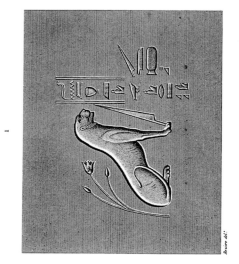

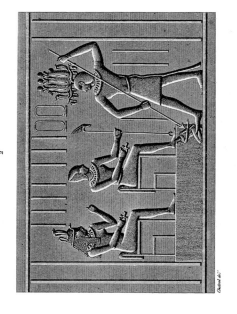

1. 3. 4. SCULPTURES DE LA GALERIE DE L'EST. 2. BAS~RELIEF DU TEMPLE DE L'OUEST.

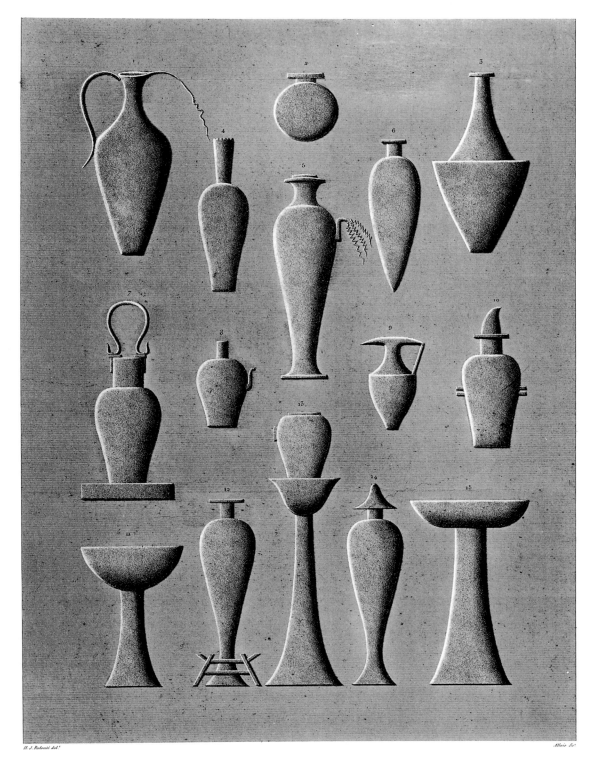

COLLECTION DE VASES SCULPTÉS DANS DIVERS ÉDIFICES.

Pl. 15.

VUE PERSPECTIVE DU SECOND PYLONE ET DE LA COUR QUI LE PRÉCÈDE.

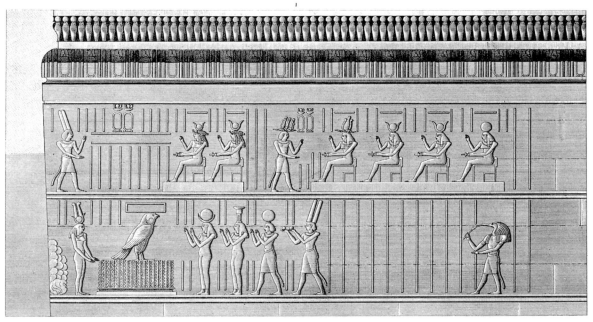

1.2. BAS-RELIEFS DE L'ÉDIFICE RUINÉ DE L'OUEST. 3 SCULPTURE DU GRAND TEMPLE.

Pl. 20.

ÎLE DE PHILÆ.

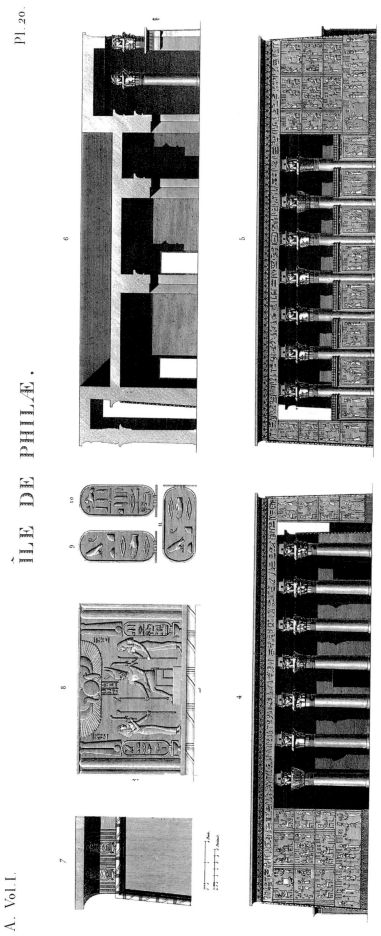

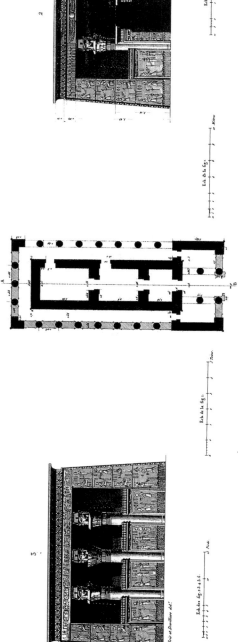

PLAN, ÉLÉVATIONS, COUPES ET DÉTAILS DU TEMPLE DE L'OUEST.

ÎLE DE PHILÆ.

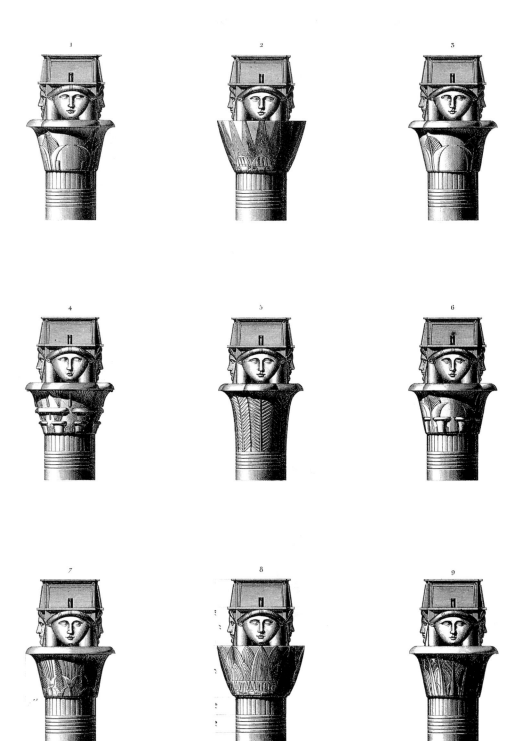

DÉTAILS DES CHAPITEAUX DU TEMPLE DE L'OUEST.

ÎLE DE PHILÆ.

Pl. 22.

BAS-RELIEFS SCULPTÉS SOUS LA GALERIE DU TEMPLE DE L'OUEST.

ÎLE DE PHILÆ.

Pl.23.

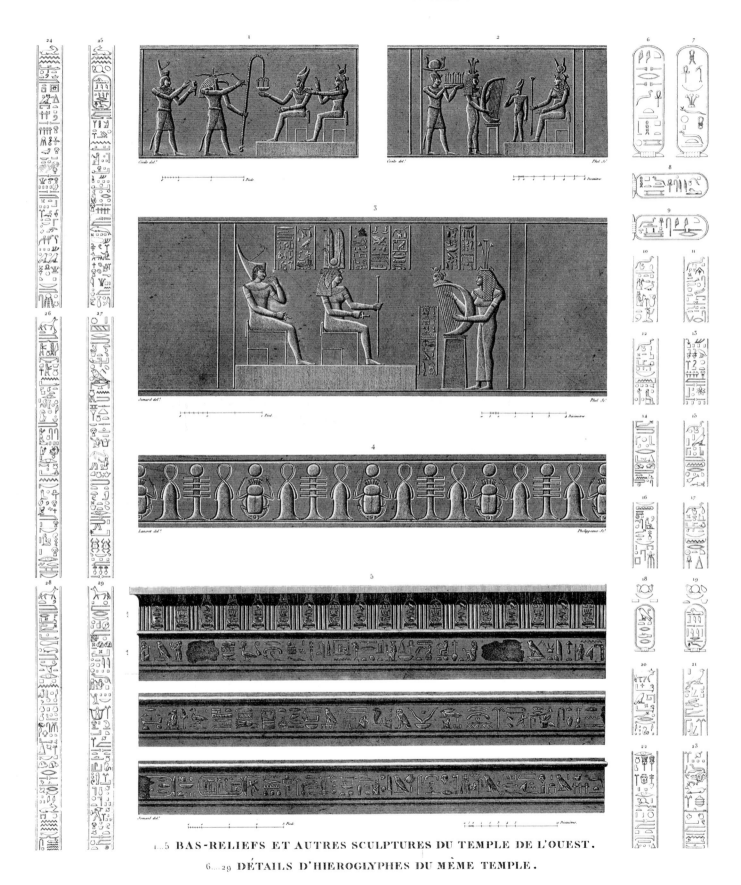

1...5 BAS-RELIEFS ET AUTRES SCULPTURES DU TEMPLE DE L'OUEST.

6....29 DÉTAILS D'HIEROGLYPHES DU MÊME TEMPLE.

Pl. 24.

ÎLE DE PHILÆ.

VUE PERSPECTIVE DU TEMPLE DE L'OUEST ET DE PLUSIEURS AUTRES ÉDIFICES.

ÎLE DE PHILÆ.

Pl. 25

Cécile del.

Adam sculp.

VUE DE L'ÉDIFICE DE L'EST ET DE PLUSIEURS MONUMENS.

Pl. 26.

ÎLE DE PHILÆ.

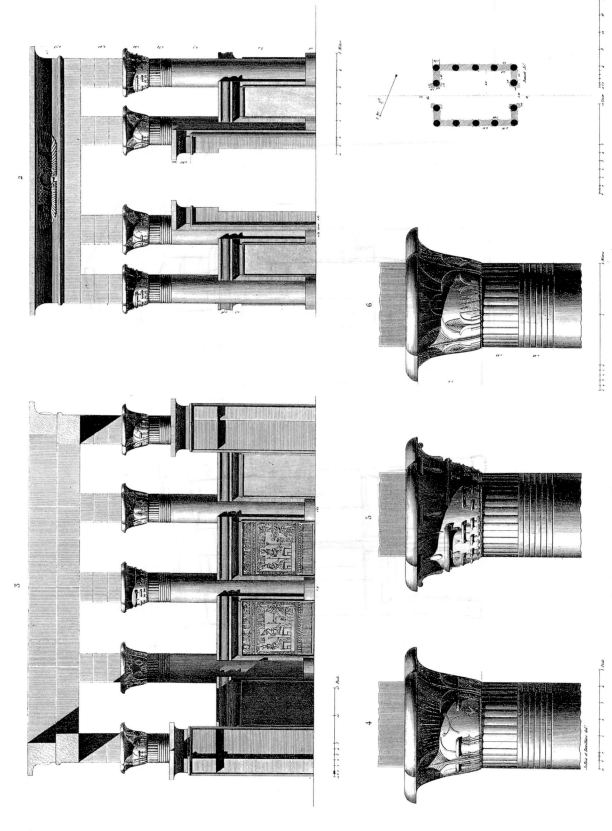

PLAN, COUPE, ÉLÉVATION ET DÉTAILS DE TROIS CHAPITEAUX DE L'ÉDIFICE DE L'EST.

Pl. 27.

ÎLE DE PHILÆ.

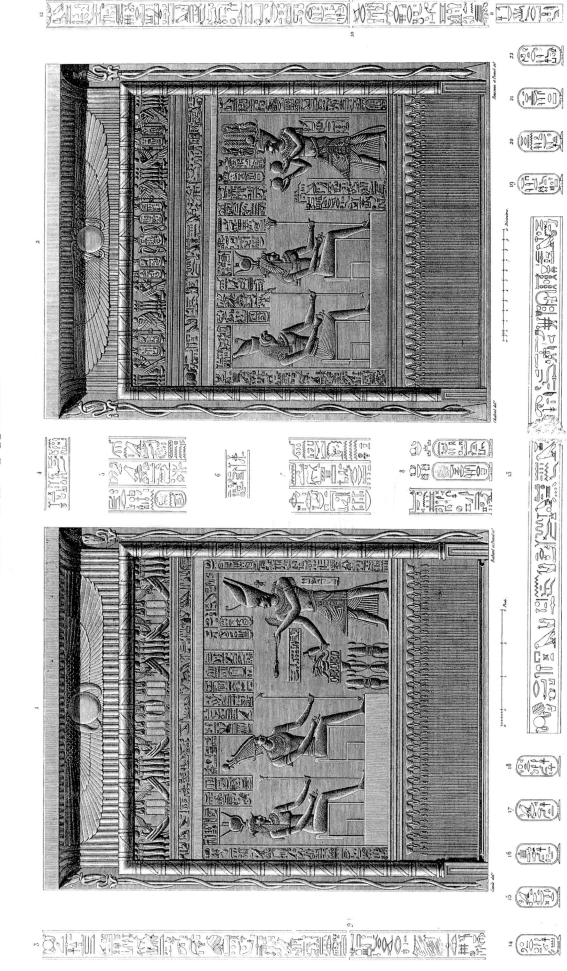

1. 2. DÉCORATIONS INTÉRIEURES DE DEUX MURS D'ENTRECOLONNEMENT DE L'ÉDIFICE DE L'EST. 3...22 DÉTAILS D'HIÉROGLYPHES.

Pl. 28.

ÎLE DE PHILÆ.

VUE PERSPECTIVE DE L'ÉDIFICE DE L'EST.

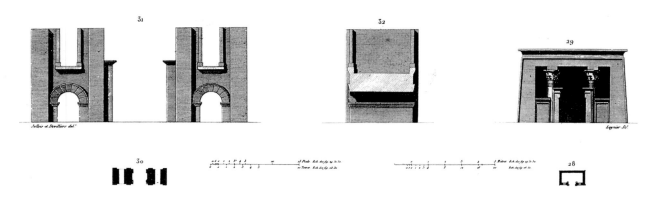

1.2.3. VUE ET PLANS DE LA CATARACTE DE SYÈNE ET DES ENVIRONS. 4 VUE DES RUINES D'ÉLÉPHANTINE.

Pl. 31.

ÎLE D'ÉLÉPHANTINE ET SYÈNE.

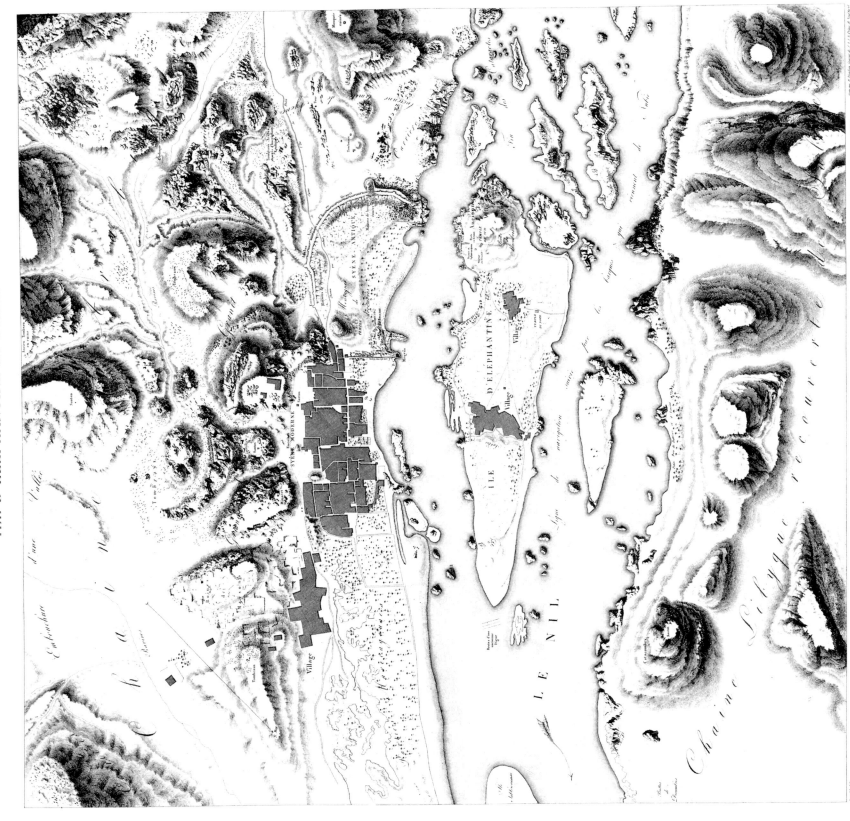

1. VUE DE L'ÎLE ET DES ENVIRONS. 2. VUE DE SYÈNE. 3. VUE D'UN ROCHER DE GRANIT
PORTANT LES TRACES DE L'EXPLOITATION.

Pl. 33.

ÎLE D'ÉLÉPHANTINE.

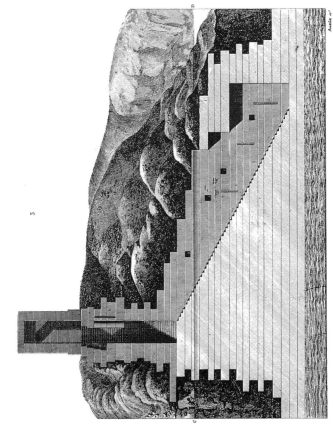

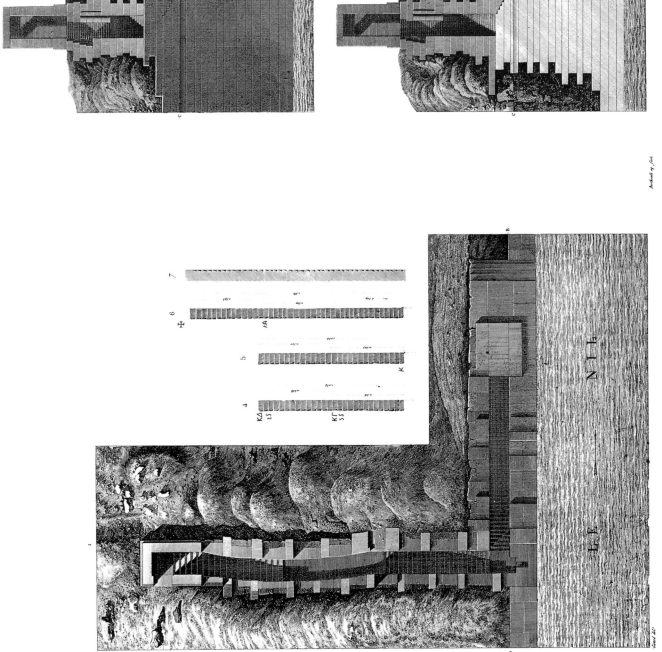

PLAN, ÉLÉVATION, COUPE ET DÉTAILS D'UN NILOMÈTRE.

Pl. 54.

ÎLE D'ÉLÉPHANTINE.

VUE DU TEMPLE DU SUD.

Pl. 35.

ÎLE D'ÉLÉPHANTINE.

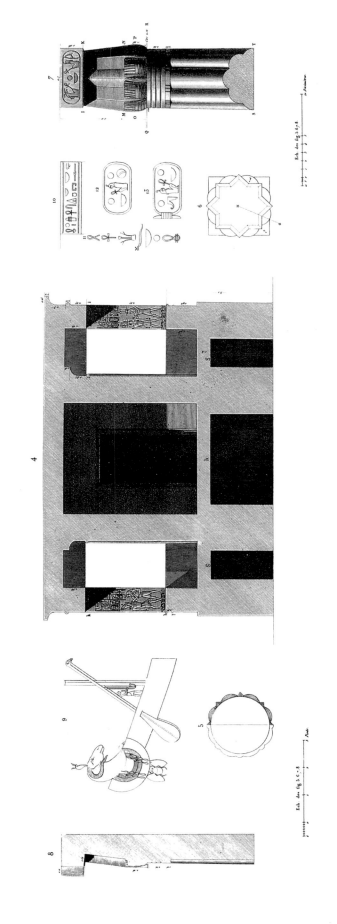

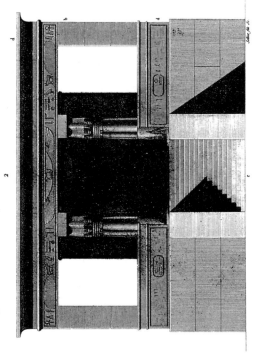

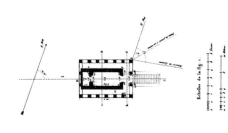

PLAN, COUPE, ÉLÉVATIONS, DÉTAILS ET BAS-RELIEFS DU TEMPLE DU SUD.

Pl. 36.

ÎLE D'ÉLÉPHANTINE.

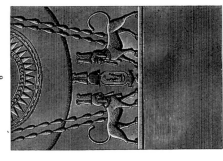

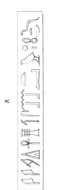

COUPES ET BAS-RELIEFS DU TEMPLE DU SUD.

ÎLE D'ÉLÉPHANTINE.

Pl. 37.

1

2

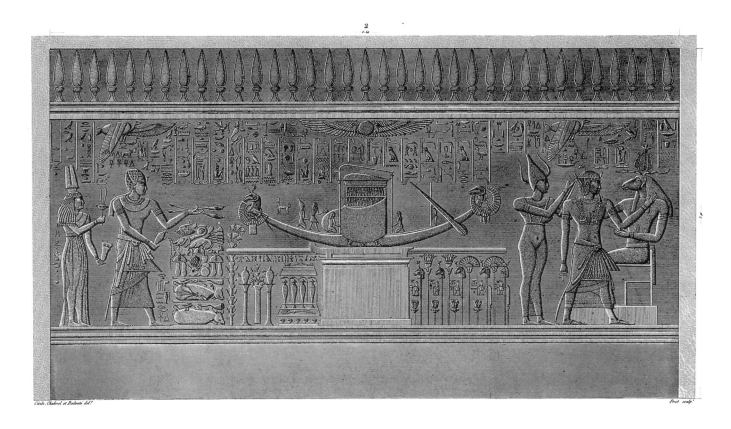

BAS-RELIEFS DU TEMPLE DU SUD.

ÎLE D'ÉLÉPHANTINE ET SYENE.

Pl. 38.

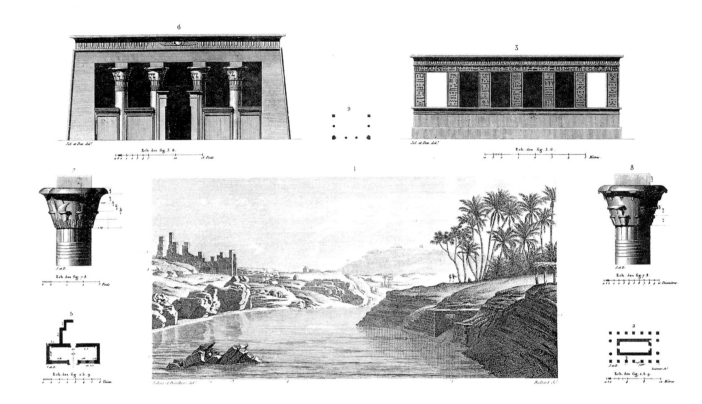

1 VUE PERSPECTIVE DU TEMPLE DU SUD A ELEPHANTINE. 2.3 TEMPLE DU NORD. 4 VUE DE L'ILE ET DES ENVIRONS

5.6.7.8 PLAN, ÉLÉVATION ET CHAPITEAUX D'UN TEMPLE A SYENE. 9 PLAN D'UN ÉDIFICE RUINÉ A SYEN.

Pl. 39.

A. Vol. I.

KOUM OMBOÛ (OMBOS.)

PLAN GÉNÉRAL DES RUINES ET DES ENVIRONS.

Pl. 40.

KOUM OMBOU (OMBOS.)

Cécile del.

Baltard sc.

VUE DU GRAND TEMPLE.

KOUM OMBOÛ (OMBOS.)

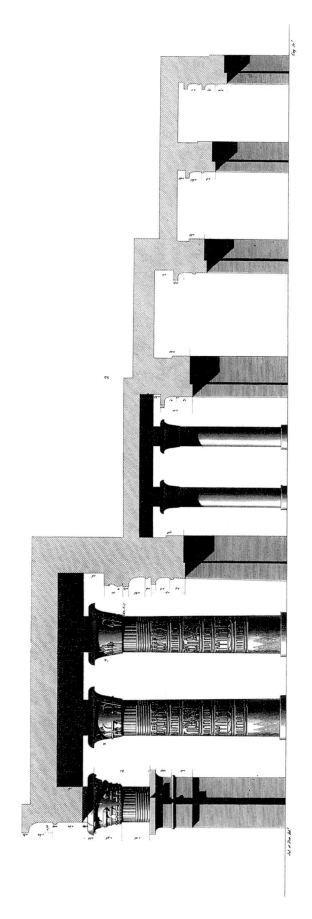

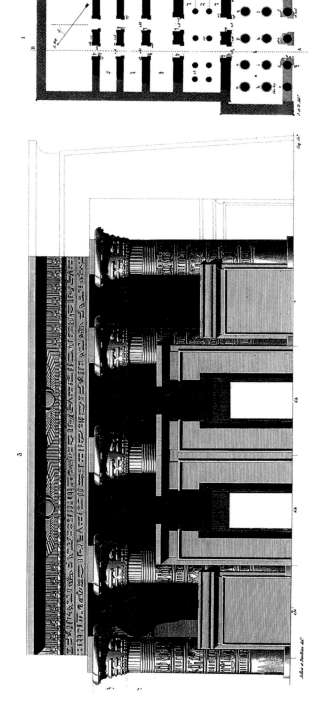

1 2 3 PLAN, COUPE, ET ÉLÉVATION DU GRAND TEMPLE 4 BAS-RELIEF DU MÊME TEMPLE.

5.6 DETAILS D'HIEROGLYPHES.

Pl. 42.

A. Vol. I.

KOUM OMBOÛ (OMBOS.)

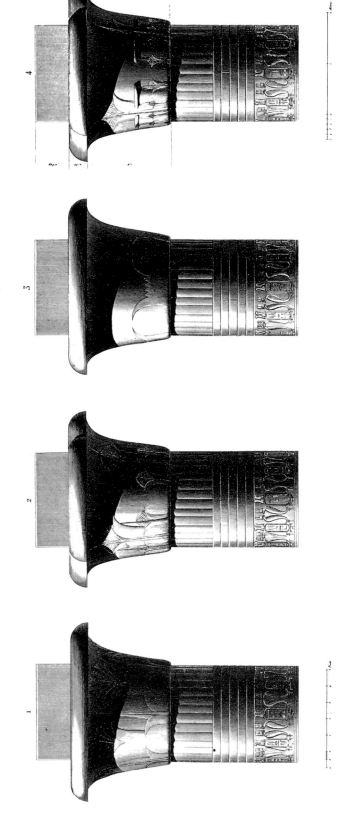

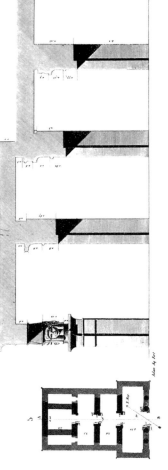

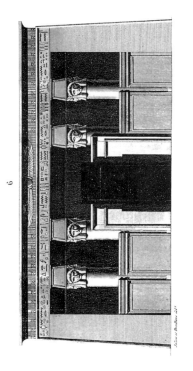

1. 2. 3. 4. CHAPITEAUX DU GRAND TEMPLE. 5. 6. 7. PLAN, ÉLÉVATION ET COUPE DU PETIT TEMPLE.

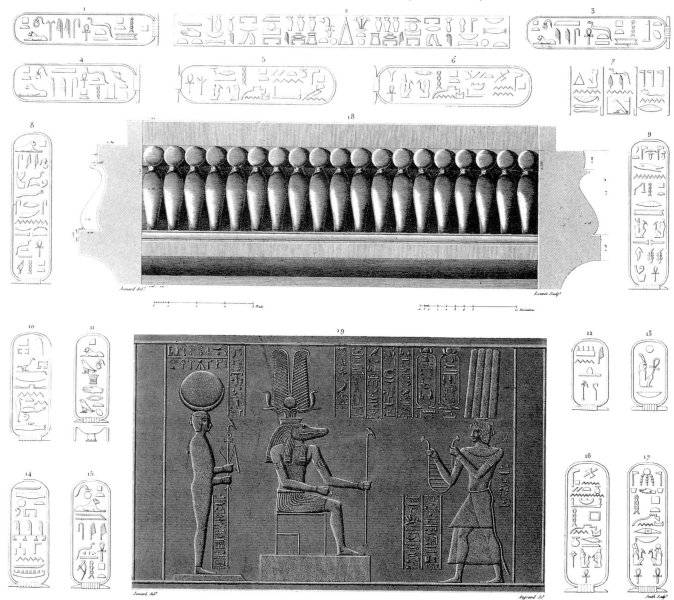

INSCRIPTIONS HIÉROGLYPHIQUES. 18.19.20 DÉTAILS D'ARCHITECTURE ET DE BAS-RELIEFS
DU PORTIQUE DU GRAND TEMPLE.

Pl. 44.

KOUM OMBOÛ (OMBOS.)

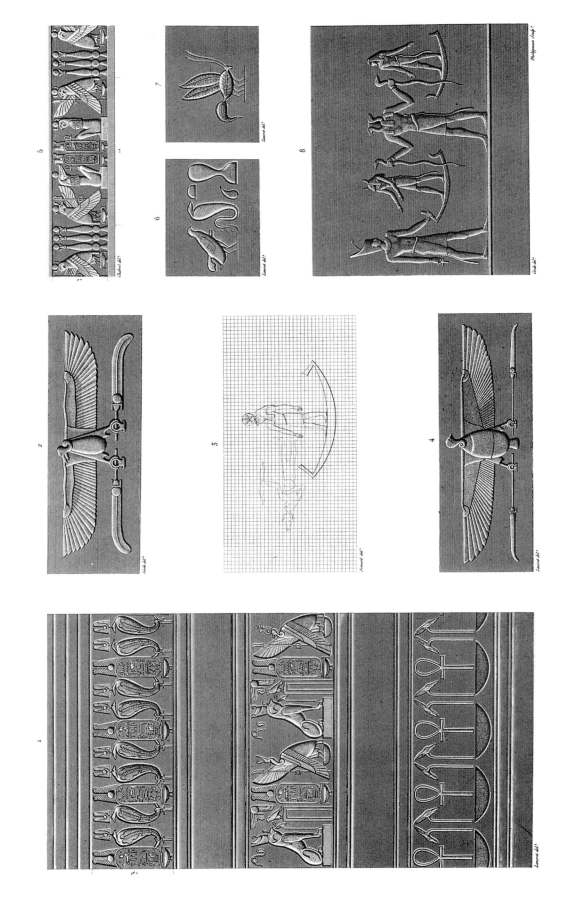

SCULPTURES ET DÉTAILS DU GRAND TEMPLE.

KOUM OMBOÛ (OMBOS.)

Pl. 45

1....5 BAS - RELIEFS DU PETIT TEMPLE. 6.......15 COEFFURES SYMBOLIQUES.

14 BAS - RELIEF DES GROTTES DE SELSELEH.

Pl. 46

KOUM OMBOÛ (OMBOS.)

VUE PERSPECTIVE DES DEUX TEMPLES ET DE L'ENCEINTE.

Pl. 47.

SELSELEH (SILSILIS.)

V.^{TE} DES GROTTES TAILLÉES A L'ENTRÉE DES ANCIENNES CARRIERES.

Pl. 48

EDFOU (APOLLINOPOLIS MAGNA.)

VUE GÉNÉRALE.

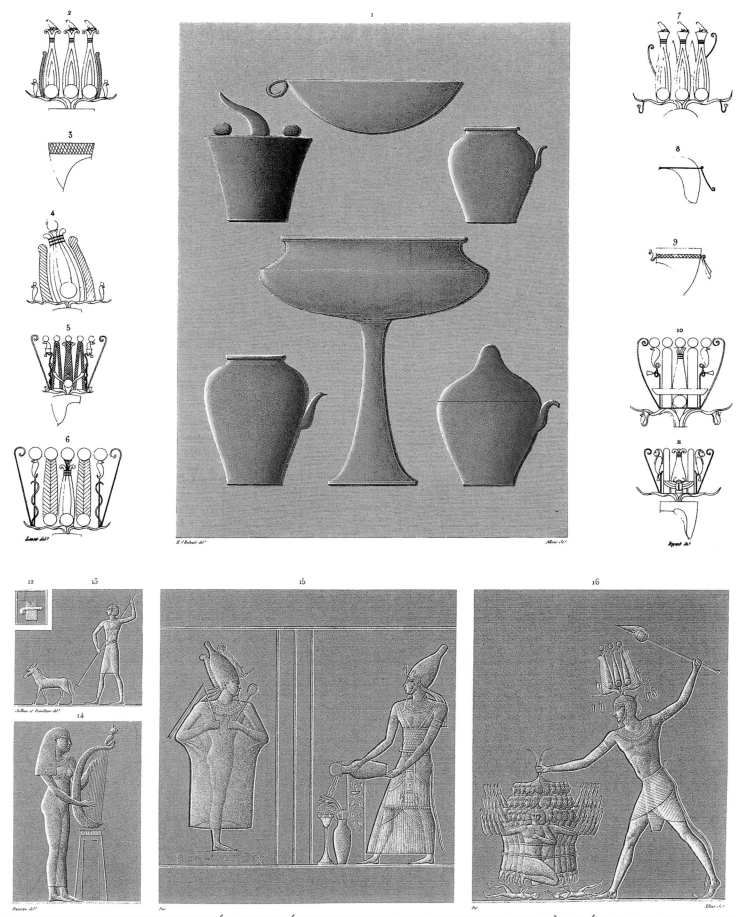

1 COLLECTION DE VASES COLORIÉS, SCULPTÉS ET PEINTS DANS LE GRAND TEMPLE. 2 À 11 DÉTAILS DE COEFFURES SYMBOLIQUES. 12.13.15.16 SCULPTURES DU GRAND TEMPLE. 14 BAS-RELIEF DU TEMPLE DE L'OUEST.

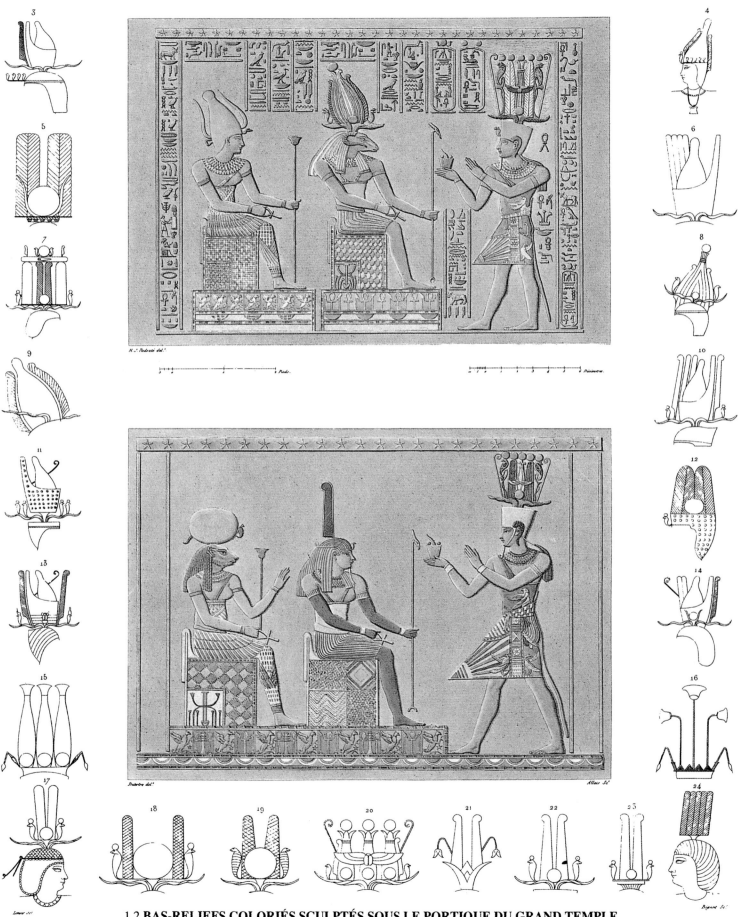

1.2 BAS-RELIEFS COLORIÉS SCULPTÉS SOUS LE PORTIQUE DU GRAND TEMPLE.
3 À 24 DÉTAILS DE COEFFURES SYMBOLIQUES.

VUE PERSPECTIVE INTÉRIEURE COLORIÉE, PRISE SOUS LE PORTIQUE DU GRAND TEMPLE.

BAS-RELIEFS DE PLUSIEURS GROTTES.

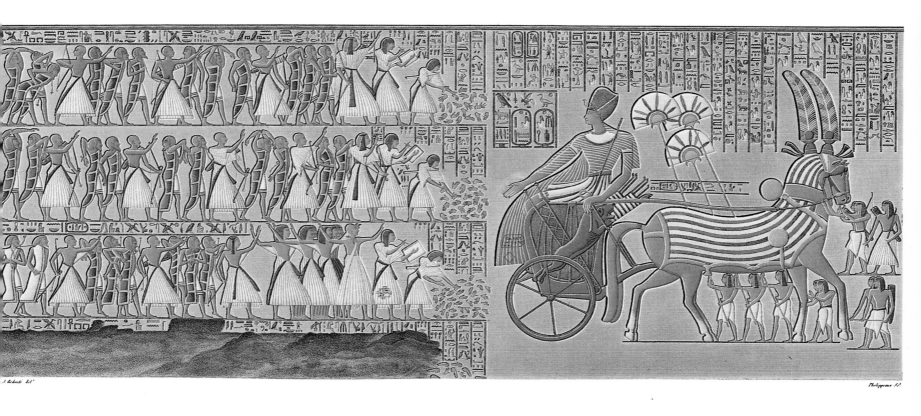

BAS-RELIEF COLORIÉ, SCULPTÉ DANS LA GALERIE SUD DU PÉRISTYLE DU PALAIS.

Le Père arch. del.   Allais Sc.

VUE PERSPECTIVE INTÉRIEURE COLORIÉE DU TEMPLE DE L'OUEST.

FRAGMENTS EN PIERRE ET EN BOIS PEINT, BAS-RELIEFS COLORIÉS ET PEINTURES DIVERSES.

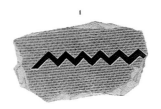

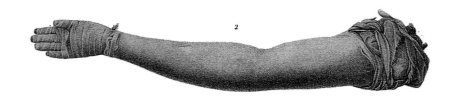

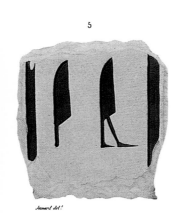

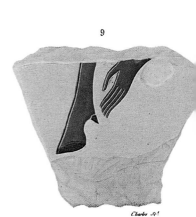

1.3.5.9 **FRAGMENTS COLORIÉS.** 2.4 **BRAS ET BANDELETTE DE MOMIE.**
6.7.8 **BRIQUES PORTANT DES HIÉROGLYPHES IMPRIMÉS.**

1

2

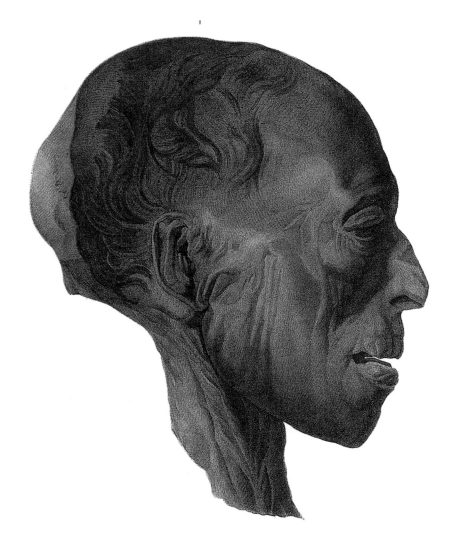
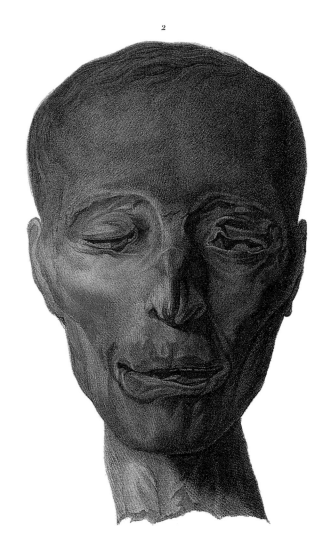

Tiré de la Collection de M.ʳ Drôle et dessiné par M.M Dutertre et H.J Redouté.

Montvalebé Sc.

PROFIL ET FACE D'UNE TÊTE DE MOMIE D'HOMME.

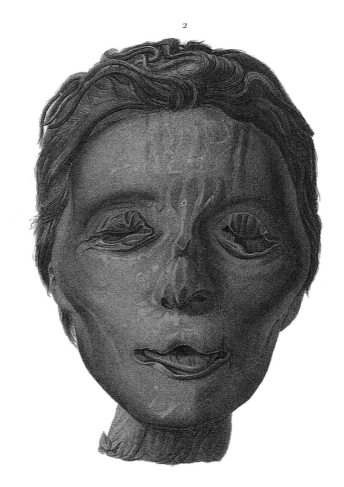

Tiré de la Collection de M⁰ Delile et dessiné par MM. Dutertre et H.J.Redouté

PROFIL ET FACE D'UNE TÊTE DE MOMIE DE FEMME.

PEINTURES DESSINÉES D'APRÈS DES ENVELOPPES DE MOMIES.

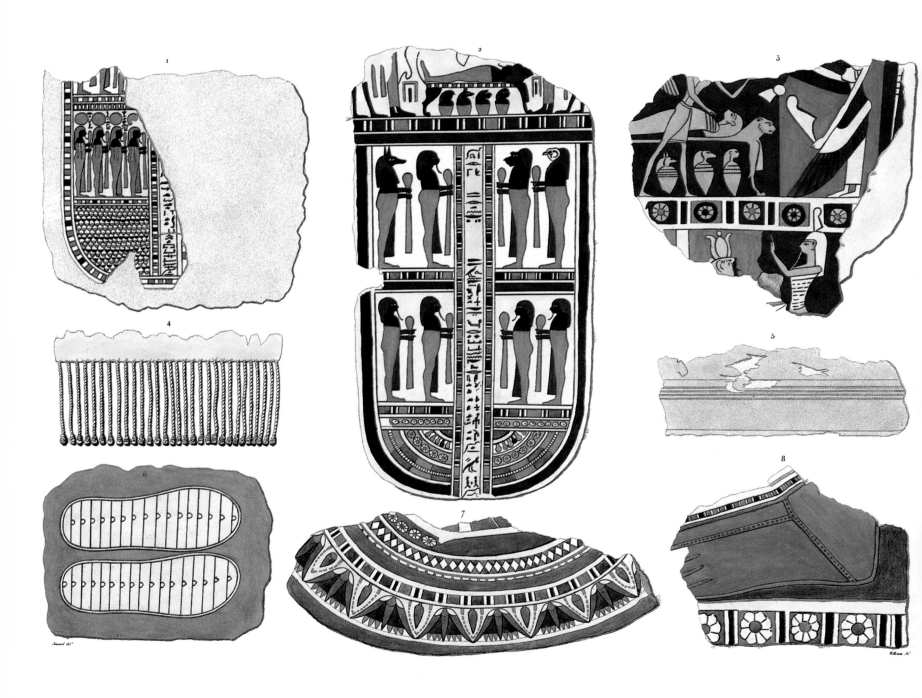

1.2.3.6.7.8 PEINTURES DESSINÉES D'APRÈS DES ENVELOPPES DE MOMIES.
4.5 DÉTAILS D'UNE FRANGE ET D'UNE TOILE RAYÉE. TROUVÉES SUR DES MOMIES.

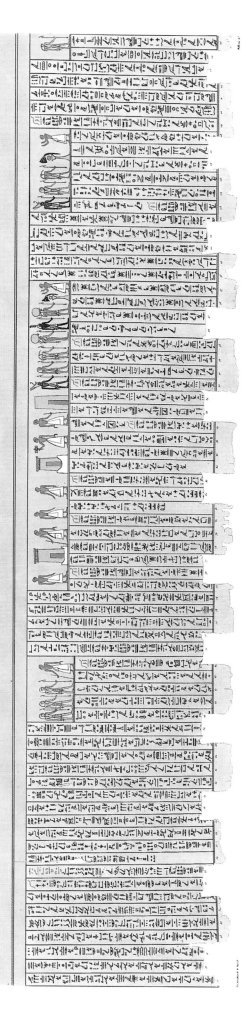

PREMIÈRE PARTIE

MANUSCRIT SUR PAPYRUS EN CARACTÈRES HIÉROGLYPHIQUES.

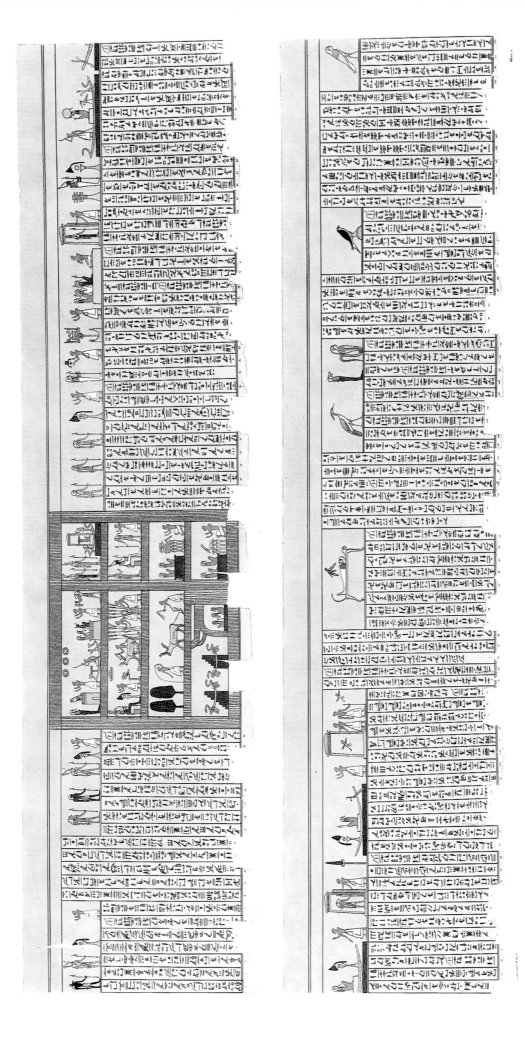

DEUXIÈME PARTIE

MANUSCRIT SUR PAPYRUS EN CARACTÈRES HIÉROGLYPHIQUES.

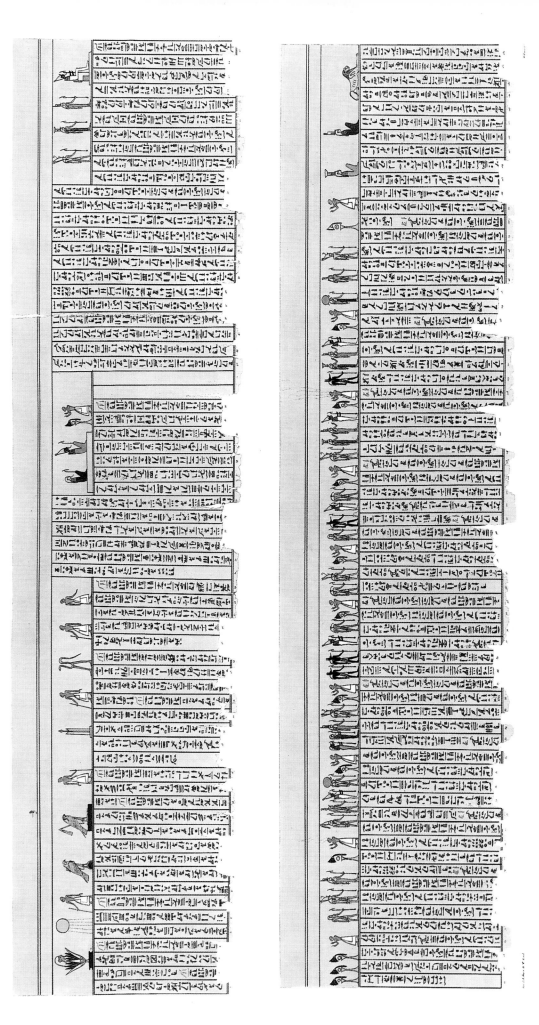

TROISIÈME PARTIE

MANUSCRIT SUR PAPYRUS EN CARACTÈRES HIÉROGLYPHIQUES.

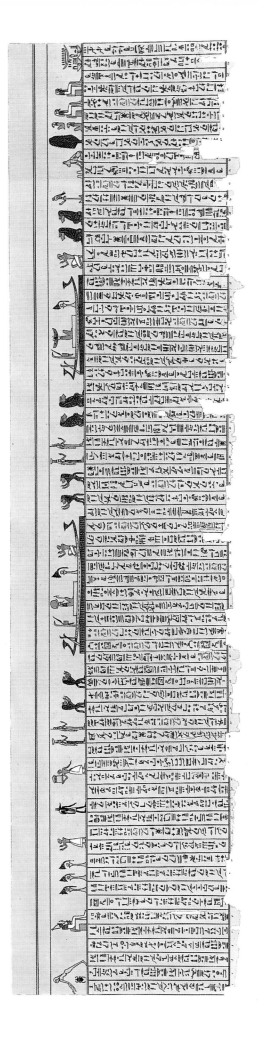

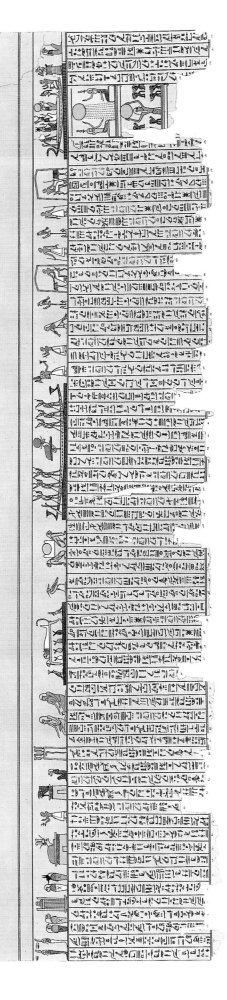

QUATRIÈME PARTIE

MANUSCRIT SUR PAPYRUS EN CARACTÈRES HIÉROGLYPHIQUES.

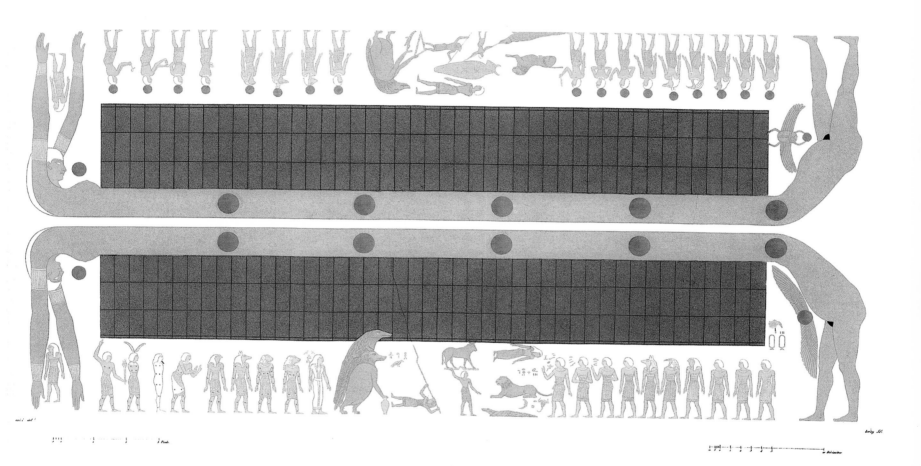

TABLEAU ASTRONOMIQUE PEINT AU PLAFOND DU 1er TOMBEAU DES ROIS À L'OUEST

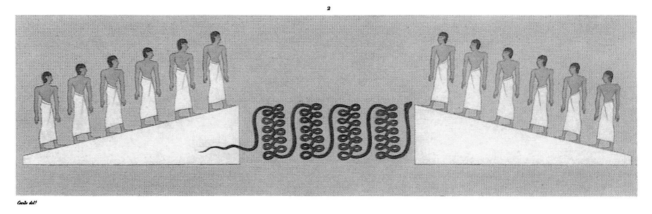

1 TABLEAU PEINT À L'ENTRÉE DU 5ᵉ TOMBEAU DES ROIS À L'OUEST.
2 À 7 AUTRES PEINTURES DES TOMBEAUX.

Pl. 86.

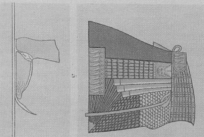

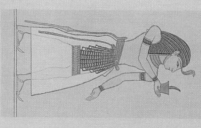

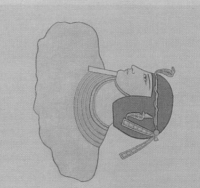

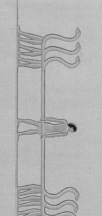

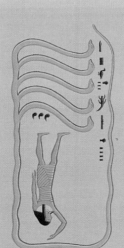

SUJETS MYSTÉRIEUX ET DÉTAILS DE COSTUMES, PEINTS DANS LE 5.ᵉ TOMBEAU DES ROIS À L'EST ET DANS D'AUTRES TOMBEAUX.

THÈBES. BYBÂN EL MOLOUK.

Pl. 87.

1. 6 PEINTURES DU 5.ᵉ TOMBEAU DES ROIS A L'EST. 7 BAS-RELIEF DE L'ENTRÉE DU MÊME TOMBEAU.

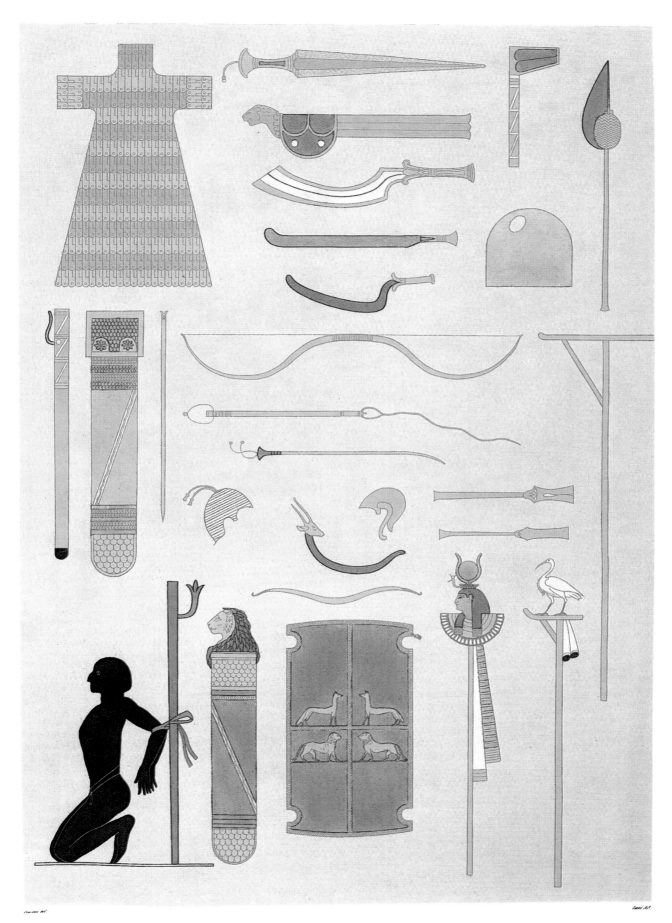

ENSEIGNES, ARMES ET INSTRUMENTS PEINTS DANS LE 5ᵉ TOMBEAU DES ROIS À L'EST.

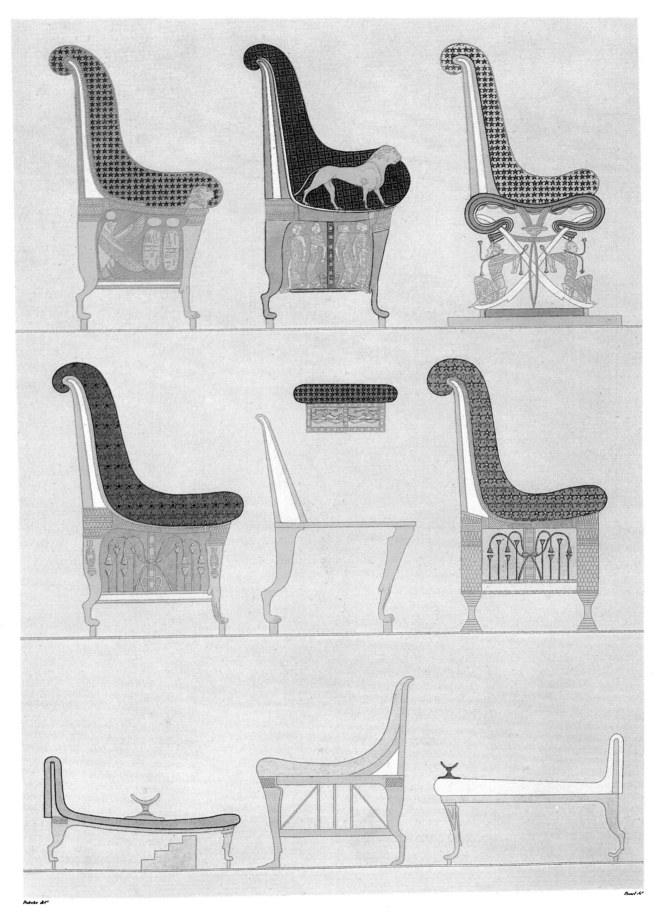

DIVERS SIEGES ET FAUTEUILS PEINTS DANS LE 5ᵉ TOMBEAU DES ROIS À L'EST.

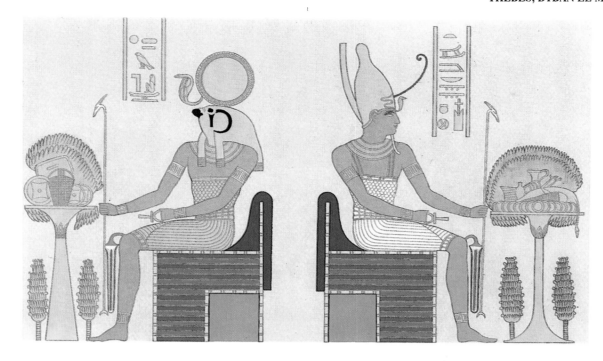

1. TABLEAU PEINT SUR LE FOND DE LA SALLE DES HARPES DANS LE 5ᵉ TOMBEAU DES ROIS À L'EST.
2.3.4 PEINTURE DE L'UNE DES SALLES DU MÊME TOMBEAU.

1.2 TABLEAUX DE LA SALLE DES HARPES DANS LE 5e TOMBEAU DES ROIS À L'EST.
3 À 8 PEINTURES DES TOMBEAUX.

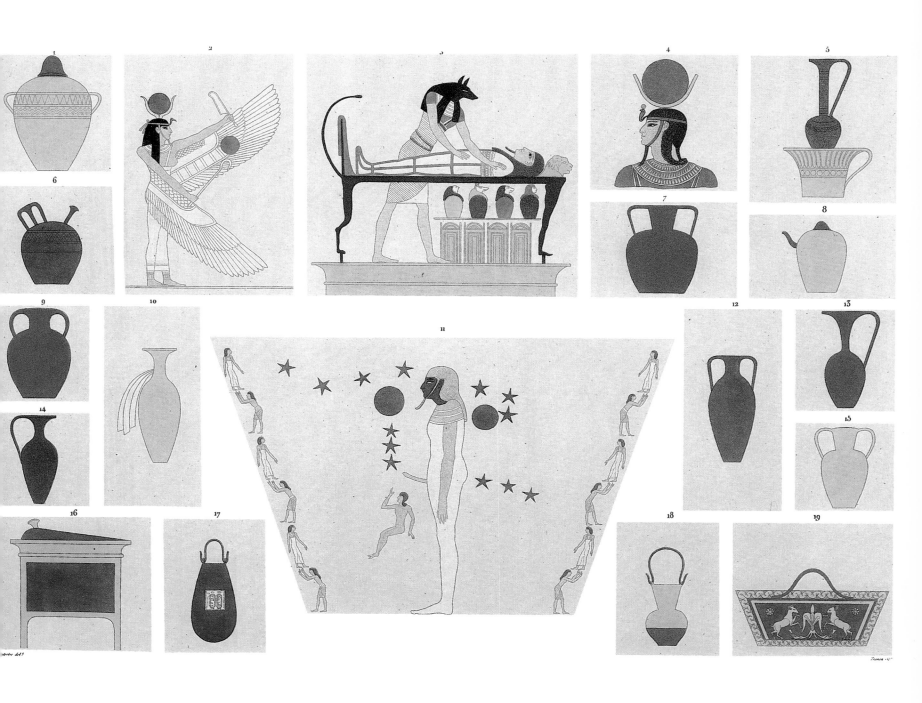

VASES, MEUBLES ET SUJETS DIVERS PEINTS DANS LES TOMBEAUX DES ROIS.

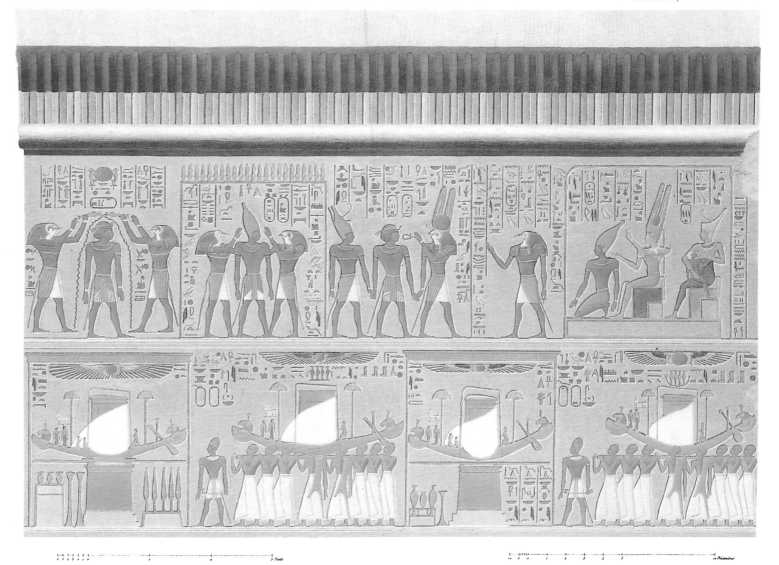

2

5

SCULPTURES COLORIÉES RECUEILLIES DANS LES APPARTEMENTS DE GRANIT
ET DANS LA GALERIE DU PALAIS.

1. DÉTAIL COLORIÉ D'UNE COLONNE DU PORTIQUE. 2....7 PROFIL ET PLANS DE LA COLONNE.

EDFOU (APOLLINOPOLIS MAGNA.)

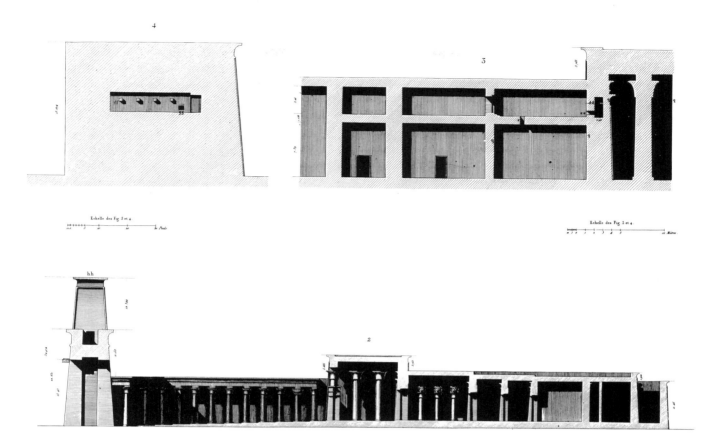

Echelle des Fig. 3 et 4.

Echelle des Fig. 3 et 4.

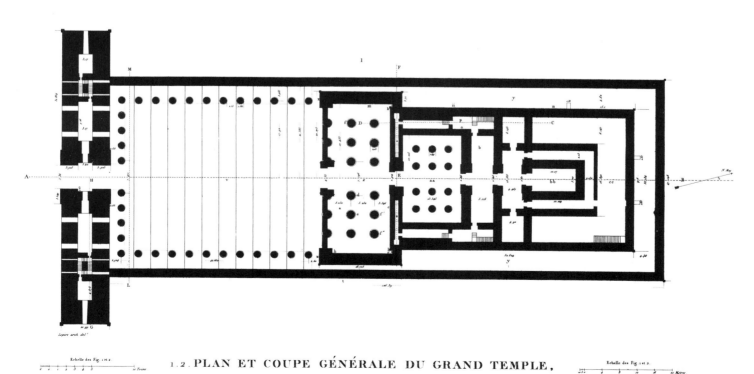

Echelle des Fig. 1 et 2.

Echelle des Fig. 1 et 2.

1.2. PLAN ET COUPE GÉNÉRALE DU GRAND TEMPLE,
3.4. DÉTAILS DE CONSTRUCTIONS INTÉRIEURES.

PLE.

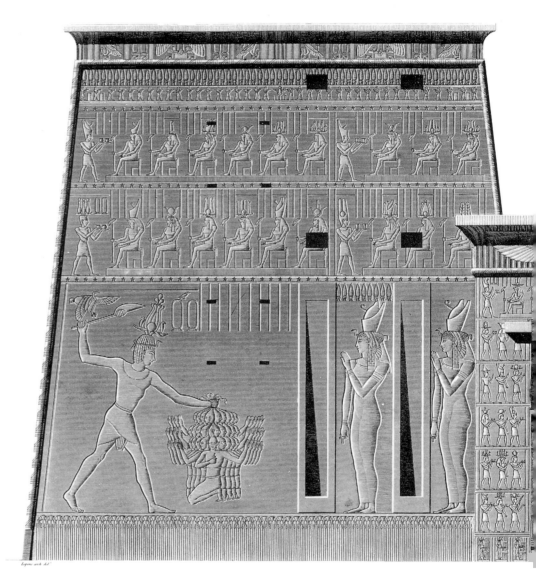

Lepère arch. del.

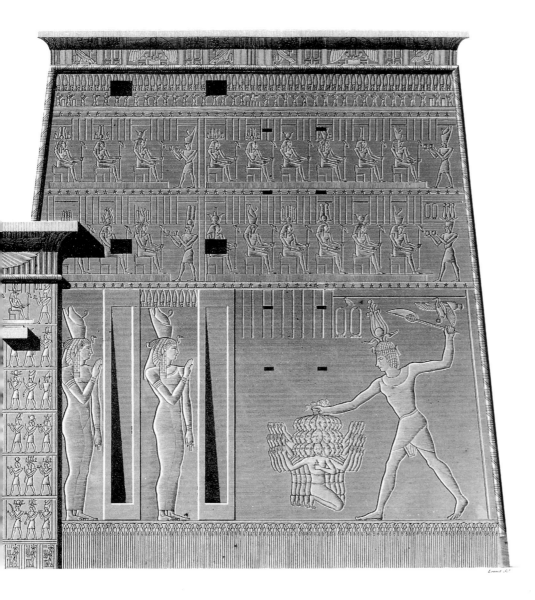

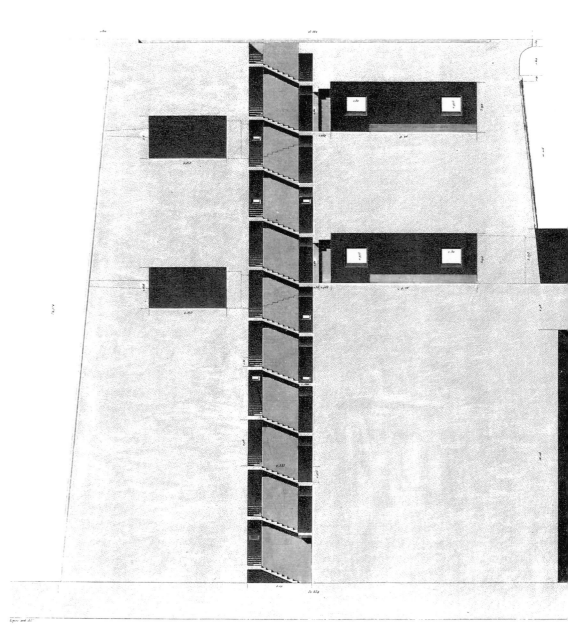

COUPE ET ÉLÉVATION INTÉ

PYLÔNE DU GRAND TEMPLE.

Pl. 53.

EDFOU (APOLLINOPOLIS MAGNA.)

ÉLÉVATION DU PORTIQUE DU GRAND TEMPLE.

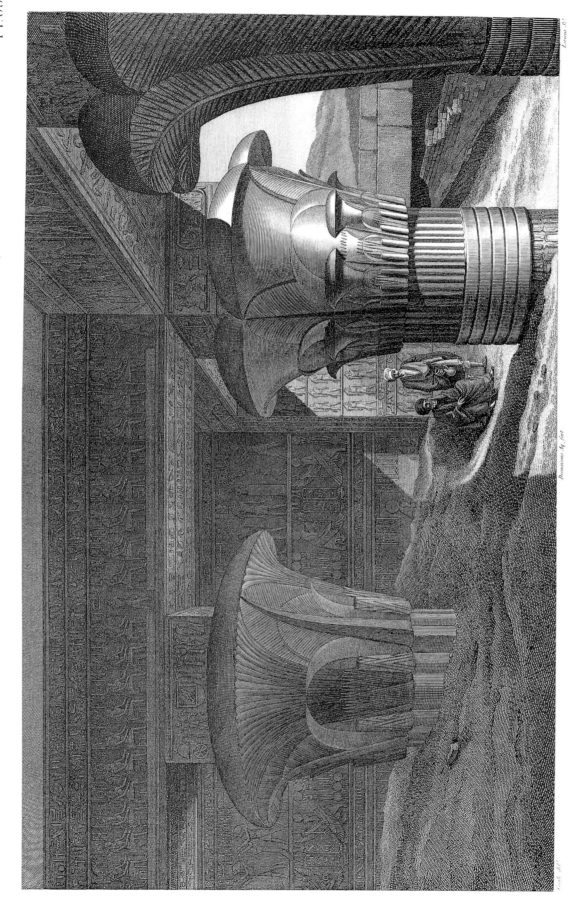

EDFOU (APOLLINOPOLIS MAGNA.)

Pl. 55.

VUE DE L'INTÉRIEUR DU PORTIQUE DU GRAND TEMPLE.

Dimensions 14 feet.

Leroux R.

Pl. 54.

POLIS MAGNA.)

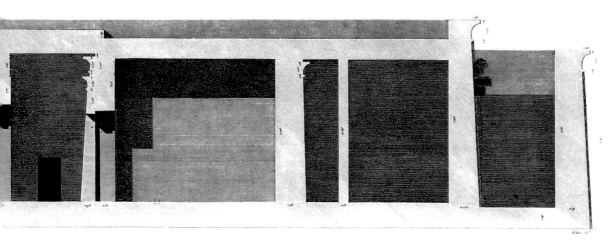

GRAND TEMPLE.

Pl. 56.

EDFOU (APOLLINOPOLIS MAGNA.)

DÉTAILS D'ARCHITECTURE DU GRAND TEMPLE.

EDFOU (APOLLINOPOLIS MAGNA.)

BAS-RELIEFS ET SCULPTURES DU GRAND TEMPLE.

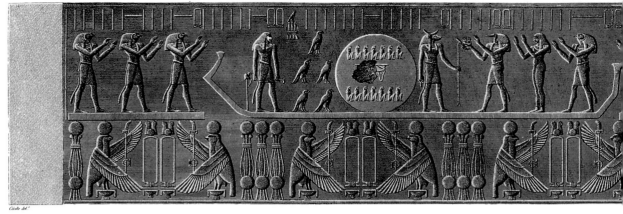

Cécile del.

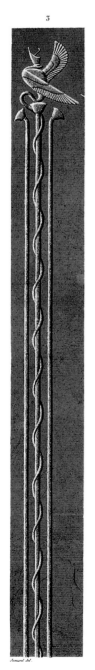

Jomard del.

Jomard, Chabrol, Lancret Balzac del.

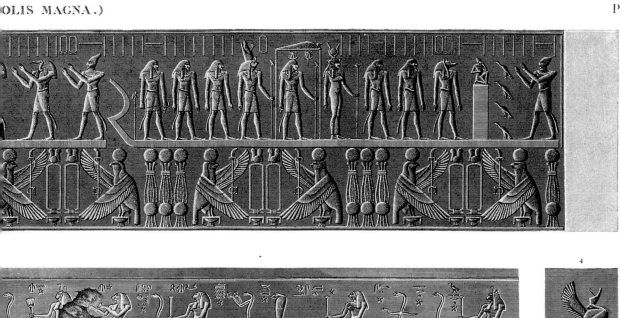

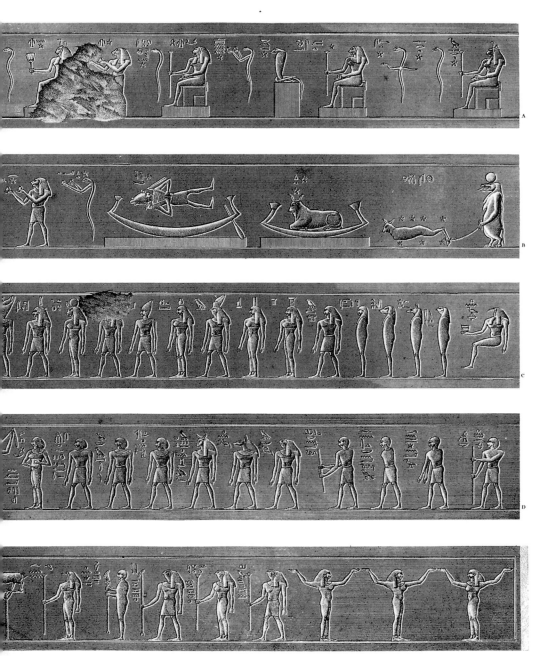

Pl. 59.

EDFOU (APOLLINOPOLIS MAGNA.)

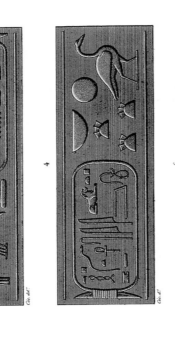

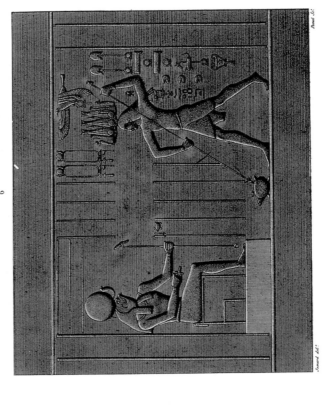

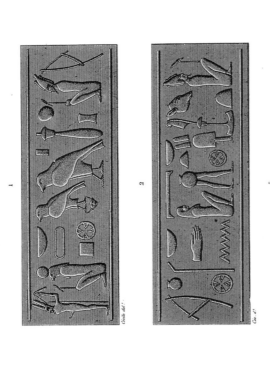

BAS-RELIEFS ET DÉTAILS DU GRAND TEMPLE.

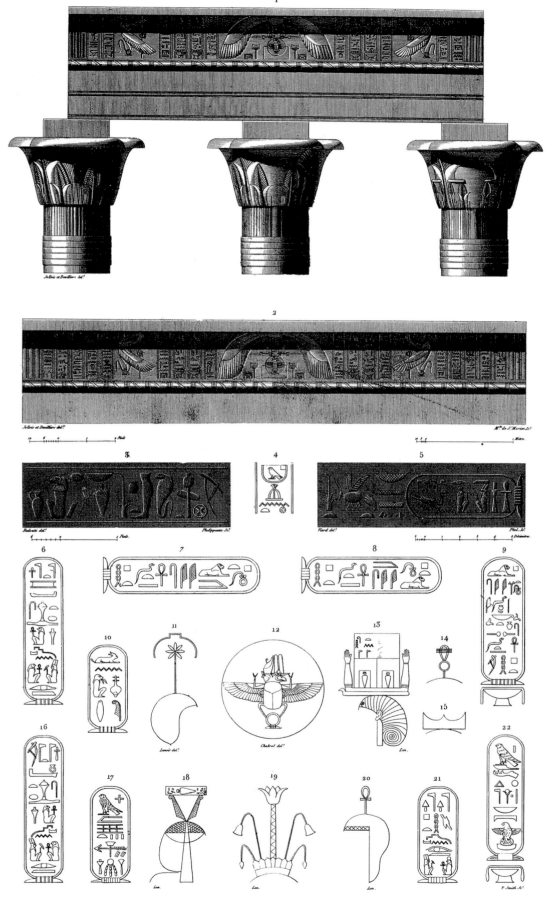

1.2.12. DÉTAILS D'ARCHITECTURE DU GRAND TEMPLE   3.5. DÉS DE CHAPITEAUX DU PORTIQUE.

4.6.7......22 DÉTAILS D'HIÉROGLYPHES ET DE COEFFURES SYMBOLIQUES.

COUR DU GRAND TEMPLE.

Sellier, fils Sc.

Pl. 62.

EDFOU (APOLLINOPOLIS MAGNA.)

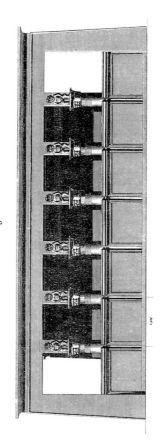

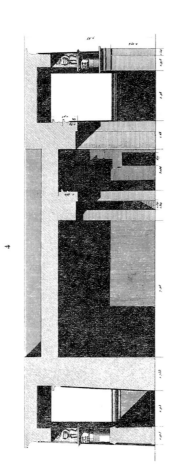

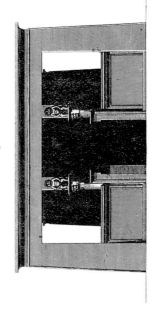

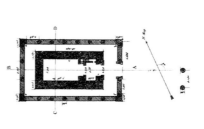

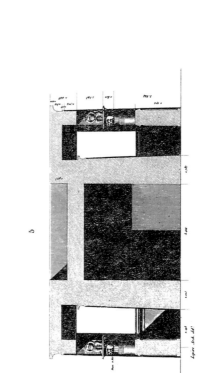

PLAN, COUPES ET ÉLÉVATIONS DU PETIT TEMPLE.

EDFOU (APOLLINOPOLIS MAGNA.)

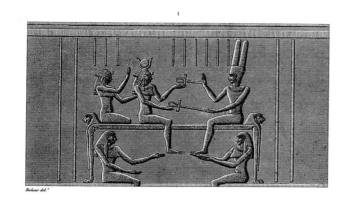

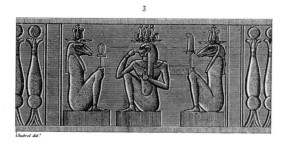

FRISES ET AUTRES SCULPTURES DU PETIT TEMPLE.

Pl. 64.

EDFOU (APOLLINOPOLIS MAGNA.)

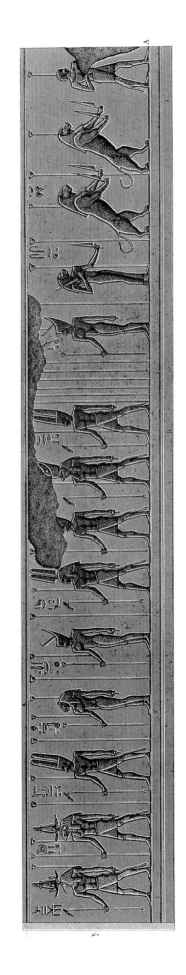

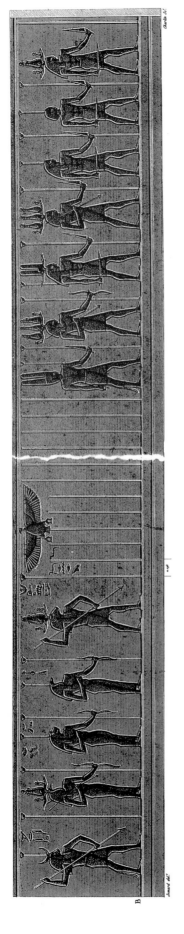

FRISE SCULPTÉE SOUS LA GALERIE NORD, DU PETIT TEMPLE.

EDFOU (APOLLINOPOLIS MAGNA.)

VUE PERSPECTIVE DU PETIT TEMPLE.

EL KAB (ELETHYIA.)

Pl. 66

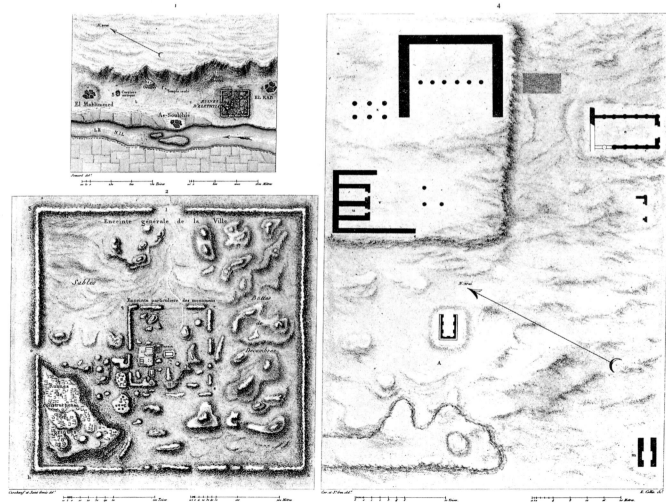

1.2 PLANS DES RUINES ET DES ENVIRONS. 3.4 VUE ET PLAN PARTICULIER DES ÉDIFICES.

1. VUE DE L'INTÉRIEUR DE LA GROTTE PRINCIPALE.

2. VUE D'UNE ANCIENNE CARRIERE.

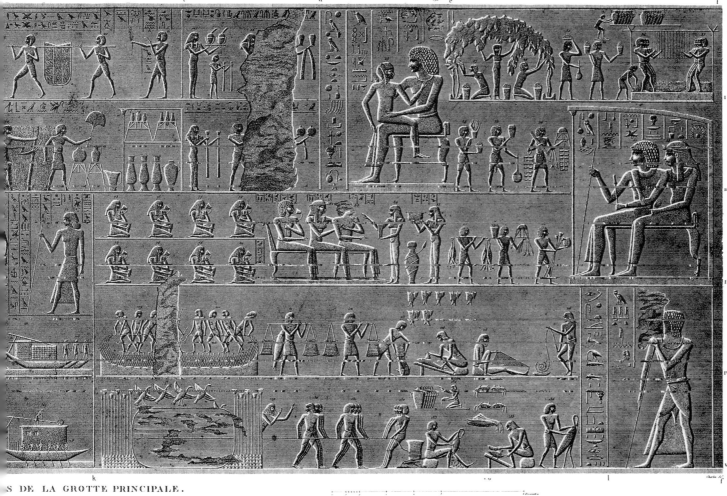

Pl. 69.

EL KAB (ELETHYIA.)

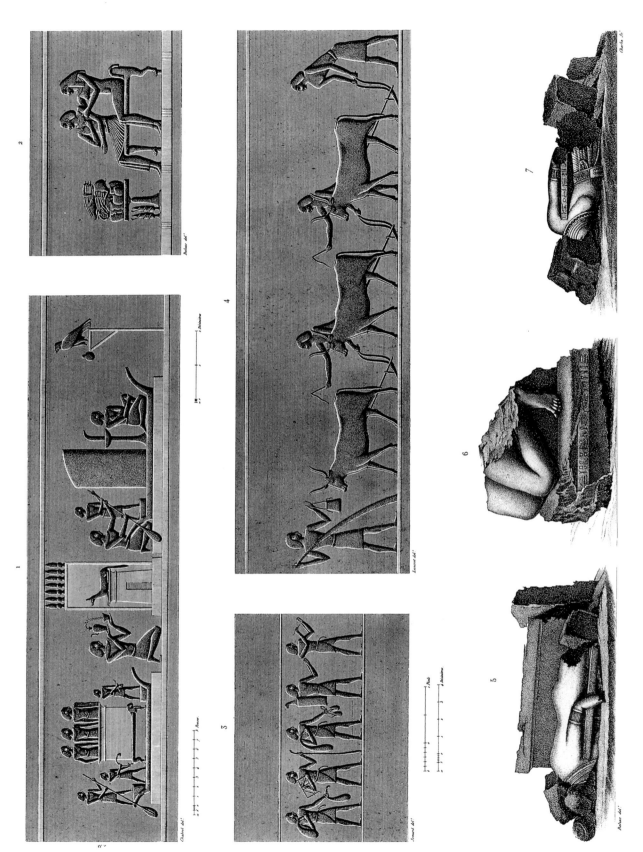

1.2.3.4 BAS-RELIEFS DES GROTTES. 5.6.7 FRAGMENS DE STATUES TROUVÉES DANS LES RUINES DE LA VILLE.

EL KAB (ELETHYIA.)

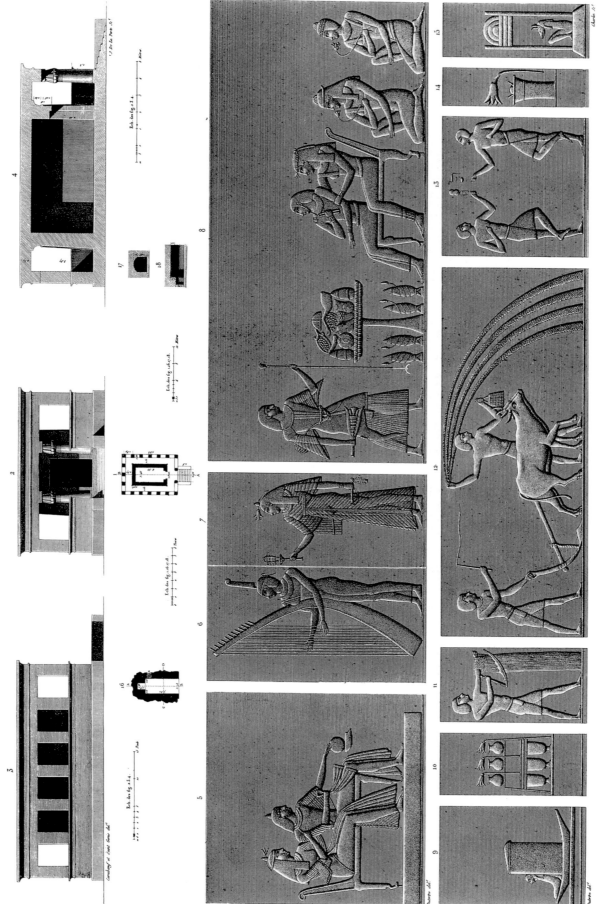

1, 2, 3, 4 PLAN, COUPE ET ÉLÉVATIONS D'UN PETIT TEMPLE ISOLÉ. 5.....15 BAS-RELIEFS DES GROTTES.

16, 17, 18 PLAN ET COUPES DE LA GROTTE PRINCIPALE.

ESNÉ (LATOPOLIS.)

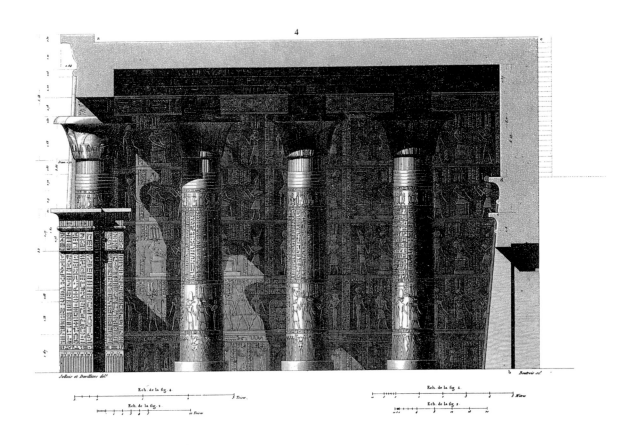

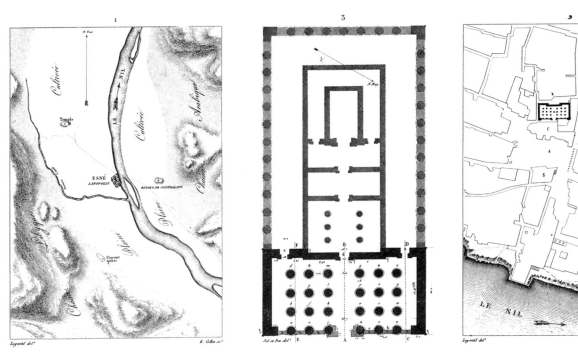

1.2 PLANS DES ENVIRONS D'ESNÉ ET D'UNE PARTIE DE LA VILLE.

3 PLAN DU TEMPLE. 4 COUPE DU PORTIQUE.

ESNÉ (LATOPOLIS.)

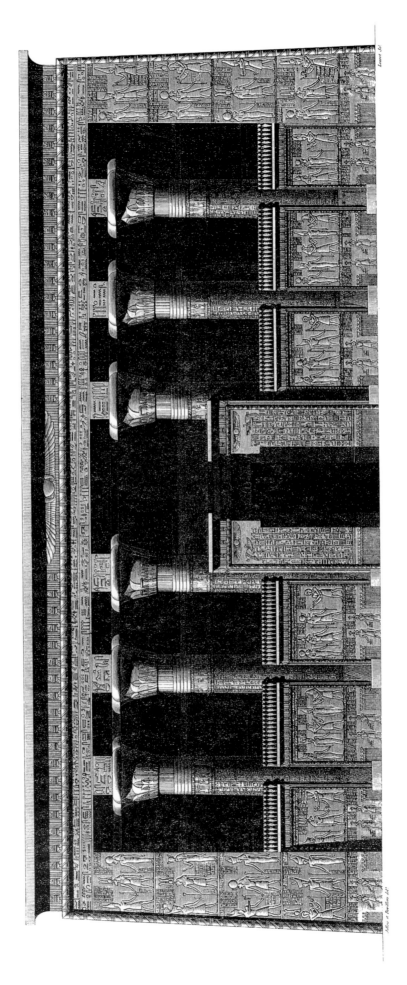

ÉLÉVATION DU PORTIQUE.

Pl. 74.

ESNÉ (LATOPOLIS.)

FACE LATÉRALE DE L'INTÉRIEUR DU PORTIQUE.

ESNÉ (LATOPOLIS.)

Pl. 75.

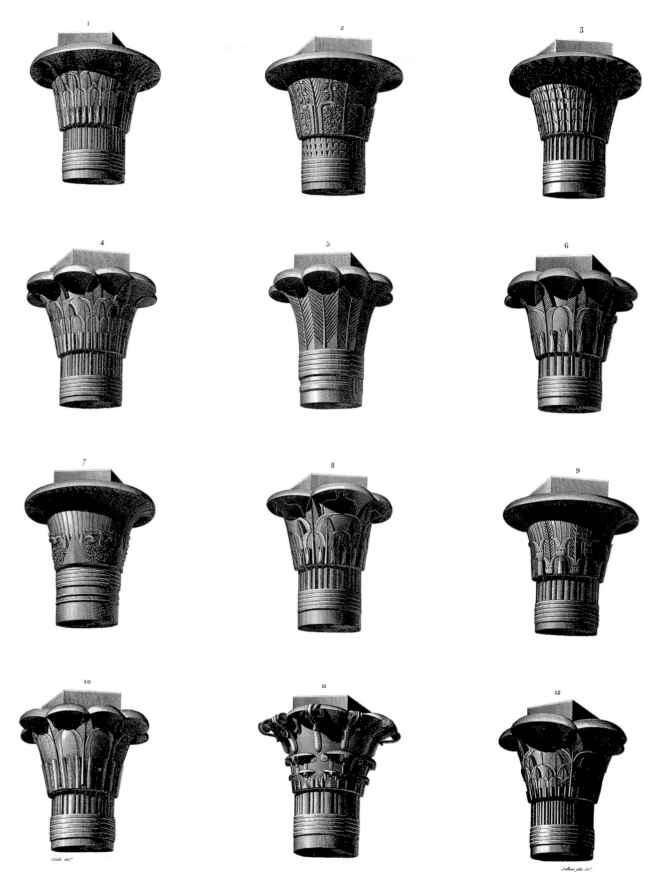

VUES DE DOUZE CHAPITEAUX DU PORTIQUE.

ESNÉ (LATOPOLIS.)

Pl. 76.

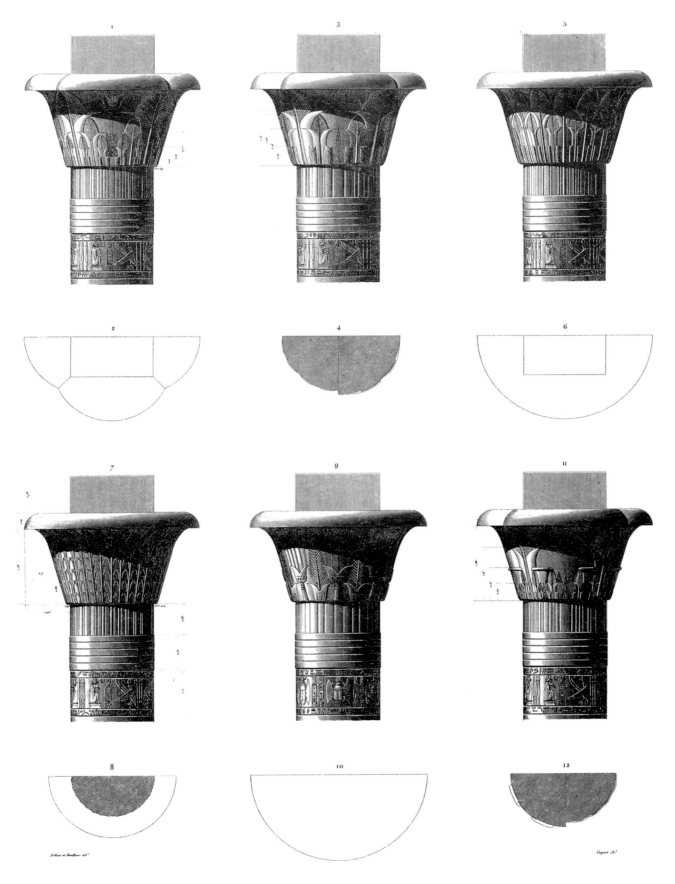

PLANS ET ÉLÉVATIONS DE SIX CHAPITEAUX DU PORTIQUE.

ESNÉ (LATOPOLIS.)

Pl. 77.

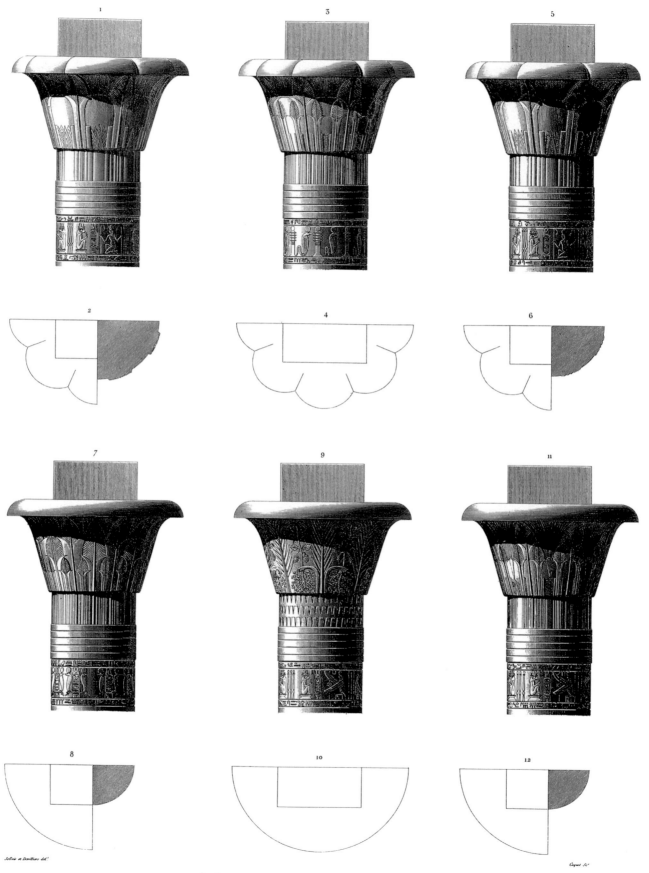

PLANS ET ÉLÉVATIONS DE SIX CHAPITEAUX DU PORTIQUE.

ESNÉ (LATOPOLIS.)

Pl. 78.

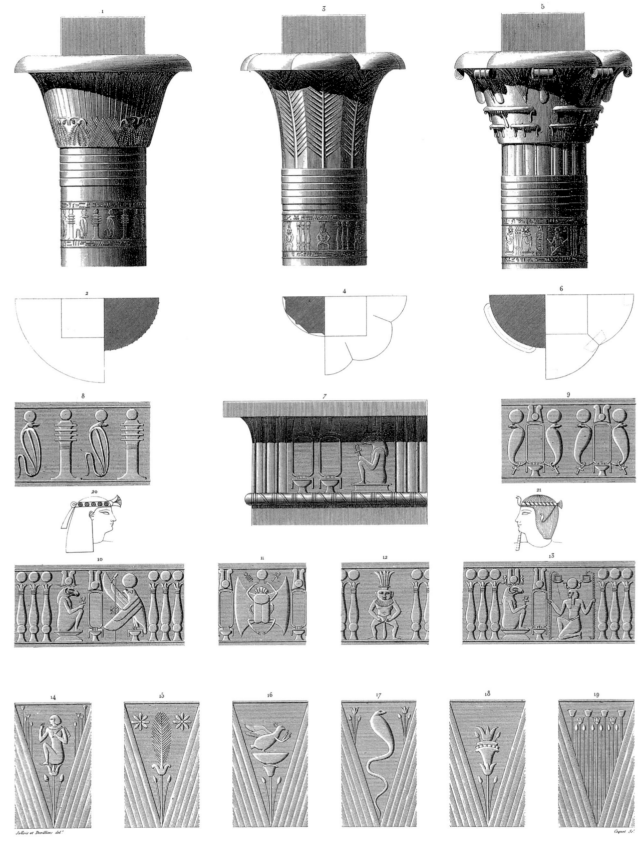

1...6 PLANS ET ÉLÉVATIONS DE TROIS CHAPITEAUX DU PORTIQUE. 7 CORNICHE DE L'INTÉRIEUR DU PORTIQUE.

8....19 DÉCORATIONS DE COLONNES. 20.21 DÉTAILS DE COEFFURES.

Pl. 80.

ESNÉ (LATOPOLIS.)

DÉTAILS D'ARCHITECTURE, BAS-RELIEFS ET INSCRIPTIONS HIÉROGLYPHIQUES DU PORTIQUE.

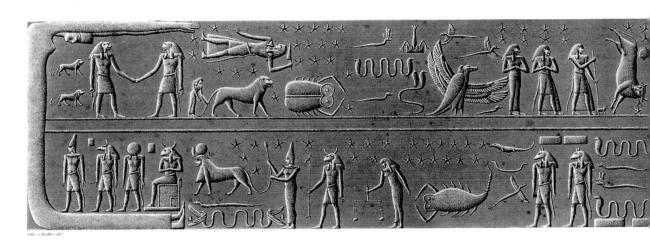

ESNÉ (LATOPOLIS.)

DÉCORATION INTÉRIEURE D'UN MUR D'ENTRECOLONNEMENT DU PORTIQUE.

ESNÉ (LATOPOLIS.)

Pl. 82

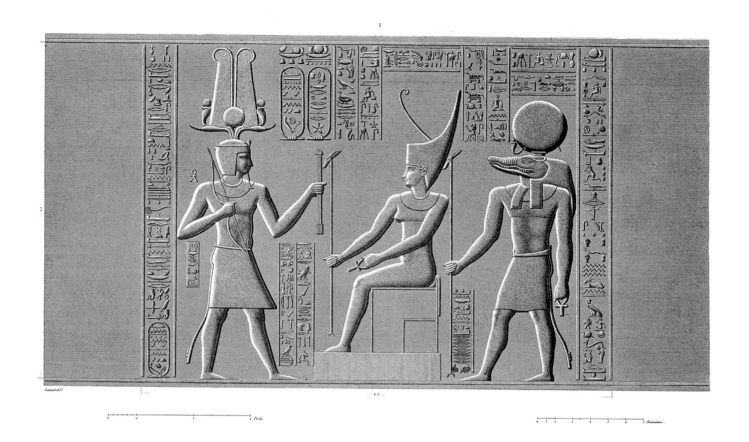

BAS-RELIEFS DU PORTIQUE.

ESNÉ (LATOPOLIS.)

VUE PERSPECTIVE DE L'INTÉRIEUR DU PORTIQUE.

ENVIRONS D'ESNÉ (LATOPOLIS.)

1

2

1 VUE D'UN TEMPLE A CONTRALATO. 2 VUE DU TEMPLE AU NORD D'ESNÉ.

Pl. 85.

A. Vol. I.

ENVIRONS D'ESNÉ (LATOPOLIS.)

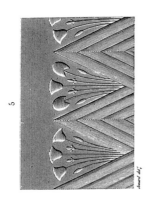

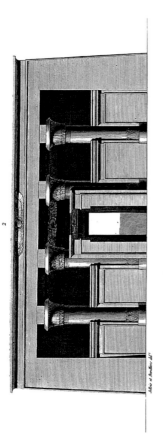

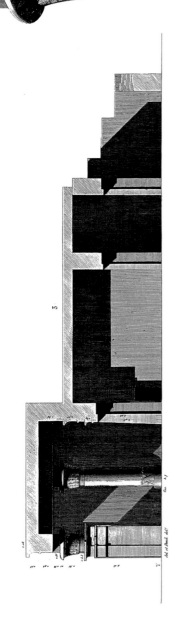

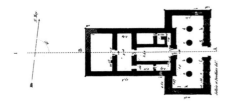

PLAN, COUPE, ÉLÉVATION ET DÉTAILS DU TEMPLE AU NORD D'ESNÉ.

ENVIRONS D'ESNÉ (LATOPOLIS.)

Pl. 86.

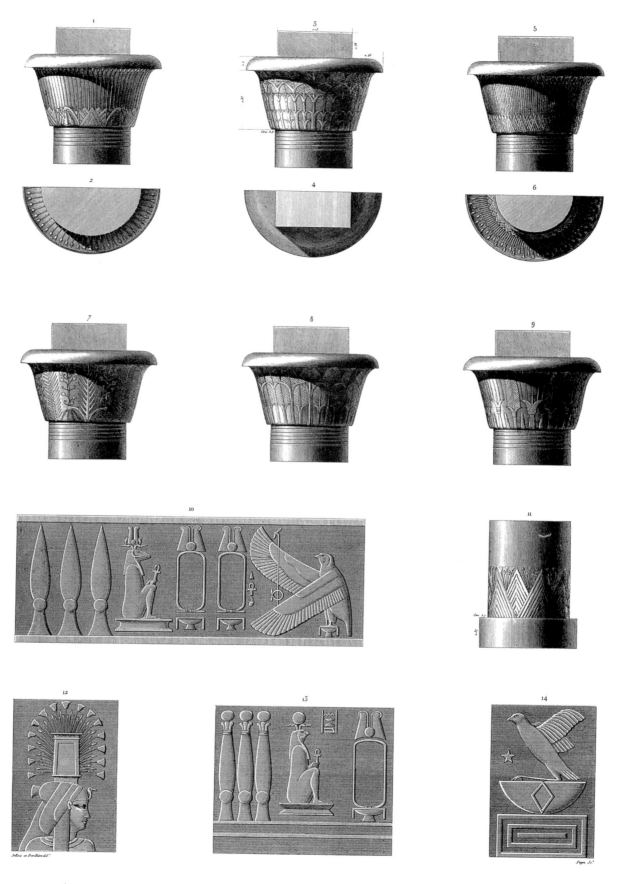

DÉTAILS D'ARCHITECTURE ET BAS-RELIEFS DU TEMPLE AU NORD D'ESNÉ.

Pl 87

ENVIRONS D'ESNÉ (LATOPOLIS.)

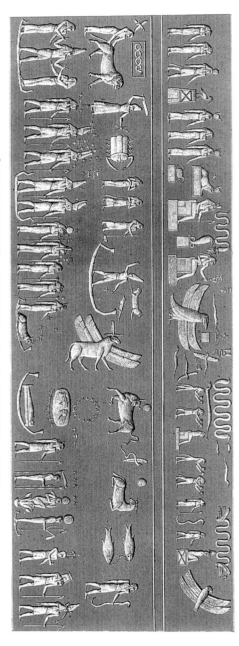

ZODIAQUE SCULPTÉ AU PLAFOND DU TEMPLE AU NORD D'ESNÉ.

ENVIRONS D'ESNÉ (LATOPOLIS.)

Pl. 88.

VUE PERSPECTIVE DU TEMPLE AU NORD D'ESNÉ.

Arthus et Bouillon del.

Bouteux sq. fect.

Lerouge.

Pl. 89.

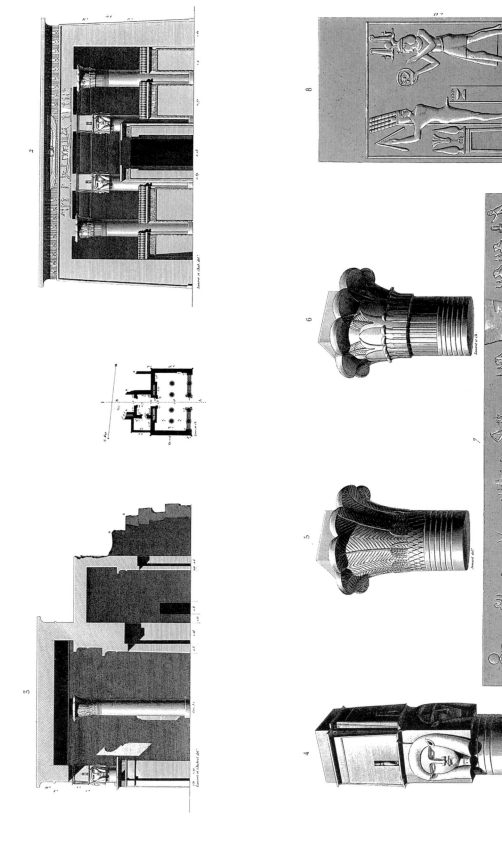

ENVIRONS D'ESNÉ (CONTRALATO.)

PLAN, COUPE, ÉLÉVATION ET DÉTAILS D'UN TEMPLE A CONTRALATO.

Pl. 90.

ENVIRONS D'ESNÉ (CONTRALATO.)

VUE PERSPECTIVE D'UN TEMPLE A CONTRALATO.

Pl. 91.

ERMENT (HERMONTHIS.)

Viuli del.   *Bouclaine aqfiul.*   *Lienard Sc.*

VUE DU TEMPLE PRISE AU SUD-OUEST.

Pl. 92.

ERMENT (HERMONTHIS.)

Dumontier ap. fecit

Loireau et Barbault sc.

Dupuis del.

VUE DU TEMPLE PRISE A L'OUEST.

Pl. 93.

ERMENT (HERMONTHIS.)

VUE DU TEMPLE PRISE AU NORD~OUEST.

Pl. 94.

ERMENT (HERMONTHIS.)

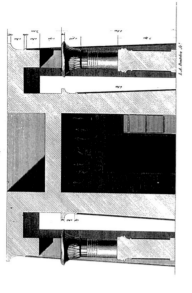

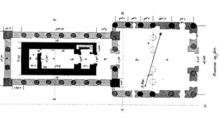

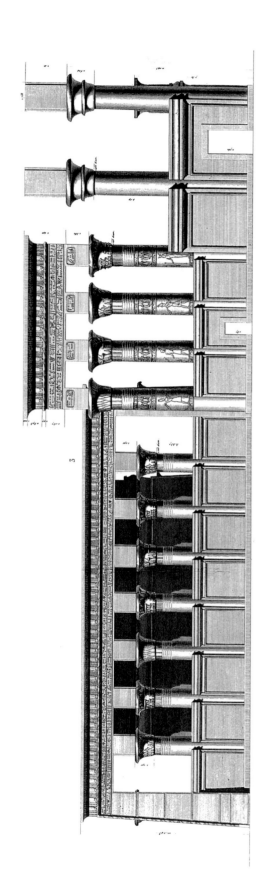

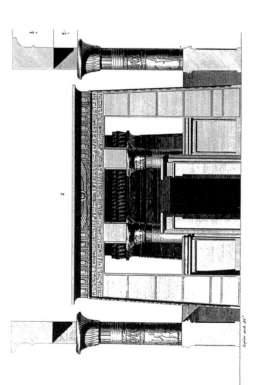

PLAN COUPE ET ÉLÉVATIONS DU TEMPLE.

ERMENT (HERMONTHIS.)

Pl. 95.

1

2

3

4

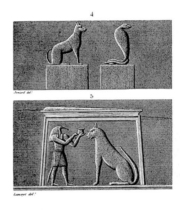

5

6

7

8

BAS-RELIEFS DE L'INTÉRIEUR ET DE L'EXTÉRIEUR DU TEMPLE.

BAS-RELIEFS SCULPTÉS DANS LE SANCTUAIRE DU TEMPLE.

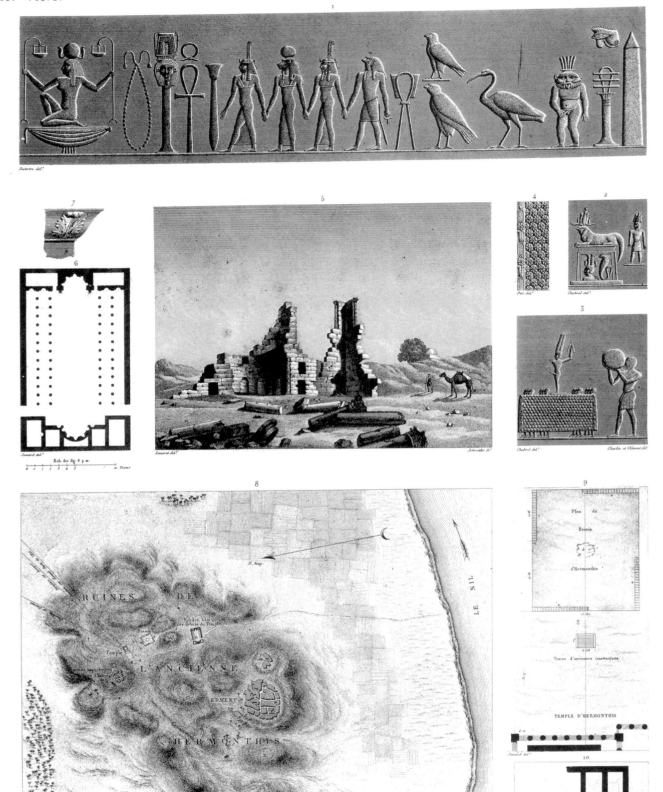

1.2.3.4.BAS-RELIEFS DU TEMPLE D'ERMENT,   5.6.7. VUE, PLAN ET DÉTAIL D'UN ÉDIFICE BÂTI DES DÉBRIS DU TEMPLE,
8.9.PLAN GÉNÉRAL DES RUINES ET D'UN BASSIN ANTIQUE,   10.PLAN DES RESTES D'UN ÉDIFICE A TÔD.

Pl. 2.

THÈBES. MEDYNET-ABOU

Extremité des ruines de la Memnonium de Strabon

Extremité de la chaine Libyque

couverte de sables

Torrent

Extremité de la chaine Libyque

couverte de villa

PLAN TOPOGRAPHIQUE DES RUINES ET DES ENVIRONS.

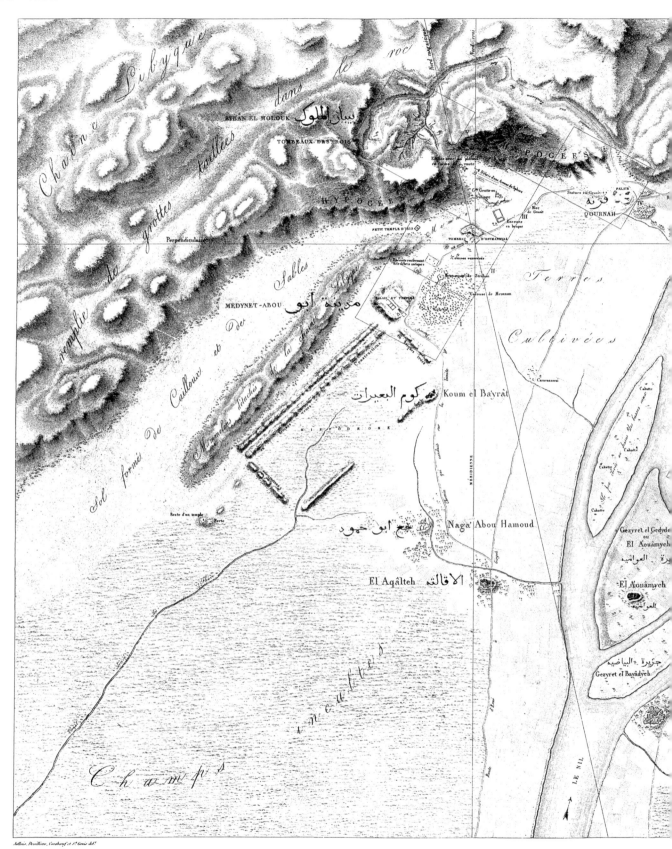

Pl.1.

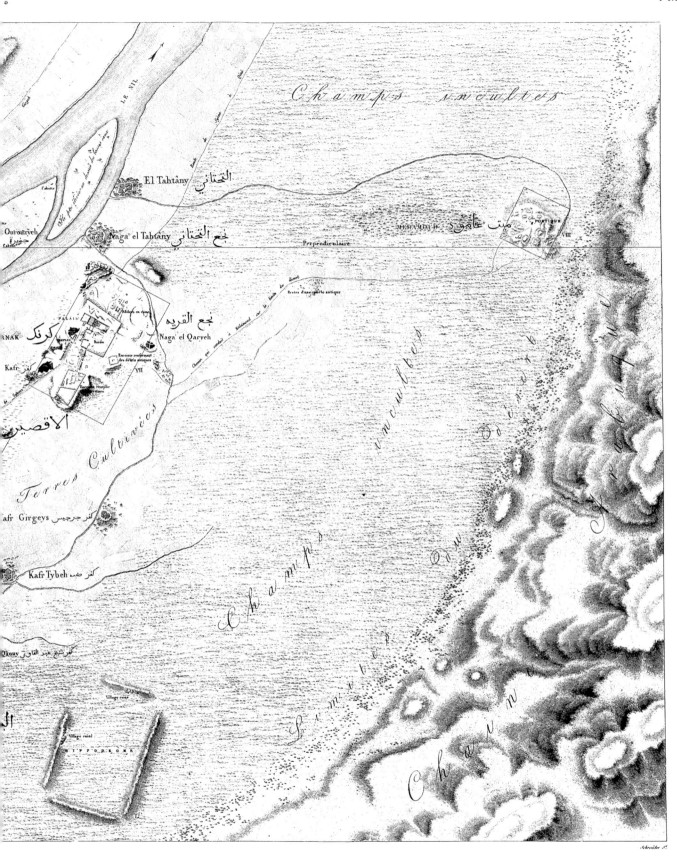

LE NIL

Champs incultes

El Tahtâny التحتاني

Ourouzyeh

Naga' el Tahtâny نجع التحتاني

MEHAMOUD منت عامود PORTIQUE

VIII

Perpendiculaire

Restes d'une porte antique

PALAIS كرنك

ANAK

Naga' el Qaryeh نجع القريه

Kafr كفر

VII

Enceinte renfermant des débris antiques

الأقصر

Terres Cultivées

incultes

Désert

Arabique

afr Girgeys كفر جرجس

Kafr Tybeh كفر طبه

Champs

Daouy

Village ruiné

Limite?

Chaine

HIPPODROME

Village ruiné

Schroeder Sc.

Mille Mètres

VUE DES PROPYLÉES DU TEMPLE

Limard Sc.

ON, PRISE DU CÔTÉ DU SUD.

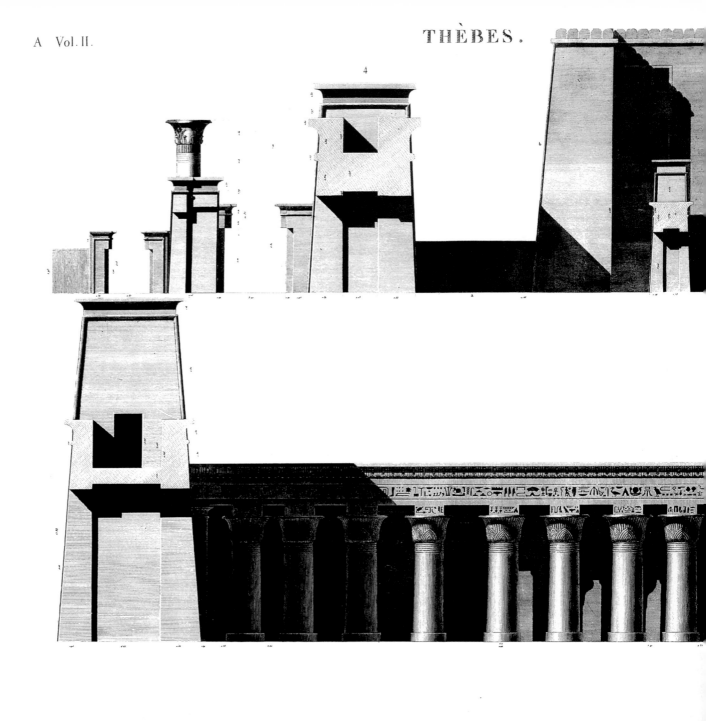

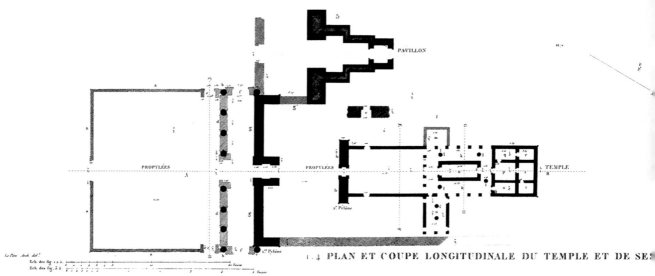

PAVILLON

PROPYLÉES

PROPYLÉES

TEMPLE

Le Père Arch. del.

1.4 PLAN ET COUPE LONGITUDINALE DU TEMPLE ET DE SE

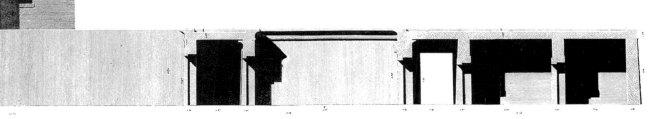

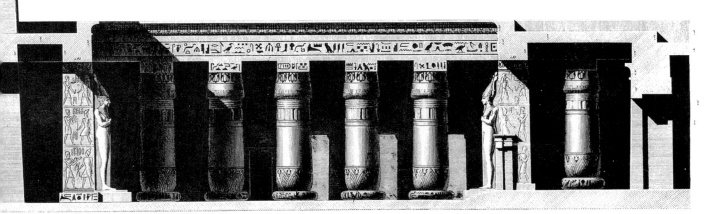

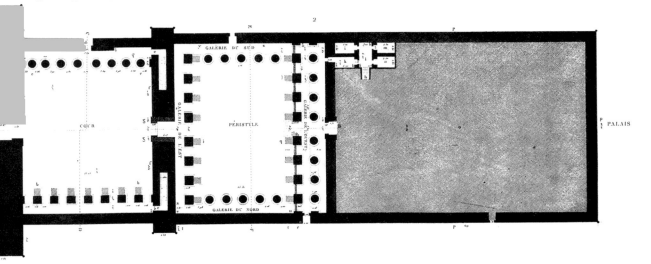

2.3 PLAN ET COUPE LONGITUDINALE DU PALAIS. 5 PLAN DU PAVILLON.

Pl. 5.

THÈBES. MEDYNET-ABOU.

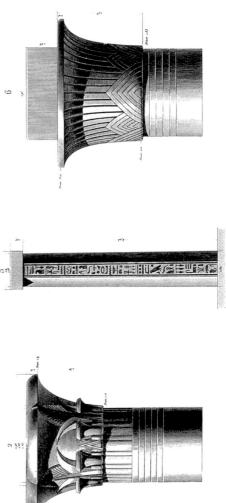

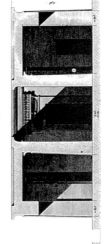

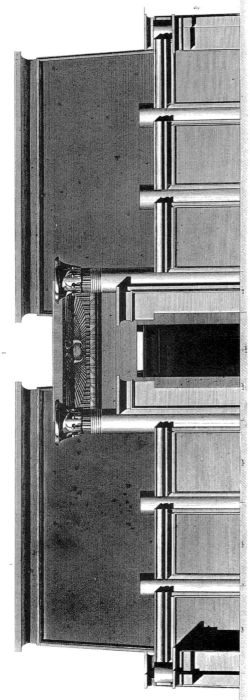

1.2.3.4.5. ÉLÉVATION ET CHAPITEAU DES PROPYLÉES, COUPES TRANSVERSALES ET DÉTAIL D'UNE COLONNE DU TEMPLE.

6. DÉTAIL DU CHAPITEAU DES COLONNES DE LA COUR DU PALAIS.

THÈBES. MEDYNET-ABOU.

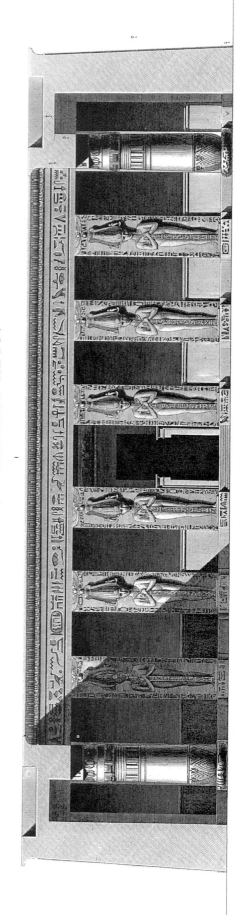

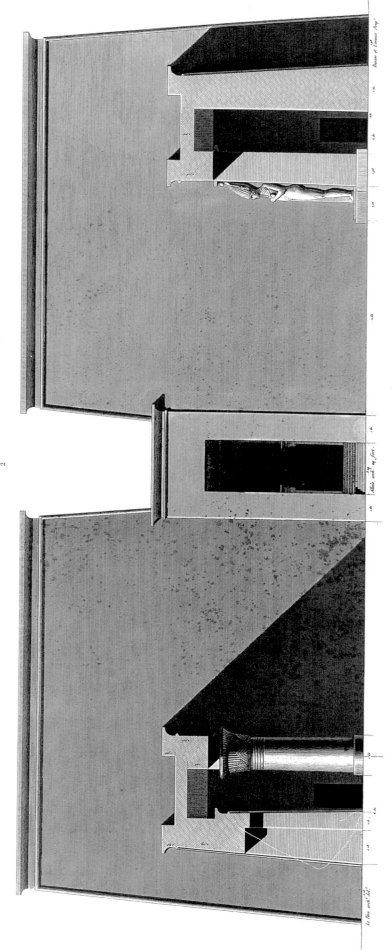

COUPES TRANSVERSALES DE LA COUR ET DU PÉRISTYLE DU PALAIS.

THÈBES. MEDINET-ABOU.

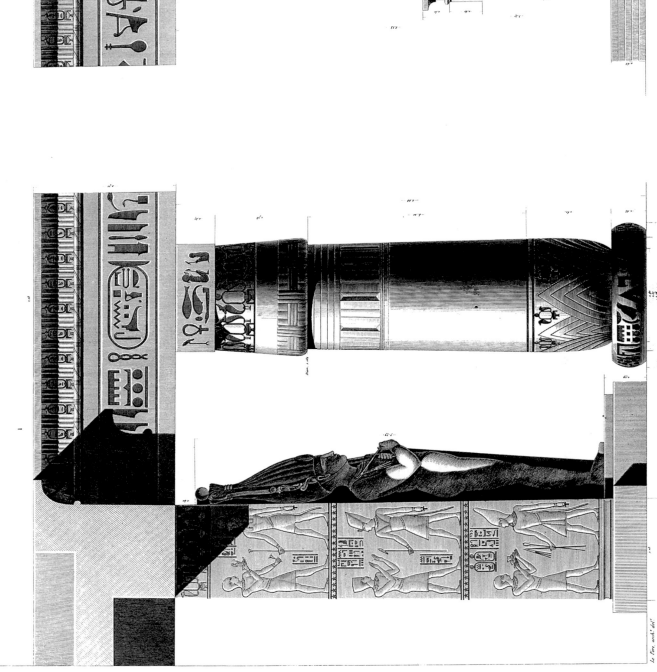

DÉTAILS D'UN PILIER CARYATIDE ET D'UNE COLONNE DU PÉRISTYLE DU PALAIS.

THÈBES. MEDYNET-ABOU.

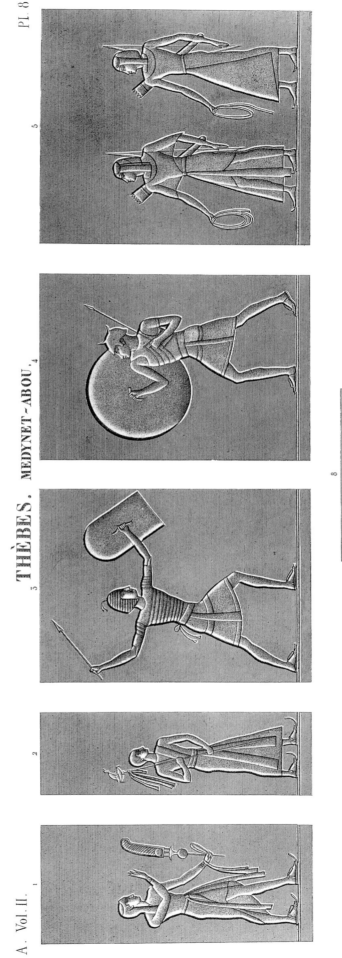

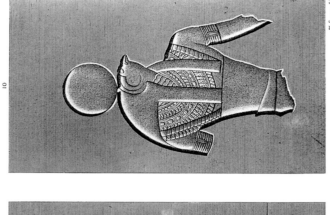

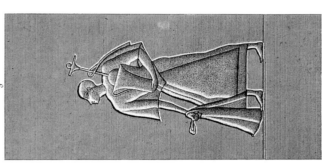

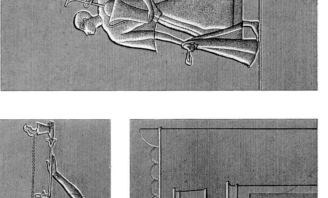

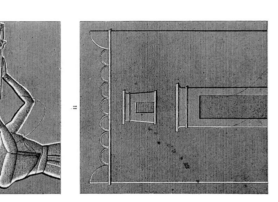

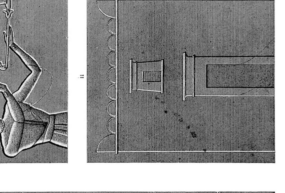

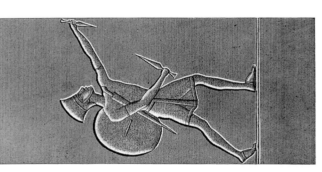

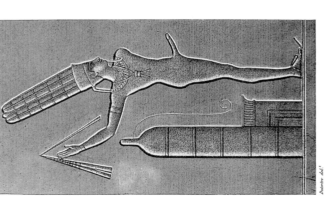

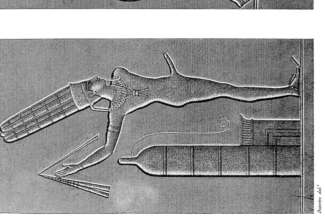

BAS-RELIEFS SCULPTÉS SUR LES MURS DU PALAIS.

Philippeaux del.

Dutertre del.

COMBAT NAVAL SCULPTÉ SUR LA

Pl. 10.

URE DU PALAIS EXPOSÉE AU NORD.

Philippeaux Sculp.

Lancret del.

A

Jollois et Devilliers del.

B

Jollois et Devilliers del.

MARCHE TRIOMPHALE SCULPTÉE DA

Panel Sc.t

Chabrol del.

Philippeaux Sc.

Delertre del.

Philippeaux Sc.

Jomard del.

Leisnier Sc.

Jomard del.

Leisnier Sc.

1 BAS - RELIEF SCULPTÉ SUR LA FACE EXTÉRIEURE DU PALAIS EXPOSÉE AU NORD . 2 BAS - RELIEF DE LA GALERIE - SUD
DU PÉRISTYLE DU PALAIS . 3.4 FRAGMENS TROUVÉS SOUS LE PREMIER PYLÔNE DES PROPYLÉES DU TEMPLE .

THÈBES. MEDYNET-ABOU.

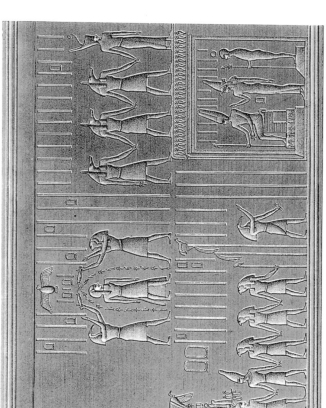

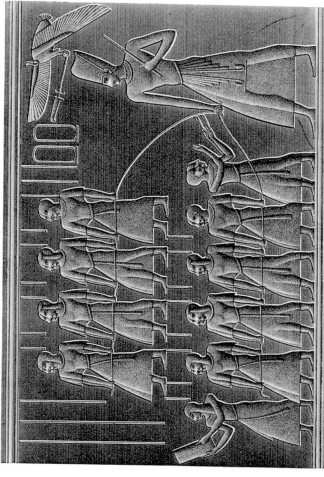

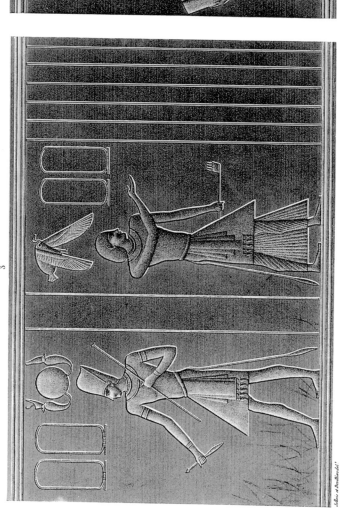

BAS-RELIEFS SCULPTÉS DANS LES GALERIES EST ET SUD DU PÉRISTYLE DU PALAIS.

Palm. del.

VUE DU PAVILL

Pl. 14.

THÈBES. MEDYNET-ABOU.

VUE INTERIEURE DU PERISTYLE DU PALAIS.

THÈBES. MEDYNET-ABOU.

2

3

4

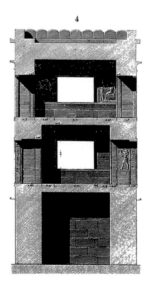

5

6

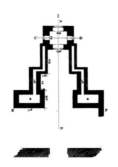

PLAN, ÉLÉVATION, COUPES ET DÉTAILS DE BAS-RELIEFS DU PAVILLON.

THÈBES. MEDYNET-ABOU.

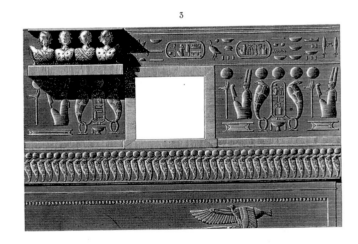

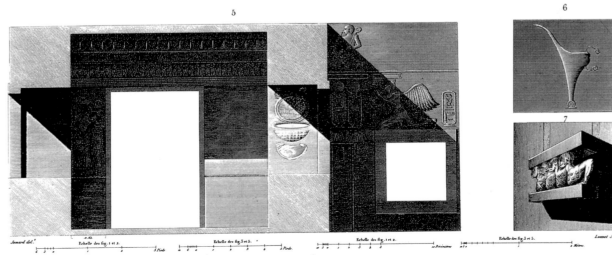

1 COUPE DU SECOND ÉTAGE DU PAVILLON. 2.3.4.5.6.7 DÉTAILS DE COUPES ET DE SCULPTURES DU PAVILLON.

THÈBES. MEDYNET-ABOU.

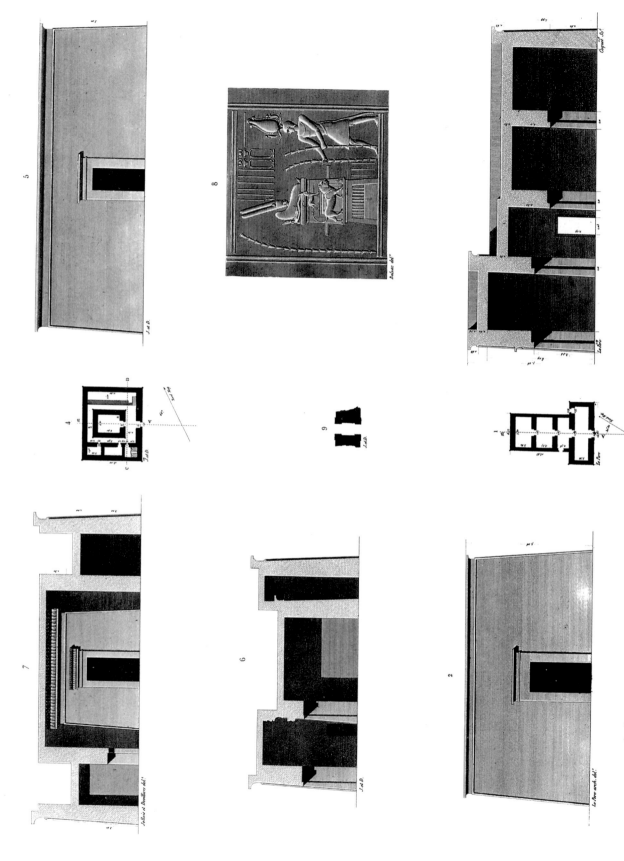

1.2.3 PLAN, ÉLÉVATION ET COUPE D'UN TEMPLE SITUÉ À L'ANGLE SUD-EST DE L'ENCEINTE. 4.5.6.7.8 PLAN, ÉLÉVATION, COUPES

ET BAS-RELIEF D'UN TEMPLE AU SUD DE L'HIPPODRÔME. 9 PORTE SITUÉE EN AVANT DU TEMPLE.

THÈBES. MEMNONIUM.

Pl.19.

PLAN TOPOGRAPHIQUE DU TOMBEAU D'OSMANDYAS, DES DEUX COLOSSES DE LA PLAINE ET DES RUINES ENVIRONNANTES.

Pl. 20.

THÈBES. MEMNONIUM.

Delarue del.

Baltard sc.

VUE DES DEUX COLOSSES.

VUE GÉNÉRALE DU TOMBEAU D'OSYMANDYAS ET D'U

Pl. 25.

LA PLAINE DE THÈBES, PRISE DU NORD-OUEST.

VUE GÉNÉRALE DU TOMBE

YAS, PRISE DU SUD-OUEST.

VUE DU PÉRISTYLE DU TOMBEAU ET DE

A STATUE COLOSSALE D'OSYMANDYAS, PRISE DE L'OUEST.

VUE DU TOMBEAU D'OSYMANDYAS ET D'UNE

Pl. 21.

A. Vol. II.

THEBES. MEMNONIUM.

DÉTAILS DU COLOSSE DU SUD.

Thomas et Aubert del.￼

Jollois et Devilliers del.￼

Pl. 22.

THÈBES. MEMNONIUM.

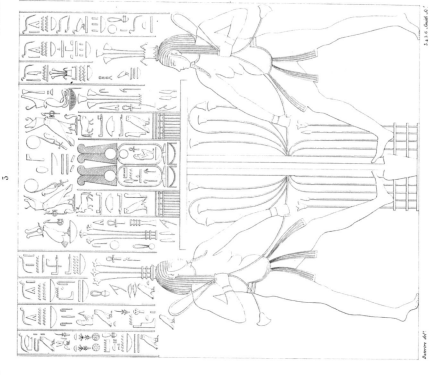

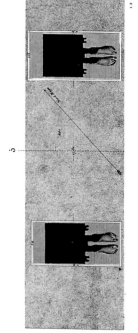

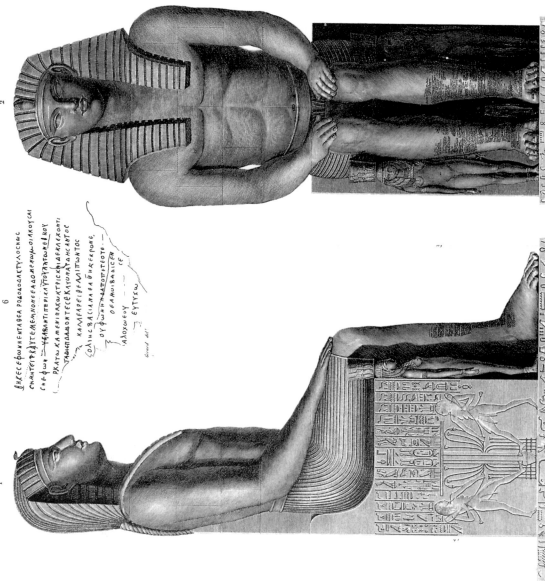

DÉTAILS DE LA STATUE COLOSSALLE DE MEMNON.

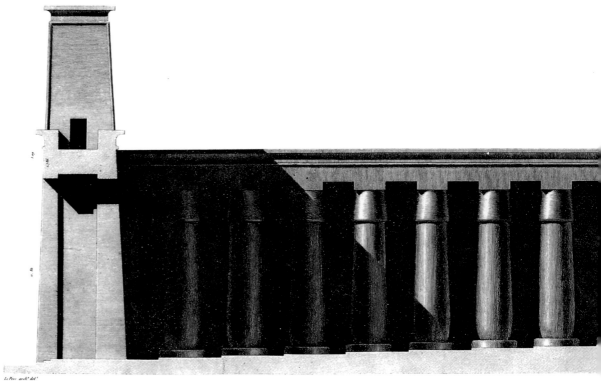

Le Père arch.ᵗ del.ᵗ

BEAU D'OSYMANDYAS.

Ballard Sc.

THÈBES. MEMNONIUM.

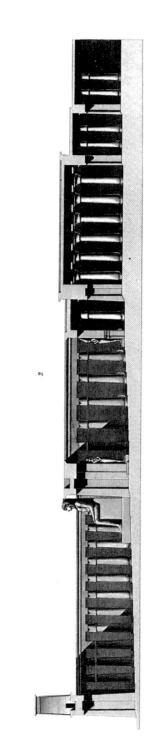

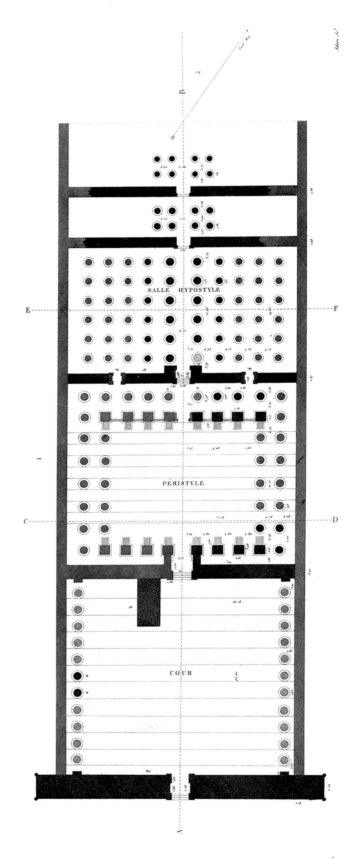

SALLE HYPOSTYLE

PÉRISTYLE

COUR

PLAN ET COUPE DU TOMBEAU D'OSYMANDYAS.

Pl. 29.

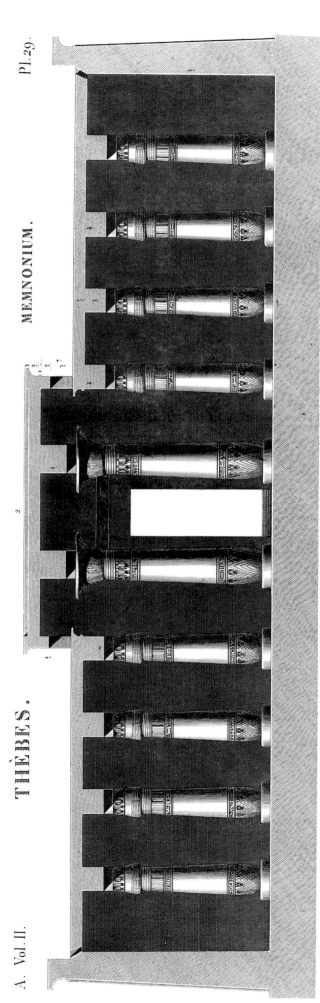

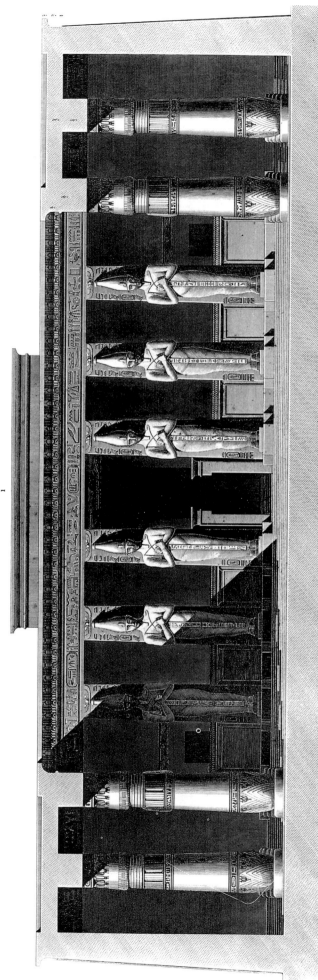

1, 2. COUPES TRANSVERSALES DU PÉRISTYLE ET DE LA SALLE HYPOSTYLE DU TOMBEAU D'OSYMANDYAS.

DÉTAILS DES CHAPITEAUX DE LA SALLE HYPOSTYLE, D'UN PILIER-CARYATIDE

ET DE L'ENTABLEMENT DU PÉRISTYLE DU TOMBEAU D'OSYMANDYAS.

BAS-RELIEFS SCULPTÉS DANS LA SALLE HYPOSTYLE ET SUR LE PREMIER PYLÔNE DU TOMBEAU D'OSYMANDYAS.

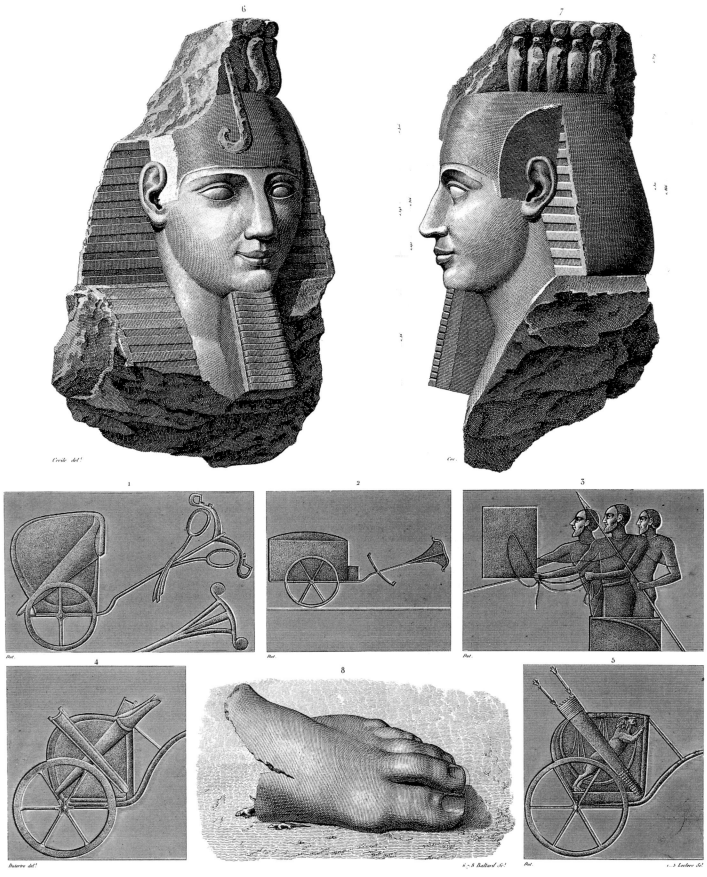

6

7

Cécile del.

Céc.

1

2

3

4

8

5

Dutertre del.

Dut.

Dut.

Dut.

6. - 8 *Baltard Sc.*

Dut.

1. - 5 *Leclerc Sc.*

1. 2. 3. 4. 5. 6. 7. DÉTAILS DE CHARS SCULPTÉS SUR LE 1.ᵉʳ PYLONE ET TÊTE DE L'UNE DES STATUES DU TOMBEAU D'OSYMANDYAS.
8 DÉBRIS DU PIED GAUCHE DE LA STATUE COLOSSALE D'OSYMANDYAS.

THÈBES. MEMNONIUM.

Κοινὸν ὑαρχεις

Κοινὸν ὑαρχεις

3.

5.

2.

Échelle de l'ombre du Némastère de Karac.

1.

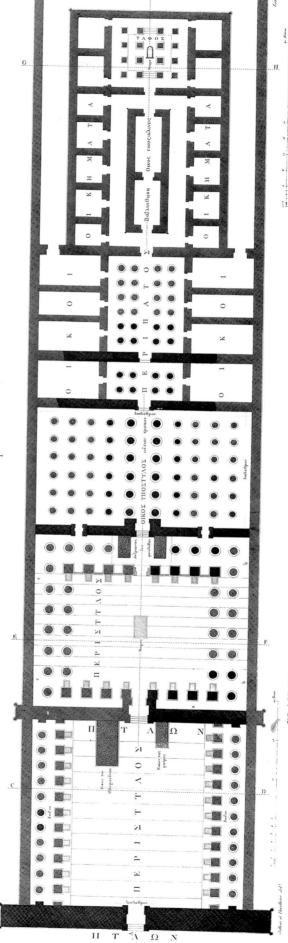

Échelle de l'ombre du Némastère d'Eléphantine.

PLAN ET COUPES DU TOMBEAU D'OSYMANDYAS RESTAURÉ D'APRÈS DIODORE DE SICILE.

Pl. 34.

THÈBES. MEMNONIUM.

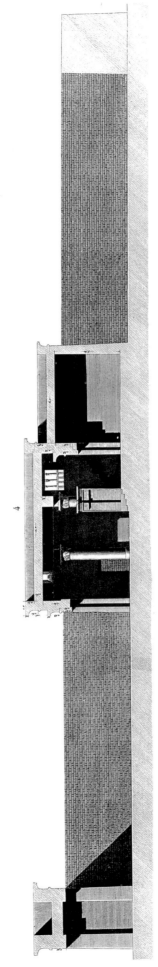

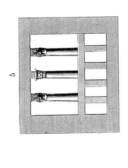

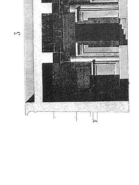

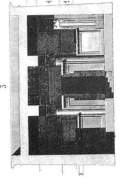

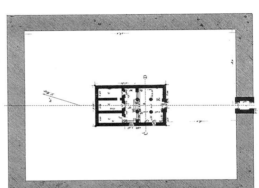

PLAN, ÉLÉVATION, COUPES ET DÉTAILS DE CHAPITEAUX ET DE PILASTRE DU TEMPLE DE L'OUEST.

Pl. 33.

THEBES. MEMNONIUM.

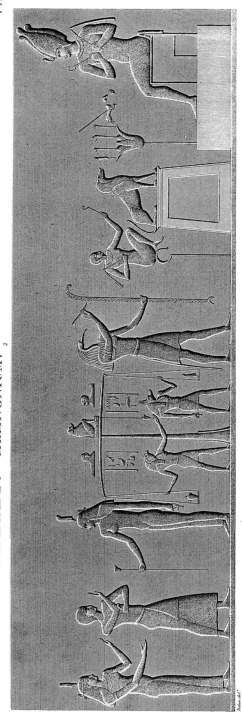

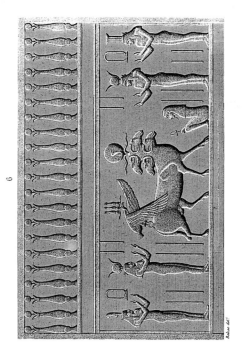

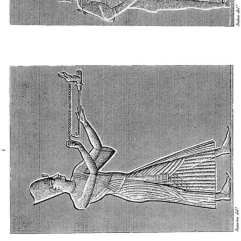

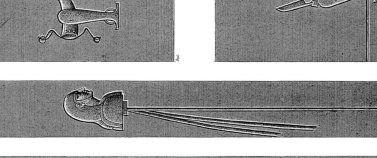

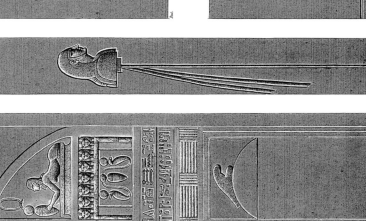

BAS-RELIEFS DU TEMPLE DE L'OUEST ET D'UNE GROTTE VOISINE.

1

2

4

5

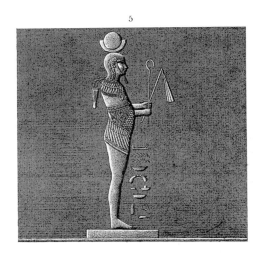

6

7

PILASTRE ET BAS-RELIEFS DU TEMPLE DE L'OUEST.

Pl. 38.

THÈBES. MEMNONIUM.

Le couvert de Sables

Les couvert de Sables

Sol couvert de Sables

Sol couvert de Sables

Débris d'une avenue de Sphinx

PLAN TOPOGRAPHIQUE DE DIVERS MONUMENS SITUÉS AU NORD DU TOMBEAU D'OSYMANDYAS.

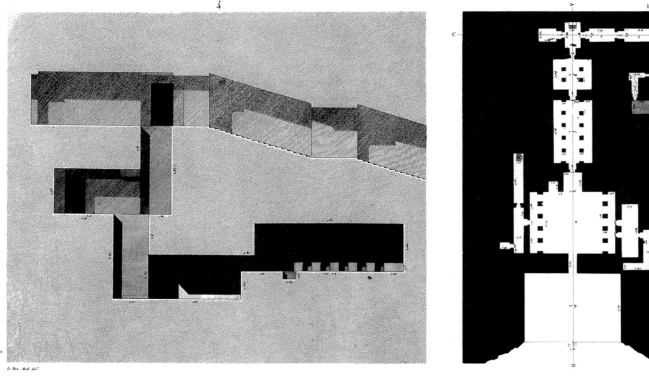

1.2.3.4 PLAN ET COUPES D'UN GRAND HYPOGÉE OU SYRINGE. 5 DÉTAIL DE SCULPTURE D

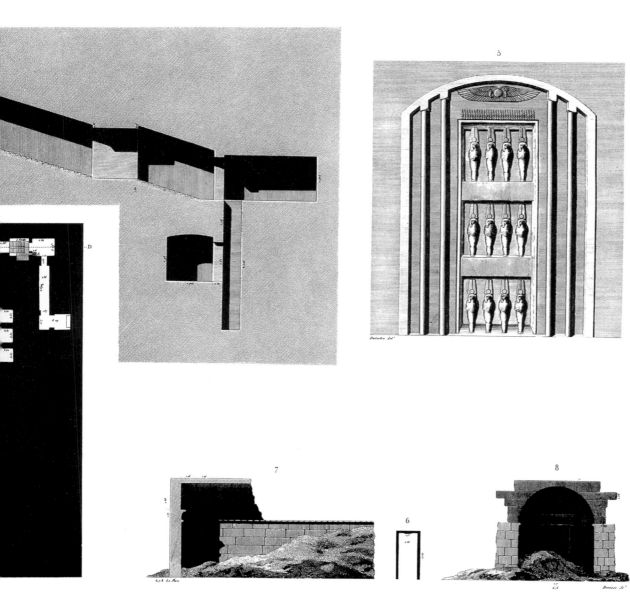

GÉE. 6.7.8 PLAN ET COUPES D'UN ÉDIFICE AYANT UN PLAFOND EN FORME DE VOUTE.

THÈBES. QOURNAH.

Pl. 40.

PLAN TOPOGRAPHIQUE DES RUINES ET DES ENVIRONS.

THÈBES. QOURNAH.

Pl. 41.

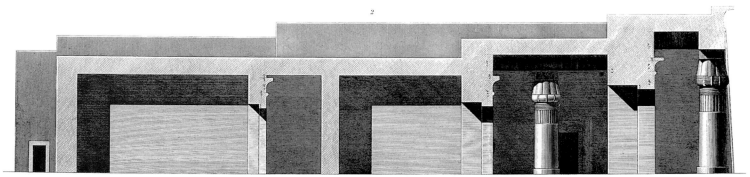

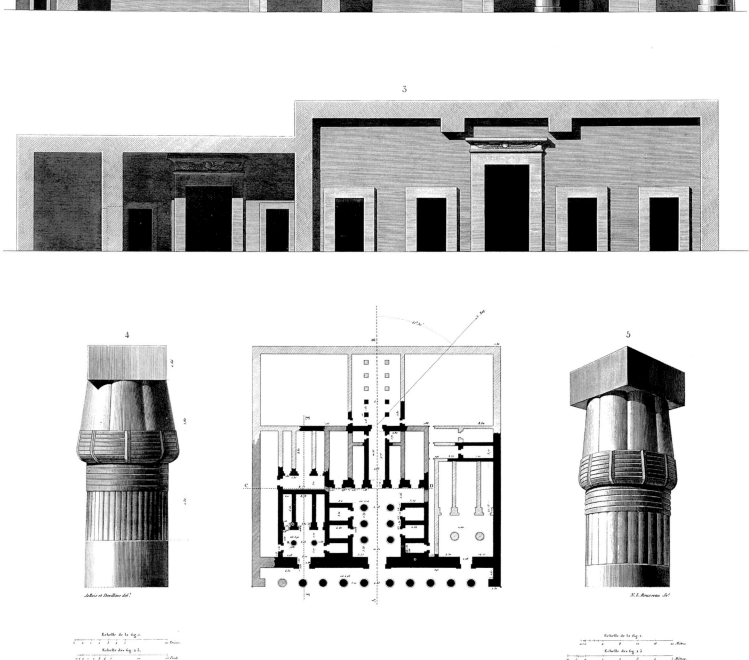

Jollois et Devilliers del.

N.L. Rousseau Sc.

PLAN, COUPES ET DÉTAILS DE CHAPITEAUX DU PALAIS.

Pl. 42.

THÈBES. QOURNAH.

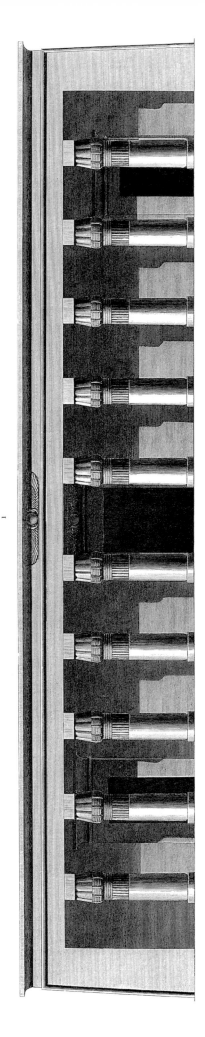

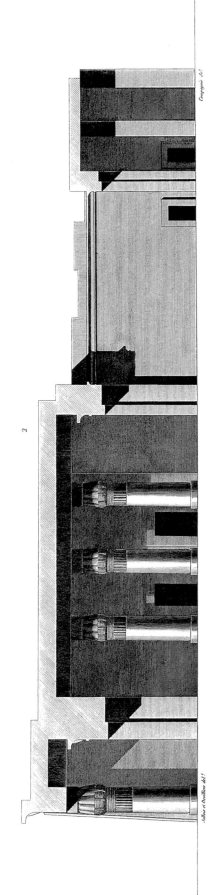

ÉLÉVATION ET COUPE LONGITUDINALE DU PALAIS.

Pl. 43.

THÈBES . QOURNAH .

VUE PERSPECTIVE DU PALAIS .

Arsher et Brullion del.t

Schroeder Sc.t

PEINTURES ET BAS RELIEFS COLORIÉS .

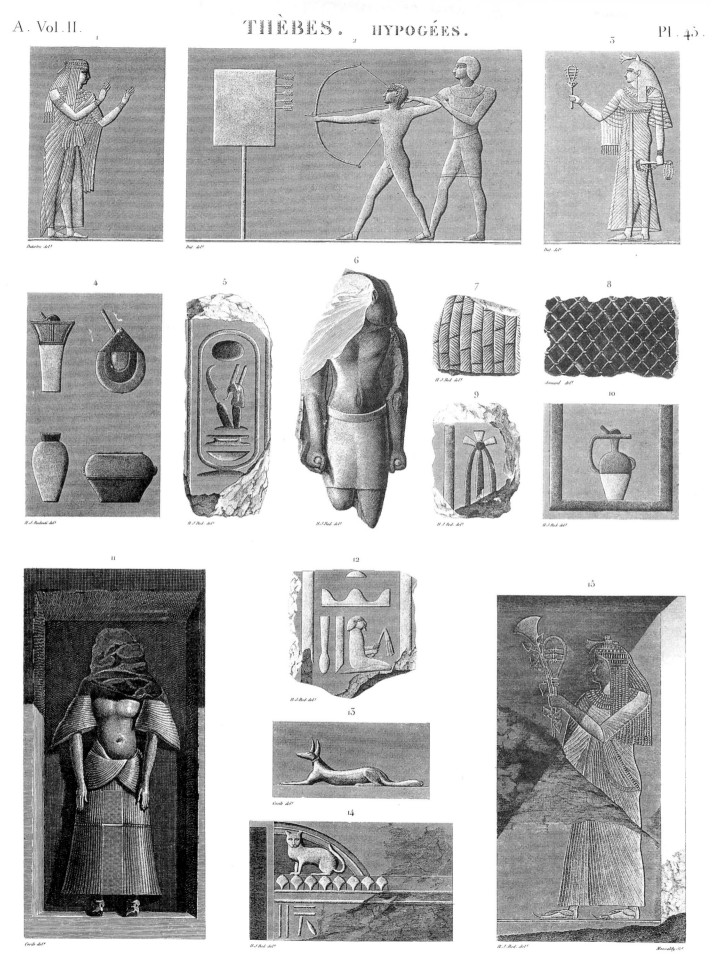

SCULPTURES, FRAGMENS ET DÉTAILS COLORIÉS.

THÈBES. HYPOGÉES.

Pl. 46

Dutertre del.

Phelippeaux Sc.t

DIVERS BAS-RELIEFS ET FRAGMENS.

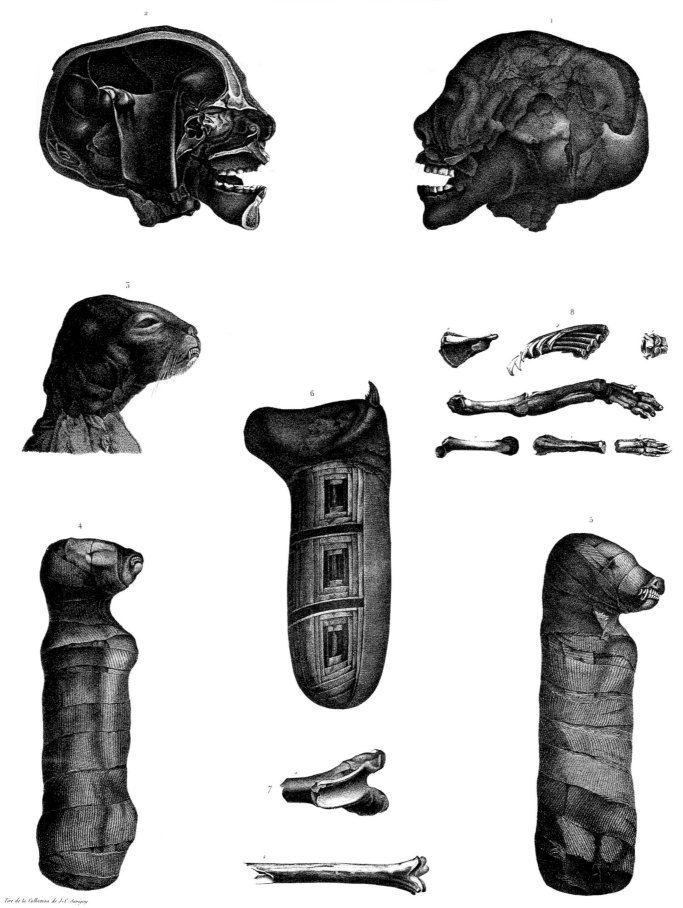

1.2 MOMIE DE FEMME 3...8 MOMIES DE CHAT ET AUTRES MAMMIFÈRES.

Pl.51.

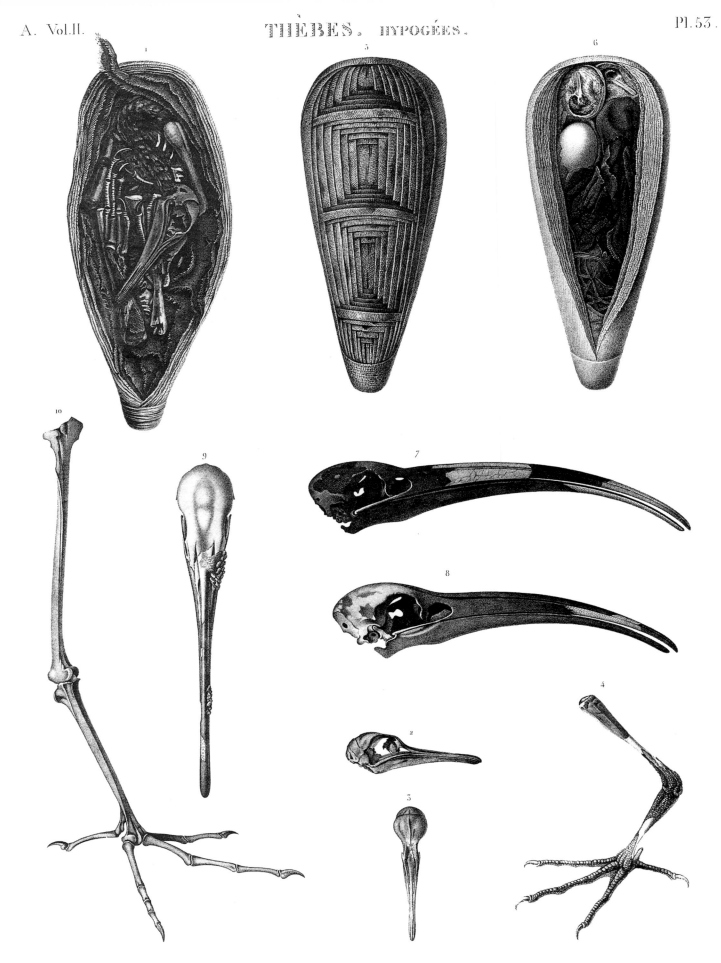

Pl. 54.

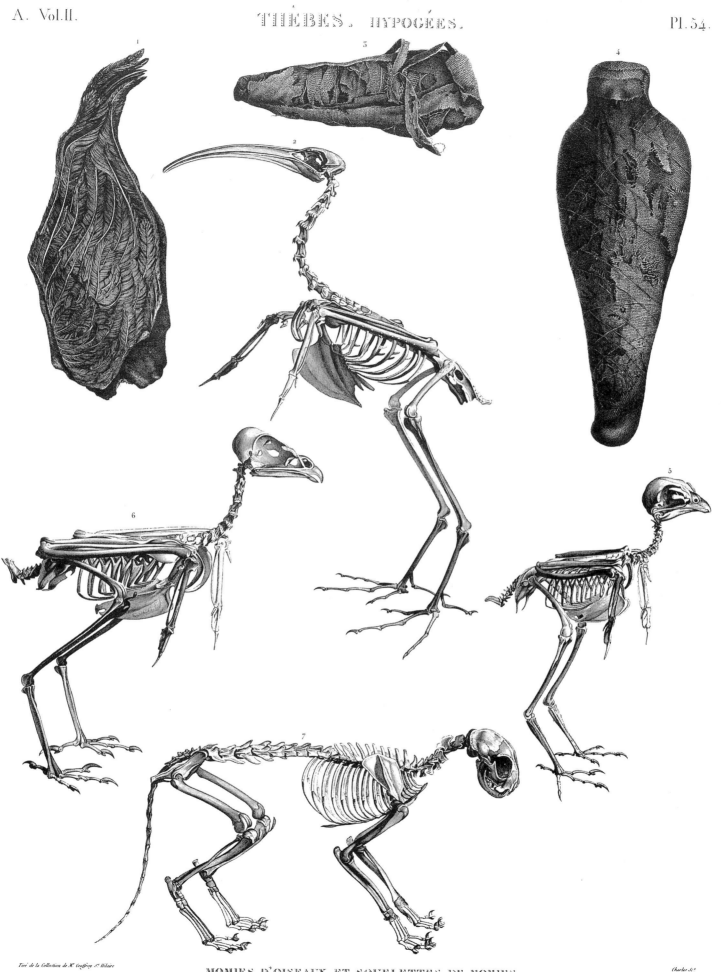

Tiré de la Collection de M.ʳ Geoffroy S.ᵗ Hilaire

Charles Sc.ᵗ

MOMIES D'OISEAUX ET SQUELETTES DE MOMIES.

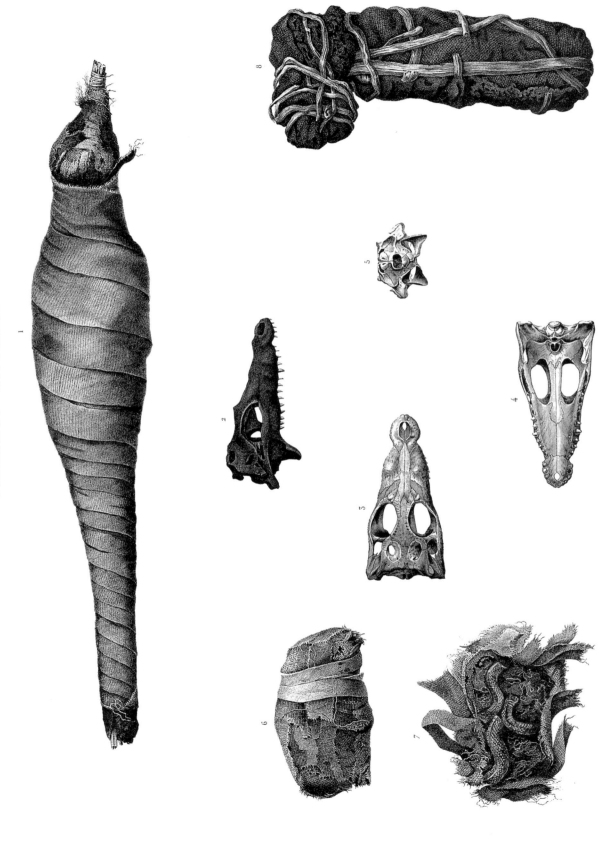

A. Vol.II.

THÈBES. HYPOGÉES.

MOMIES ET DÉTAILS DE CROCODILE, DE SERPENT ET DE CHIEN.

Lambert del.

Tiré de la Collection de M.r Geoffroy St Hilaire.

Deterbre del.'　　　　　Smith ag forti.'　　　　　Trecca Sc.'

PEINTURES D'ENVELOPPES DE MOMIES, ET DIVERS FRAGMENS EN BOIS PEINT, EN PIERRE ET EN BRONZE.

1.2 TENONS EN BOIS. 5.....9 FRAGMENS D'ENVELOPPE DE MOMIE ET AUTRES ANTIQUES.

Pl. 60.

THÈBES. HYPOGÉES.

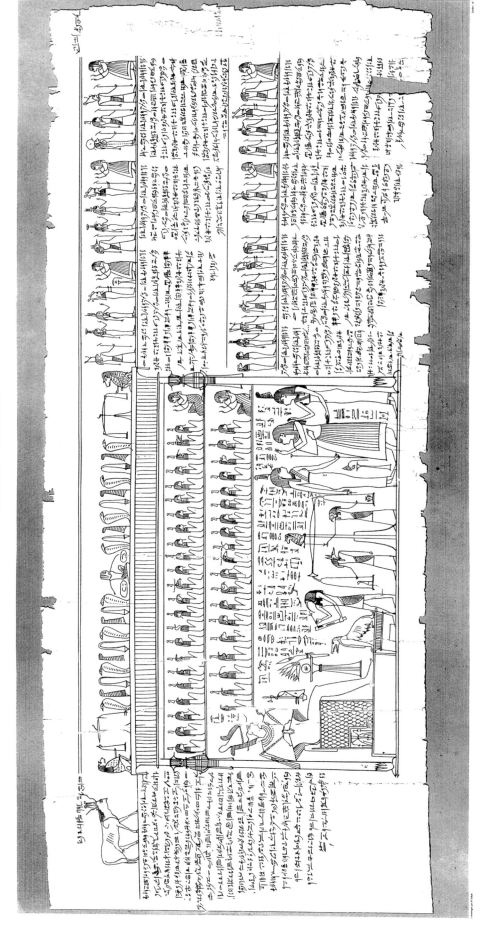

MANUSCRIT SUR PAPYRUS.

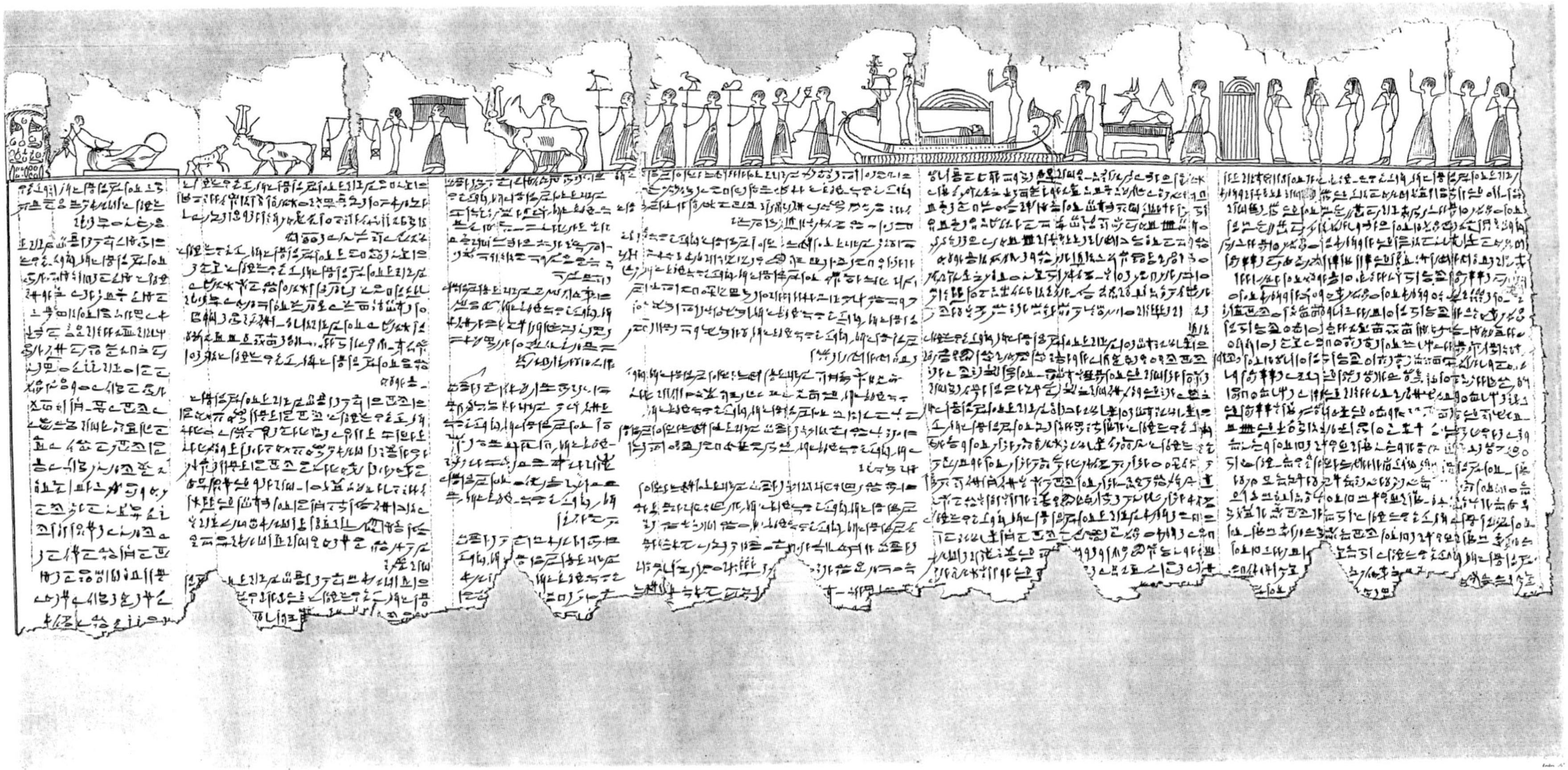

MANUSCRIT SUR PAPYRUS. 1re PARTIE.

Pl. 62.

THÈBES. HYPOGÉES.

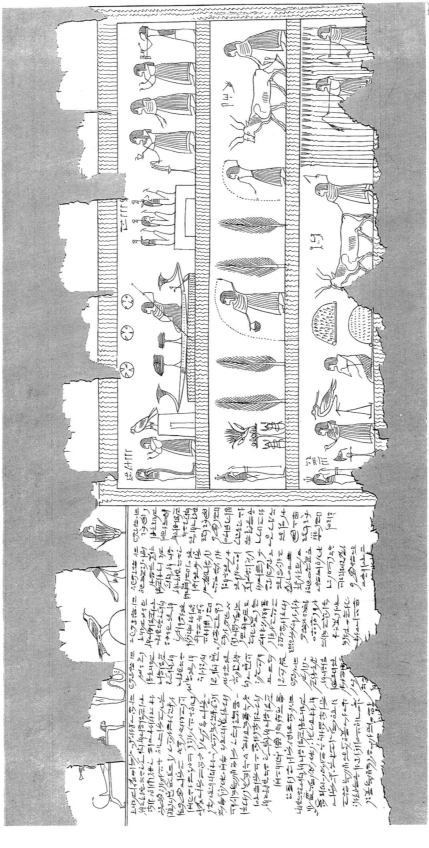

THÈBES. HYPOGÉES.

Pl. 65.

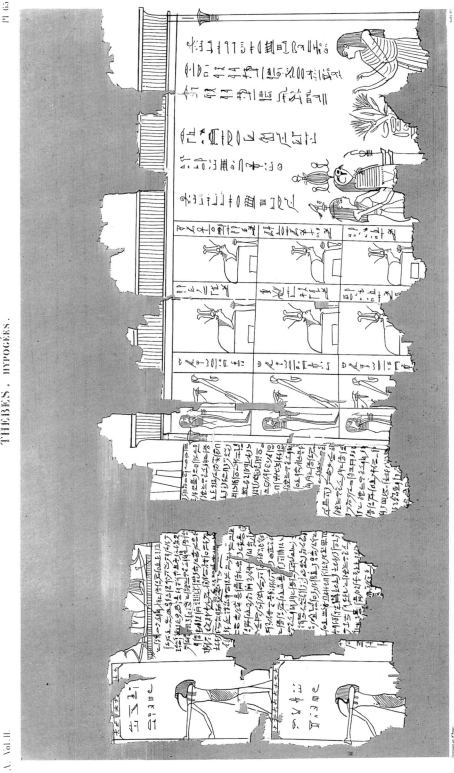

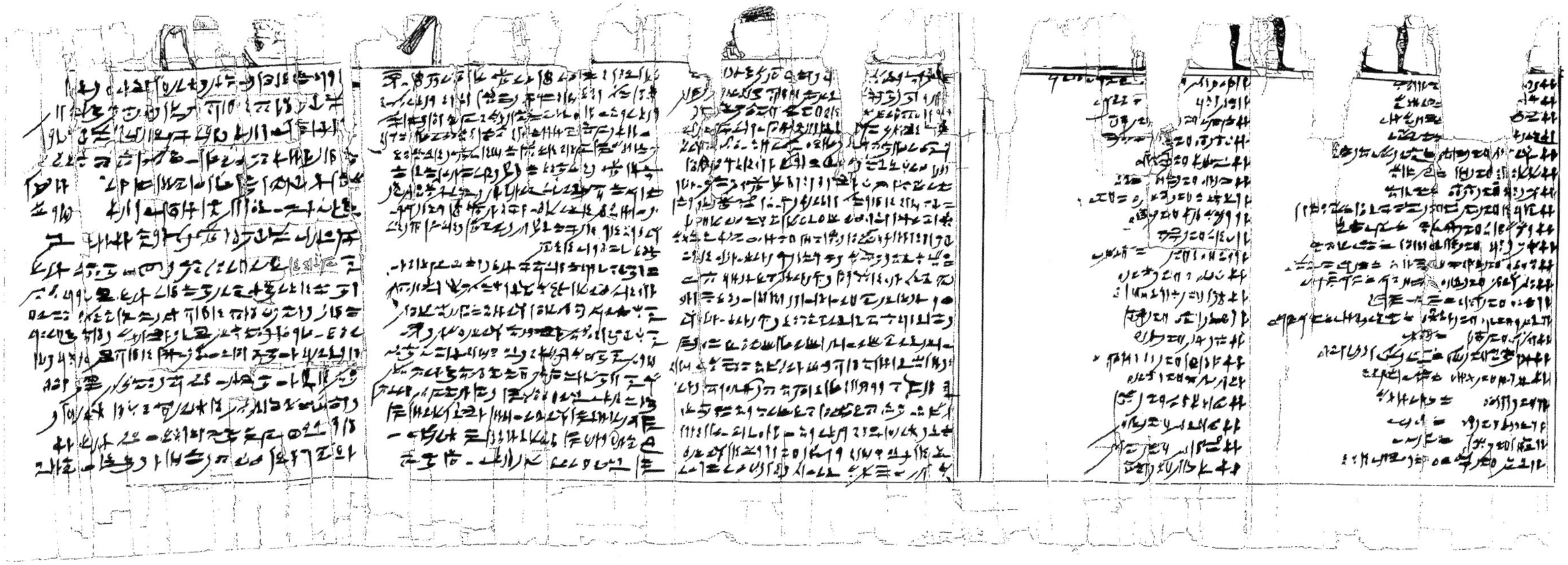

MANUSCRIT SUR PAPYRUS.

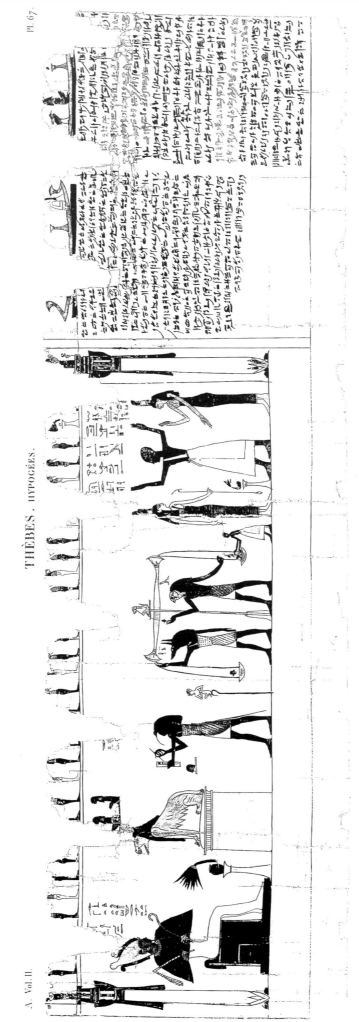

THÈBES. HYPOGÉES.

MANUSCRIT SUR PAPYRUS.

THÈBES. HYPOGÉES.

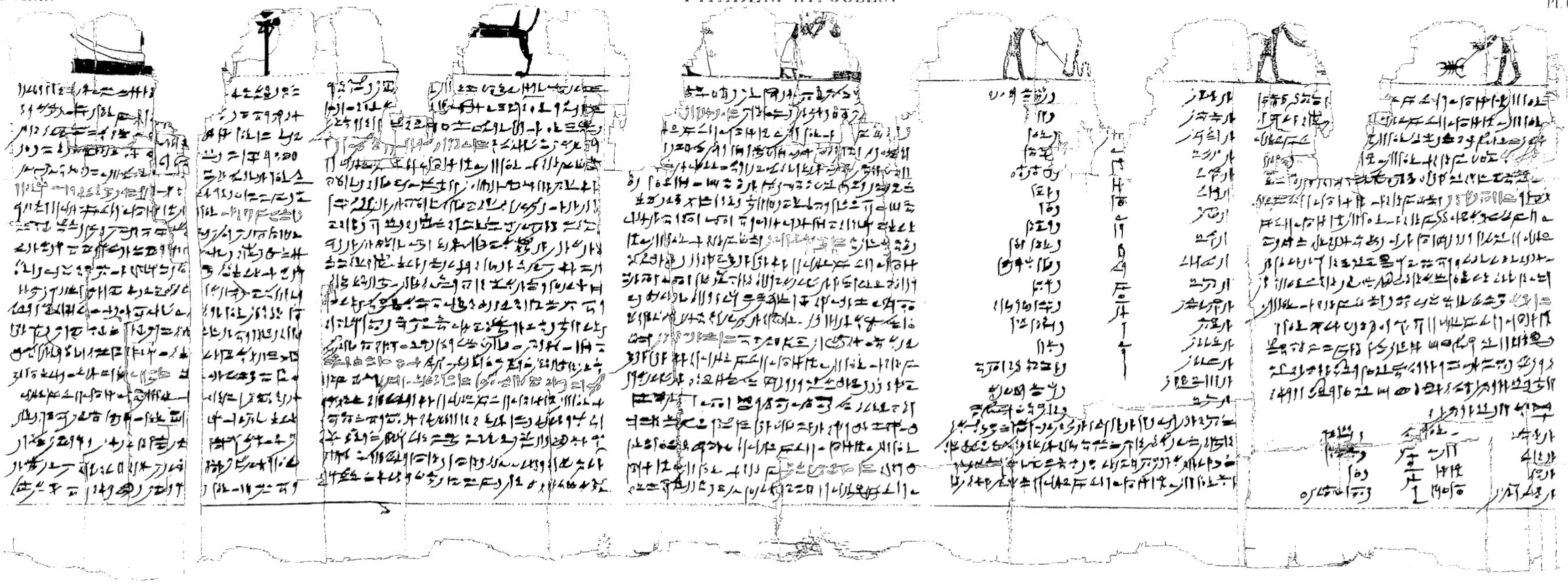

MANUSCRIT SUR PAPYRUS.

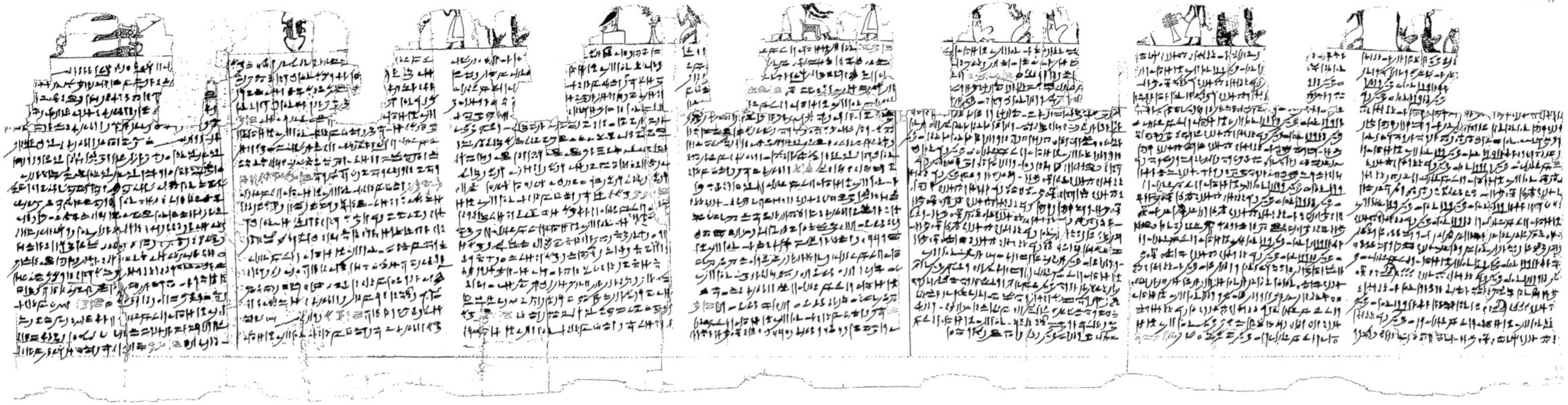

MANUSCRIT SUR PAPYRUS.

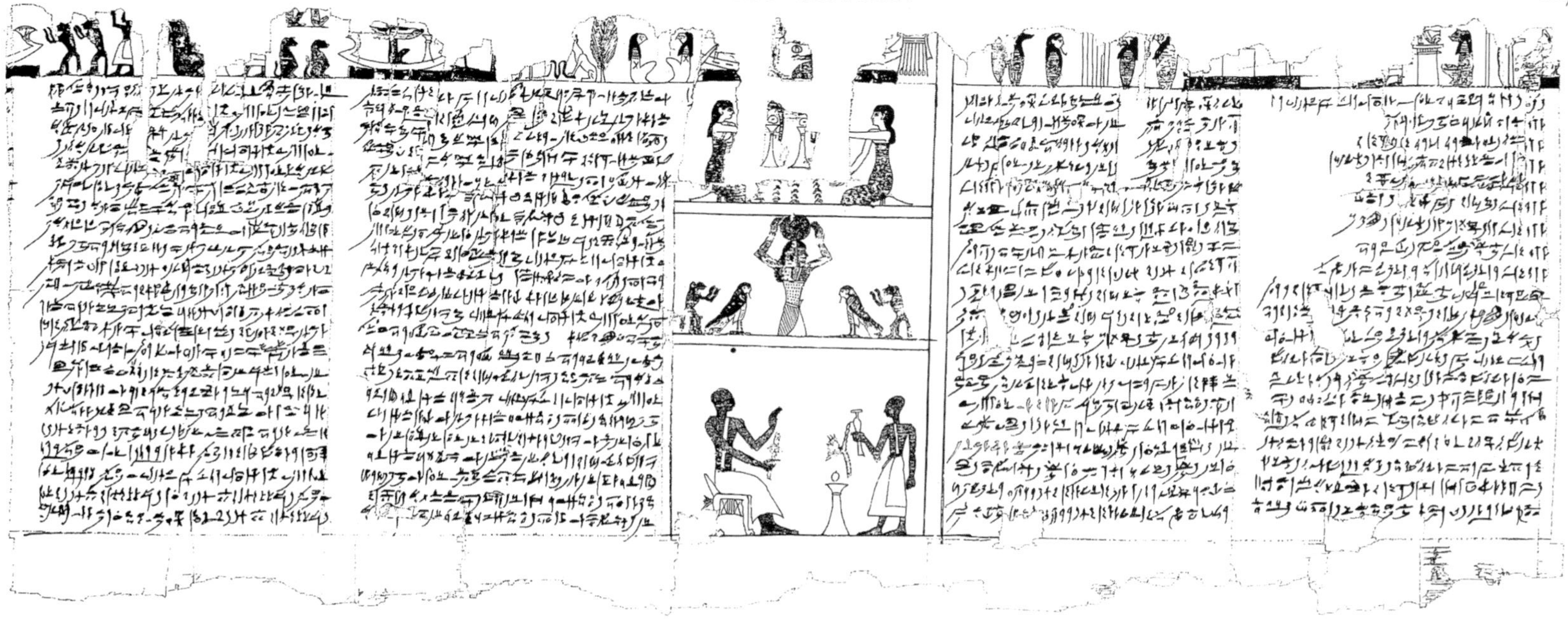

MANUSCRIT SUR PAPYRUS.

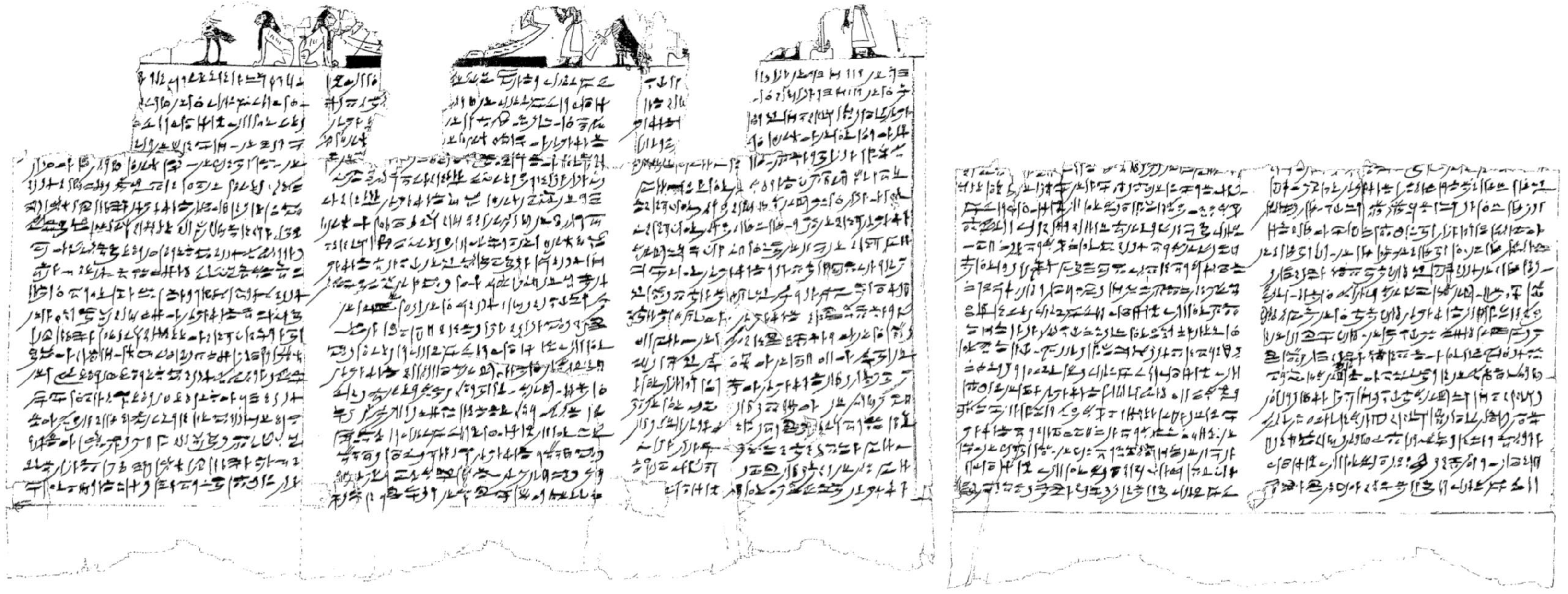

Communiqué par M. Jacobs et faisant suite au manuscrit tiré du Cabinet de la Bibliothèque Impˡᵉ

MANUSCRIT SUR PAPYRUS.

Leclerc Sc.

IDOLES ET FRAGMENS EN BOIS DE SYCOMORE PEINTS DE DIVERSES COULEURS.

Pl. 77.

Blondeau Sculp.

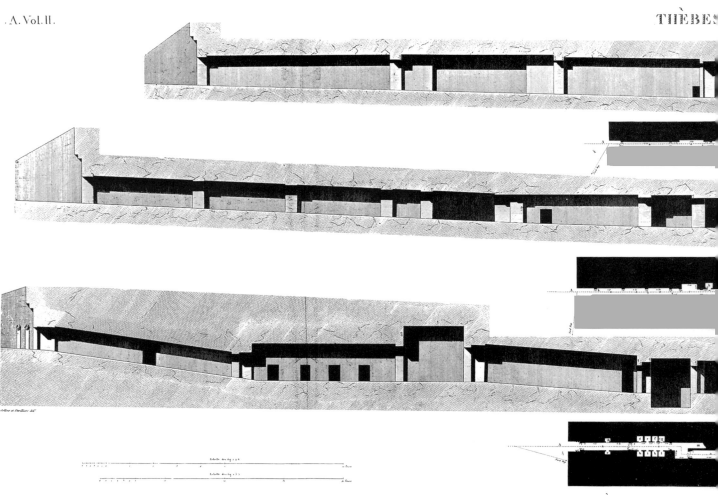

Jollois et Devilliers del.

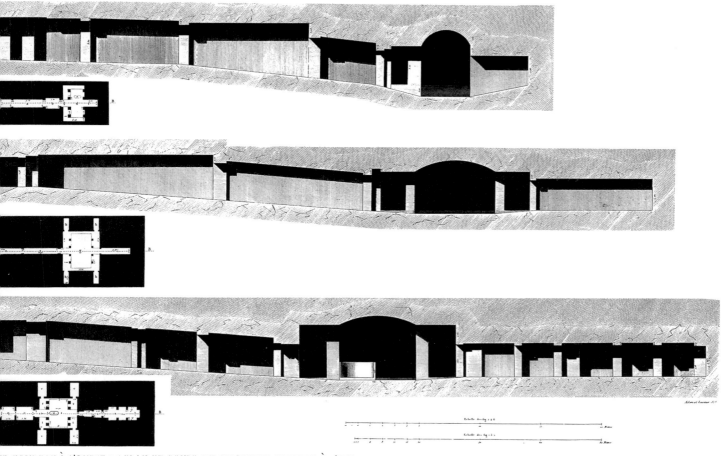

Adam et Lecomte del.

Echelle des fig. 3.4.6

Echelle des fig. 5.5.

...E TOMBEAU À L'OUEST. 5.6 PLAN ET COUPE DU CINQUIEME TOMBEAU À L'EST.

Rougent sq. fecit.

Jollois et Devilliers del.

Echelle des fig. 1
Echelle des fig. 8.9.10.
Echelle des fig. 11.12.13.

1.2.4.6 PLANS DES 5.4.2.ET 1.TOMBEAUX DES ROIS À L'EST. 5 PLAN DU 5.TOMBEAU À L'OUEST. 3 PLAN D
13.14 PLAN ET COUPE DU 1.TOMBEAU

Pl. 79.

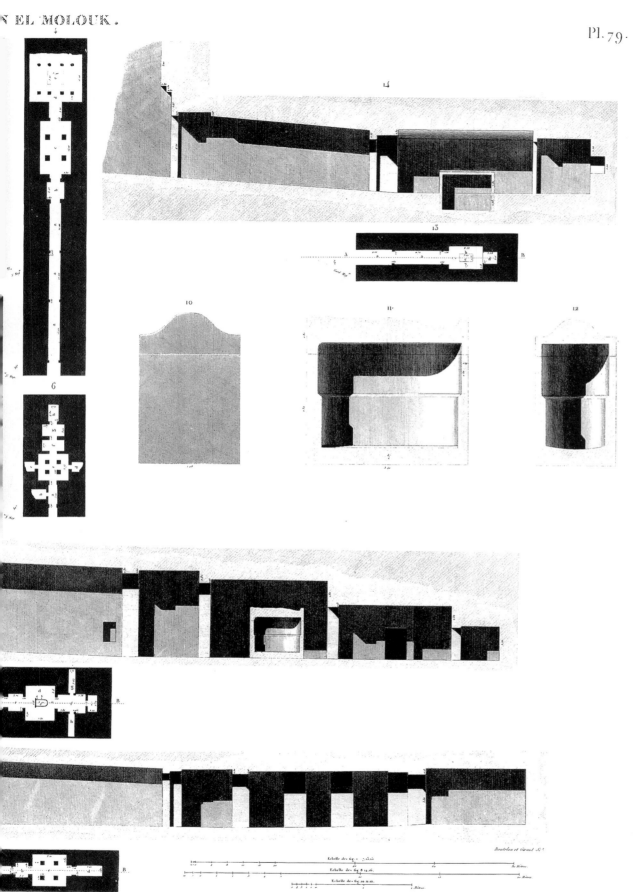

Bouclefou et Giraud Sc.t

DE L'OUEST. 7...12 PLAN, COUPE ET DÉTAILS DE L'ENTRÉE ET DU SARCOPHAGE DU 2.e TOMBEAU À L'OUEST.
N ET COUPE DU 6.e TOMBEAU À L'OUEST.

IDOLE ET FRAGMENS D'ANTIQUITÉS EN SERPENTINE, EN ALBÂTRE ET EN GRÈS
TROUVÉS DANS LE TOMBEAU ISOLÉ DE L'OUEST.

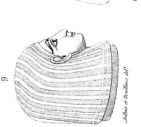

Pl. 81.

A. Vol. II.

THÈBES. BYBÂN EL MOLOUK.

1....6 STATUES ET FRAGMENS DE GRANIT NOIR ET DE GRANIT ROUGE TROUVÉS DANS LES TOMBEAUX DES ROIS À L'OUEST,
7...13 COUVERCLES DE VASES TROUVÉS DANS LES HYPOGÉES.

Le Rey sc.

Adhie et Rouillère del.

THEBES. BYBAN EL MOLOUK.

1...6. BAS~RELIEFS SCULPTÉS ET PEINTS DANS LES 5ᵉ ET 4ᵉ TOMBEAUX DES ROIS A L'OUEST. 7. BAS~RELIEF DU 5ᵉ TOMBEAU A L'EST.

Balzac del.

Darmairon et

VUE GÉNÉRALE PRISE D'UNE ILE

Pl. 2.

Berthault Sc.

JINES DU PALAIS.

Pl.1.

THÈBES. LOUQSOR.

PLAN TOPOGRAPHIQUE DES RUINES.

Pl. 6.

THÈBES. LOUQSOR.

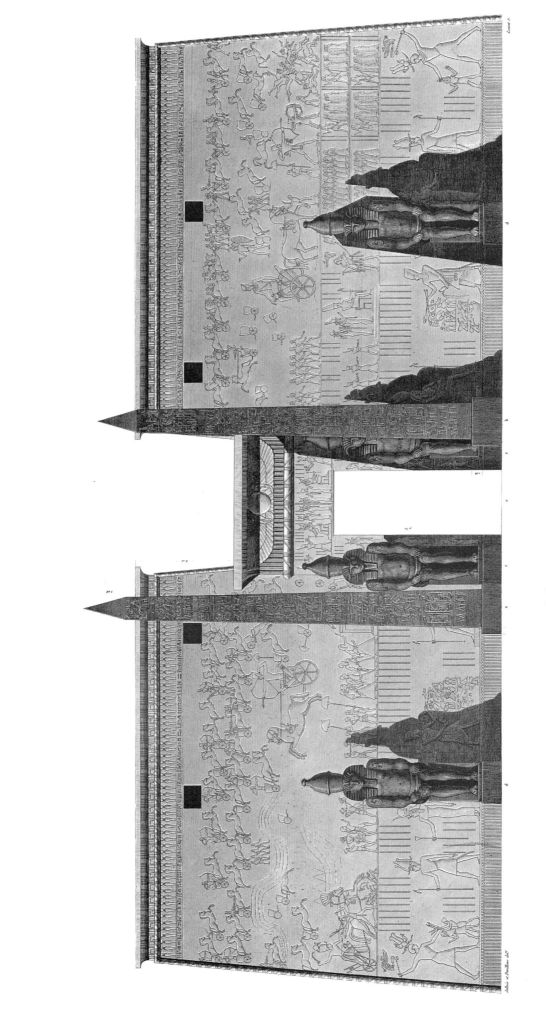

ÉLÉVATION DE LA FAÇADE DU PALAIS.

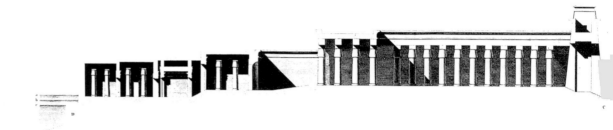

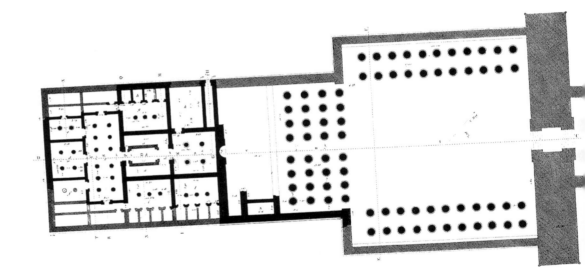

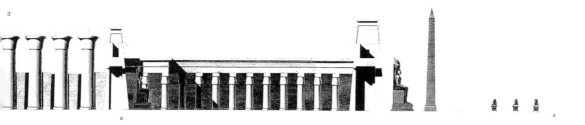

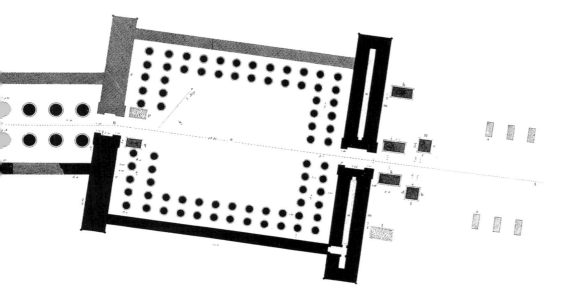

E DU PALAIS .

a   b   c

Jollois et Devilliers del.

PREMIERE ET SECONDE PAR

PE LONGITUDINALE DU PALAIS.

Adam .Sc.

Pl. 8.

THÈBES. LOUQSOR.

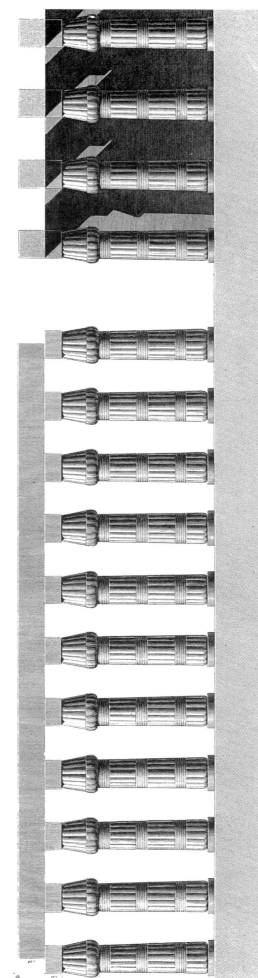

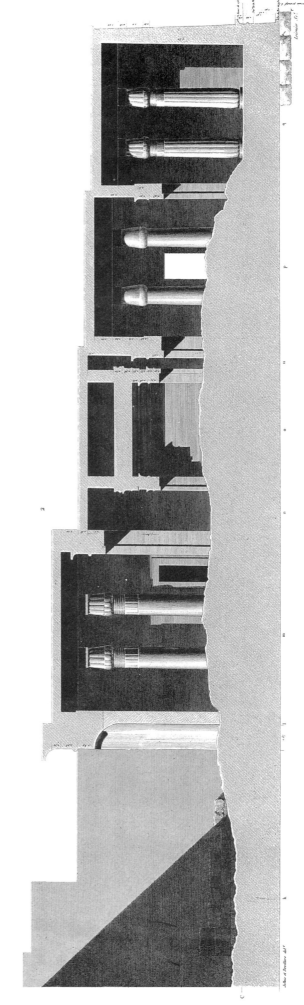

TROISIEME ET QUATRIEME PARTIES DE LA COUPE LONGITUDINALE DU PALAIS.

A. Vol.III.

Pl.9.

THÈBES. LOUQSOR.

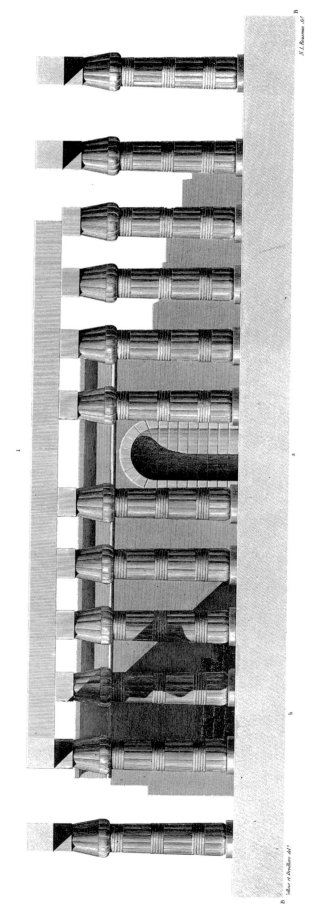

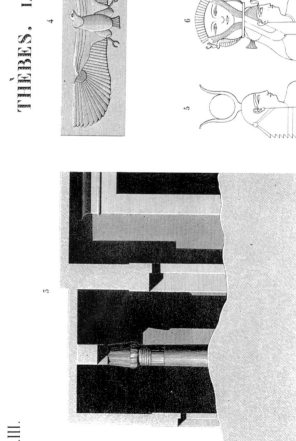

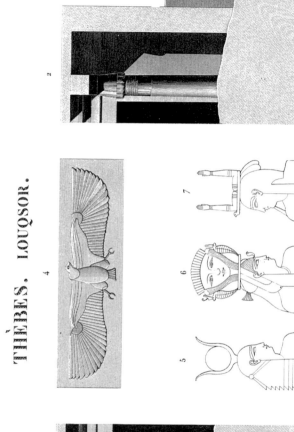

1.2.3 COUPES TRANSVERSALES DU PALAIS. 4.5.6.7 DÉTAILS RECUEILLIS DANS LES SALLES INTÉRIEURES.

DÉTAILS DE TROIS FACES DE L'OBÉLISQUE ORIENTAL DU PALAIS.

DÉTAILS DE TROIS FACES DE L'OBÉLISQUE OCCIDENTAL DU PALAIS.

Pl. 10.

THÈBES. LOUQSOR.

1.2.3.4.5.6 SUITE DES COUPES TRANSVERSALES.—7.7.8.9 DÉTAILS D'UNE COLONNE D'UNE FRISE ET D'UNE CORNICHE DU PALAIS.

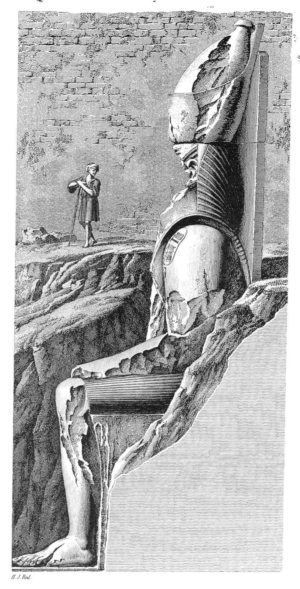

DÉTAILS DES COLOSSES ORIENTAL ET OCCIDENTAL PLACÉS PRÈS DE LA PORTE DU PALAIS.

THÈBES. LOUQSOR.

Pl. 14.

1

2

3

4

5

6

7

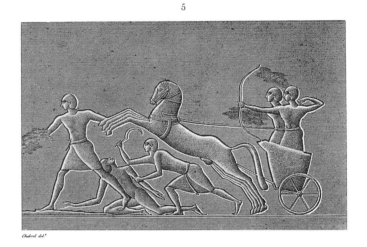

BAS-RELIEFS RECUEILLIS SUR LES MURS INTÉRIEURS ET EXTÉRIEURS DU PALAIS.

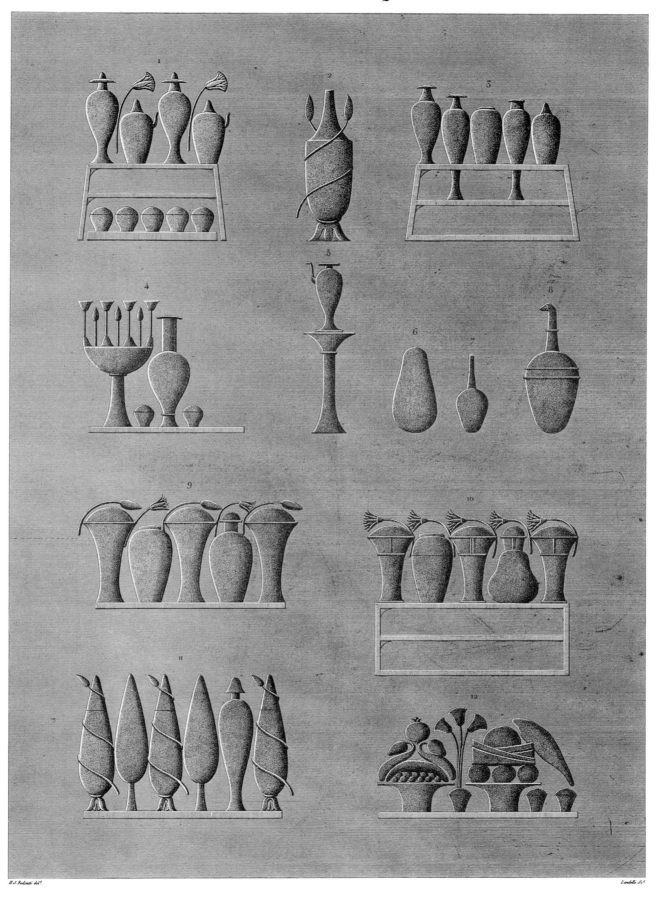

DIVERS VASES SCULPTÉS SUR LES MURS DU PALAIS.

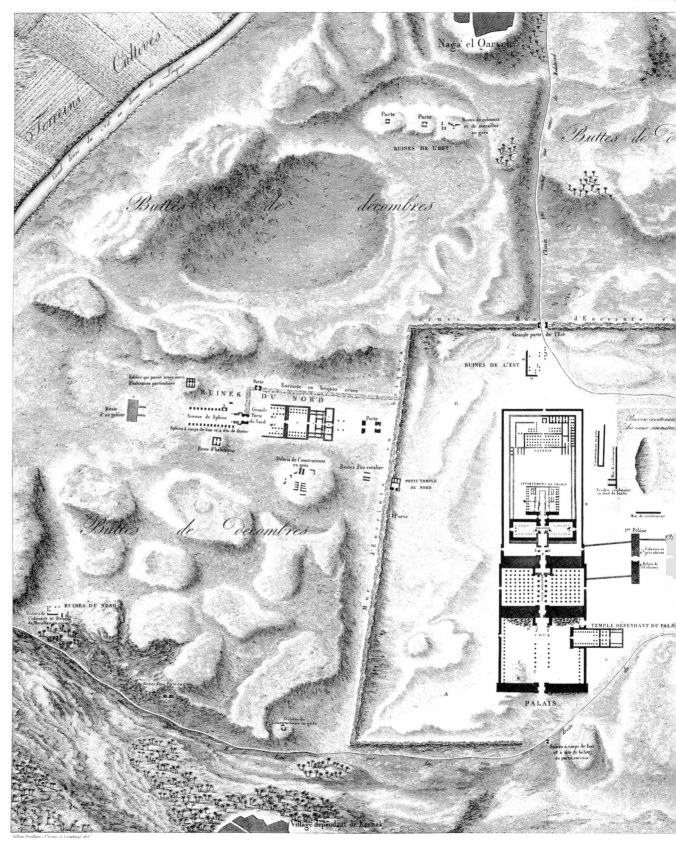

Naga' el Qarneh

Buttes de Dé

Porte   Porte   Restes de colonnes
                     et de murailles
                     en grès
RUINES DE L'EST

Buttes   de   décombres

Grande porte de l'Est

RUINES DE L'EST

Édifice qui parut avoir servi   Porte   Enceinte en briques crues
d'habitation particulière
                                        G
                    RUINES   DU NORD
                              Grande
                              Porte   Porte
Reste   du Nord
d'un pylône
                    Avenue de Sphinx
              Sphinx à corps de lion et à tête de femme   Bassin contenan
                                                                     des eaux saumâtre
              Reste d'habitation
                                        PETIT TEMPLE
              Débris de Constructions DU NORD   Escalier conduisant
              en grès   au fond du bassin
                              Restes d'un escalier
                                                                     Mur de revêtement
Buttes   de   Décombres
                                        Porte   1er Pylône   2e P
                                                                     Colonnes en
                                                                     grès siliceux
                                                                     Débris de
                                                                     5 Colonnes

                                                                     TEMPLE DÉPENDANT DU PALA
RUINES DU NORD
Restes de
Colonnes et Débris
de Murailles   COUR

                                                                     A
                                                         PALAIS

Restes d'un Portique

Débris de
Constructions en grès   Sphinx à corps de lion
                                                          et à tête de bélier
                                                          en partie enfouie

Village dépendant de Karnak

Cécile et Balzac del.

VUE DES RUINES DE LA SALLE HY

DES APPARTEMENS DE GRANIT DU PALAIS.

THÈBES. KARNAK.

Pl. 19.

Gaïté del.

Dumanoir et fils.

Liénard sc.

VUE DU PALAIS PRISE DE L'INTÉRIEUR DE LA COUR.

D'UN COLOSSE PLACÉ À L'ENTRÉE DE LA SALLE HYPOSTYLE DU PALAIS.

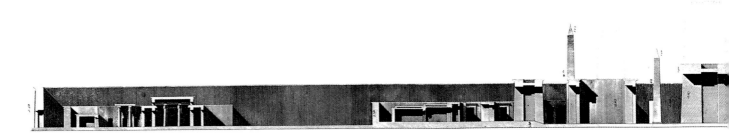

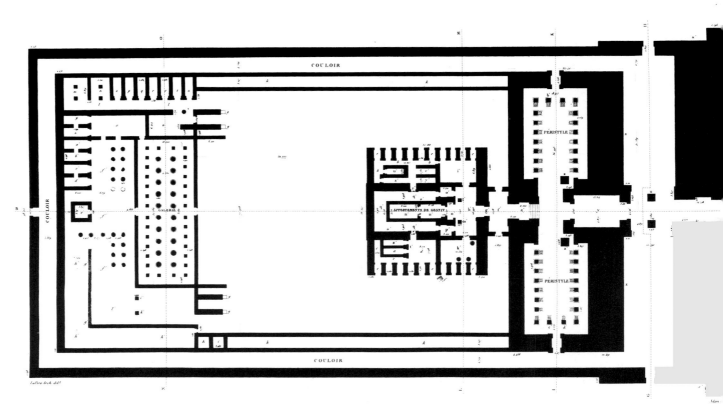

COULOIR

COULOIR

COULOIR

PÉRISTYLE

GALERIE

APPARTEMENTS DE GRANIT

PÉRISTYLE

COULOIR

Lefèvre Arch. del.

1.2.5 PLAN, COUPE GÉNÉRALE ET ÉLÉVATION DU PA

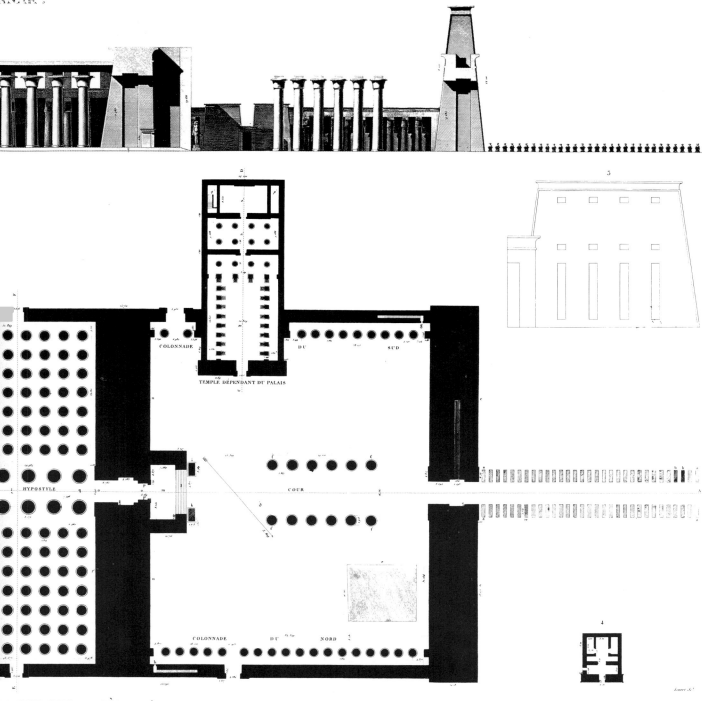

COLONNADE   DU   SUD

TEMPLE DÉPENDANT DU PALAIS

HYPOSTYLE   COUR

COLONNADE   DU   NORD

N PETIT TEMPLE PRÈS DE L'ENCEINTE DU PALAIS.

GITUDINALE DU PALAIS .

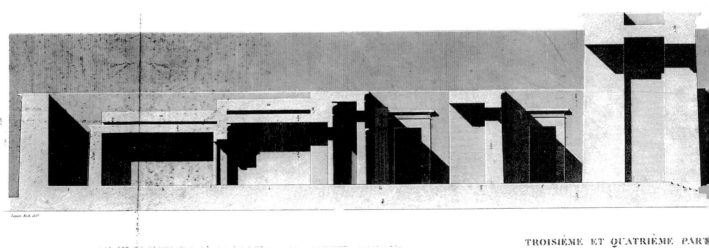

Lepère Arch.t del.t

Lepère Arch.ᵗ del.ᵗ

COUPE TRANSVERSALE

POSTYLE DU PALAIS.

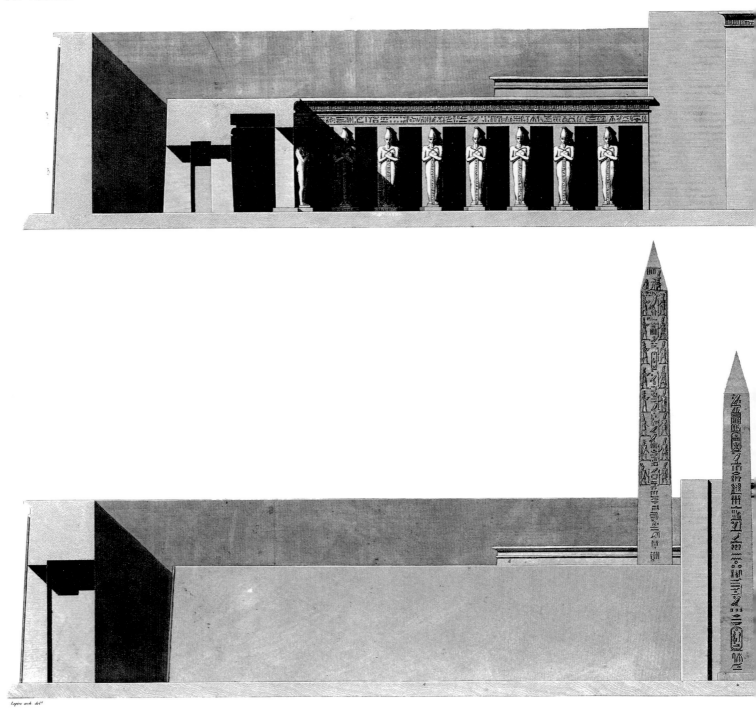

Lepère arch. del.

1. COUPÉ TRANSVERSALE DU PÉRISTYLE DU PALAIS, 2. C

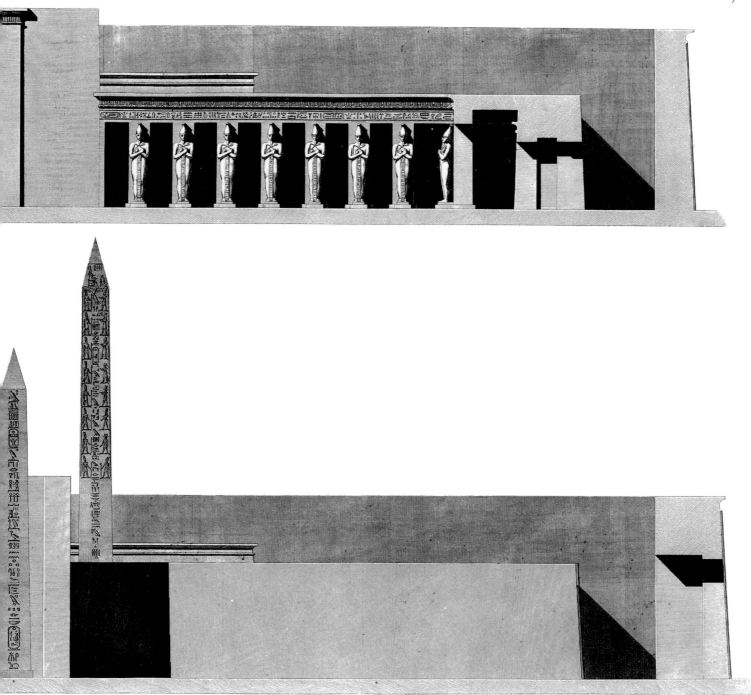

RSALE DU PALAIS PRISE EN AVANT DES OBÉLISQUES .

Pl. 25.

THÈBES. KARNAK.

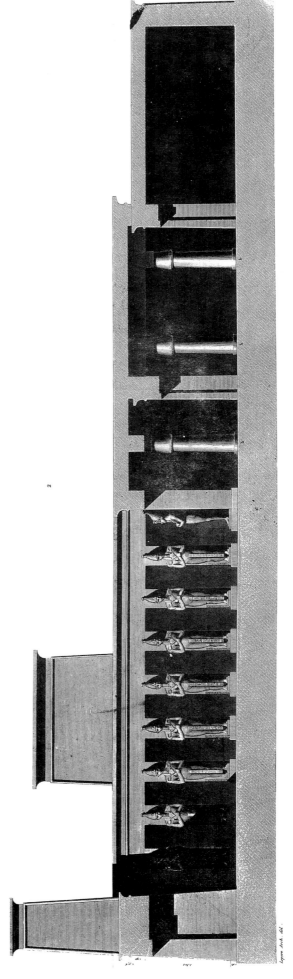

1. VUE INTÉRIEURE DU GRAND TEMPLE DU SUD. 2 COUPE LONGITUDINALE DU TEMPLE DÉPENDANT DU PALAIS.

1.2.3 VUE ET DÉTAILS DE L'UN DES SPHINX PLACÉS À L'ENTRÉE PRINCIPALE DU PALAIS, 4 DÉTAIL DE L'UN
DES SPHINX DE L'ALLÉE DU SUD. 5 PETIT TORSE EN GRANIT TROUVÉ PRÈS DE LA PORTE DU SUD .

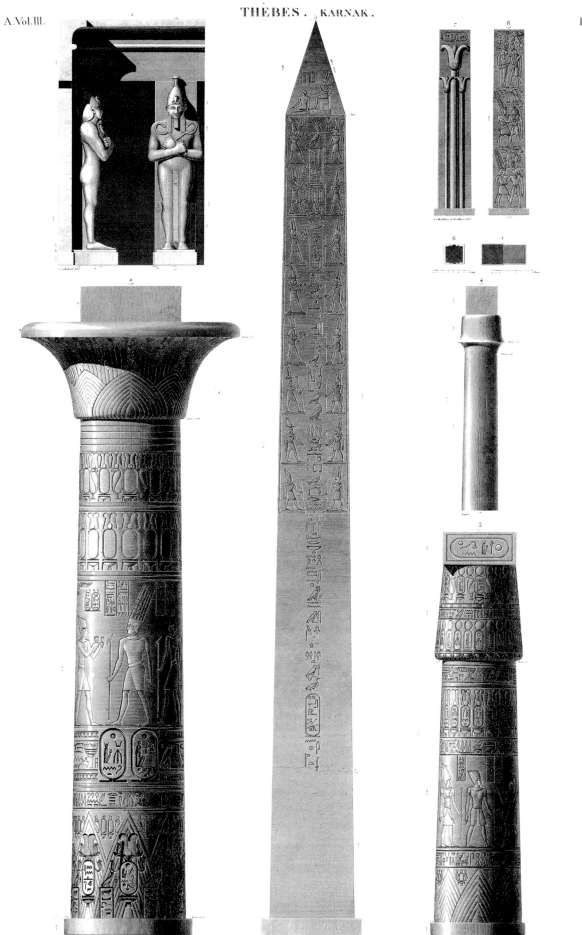

1.DÉTAILS DES PILIERS CARYATIDES DU TEMPLE DÉPENDANT DU PALAIS. 2.3.4.5.6.7.8 DÉTAILS DES COLONNES DE LA SALLE HYPOSTYLE ET
DE LA GALERIE, DU GRAND OBÉLISQUE ET DES STÈLES DU PALAIS.

Pl. 31.

THÈBES. KARNAK.

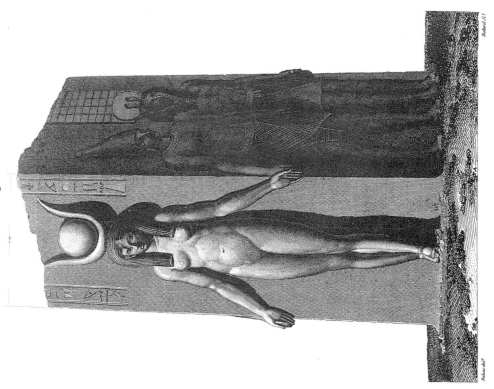

VUES D'UN BLOC EN GRANIT ORNÉ DE SIX FIGURES, TROUVÉ PRÈS DE LA GALERIE DU PALAIS.

THÈBES. KARNAK.

Pl. 32.

1

2

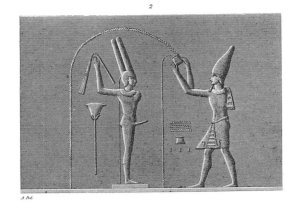

3

A. Delile del.

A. Del.

A. Del.

4

Balzac del.

5

Bals.

BAS - RELIEFS SCULPTÉS DANS L'INTÉRIEUR DE LA SALLE HYPOSTYLE ET SUR LES MURS
EXTÉRIEURS DU PALAIS.

DIVERS BAS - RELIEFS SCULPTÉS SUR LES STÈLES ET LES MURS DES APPARTEMENS DE GRANIT DU PALAIS.

Chabrol del.

Chabrol et Jomard del.

BARQUES SYMBOLIQUES FAISANT PARTIE DE LA DÉCORATION DE LA SALLE

ET SUJETS GUERRIERS SCULPTÉS SUR LES MURS EXTÉRIEURS DU PALAIS .

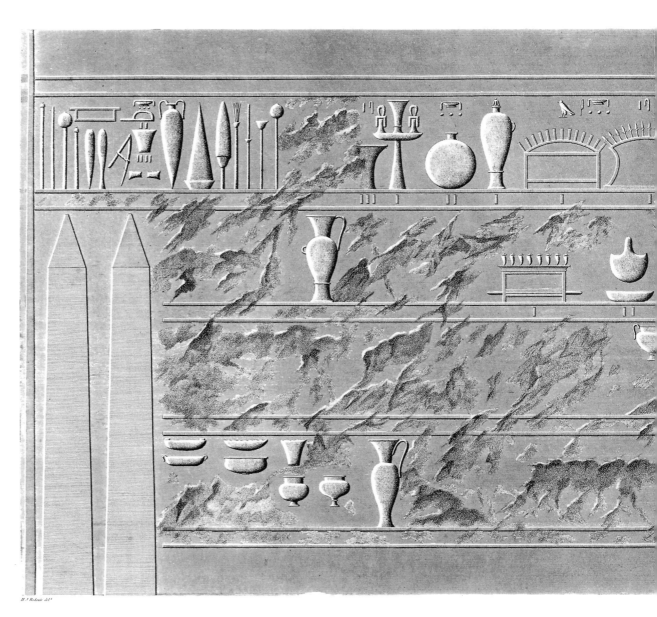

BAS‑RELIEFS SCULPTÉS DANS LE COULOIR

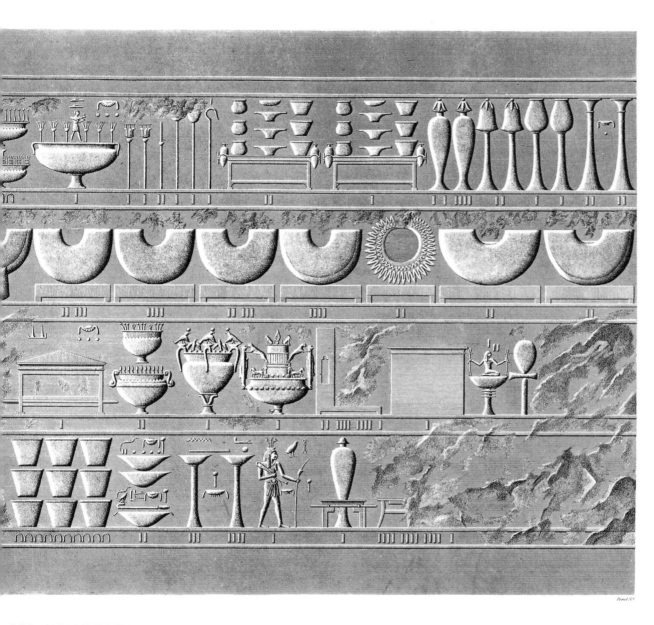

LES APPARTEMENS DE GRANIT DU PALAIS.

BAS~RELIEFS SCULPTÉS DANS L'INTÉRIEUR DU PALAIS ET DANS LES ÉDIFICES DU SUD .

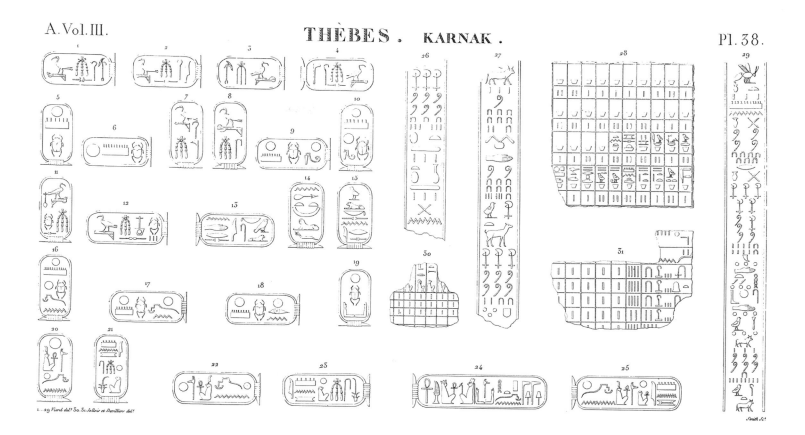

1....31 HIÉROGLYPHES RECUEILLIS DANS LES DIVERS MONUMENS . 32 SUJET MILITAIRE SCULPTÉ SUR LE MUR

EXTÉRIEUR DU PALAIS, EXPOSÉ AU NORD .

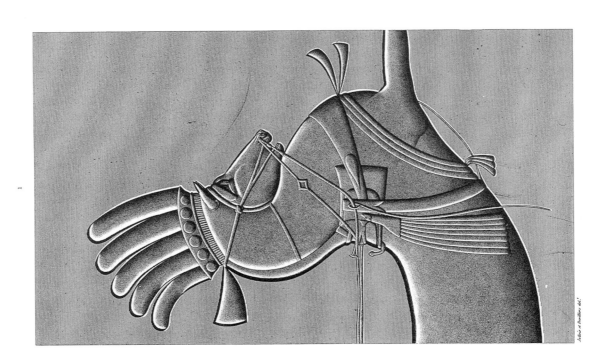

Pl. 39.

THÈBES . KARNAK .

1 HARNACHEMENT D'UN CHEVAL. 2 COMBAT SCULPTÉ SUR LES MURS EXTÉRIEURS DU PALAIS .

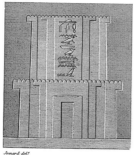

SCÈNES GUERRIERES SCULPTÉES SUR LA FACE NORD DU PALAIS.

A. Le Père arch.del.￼　　　　　　　　　　　　　　　　　　　　　　　　　Coquet Sc.

VUE PERSPECTIVE INTÉRIEURE DU PALAIS, PRISE DE L'EST

THÈBES. KARNAK.

VUE DES PROPYLÉES PRISE DU SUD.

VUE GÉNÉRALE DES PROPYLÉ

INES DU PALAIS PRISE DU NORD-EST .

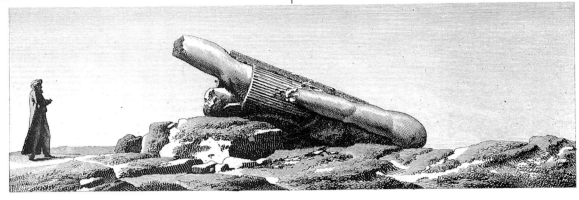

2

5

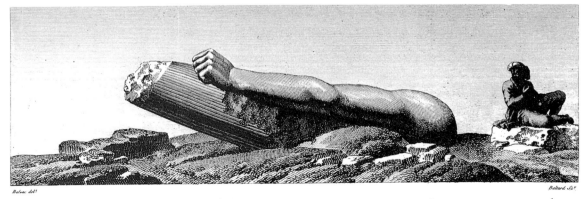

1. VUE DE DEUX COLOSSES SITUÉS AU DEVANT DE L'UN DES PYLÔNES DES PROPYLÉES,

2.3 FRAGMENS DE COLOSSES TROUVÉS DANS L'ENCEINTE DU SUD.

VUE ET DÉTAILS DES SPHINX DE L'AVENUE DES PROPYLÉES DU PALAIS.

Pl. 4.

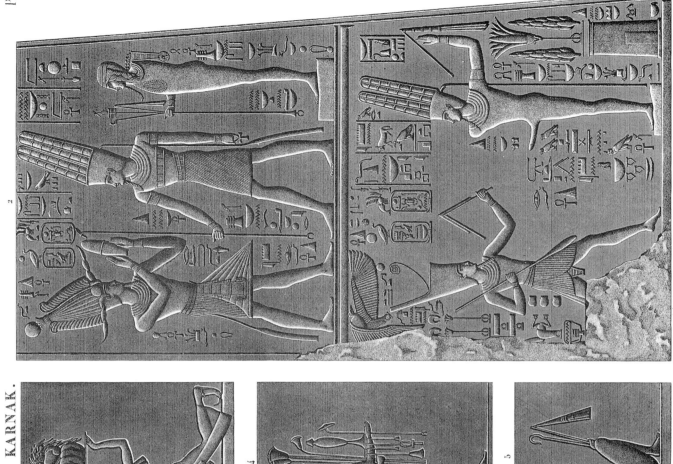

2

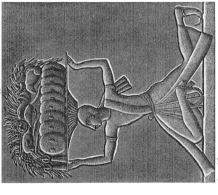

THÈBES. KARNAK.

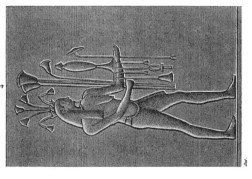

4

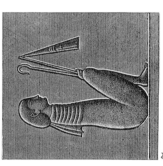

5

1

Jollois et Devilliers del.t.

1. 2. DÉCORATION INTÉRIEURE DE LA PORTE DE GRANIT DES PROPYLÉES. 3. 4. 5. SUJETS RECUEILLIS DANS DIVERS ÉDIFICES.

Pl. 48.

1.2.3.4.5 STATUES DE GRANIT NOIR TROUVÉES DANS L'ENCEINTE DU SUD. 6 VUE DU COLOSSE
PLACÉ À L'ENTRÉE DE LA SALLE HYPOSTYLE DU PALAIS.

2

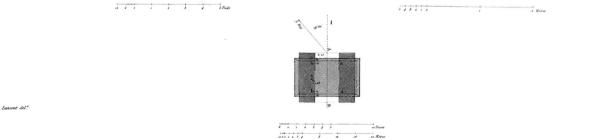

Lancret del.

Pomel Sc.

PLAN ET DÉTAIL DU PLAFOND DE LA PORTE DU SUD .

COUPE DE LA PORTE DU SUD.

Pl. 53.

THÈBES. KARNAK.

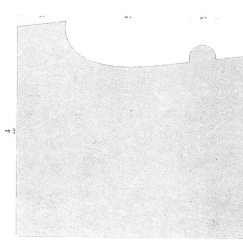

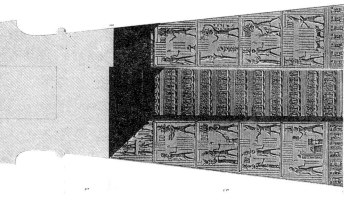

COUPE, DÉTAIL ET BAS-RELIEFS INTÉRIEURS DE LA PORTE DU SUD.

VUE INTÉRIEURE ET PLAN DU GRAND TEMPLE DU SUD .

VUE ET DÉTAILS DES BÉLIERS DE L'AVENUE DU GRAND TEMPLE DU SUD.

Echelle des fig. 1 à 5

Echelle des fig. 4 à 6

1, 2, 3 COUPES LONGITUDINALES ET TRANSVERSALES.

2

4

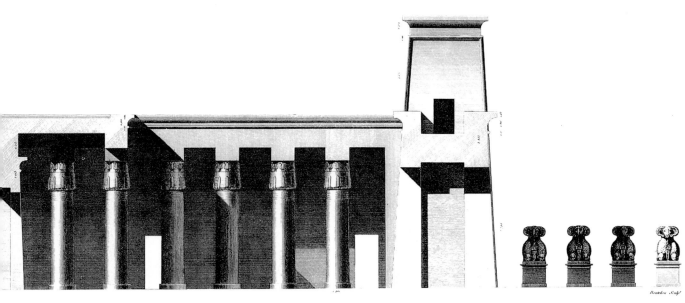

DE CHAPITEAUX DU GRAND TEMPLE DU SUD .

Echelle des fig. 1 y 3

Echelle des fig. 4 5 6

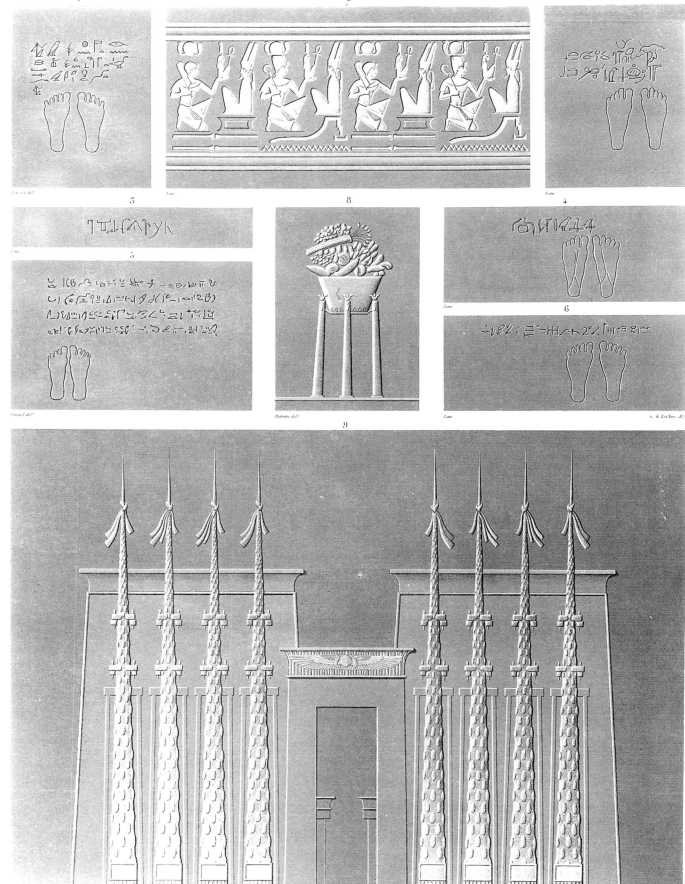

Pl.58.

THEBES. KARNAK.

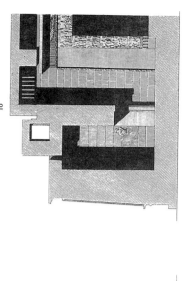

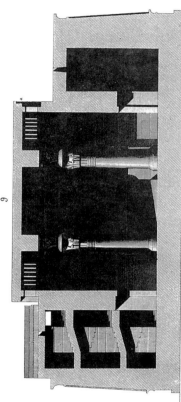

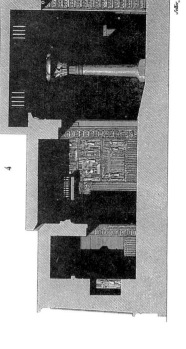

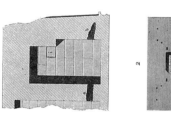

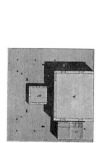

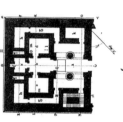

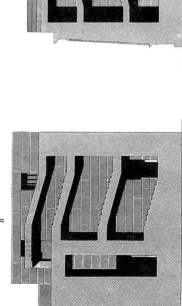

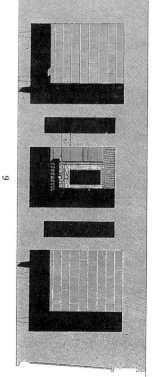

PLANS ÉLÉVATION COUPES ET DÉTAILS DU PETIT TEMPLE DU SUD.

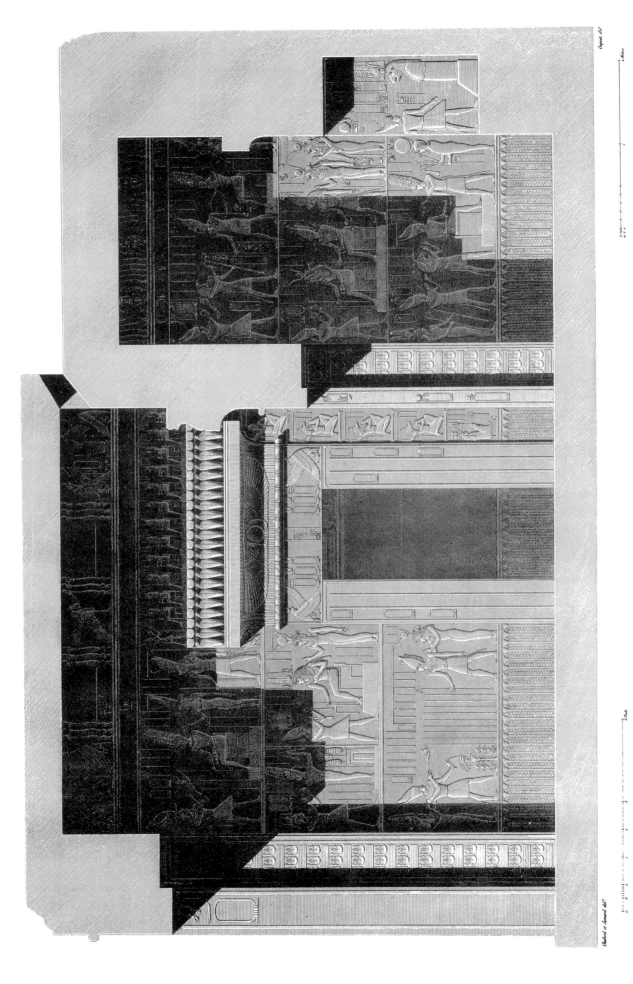

PORTION DE LA COUPE LONGITUDINALE DU PETIT TEMPLE DU SUD.

2

3

Chabrol et Jomard del.t   Echelle des fig. 2. 3   Lesieur Sc.t

ÉLÉVATION DE LA PORTE EXTÉRIEURE ET BAS-RELIEFS DU PETIT TEMPLE DU SUD.

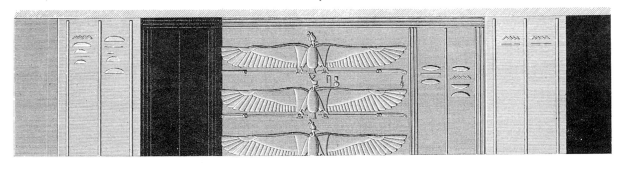

2

ÉLÉVATION DE LA FAÇADE INTÉRIEURE ET BAS-RELIEFS DU PETIT TEMPLE DU SUD.

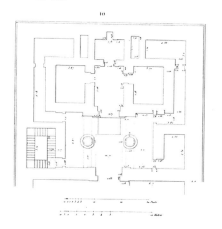

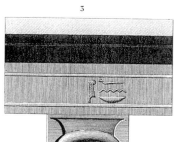

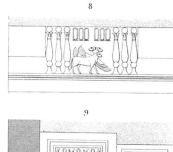

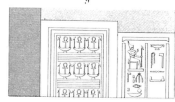

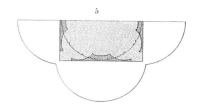

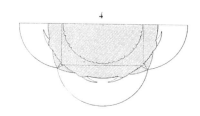

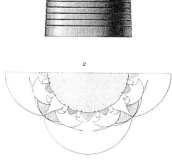

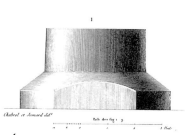

Chabrol et Jomard del.

Meszy Sc.

DÉTAILS D'ARCHITECTURE, COUPE DU SANCTUAIRE ET BAS-RELIEFS DU PETIT TEMPLE DU SUD.

Chabrol et Jomard del.

COUPE TRANSVERSA

Pl.64.

THÈBES. KARNAK.

BAS RELIEF SCULPTÉ DANS L'UNE DES SALLES LATÉRALES DU PETIT TEMPLE DU SUD.

THÈBES. KARNAK.

Pl. 65.

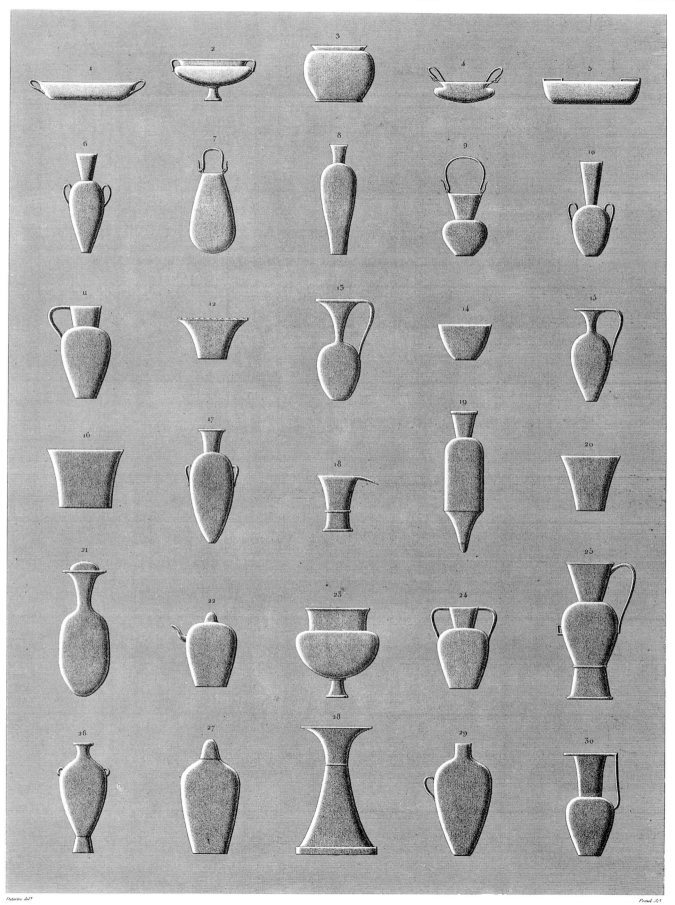

Laborde del.   Pomel sc.t

COLLECTION DE VASES RECUEILLIS DANS DIVERS ÉDIFICES.

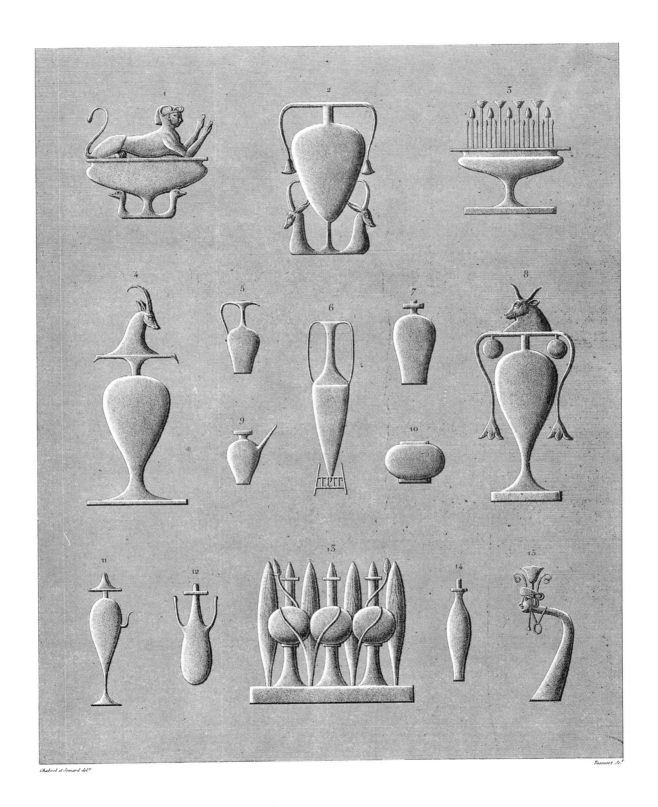

Chabrol et Jomard del.t   Fossart Sc.t

VASES DESSINÉS DANS PLUSIEURS MONUMENS .

Pl. 67.

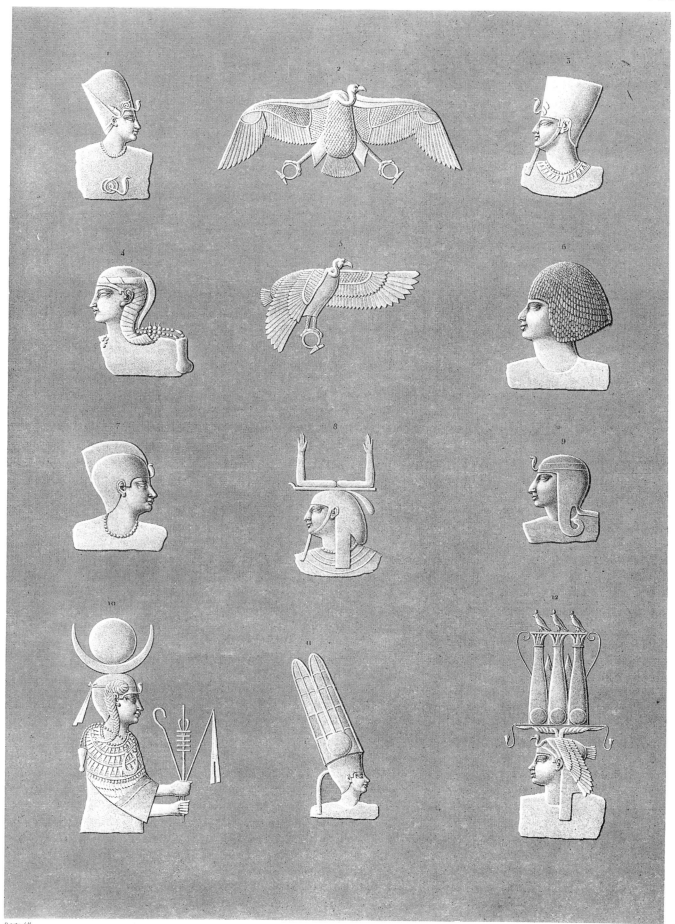

Duterte del.

Tassaert Sc.t

DÉTAILS DE FIGURES, TIRÉS DES BAS-RELIEFS DE DIVERS ÉDIFICES .

THÈBES . MED-A'MOUD .

Pl.68.

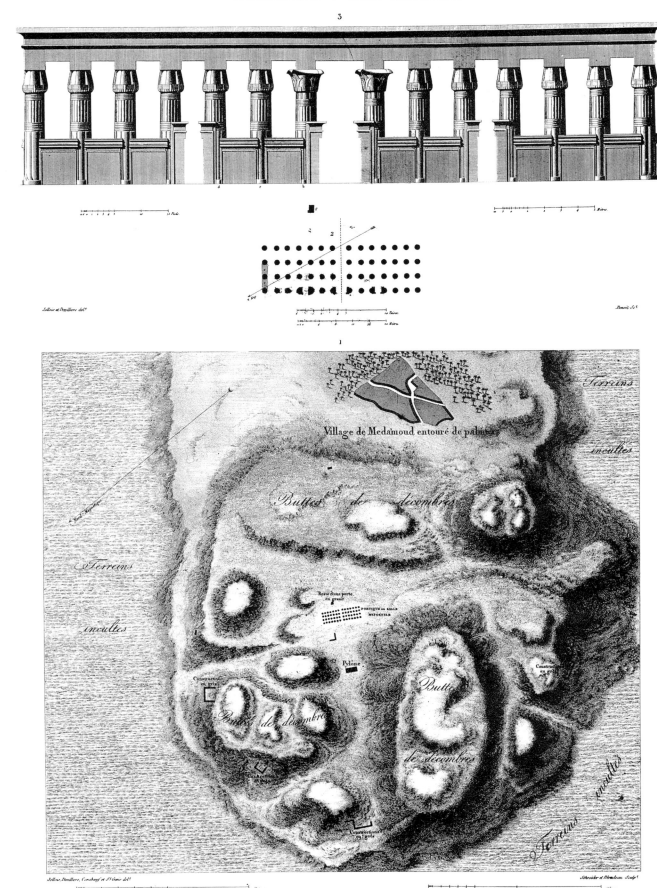

1. PLAN TOPOGRAPHIQUE DES RUINES, 2.3 PLAN ET ÉLÉVATION DES RESTES D'UN PORTIQUE.

THÈBES.

Pl. 69.

COLLECTION DE LÉGENDES HIÉROGLYPHIQUES RECUEILLIES DANS LES ÉDIFICES.

ΒΑΣΙΛΙΣΣΑΚΛΕΟΠΑΤΡΑΚΑΙΒΑΣΙΛΕΥΣΠΤΟΛΕΜΑΙΟΣΘΕΟΙΜΕΓΑΛΟΙΦΙΛΟΜΗΤΟΡΕΣ
ΑΡ ΣΚΑΙΤΑΤΕΚΝΑΗ ΔΙΟΙΘΕΟΙΜΕΠΙΣΤΩΙΚΑΙΤΟΙΣΣΥΝΝΑΟΙΣΘΕΟΙΣ

1. 2. 3. 4 COURONNEMENT D'UNE PORTE, PLAN, ÉLÉVATION ET COUPE D'UN MONOLITHE DE QOUS.

5...9 FRISE ET BAS-RELIEFS DESSINÉS A KEFT.

DENDERAH. (TENTYRIS)

Pl. 2.

Petite Enceinte de l'Est renfermant des débris antiques

Monticules

Maison moderne

Débris de Maisons modernes

Débris de Maison Modernes

GRAND TEMPLE

Débris de Maisons Modernes

PETIT TEMPLE ou TYPHONIUM

Débris de Maisons modernes

PORTE DU NORD

EDIFICE DU NORD

Buttes

Buttes

PLAN TOPOGRAPHIQUE DES RUINES.

ISE DE L'OUEST.

PL. 4.

DENDERAH. (TENTYRIS.)

VUE DE LA PORTE DU NORD.

Lereux [?].

Protain del.[?]

Chabrol et Jomard del.　　　Echelle de la fig. 2.　　　　　Echelle de la fig. 4.　　　Plée Sc.

PLAN, COUPE ET DÉTAIL DE LA PORTE DU NORD.

DENDERAH. (TENTYRIS) Pl. 6.

ÉLÉVATION PERSPECTIVE DE LA PORTE DU NORD.

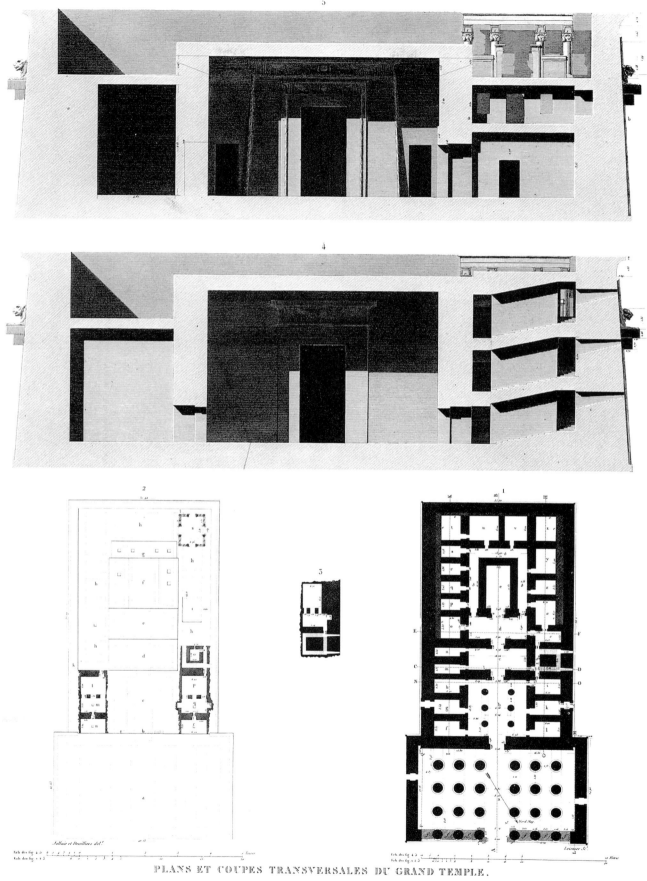

PLANS ET COUPES TRANSVERSALES DU GRAND TEMPLE.

AND TEMPLE.

Jollois et Devilliers del.

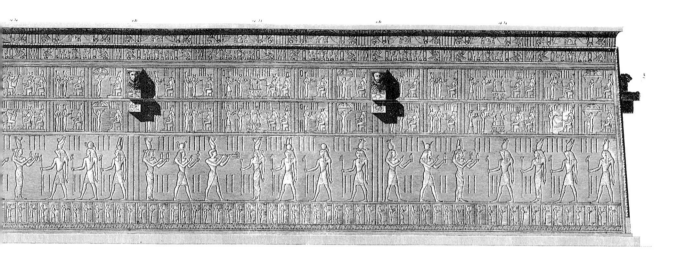

'DINALE DU GRAND TEMPLE.

Pl. 9.

DENDERAH. (TENTYRIS.)

ÉLÉVATION DU PORTIQUE DU GRAND TEMPLE.

DENDERAH. (TENTYRIS)

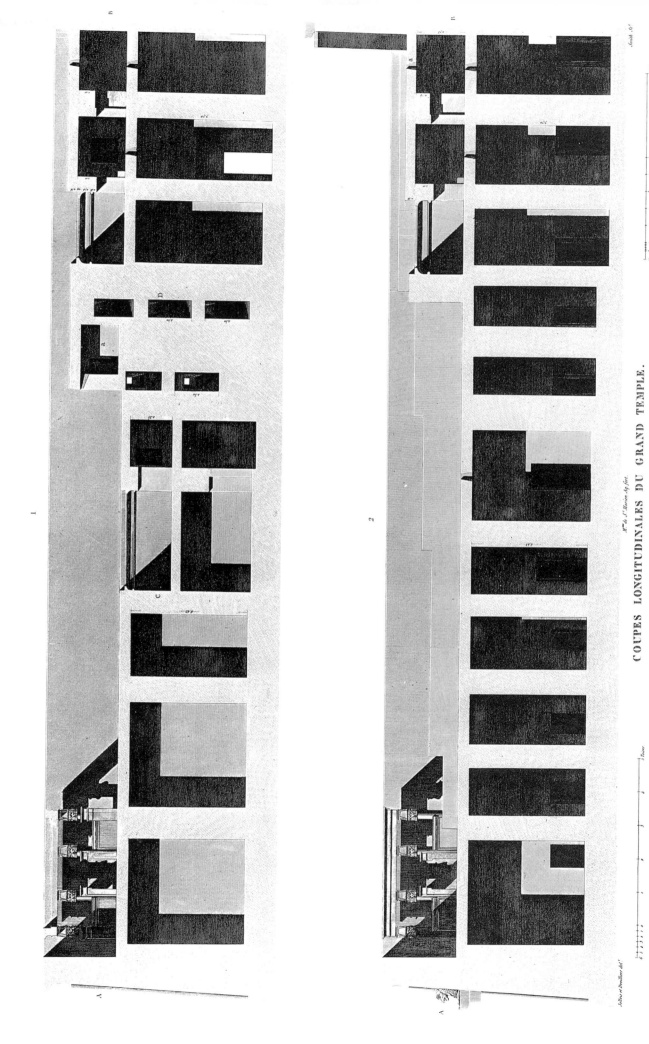

Jollois et Desilliers del.

N.ͤ de S.ͭ Morien del fecit.

Smith Sc.ͭ

COUPES LONGITUDINALES DU GRAND TEMPLE.

Pl. 15.

DENDERAH. (TENTYRIS)

DÉTAILS DE DEUX MURS D'ENTRECOLONNEMENT DU PORTIQUE

ET BAS - RELIEFS RECUEILLIS DANS LE GRAND TEMPLE.

PL.14.

DENDERAH. (TENTYRIS)

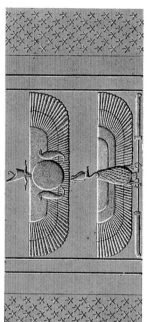

DÉCORATION DES ANTES ET D'UN SOFFITE, ET BAS-RELIEF DE L'EXTÉRIEUR DU PORTIQUE DU GRAND TEMPLE.

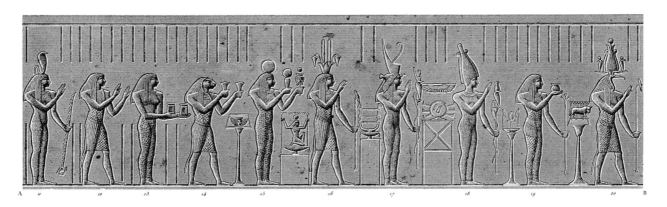

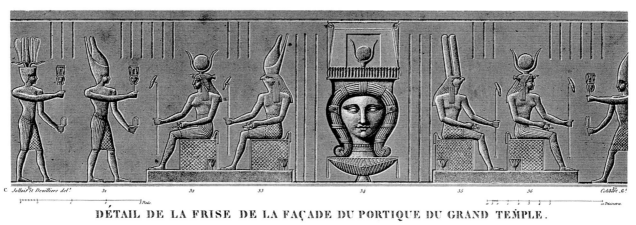

DÉTAIL DE LA FRISE DE LA FAÇADE DU PORTIQUE DU GRAND TEMPLE.

Pl. 17.

DENDÉRAH. (TENTYRIS.)

DÉTAIL DE LA FACE LATÉRALE DE L'EST DANS LE PORTIQUE DU GRAND TEMPLE.

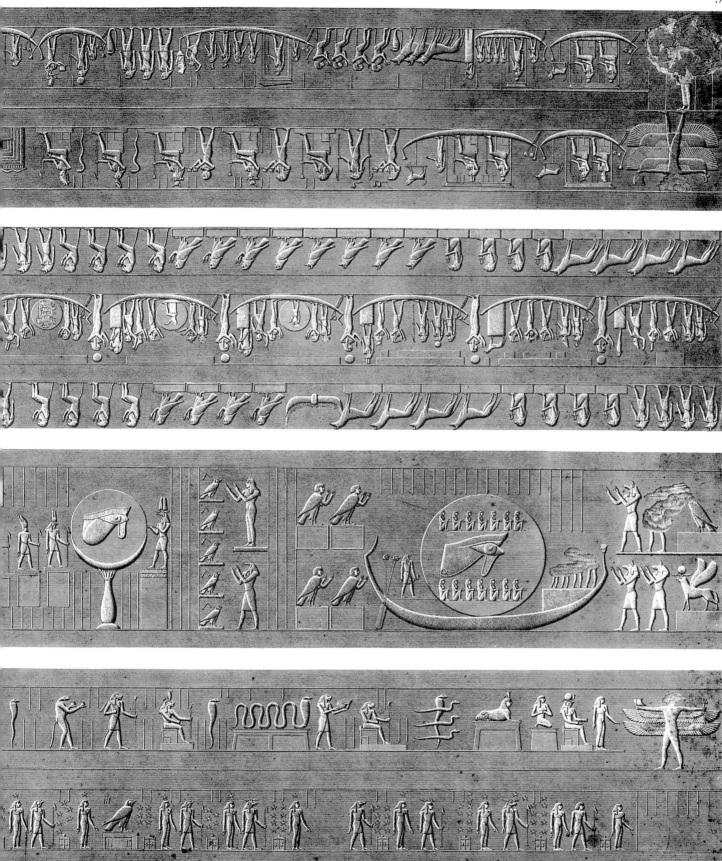

Sellier et Devilliers del.

Charlin Sc.

DENDERAH. (TENTYRIS)

PLAFOND DU PORTIQUE DU GRAND TEMPLE.

Pl. 21.

ZODIAQUE SCULPTÉ AU PLAFOND DE L'UNE DES SALLES SUPÉRIEURES DU GRAND TEMPLE.

ZODIAQUE SCULPTÉ AU PLAFOND DE L'UNE DES SALLES SUPÉRIEURES DU GRAND TEMPLE.

DENDERAH. (TENTYRIS)

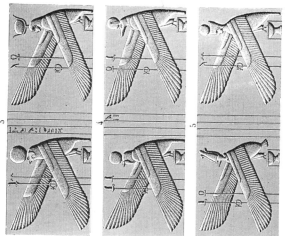

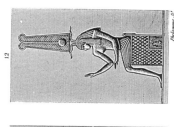

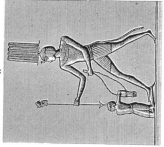

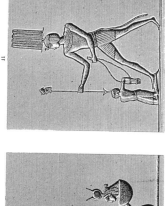

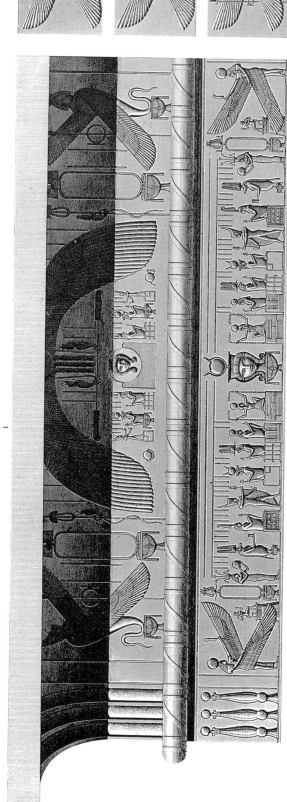

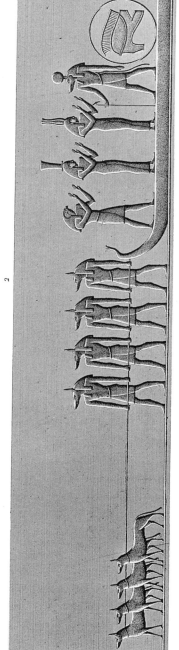

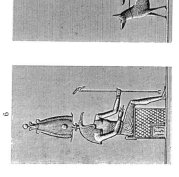

1 CORNICHE ET FRISE DES FACES LATÉRALES DU PORTIQUE DU GRAND TEMPLE. 2.3.4.5 BAS - RELIEFS DE L'APPARTEMENT DU ZODIAQUE.

6...12 DÉTAILS DESSINÉS SUR LES MURS DU GRAND TEMPLE.

Jollois et Devilliers del.

Philippeau Sc.

Pl. 23.

DENDERAH. (TENTYRIS.)

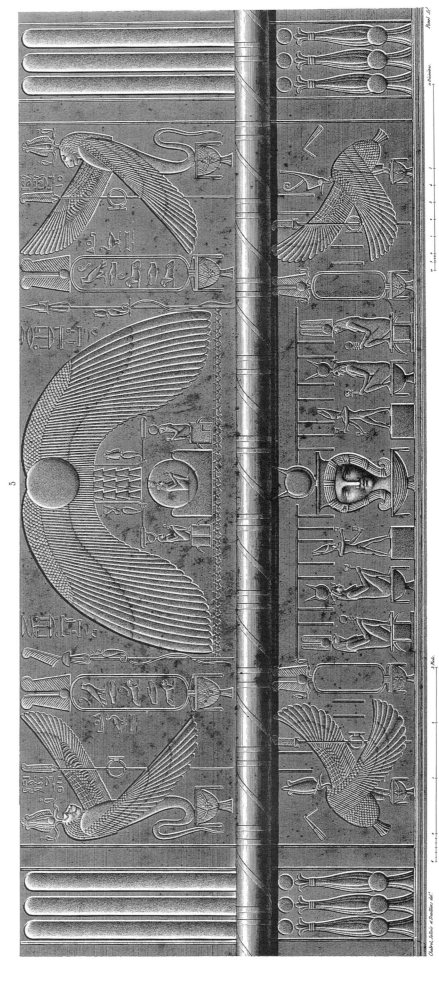

1. FRISE DE LA PARTIE POSTÉRIEURE DU PORTIQUE. 2. CORNICHE DE LA 1re SALLE DE L'APPARTEMENT DU ZODIAQUE. 3. FRISE ET CORNICHE DU GRAND TEMPLE.

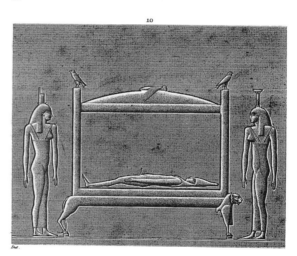

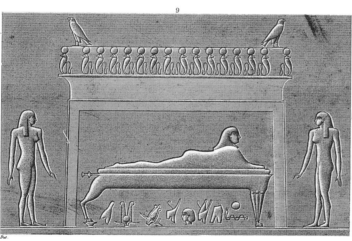

1.2.3.8.9.10 BAS-RELIEFS DE L'APPARTEMENT DU ZODIAQUE. 4.5.6.7.11.13 DÉTAILS DU GRAND TEMPLE ET DE LA PORTE DU NORD.
12 COURONNEMENT DE LA PORTE DU PORTIQUE DU GRAND TEMPLE.

PL.25.

DENDERAH. (TENTYRIS.)

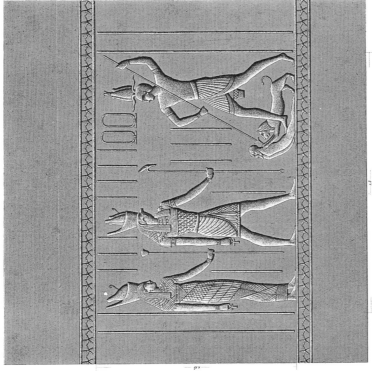

3

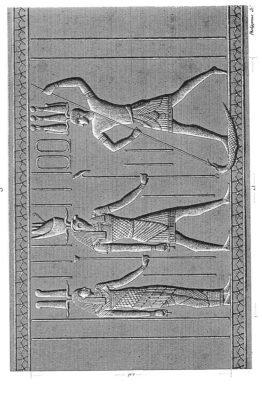

5

1

2

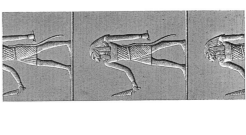

4

Jomard del.

Philippeau sc.

BAS-RELIEFS DU GRAND TEMPLE, DE LA PORTE DU NORD, ET DE CELLE DE L'ENCEINTE DE L'EST.

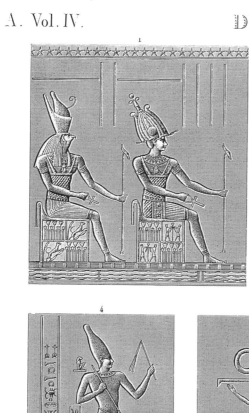

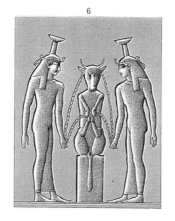

Dutertre del.

Pomel Sc.

DIVERS BAS-RELIEFS DESSINÉS DANS L'APPARTEMENT DU ZODIAQUE ET DANS LES TEMPLES.

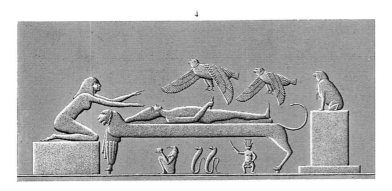

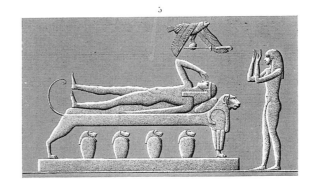

Duterte del.'   Charlin Sc.'

COSTUMES ET BAS-RELIEFS SCULPTÉS DANS L'APPARTEMENT DU ZODIAQUE ET SUR LES MURS DU GRAND TEMPLE.

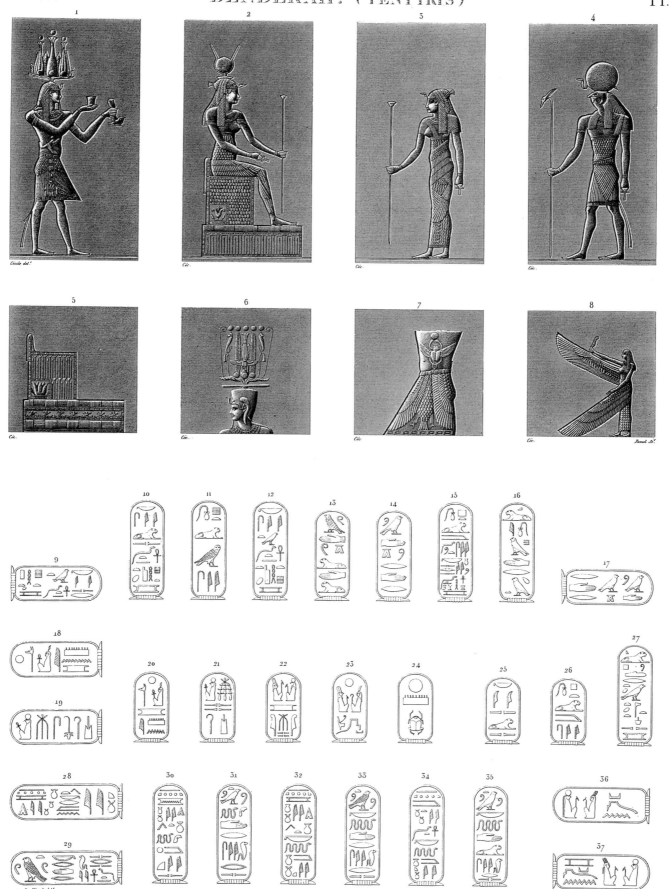

DÉTAILS DE FIGURES ET DE COSTUMES, ET LÉGENDES HIÉROGLYPHIQUES RECUEILLIS DANS LES TEMPLES.

Le Père Architecte del.'

QUE DU GRAND TEMPLE.

Pl. 3.

VUE PERSPECTIVE DE L'INTÉRIEUR DU PORTIQUE DU GRAND TEMPLE.

DENDERAH. (TENTYRIS)

Pl. 31.

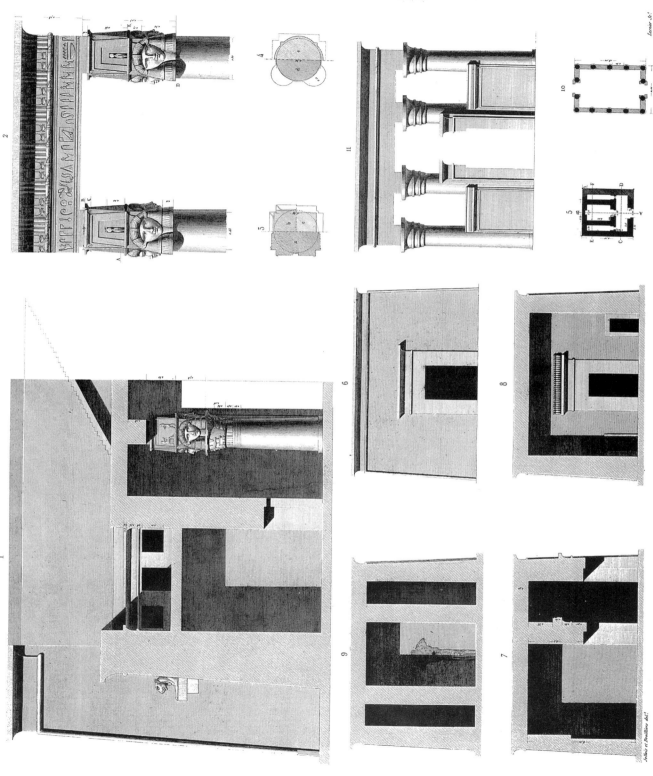

1 COUPE DU 2ème PORTIQUE DU GRAND TEMPLE. 2.3.4 DÉTAILS DU PETIT ÉDIFICE DE LA TERRASSE. 5..9 PLAN, ÉLÉVATION
ET COUPES DE L'ÉDIFICE DU SUD. 10..11 PLAN ET ÉLÉVATION DE L'ÉDIFICE DU NORD.

Pl. 32.

DENDERAH. (TENTYRIS.)

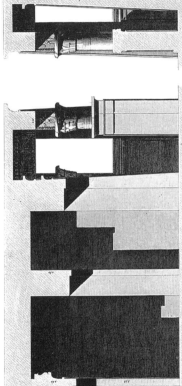

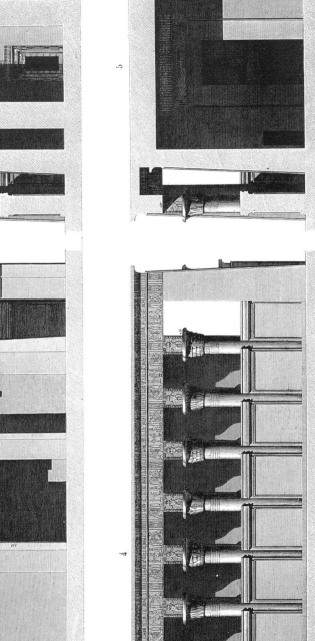

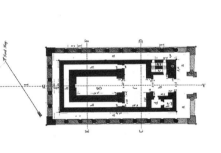

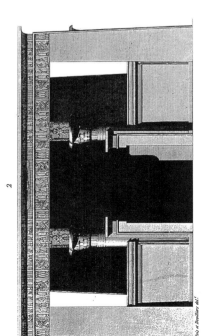

PLAN, ÉLÉVATIONS ET COUPES DU TYPHONIUM.

Jollois et Devilliers del.

Lenoir sc.

Pl. 33.

DENDERAH. (TENTYRIS)

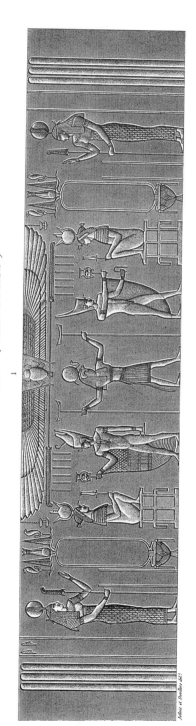

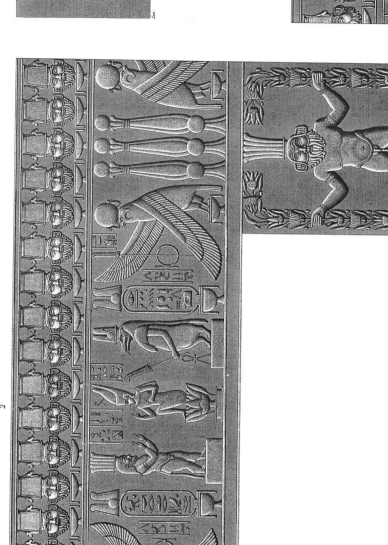

1.2 DÉCORATION DE LA CORNICHE ET DE LA FRISE INTÉRIEURE DE LA GALERIE DU TYPHONIUM.

3.4.5.6 LÉGENDES VARIÉES ET DÉTAILS DE LA MÊME FRISE.

A. Vol. IV.

DENDERAH. (TENTYRIS)

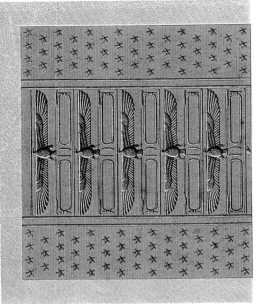

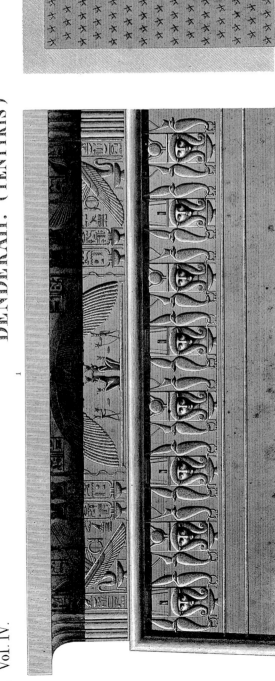

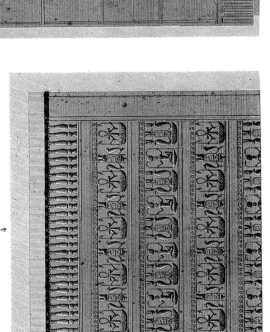

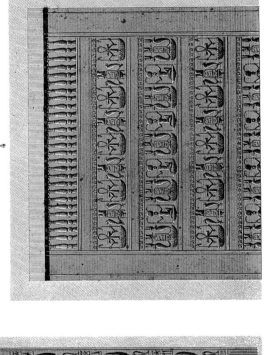

Barbier del.^t

Pomel sc.^t

1 DÉTAIL DE LA CORNICHE ET DE LA FRISE DE L'ÉDIFICE DU SUD. 2.3.4.5 SCULPTURES INTÉRIEURES DU TYPHONIUM.

ABYDUS

Pl. 35.

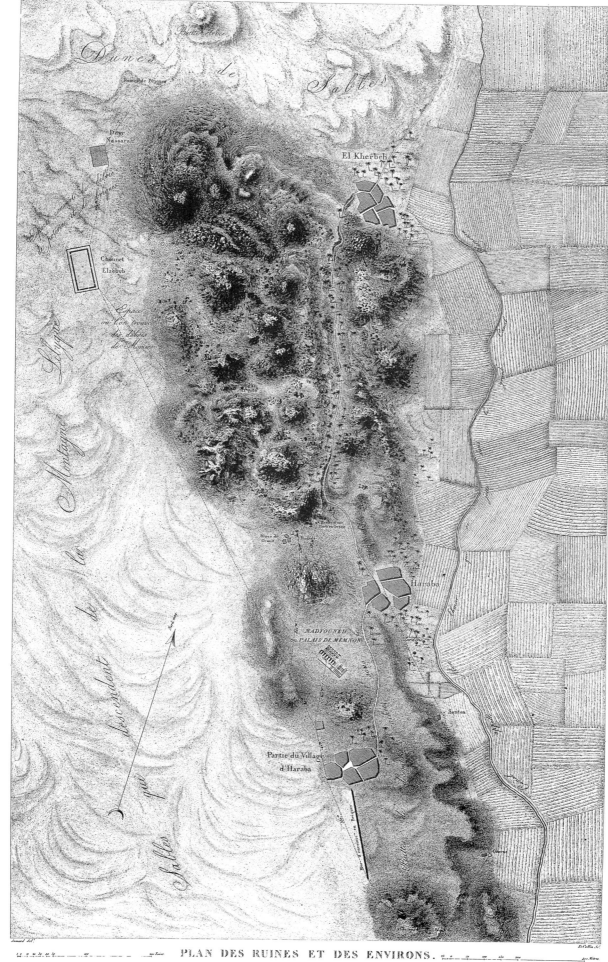

Dunes de Sables

El Kherbeh

Deyr Nassarah

Chounet el Elzebeb

Haraba

MADFOUNEH ou PALAIS DE MEMNON

Santon

Partie du Village d'Haraba

Jomard del.

Ei Collin Sc.

PLAN DES RUINES ET DES ENVIRONS.

Pl. 56.

ABYDUS.

PLAN, ÉLÉVATION ET COUPES DU PALAIS.

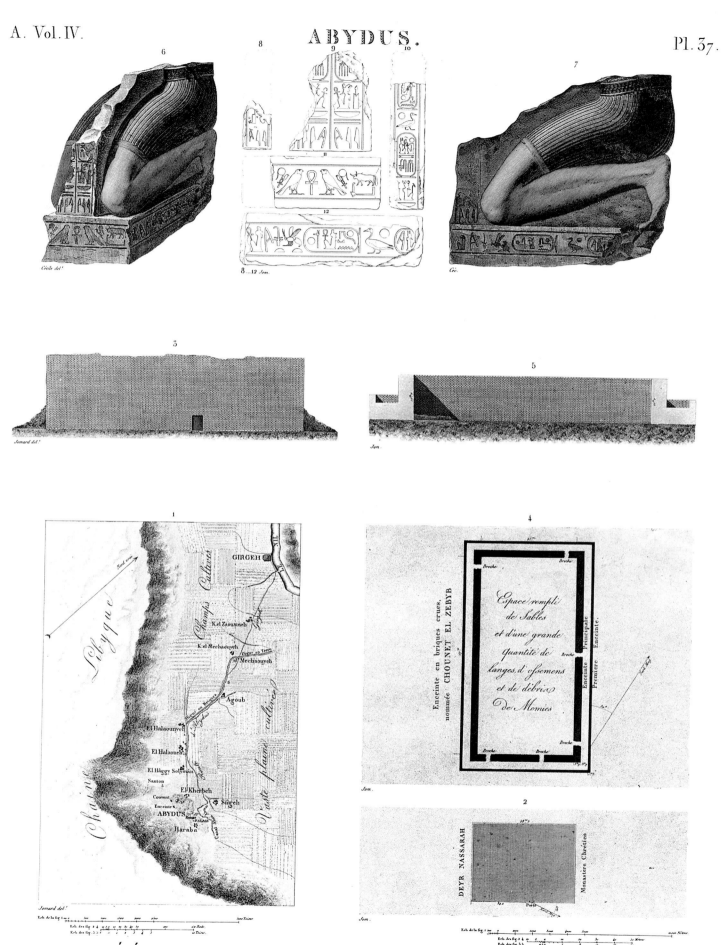

1 PLAN GÉNÉRAL DES ENVIRONS. 2.3.4.5 PLANS ET PROFILS DES BÀTIMENS DU NORD-OUEST,
6.....12 VUES ET DÉTAILS D'UN FRAGMENT DE STATUE TROUVÉ DANS LES RUINES.

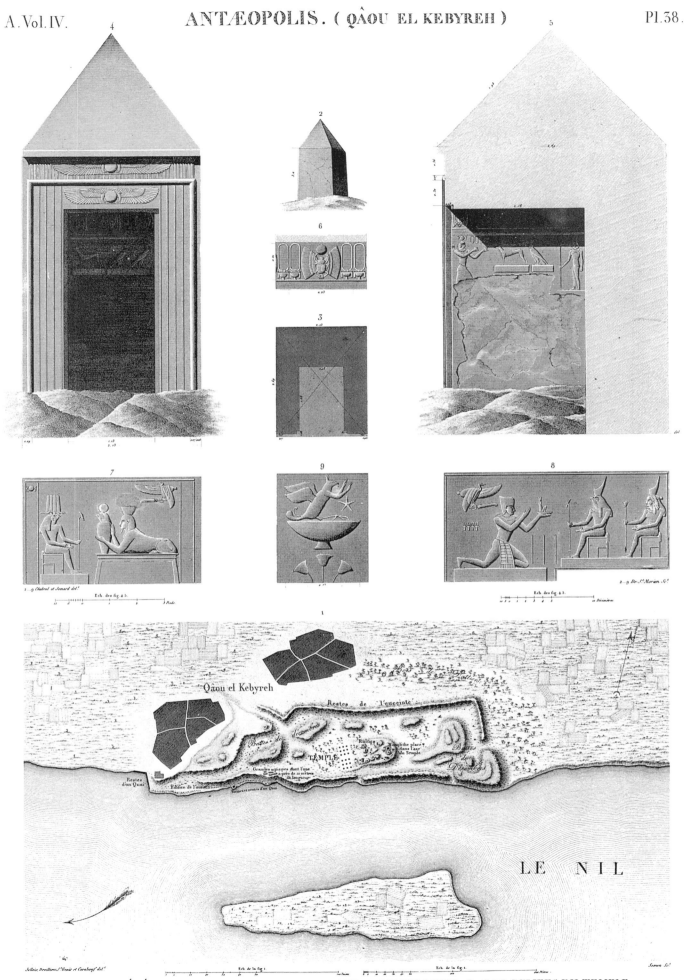

QÂOU EL KEBYREH. (ANTÆOPOLIS.)

VUE DU TEMPLE, PRISE DU CÔTÉ DE L'OUEST.

Rougeron *Sc.*

Chavrin del.

QÂOU EL KEBYRYH, (ANTÆOPOLIS?)

Pl. 40.

VUE DU TEMPLE PRISE DU CÔTÉ DU SUD-OUEST.

QÂOU EL KEBYREII. (ANTÆOPOLIS)

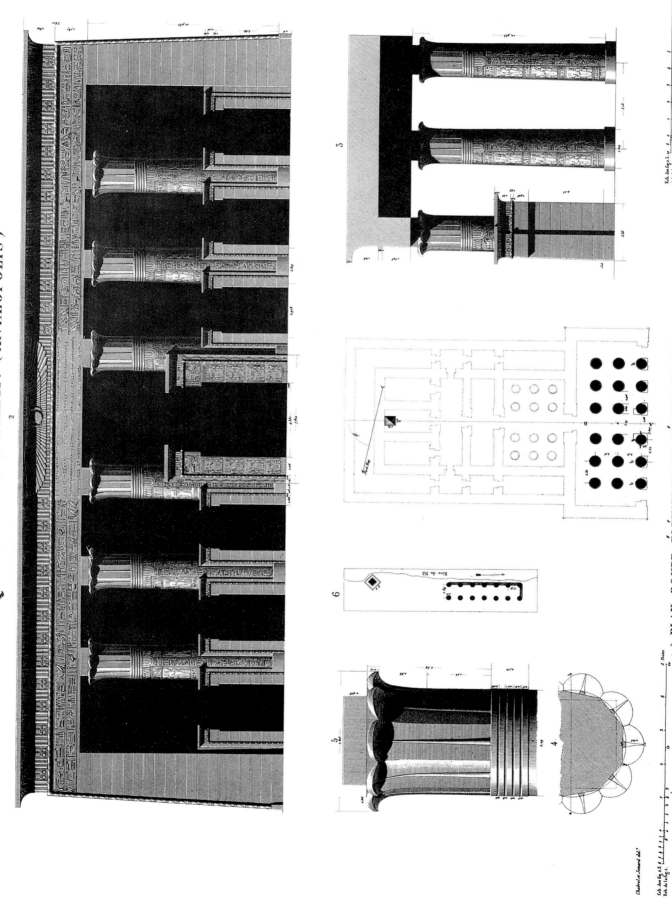

1...5 PLAN, COUPE, ÉLÉVATION ET DÉTAILS DU PORTIQUE DU TEMPLE.
6 PLAN DES RESTES DE L'ÉDIFICE DE L'OUEST.

PL. 42.

QÂOU EL KEBYREH. (ANTÆOPOLIS.)

Bralle sc. fecit

Chabrol et Jomard del.

Papier. R.t

VUE PERSPECTIVE DU TEMPLE.

Pl. 45.

SYOUT. (LYCOPOLIS)

VUE DE LA MONTAGNE ET DES HYPOGÉES PRISE A L'EXTRÉMITÉ DE LA VILLE DU CÔTÉ DE L'OUEST.

Pl. 44.

SYOUT. (LYCOPOLIS)

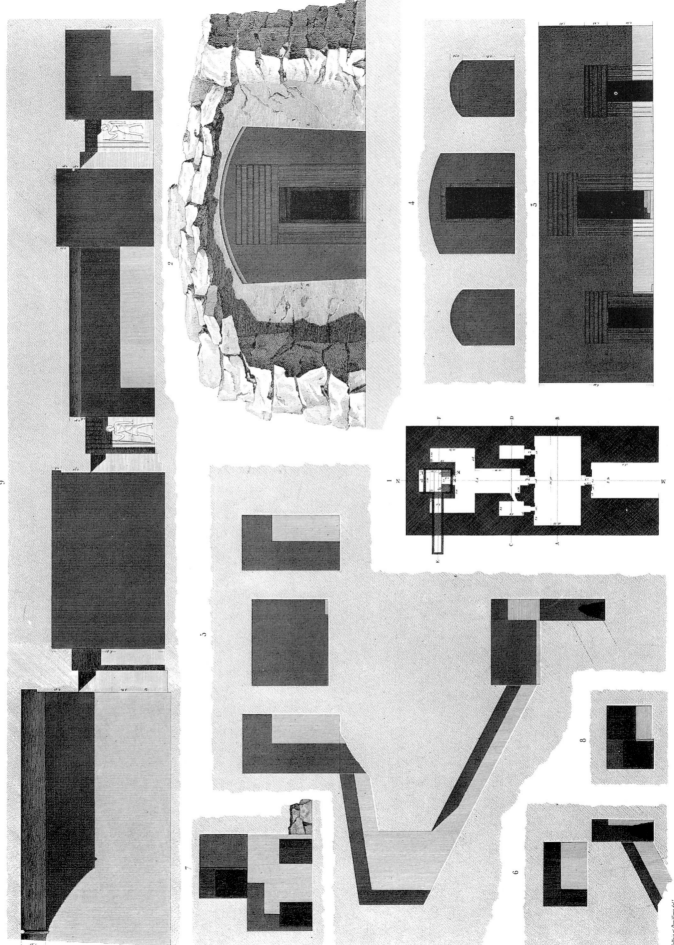

PLAN, COUPES ET ÉLÉVATION DE L'HYPOGÉE PRINCIPAL.

Jollois et Bouillard del.

SYOUT (LYCOPOLIS) Pl. 45.

BAS-RELIEFS RECUEILLIS DANS LA SALLE DU FOND DE L'HYPOGÉE PRINCIPAL.

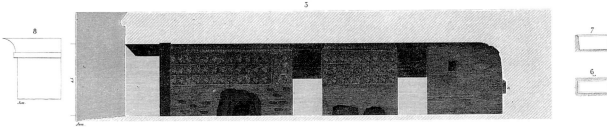

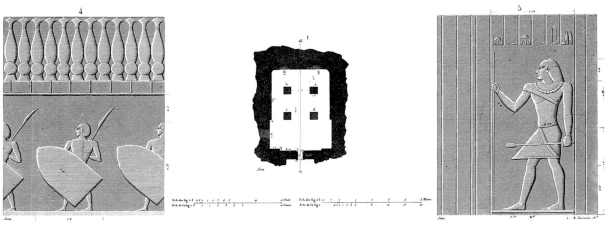

1.....8 PLAN, COUPE, ÉLÉVATION ET DÉTAILS D'UN HYPOGÉE. 9.10 VUES DE DEUX HYPOGÉES.

SYOUT. (LYCOPOLIS)

Pl. 47.

10

11

1

15

12

6

2

7

3

4

5

9

8

Jollois et Devilliers del.

10 13 Smith Sc.

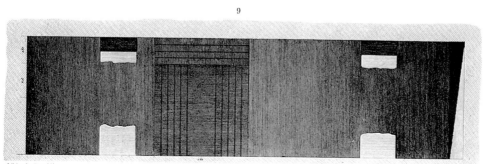

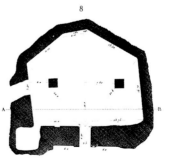

PLANS, COUPES, ÉLÉVATION ET DÉTAILS DE DIVERS HYPOGÉES.

Ech. des fig. 10 et 9.

Ech. des fig. 12 et 15.

Ech. des fig. 1, 2, 3 et 8.

Ech. des fig. 5 et 4.

SYOUT, (LYCOPOLIS)

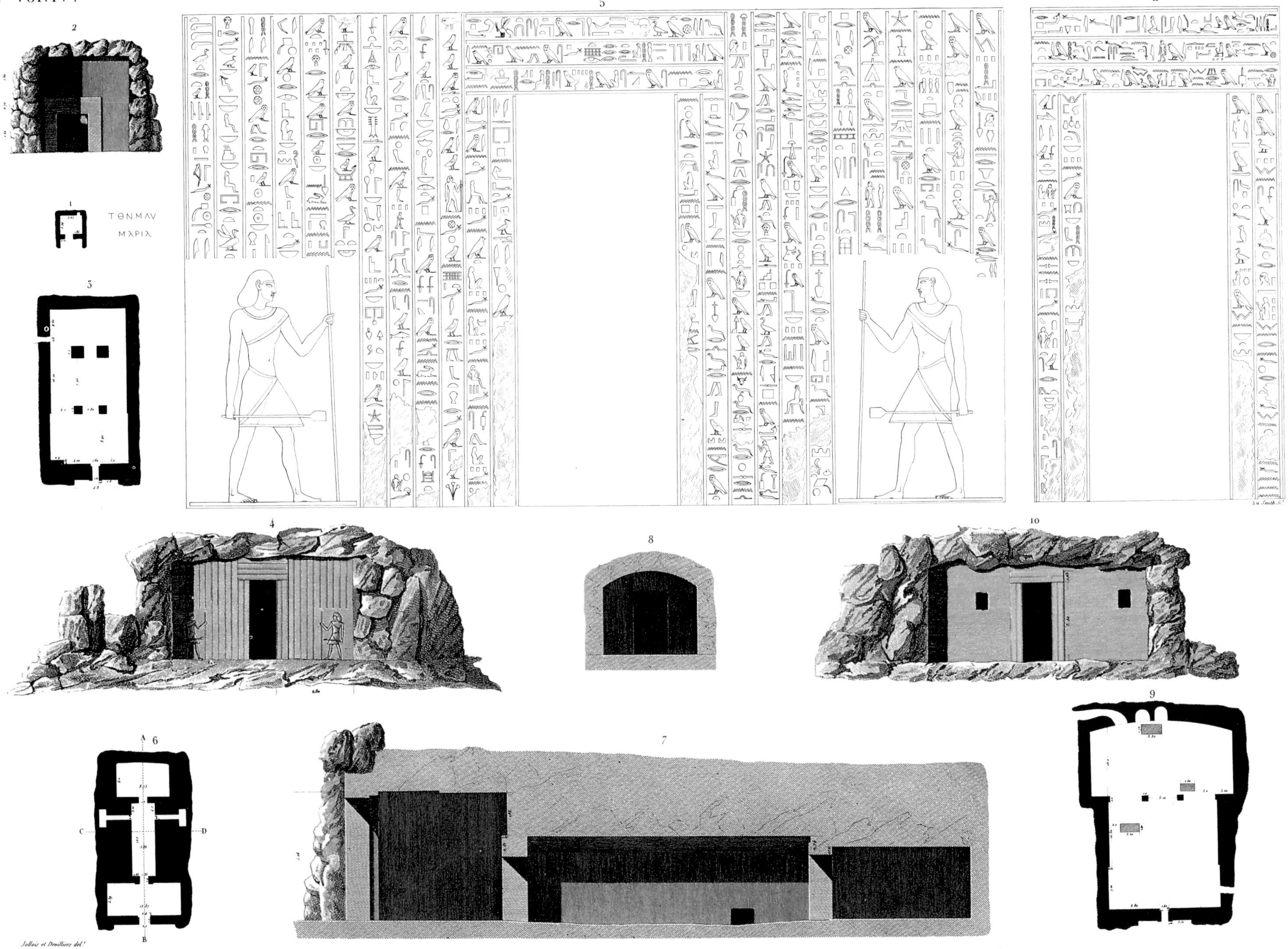

2
1
ΤΘΝΜΑΥ
ΜΑΡΙΑ
3
5
11
4
8
10
6
A
B
C
D
7
9
J.W. Smith Sc.
Jollois et Devilliers del.

PLANS, COUPES, ÉLÉVATIONS ET DÉCORATIONS HIEROGLYPHIQUES DE DIVERS HYPOGÉES.

SYOUT. (LYCOPOLIS)

Pl. 49.

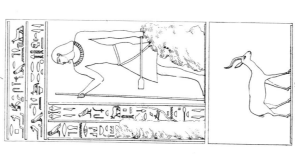

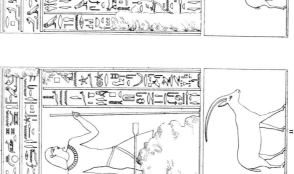

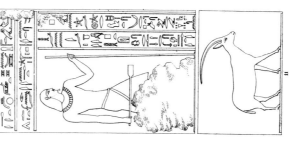

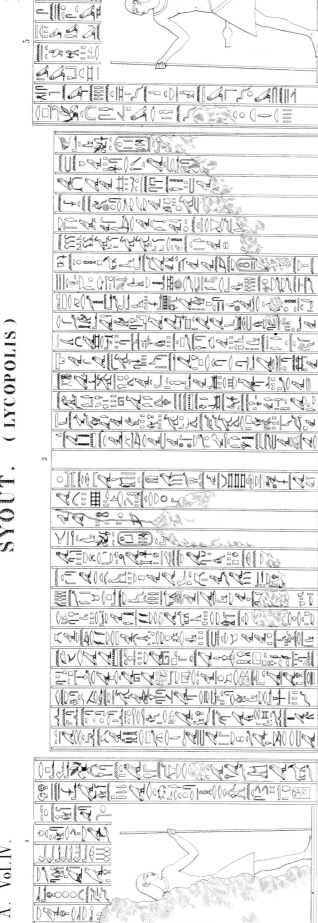

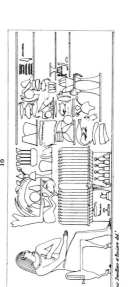

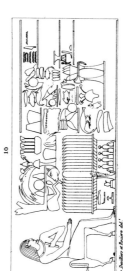

DÉCORATIONS HIÉROGLYPHIQUES ET BAS-RELIEFS RECUEILLIS DANS LES HYPOGÉES.

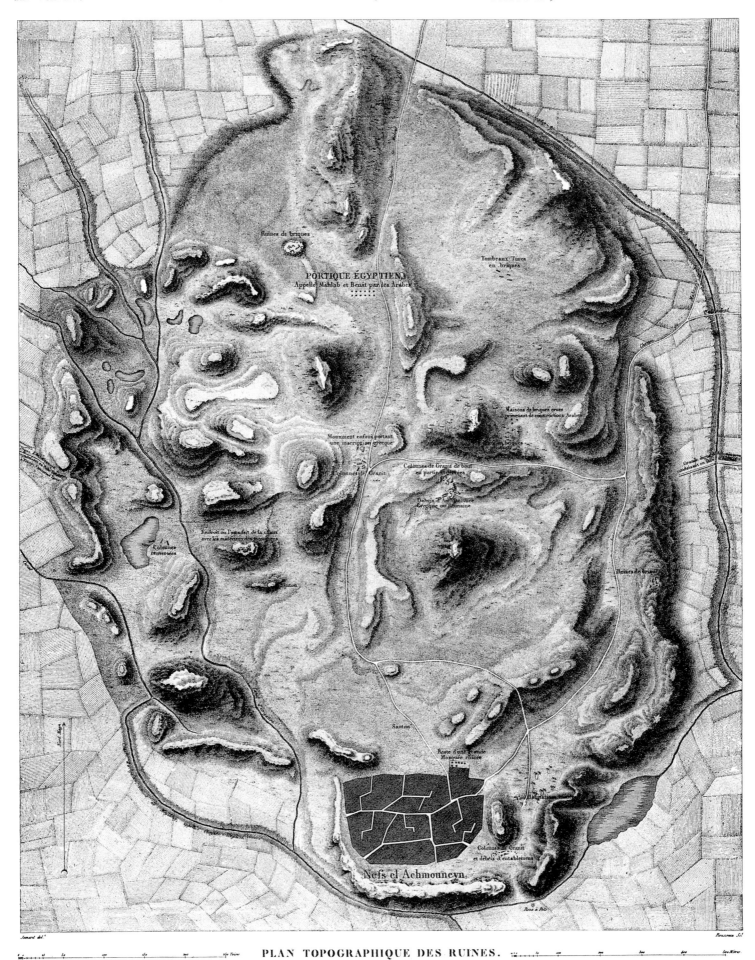

Ruines de briques

PORTIQUE ÉGYPTIEN.
Appellé Mahlab et Benat par les Arabes

Tombeaux Turcs en briques

Maisons de briques crues provenant de constructions Arabes

Monument enfoui portant une inscription grecque

Colonnes de Granit de bout en partie enterrées

Colonnes de Granit

Débris d'architecture Grecque ou Romaine

Endroit où l'on a fait de la chaux avec les matériaux des monuments

Colonnes renversées

Ruines de briques

Santon

Santon

Reste d'une Mosquée ruinée

Nefs el Achmouneyn

Colonnes de Granit et débris d'entablement

Jomard del.

Rousseau Sc.

PLAN TOPOGRAPHIQUE DES RUINES.

Pl. 51.

ACHMOUNEYN. (HERMOPOLIS MAGNA)

Ccole del.'

Baugean Aq.forti.

Dubourt Sc.

VUE DU PORTIQUE PRISE DU CÔTÉ DU MIDI.

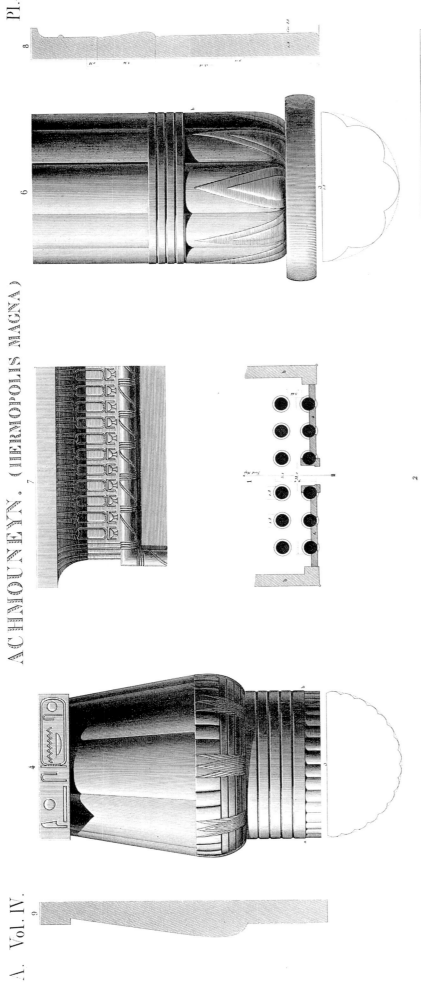

PLAN, ÉLÉVATION ET DÉTAILS DU PORTIQUE DU TEMPLE.

Pl. 55.

Cécile del.

Baville Arc. Dir.

Dubomet Sc.

VUE DU PORTIQUE DU THÉATRE.

Grande plaine lavée par les

Tombeau   Tombeaux   Tombeau

Tombeau avec dôme

Enceinte   en   briques

Ruines

Restes de l'enceinte d'une ville ruinée

briques

Ruines de
constructions en briques

Enceinte   en   briques

Chemin   Porte d'une Rue

PORTE DU NORD

Monticules   couverts   de   débris   de

constructions   de   fragmens   de

colonnes   en   marbré   et

de   poteries   romaines

grande   rue   transversale

Restes d'un cône qui paroît
avoir servi de Tombeau

Porte

COLONNES   TRIOMPHALES   COLONNES   TRIOMPHALES

Rue   principale   bordée   de   Col

DÉDIÉES A   ALEXANDRE SÉVÈRE

Chapiteau

Monticules   couverts   de   Ruines.

Grande butte

ARC DE T

Cheykh
Abadeh

Port

PORTE   DE L'E

Grec

doriqué

de   l'ordre   doriqué

Colonnes   de

rue   d'une

bordée   de   Colonnes

Grande   rue   d'Autre

Chabrol et Jomard del.

HIPPODROME
ou CIRQUE

Tombeau de
Cheikh Abâdeh

Enceinte en briques

Monticules

couverts de ruines

de

décombres

Enceinte en briques

PORTIQUE
D'ORDRE
CORINTHIEN

l'ordre dorique Grec

Porte

RESTES D'UN AMPHITHÉÂTRE

LE NIL

E L'ENCEINTE DE LA VILLE.

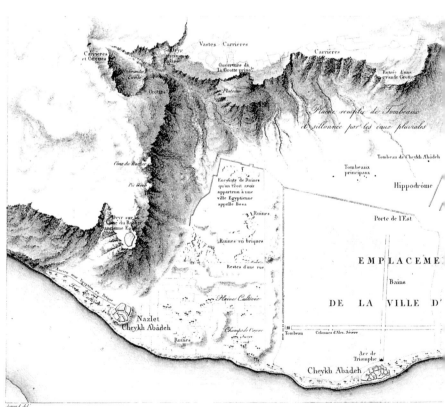

Pl. 54.

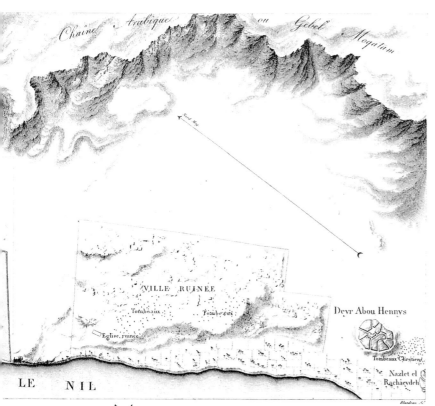

LE NIL

Deyr Abou Hennys

Tombeaux Girguent

Nazlet el
Rachaydeh

VILLE, PRISE DU CÔTÉ DU SUD-OUEST.

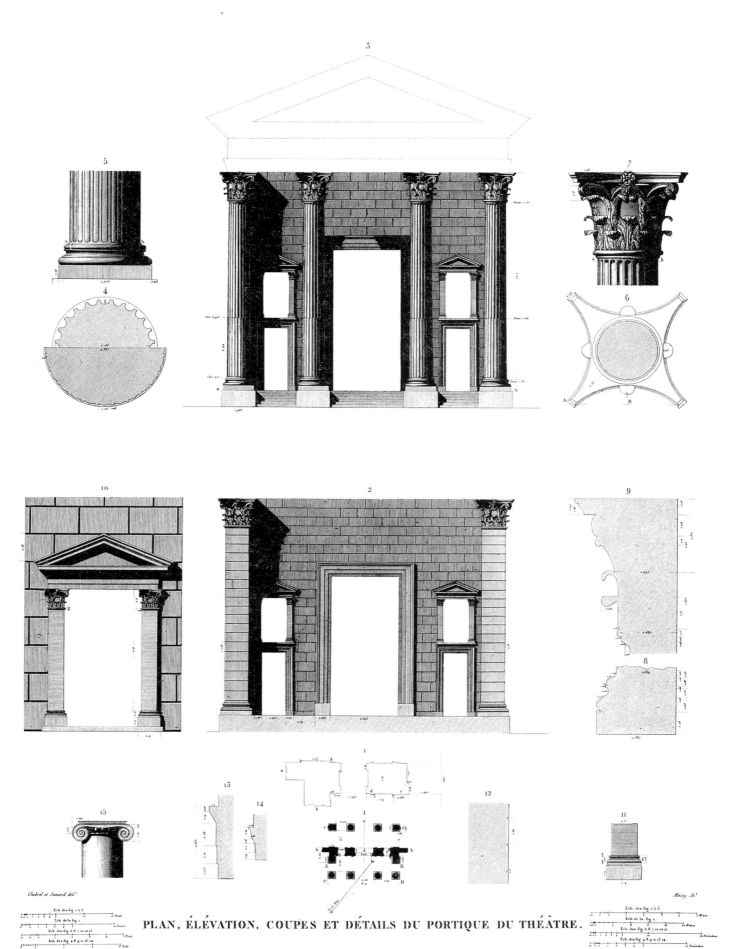

PLAN, ÉLÉVATION, COUPES ET DÉTAILS DU PORTIQUE DU THÉÂTRE.

Pl. 57.

ANTINOÉ.

Cécile del.

Pichenot. Sc.

VUE DE L'ARC DE TRIOMPHE.

Pl. 58.

ANTINOË.

PLAN, ÉLÉVATION, COUPES ET DÉTAILS DE L'ARC DE TRIOMPHE.

Chabrol et Jomard del.

Mutoy R.t

1

3

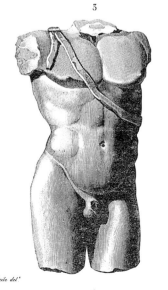

2

4

1.2 VUE ET DÉTAILS DE LA COLONNE D'ALEXANDRE SÉVÈRE.   3.4 FRAGMENT D'UNE STATUE D'ANTINOÜS.

ANTINOË

Pl. 60.

1.....9 ÉLÉVATION ET DÉTAILS DE LA COLONNE D'ALEXANDRE SÉVÈRE. 10...15 DÉTAILS D'ARCHITECTURE DE DIVERS MONUMENS. 16.17 PLAN ET COUPE DE L'HIPPODROME.

18 PLAN D'UNE PARTIE DE LA RUE PRINCIPALE.

ANTINOË.

1...20 PLANS, ÉLÉVATIONS ET DÉTAILS DE DIVERS PORTIQUES. 21..24 PLAN ET DÉTAIL D'UN BATIMENT DE BAINS.

25..28 COLONNADE DE LA RUE PRINCIPALE.

Pl. 62.

HEPTANOMIDE.

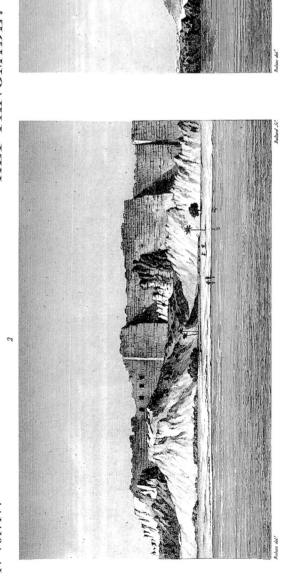

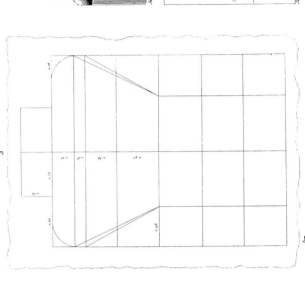

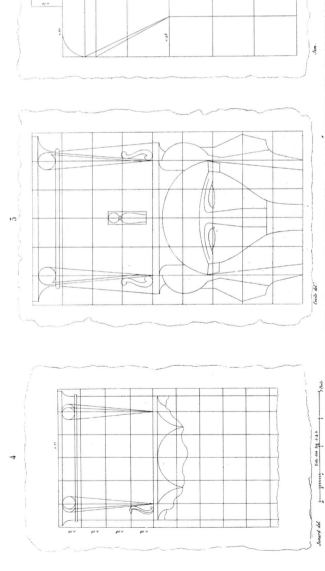

1.2 VUES DE GEBEL ABOU FEDAH ET DES ENVIRONS. 3.4.5 ÉPURES DE CHAPITEAUX TRACÉES DANS LES HYPOGÉES DE GEBEL ABOU FEDAH.
6.7.8 PLANS ET DÉTAILS DE GEBEL CHEYKII EL HARYDY.

LE NIL

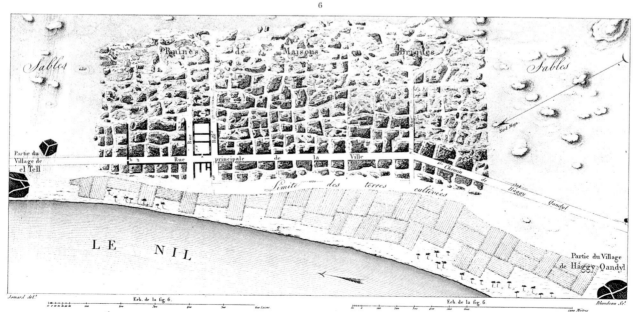

1.3.4.5 **VUE ET DÉTAILS DES RUINES D'EL DEYR.** 2 **PLAN D'UN ÉDIFICE RUINÉ À EL DEYR.** 6...10 **PLAN GÉNÉRAL**
D'UNE ANCIENNE VILLE ET DÉTAILS D'UNE PORTE EN BRIQUES, À EL TELL.

HEPTANOMIDE. BENY-HASAN.

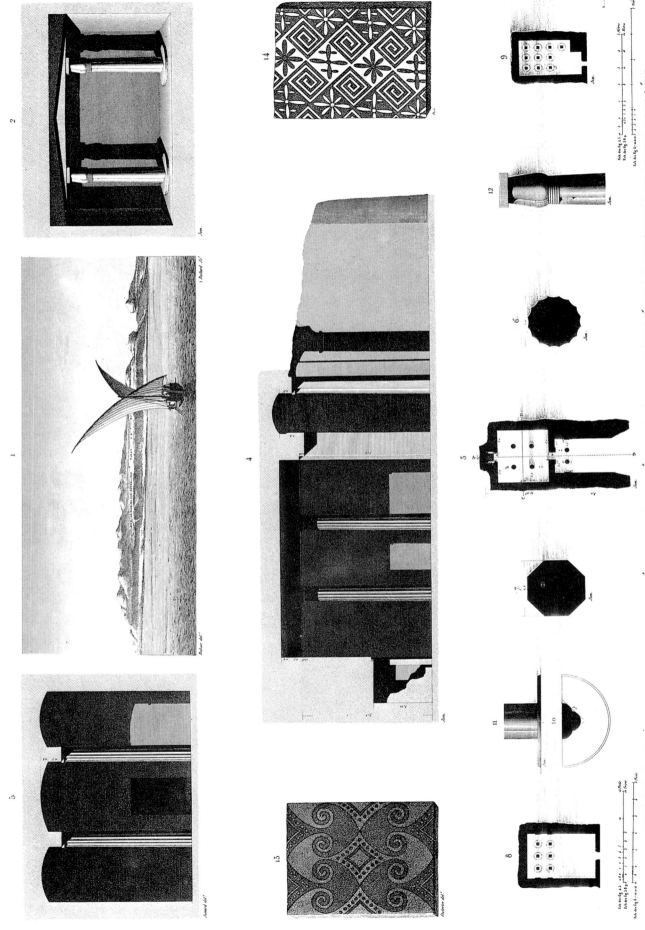

1. 2 VUES DES HYPOGÉES. 3...7 PLAN, COUPES ET DÉTAILS DE L'HYPOGÉE PRINCIPAL. 8...14 PLANS, DÉTAILS ET PEINTURES DE DIVERS HYPOGÉES.

1 VUE D'UNE ANCIENNE CARRIERE APPELLÉE ESTABL ANTAR. 2.4 BAS-RELIEFS ET PEINTURES DE DIVERS HYPOGÉES.

1

2

3

4

5

6

7

8

9

10

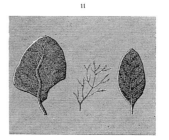

11

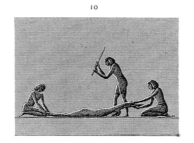

12

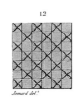

13

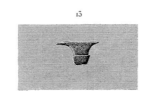

14

15

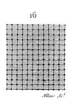

16

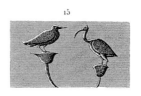

Jomard del.

Allais Sc.

BAS-RELIEFS ET PEINTURES DE DIVERS HYPOGÉES.

1 PLAN DE CUSÆ. 2...6 ANTIQUITÉS DE MEYLÀOUY ET DES ENVIRONS. 7...10 DEYR AU NORD D'ANTINOÉ. 11.12.13 DEYR ABOU-FÂNEH.
14...20 PLAN ET DÉTAILS DE TEHNÉ. 21 VUE D'OUÀDY EL TEYR.

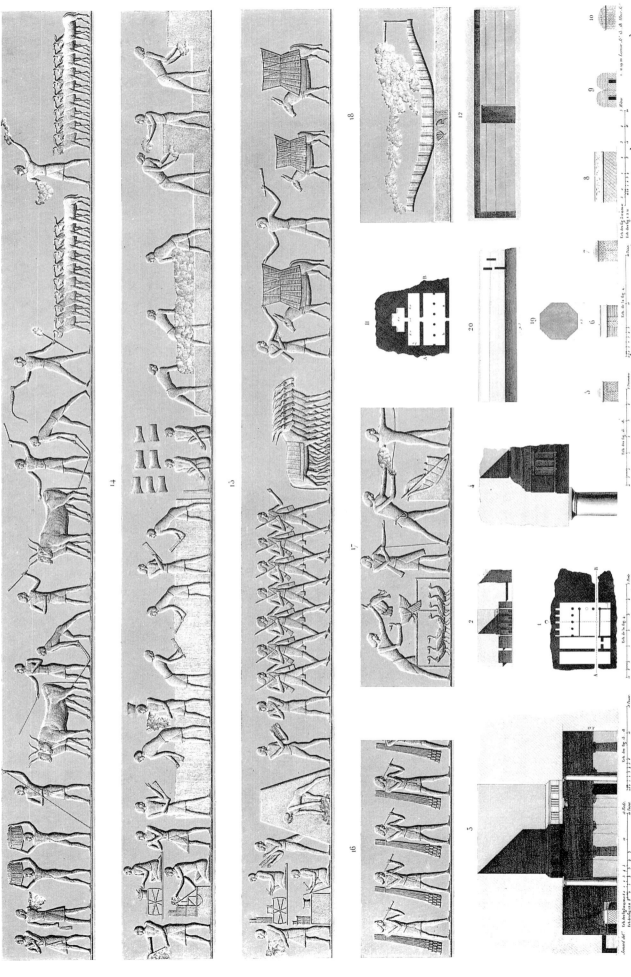

ÆGYPTIACA.

1...10 PLANS ET DÉTAILS D'UN HYPOGÉE D'ARCHITECTURE DORIQUE, SITUÉ À SAOUÀDEH.   11...19 PLAN, BAS-RELIEFS ET DÉTAILS D'UN HYPOGÉE ET D'UNE CARRIÈRE AU MIDI DE SAOUÀDEH.

VUES D'UN TEMPLE ÉGYPTIEN, SITUÉ VERS L'EXTRÉMITÉ OCCIDENTALE

DU LAC APPELÉ BIRKET EL QEROUN.

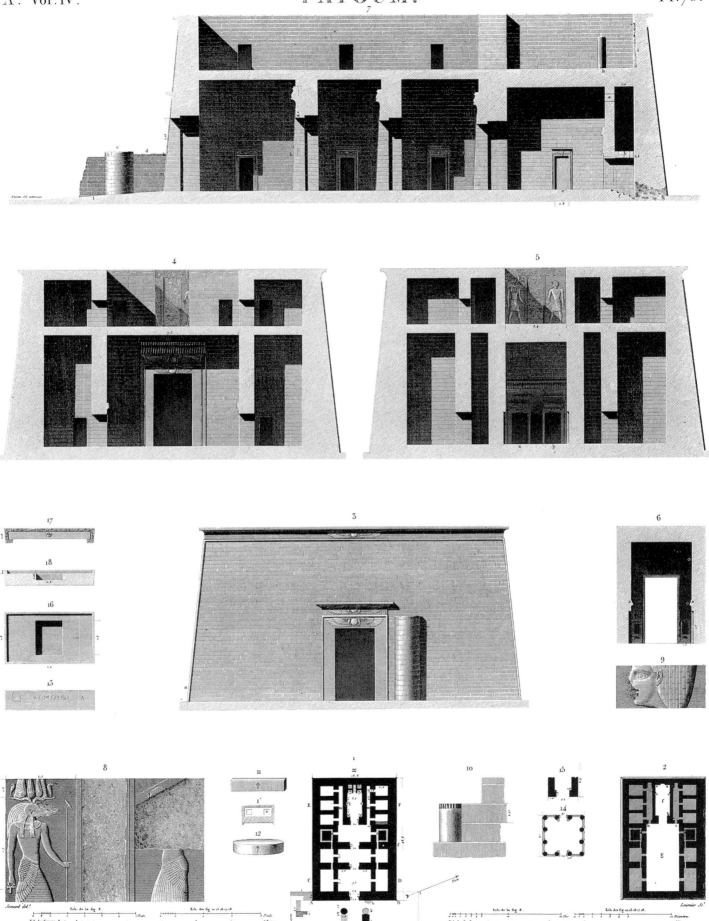

1.....13 PLANS, ÉLÉVATION, COUPES ET DÉTAILS D'UN TEMPLE ÉGYPTIEN, SITUÉ VERS L'EXTRÉMITÉ OCCIDENTALE DU LAC
APPELÉ BIRKET EL QEROUN. 14....18 PLANS ET DÉTAILS DE PLUSIEURS ANTIQUITÉS DES ENVIRONS.

Pl. 71.

FAYOUM.

VUE ET DÉTAILS DE L'OBÉLISQUE DE BEGYG.

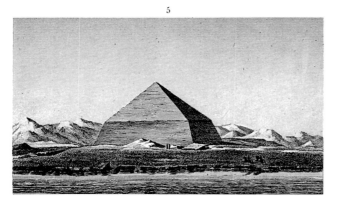

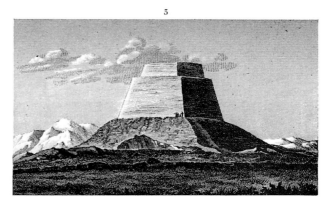

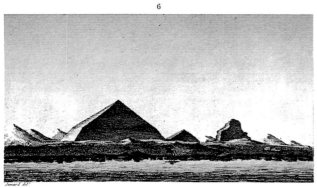

1. 2 VUES DE DEUX PYRAMIDES EN BRIQUES A L'EST DU FAYOUM. 3 PYRAMIDE DE MEYDOUNEH.
4 PYRAMIDES D'EL METANYEH. 5.6 PYRAMIDES DE SAQQARAH.

MEMPHIS ET ENVIRONS.

Pl. 1.

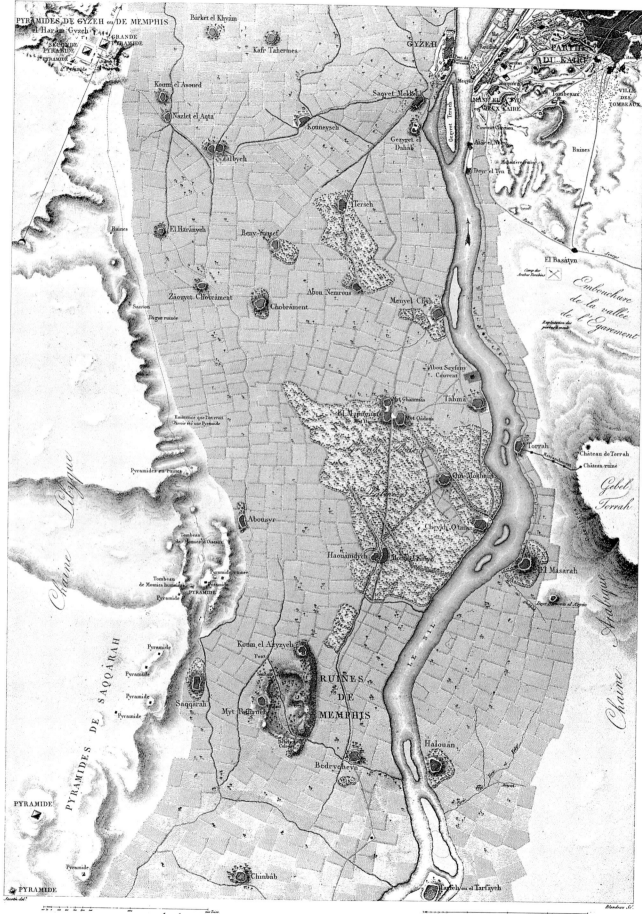

PLAN GÉNÉRAL DE L'EMPLACEMENT DE MEMPHIS ET DES ENVIRONS.

1

2

3

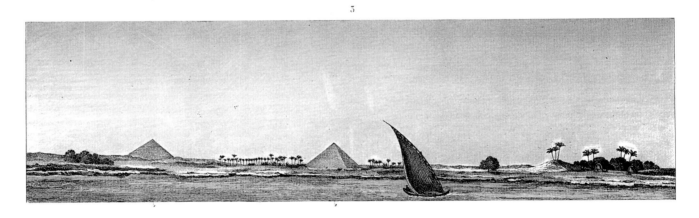

4

VUES DES PYRAMIDES DE SAQQÀRAH ET DES ENVIRONS.

Dutertre del.

Paris lig. Fol.

Delignon Sc.

VUE DES RUINES, PRISE DU SUD-EST.

MEMPHIS ET ENVIRONS.

1 POIGNET D'UN COLOSSE À MEMPHIS. 2...7 PLAN, COUPE ET DÉTAILS D'UN TOMBEAU DE MOMIES D'OISEAUX À SAQQARAH. 8 VUE DES CARRIÈRES DE TORRAH. 9 VUE D'UN MUR ANTIQUE.

MEMPHIS ET ENVIRONS.

Pl. 5.

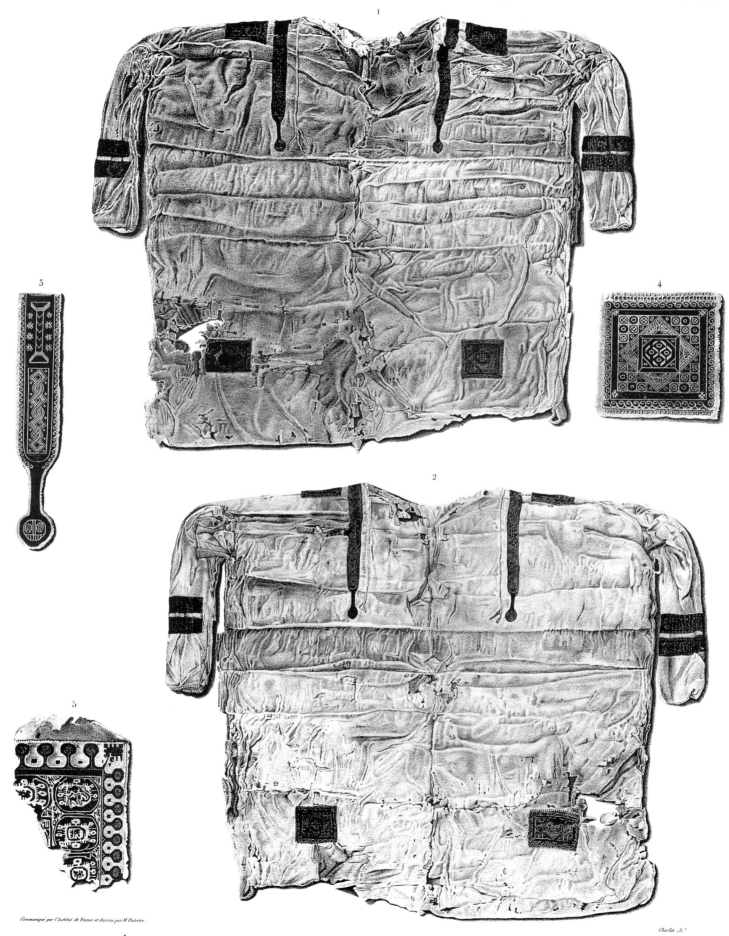

Communiqué par l'Institut de France et dessiné par M.Dulostre.

Charlin Sc.t

DÉTAILS D'UNE TUNIQUE TROUVÉE DANS UN DES TOMBEAUX DE SAQQÀRAH.

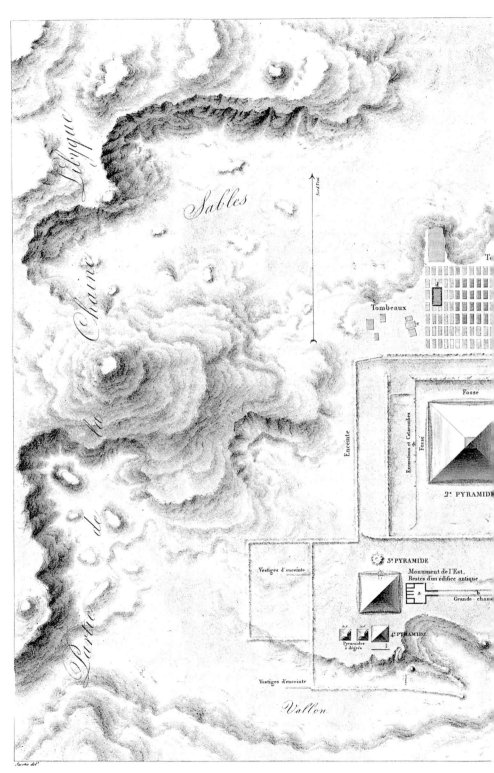

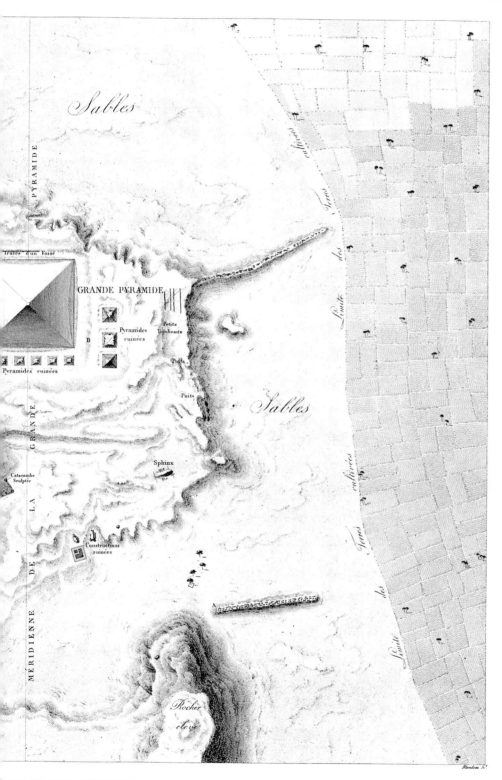

Sables

PYRAMIDE

Tracés d'un Fossé

GRANDE PYRAMIDE

B   Pyramides ruinées

Petits Tombeaux

Pyramides ruinées

Puits

Puits

Sables

GRANDE

Catacombe Sculptée

LA

Sphinx

DE

Constructions ruinées

MÉRIDIENNE

Rocher élevé

cultivées

Terres   des   Limite

Terres cultivées

Limite   des

Limite

DES ET DES ENVIRONS.

VUE GÉNÉRALE DI

PRISE DU SUD-EST.

Ballard. G.

SPHINX, PRISE AU SOLEIL COUCHANT.

Pl. 9.

PYRAMIDES DE MEMPHIS.

Cécile del.

Schroeder sc.

VUE DE L'ENTRÉE DE LA GRANDE PYRAMIDE, PRISE AU SOLEIL LEVANT.

PYRAMIDES DE MEMPHIS.

VUE DE LA SECONDE PYRAMIDE, PRISE DU COTÉ DU LEVANT.

Pl. ii.

PYRAMIDES DE MEMPHIS.

VUE DU SPHINX ET DE LA GRANDE PYRAMIDE, PRISE DU SUD-EST.

Pl. 12.

PYRAMIDES DE MEMPHIS.

VUE DU SPHINX ET DE LA SECONDE PYRAMIDE, PRISE DU LEVANT.

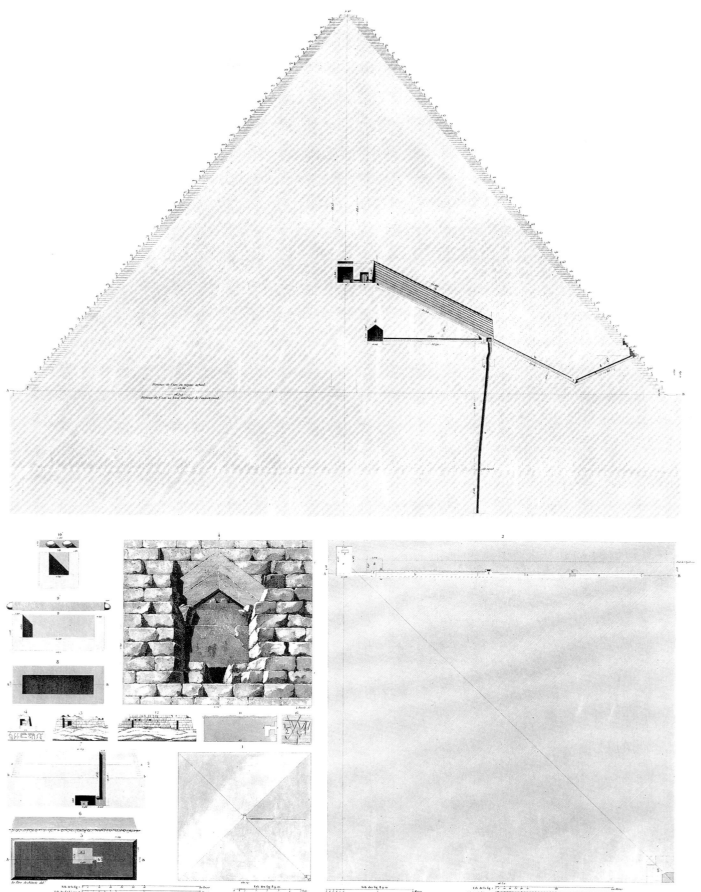

1...4 PLANS, COUPE ET ENTRÉE DE LA GRANDE PYRAMIDE. 5...10 PLAN, ÉLÉVATION, COUPE ET DÉTAILS D'UN TOMBEAU PRINCIPAL ET DE SON SARCOPHAGE.

11...13 DÉTAILS DES ENVIRONS.

1.2 PLAN ET ÉLÉVATION DE L'ANGLE NORD - EST DE LA GRANDE PYRAMIDE 3.

PES DE L'ENTRÉE, ET DÉTAILS DU SARCOPHAGE DE LA SALLE SUPÉRIEURE.

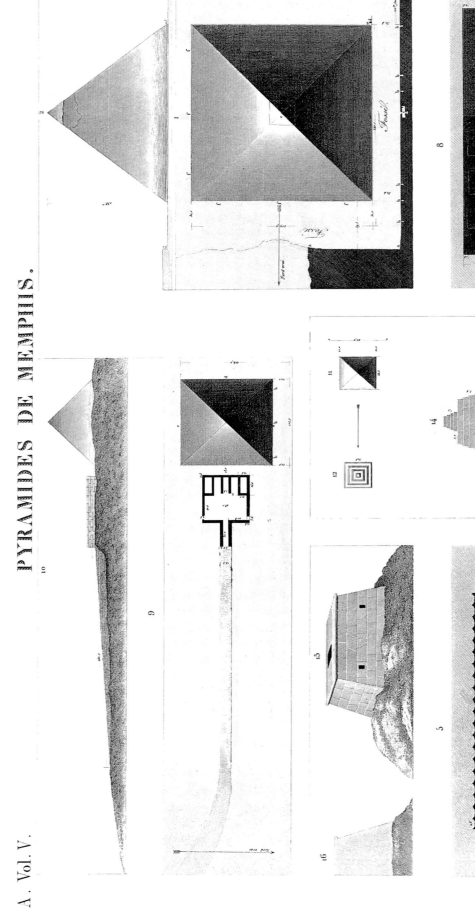

1....8 PLAN ET ÉLÉVATION DE LA 2.ᵉ PYRAMIDE, PLANS ET COUPES D'UN HYPOGÉE À L'OUEST ET D'UN AUTRE À L'EST, 9.10 PLAN ET ÉLÉVATION DE LA 3.ᵉ PYRAMIDE, DE L'ÉDIFICE
DE L'EST ET D'UNE GRANDE CHAUSSÉE. 11.14 PLANS ET ÉLÉVATION DE LA 4.ᵉ PYRAMIDE ET D'UNE PYRAMIDE À DÉGRÉS. 15.16 TOMBEAU PYRAMIDAL À L'OUEST DE LA GRANDE PYRAMIDE.

PYRAMIDES DE MEMPHIS.

Pl. 17.

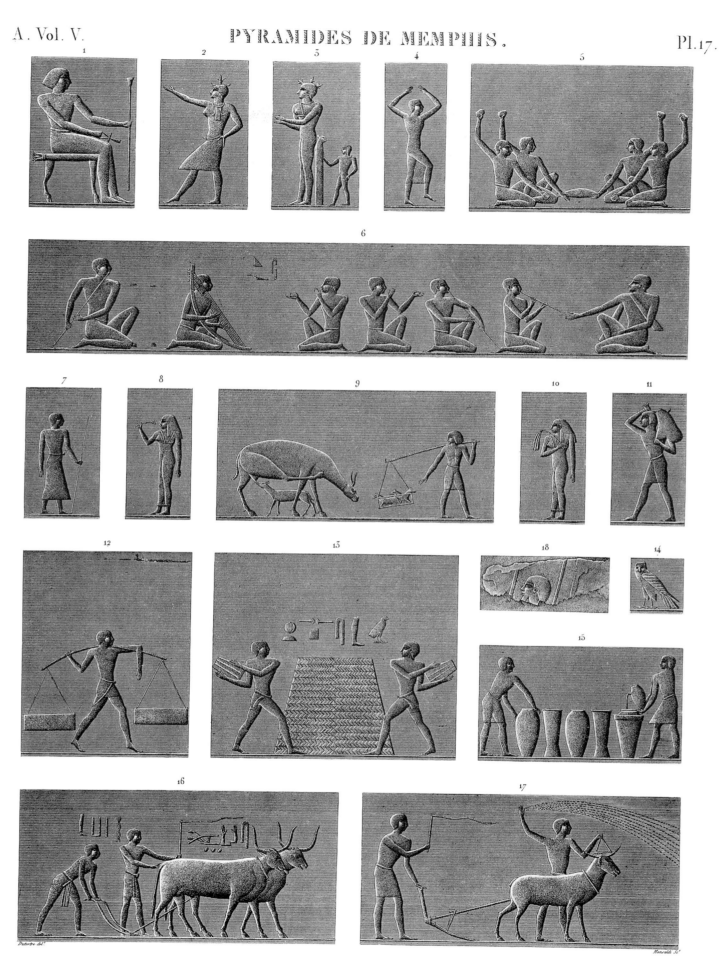

BAS-RELIEFS ET FRAGMENT D'HIÉROGLYPHES SCULPTÉS DANS LES TOMBEAUX SITUÉS À L'EST DE LA SECONDE PYRAMIDE.

PYRAMIDES DE MEMPHIS.

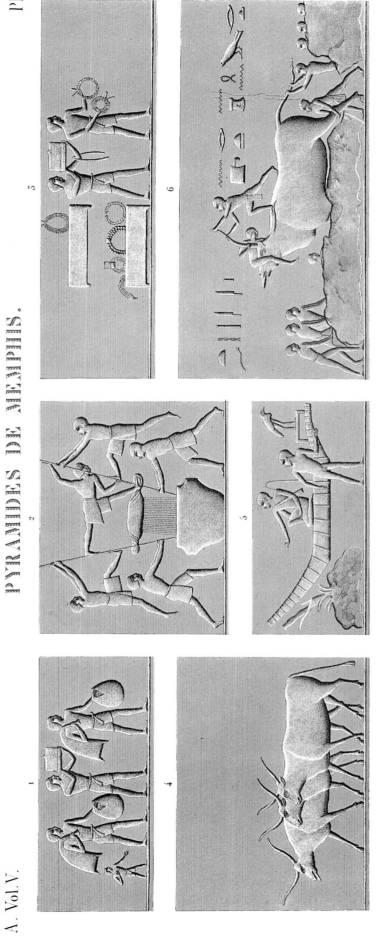

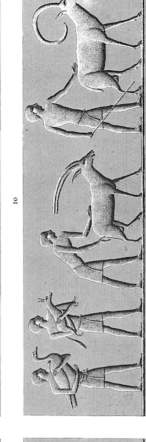

BAS RELIEFS SCULPTÉS DANS LES TOMBEAUX SITUÉS A L'EST DE LA SECONDE PYRAMIDE.

VALLÉE DU NIL ET LAC MARÉOTIS.

Pl.19.

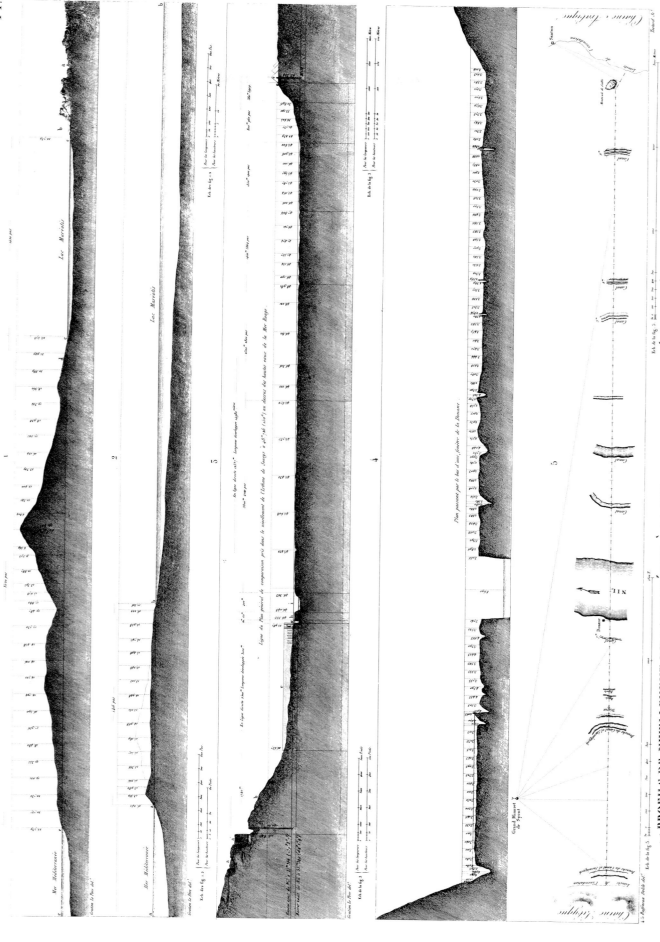

1.2 PROFILS DE NIVELLEMENT DU LAC MARÉOTIS À LA MER. 3 PROFIL DE LA VALLÉE DU NIL À LA HAUTEUR DES PYRAMIDES.

4.5 PLAN ET PROFILS DE LA VALLÉE DU NIL À SYOUT OU LYCOPOLIS.

2

Laneret et Dubois Aymé del.   Decourroux aq. fort.

3   4   5

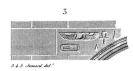   

J. L. S. Jomard del.   J. L. S. Smith sc.

1

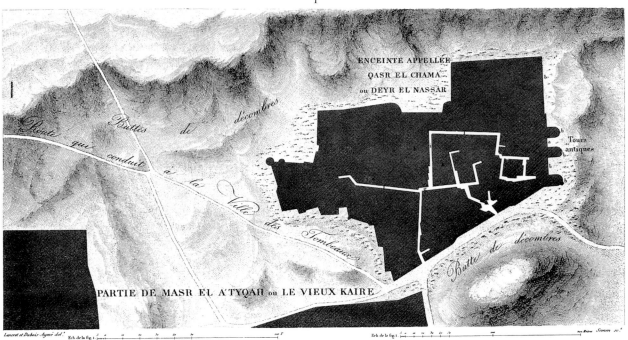

ENCEINTE APPELLÉE
QASR EL CHAMA
ou DEYR EL NASSAR

Tours
antiques

PARTIE DE MASR EL A'TYQAH ou LE VIEUX KAIRE

Laneret et Dubois Aymé del.   Ech. de la fig. 1   Ech. de la fig. 1   Semen sc.

PLAN, VUE ET DÉTAILS D'UN ÉDIFICE DE CONSTRUCTION ROMAINE.

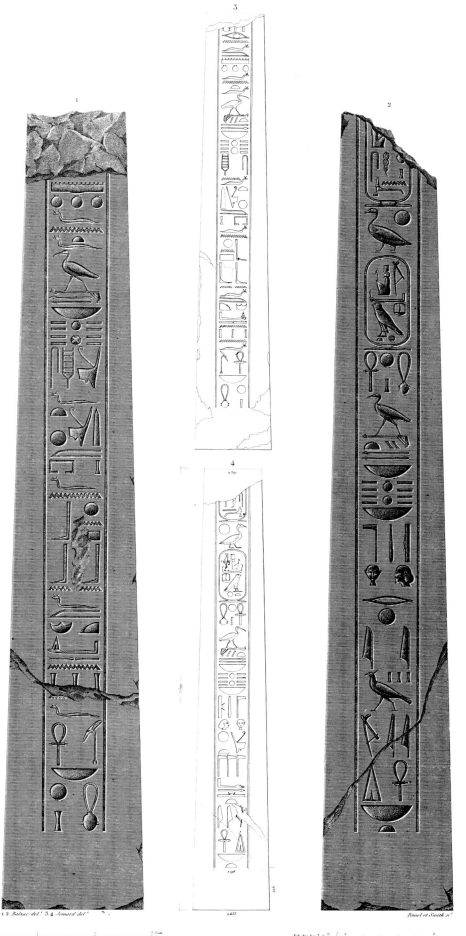

DÉTAILS DES QUATRE FACES D'UN OBÉLISQUE TROUVÉ AU KAIRE.

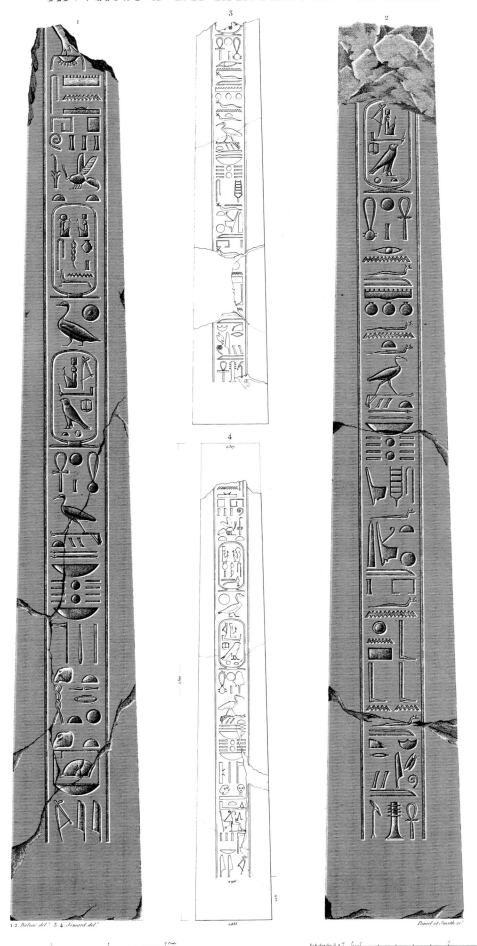

DÉTAILS DES QUATRE FACES D'UN OBÉLISQUE TROUVÉ AU KAIRE.

ENVIRONS DE BABYLONE. (LE KAIRE)

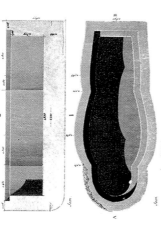

SARCOPHAGE EN FORME DE MOMIE, TROUVÉ SUR LE BORD DU NIL À BOULÂQ.

1

8

6

10

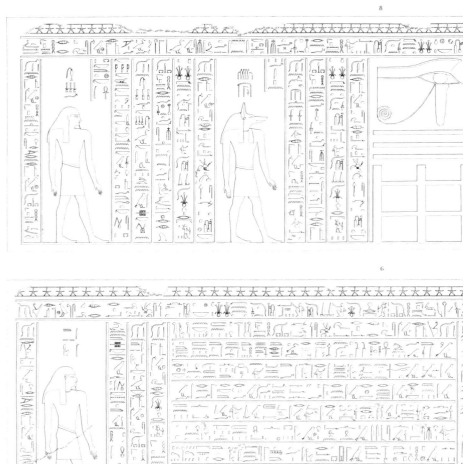

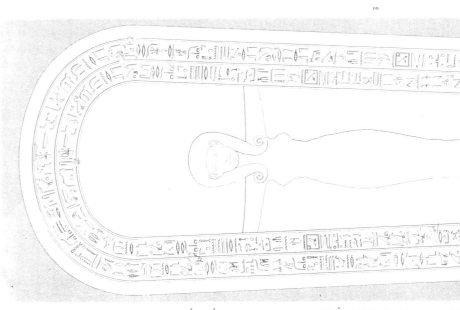

Semand del.

1. FRAGMENT TROUVÉ PRÈS DE LA PORTE DU CHÂTEAU DU KAIRE. 2..10 P
TROUVÉ À QALA'T EL K

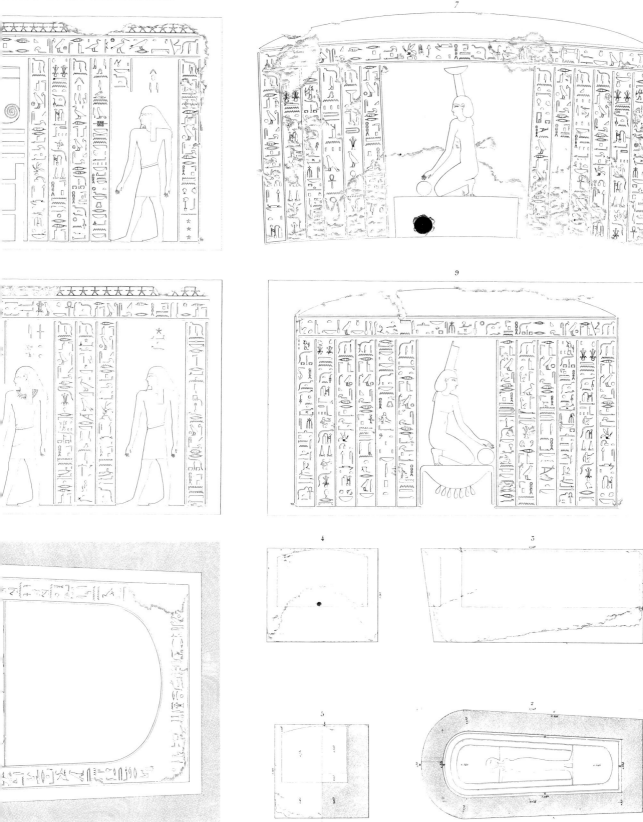

ÉLÉVATIONS ET SCULPTURES EXTÉRIEURES D'UN SARCOPHAGE EN GRANIT,
A MOSQUÉE DE TOULOUN.

1

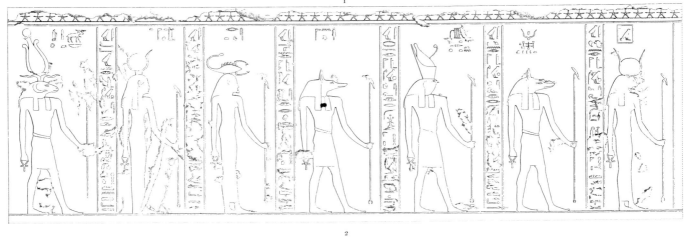

2

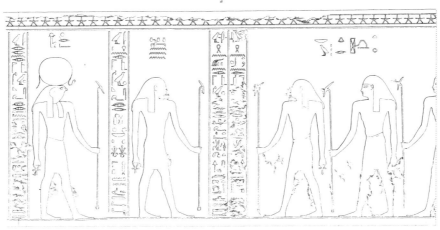

3

4

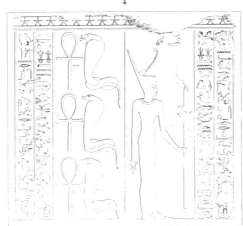

INTÉRIEUR D'UN SARCOPHAGE EN GRANIT, TROUVÉ À QALA'T EL KABCH, SOUS LA MOSQUÉE DE TOULOUN.

Pl. 26

1 PLAN DES RUINES ET DE L'ENCEINTE DE LA VILLE.
2.3.4 DÉTAILS DE L'OBÉLISQUE.

LE

A
B
C
D
E
F
G
H
I
K
L
VII
V
VI
Gâma el Hakym
Gâma el Dâher
Birket el Rotly
Ouasât el Ezbekyeh
Place Ezbekyeh
Terres labourables
Birket Faouâleh
Bâb el Hadyd
Porte de fer
Qantarat el Lymoun
Soultâny

PLAN PA

Pl. 26

LA VILLE.

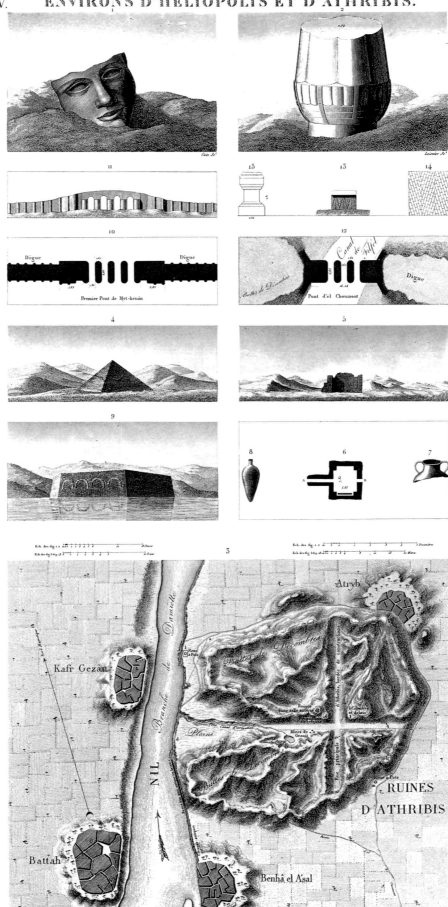

1.2.15 FRAGMENS TROUVÉS À QELYOUB 3.....9 PLAN, VUES ET DÉTAILS D'ATHRIBIS.
10..14 PONTS CONSTRUITS SUR DES FONDATIONS ROMAINES.

TANIS. (SÀN)

Pl. 28.

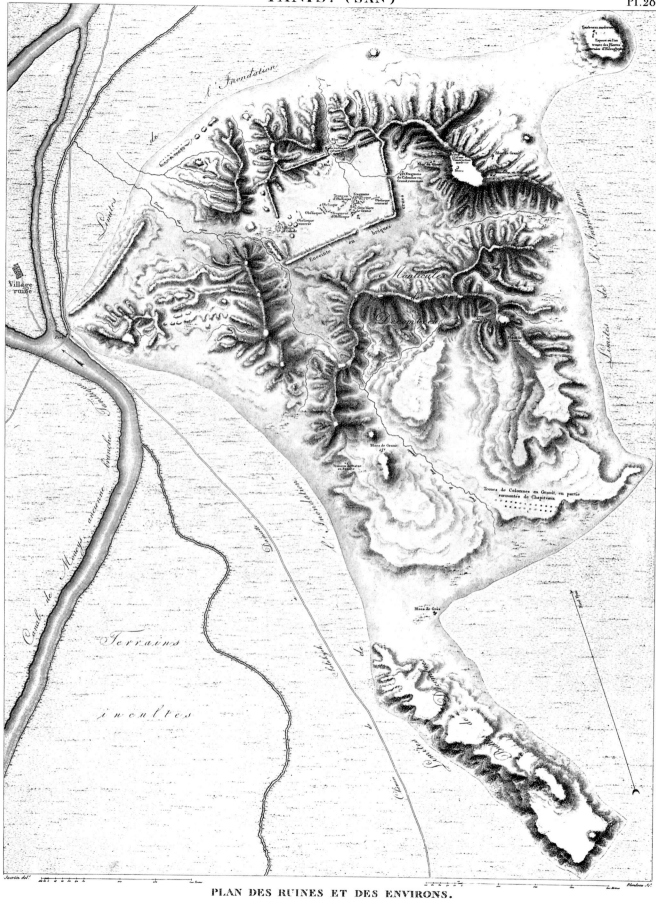

PLAN DES RUINES ET DES ENVIRONS.

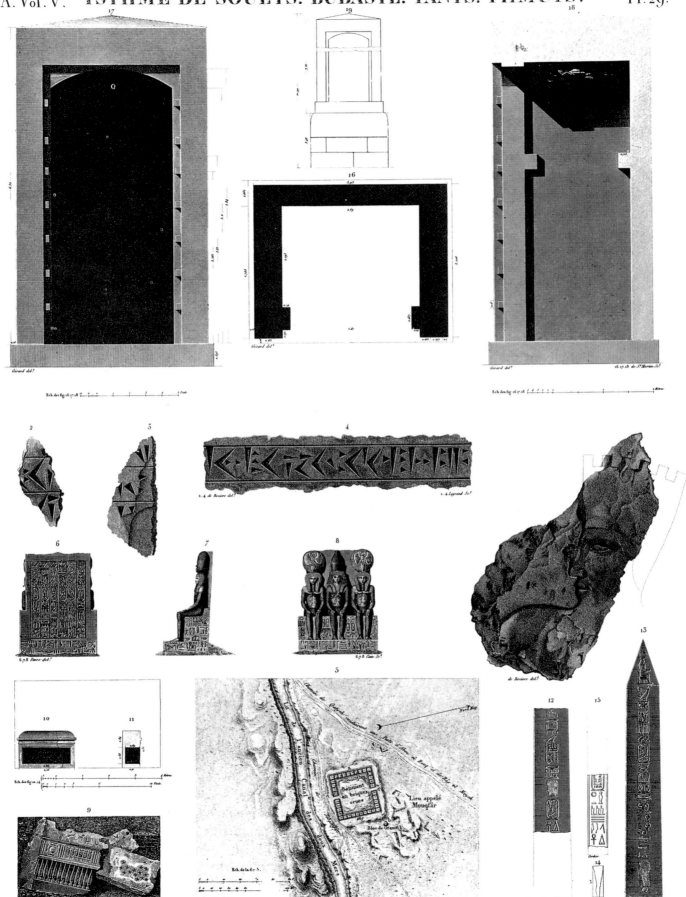

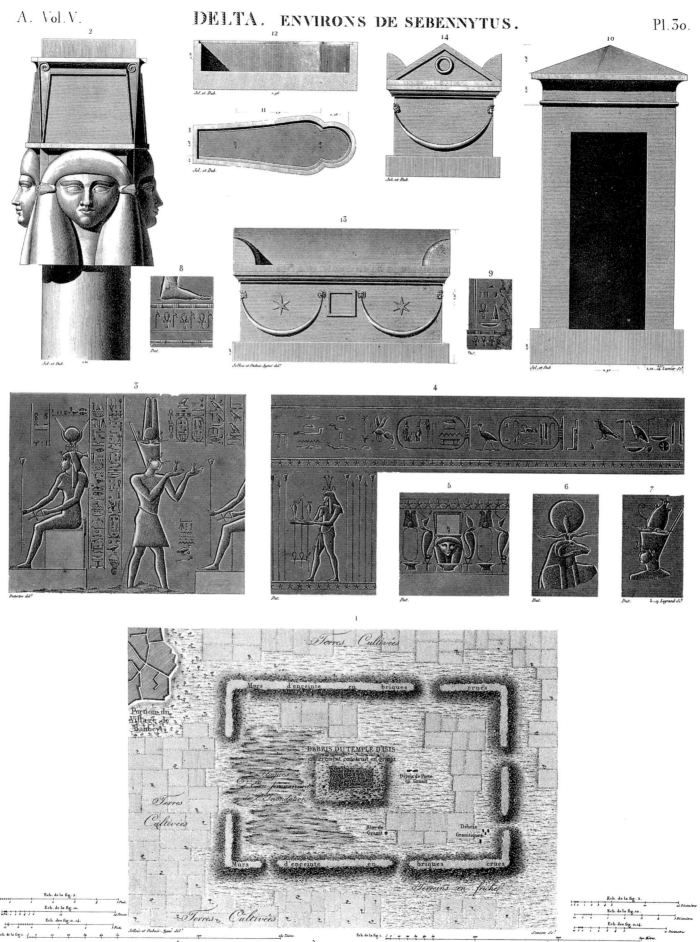

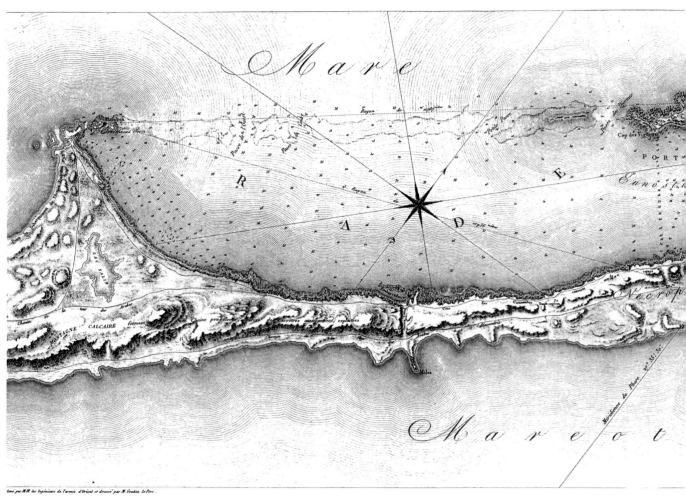

Mediterraneum

Lacus

LAC MADYEH

VILLE ET ENVIRONS D'ALEXANDRIE.

Pl. 52.

ALEXANDRIE.

V.E DE L'OBÉLISQUE APPELLÉ AIGUILLE DE CLÉOPATRE ET DE LA TOUR DITE DES ROMAINS, PRISE DU SUD-OUEST.

1.2 ÉLÉVATIONS DE DEUX FACES DE L'OBÉLISQUE APPELÉ AIGUILLE DE CLÉOPATRE.
5.5. ÉLÉVATIONS DE DEUX FACES DE L'OBÉLISQUE RENVERSÉ.

PL.34.

ALEXANDRIE.

A. Vol. V.

VUE PROFILS ET DÉTAILS DE LA GRANDE COLONNE APPELÉE COMMUNÉMENT COLONNE DE POMPÉE.

ALEXANDRIE.

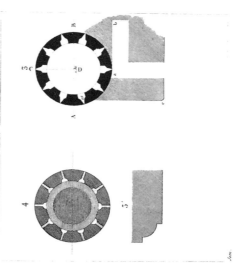

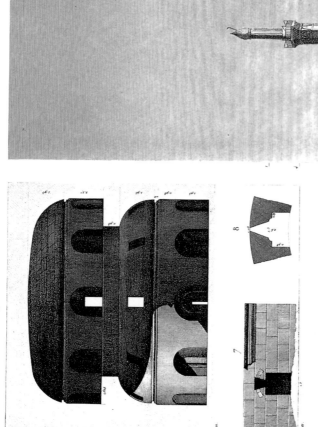

1 VUE DE TROIS COLONNES EN GRANIT, SITUÉES AU SUD DE L'ANCIENNE BASILIQUE VULGAIREMENT NOMMÉE MOSQUÉE DE St. ATHANASE. 2...9 VUE INTÉRIEURE,

PLANS, COUPES ET DÉTAILS D'UNE TOUR ANTIQUE, PLACÉE AU NORD DES DEUX OBÉLISQUES, ET CONNUE SOUS LE NOM DE TOUR DES ROMAINS.

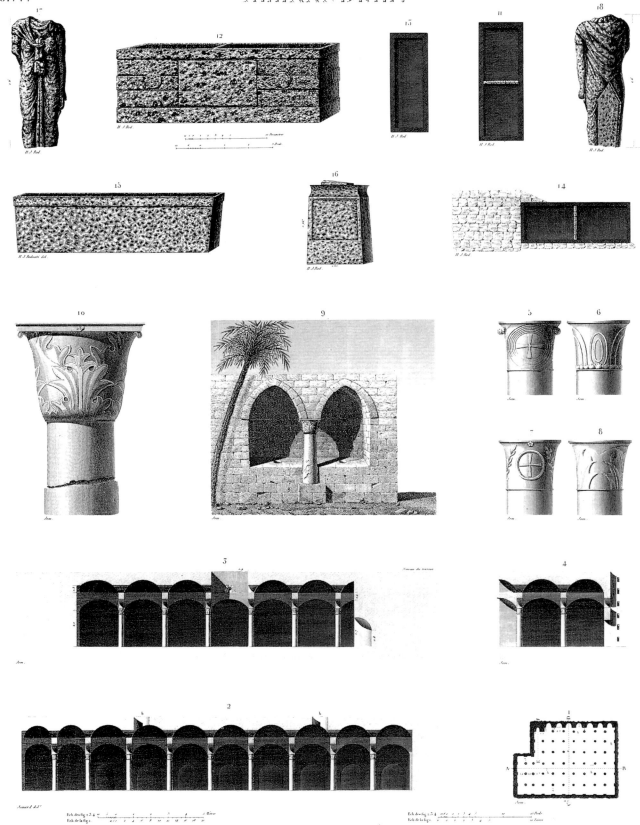

1...8 PLAN, COUPES ET DÉTAILS D'UNE GRANDE CITERNE. 9.10 DÉTAILS D'UNE COLONNE AVEC UN CHAPITEAU
EN MARBRE 11...18 SARCOPHAGES, STATUE ET SOCLE EN GRANIT.

ALEXANDRIE.

Pl. 37.

1. 2. 3. PLAN, ÉLÉVATION ET COUPE D'UNE ANCIENNE ÉGLISE DITE MOSQUÉE DES MILLE COLONNES OU DES SEPTANTE.

4...23 PLANS, COUPES ET DÉTAILS DE HUIT DES PRINCIPALES CITERNES DE L'ANCIENNE VILLE.

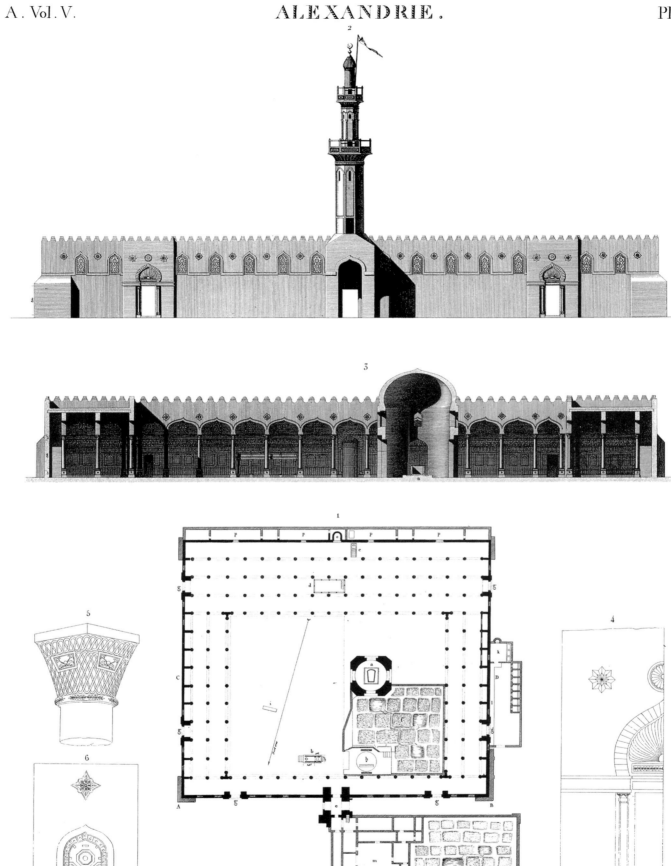

PLAN, ÉLÉVATION, COUPE ET DÉTAILS D'UNE ANCIENNE BASILIQUE, VULGAIREMENT
NOMMÉE MOSQUÉE DE St ATHANASE.

1

3

2

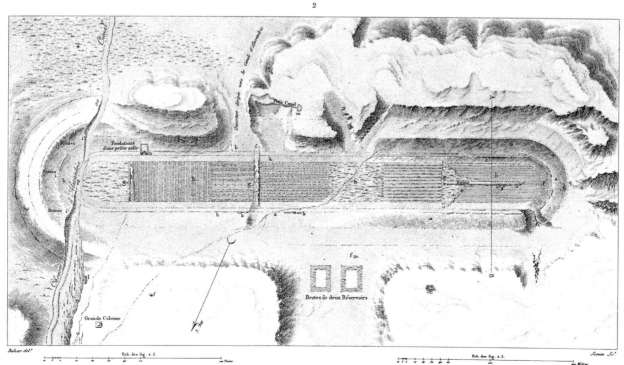

2.3 PLAN ET COUPE D'UN STADE SITUÉ AU SUD-OUEST DE LA COLONNE DITE DE POMPÉE.

1 VUE INTÉRIEURE D'UNE ANCIENNE BASILIQUE, VULGAIREMENT NOMMÉE MOSQUÉE DE Sᵗ ATHANASE.

2

3

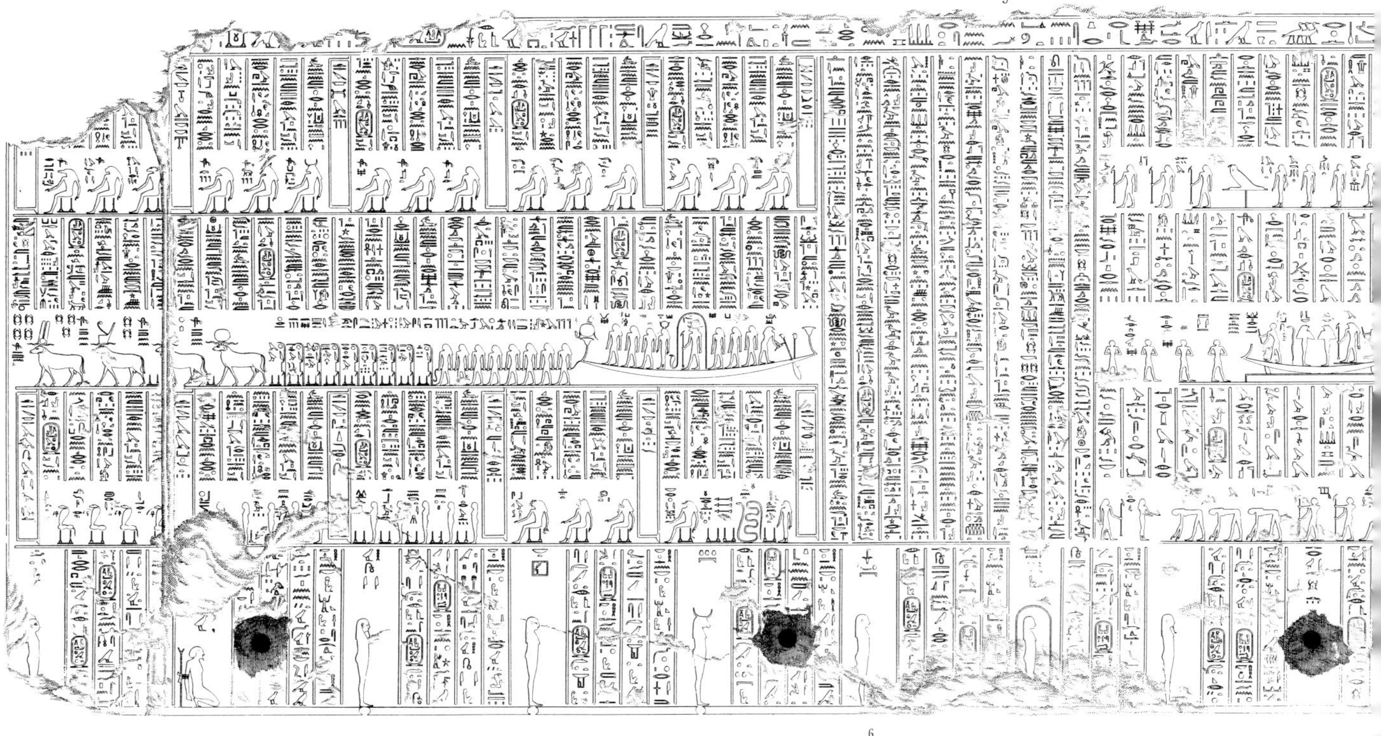

6

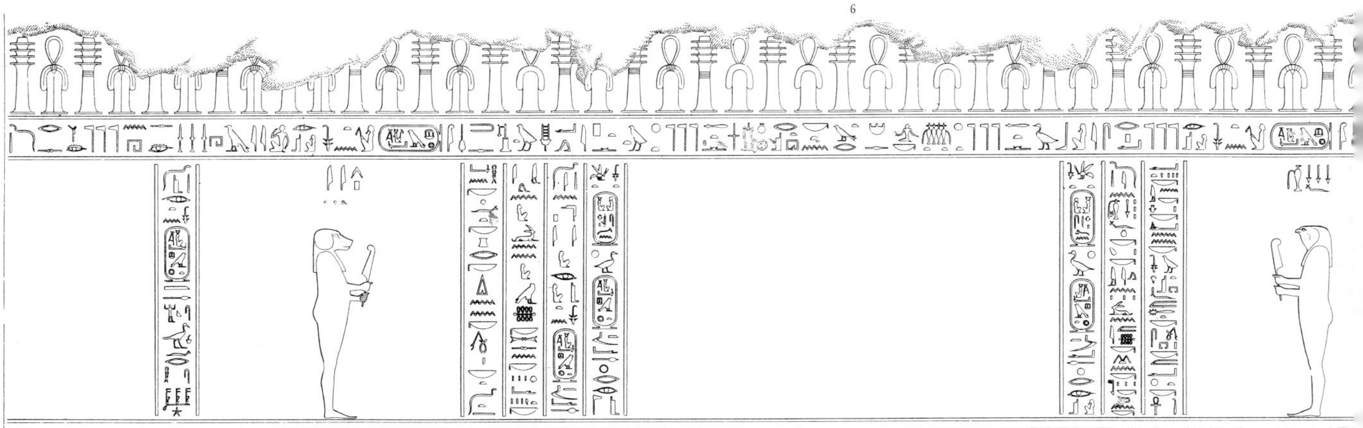

Jomard del.t

Ech. de la fig. 1 — 8 Pieds

Ech. de fig. 2..7 — 18 Pouces

1..7 PLAN ET DÉTAILS DES SCULPTURES D'UN SARCOPHAGE EN BRÈCHE ÉGYPTIENNE, TROUVÉ

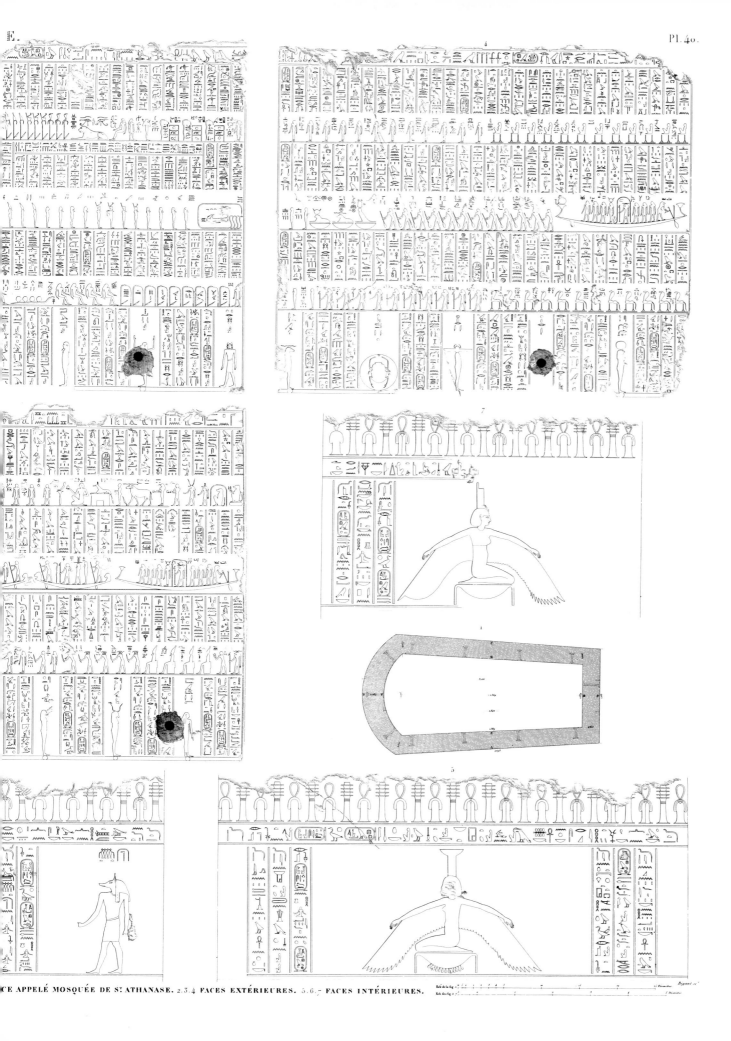

Pl.41.

ALEXANDRIE.

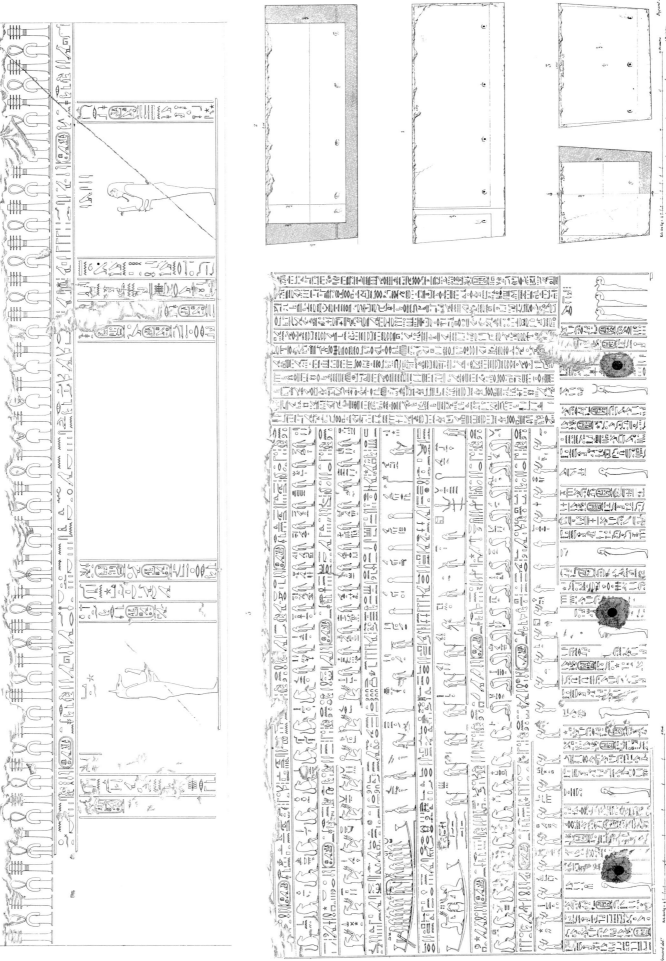

1..6 COUPES ET DÉTAILS DES SCULPTURES D'UN SARCOPHAGE EN BRÊCHE ÉGYPTIENNE, TROUVÉ DANS L'ÉDIFICE APPELÉ MOSQUÉE DE St ATHANASE. 5 FACE EXTÉRIEURE. 6 FACE INTÉRIEURE.

Pl. 42.

ALEXANDRIE.

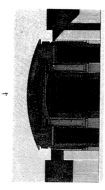

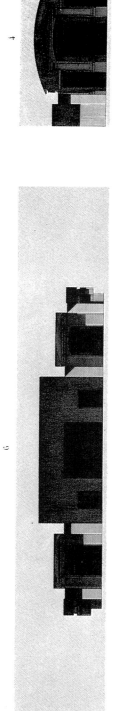

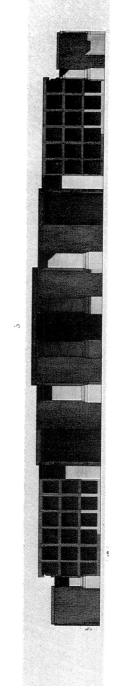

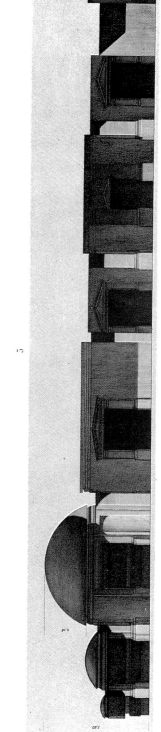

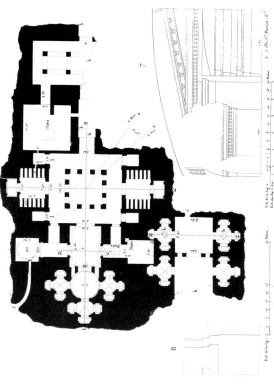

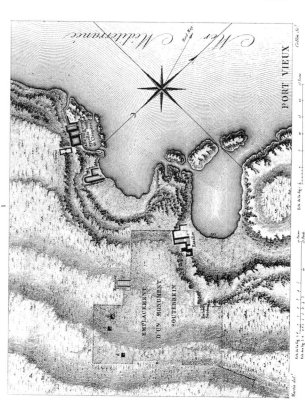

PORT VIEUX

Mer Méditerranée

PLANS, COUPES ET DÉTAILS D'UN MONUMENT SOUTERREIN, SITUÉ A L'OUEST DE LA VILLE ANTIQUE.

Pl. 45.

ENVIRONS D'ALEXANDRIE. TAPOSIRIS.

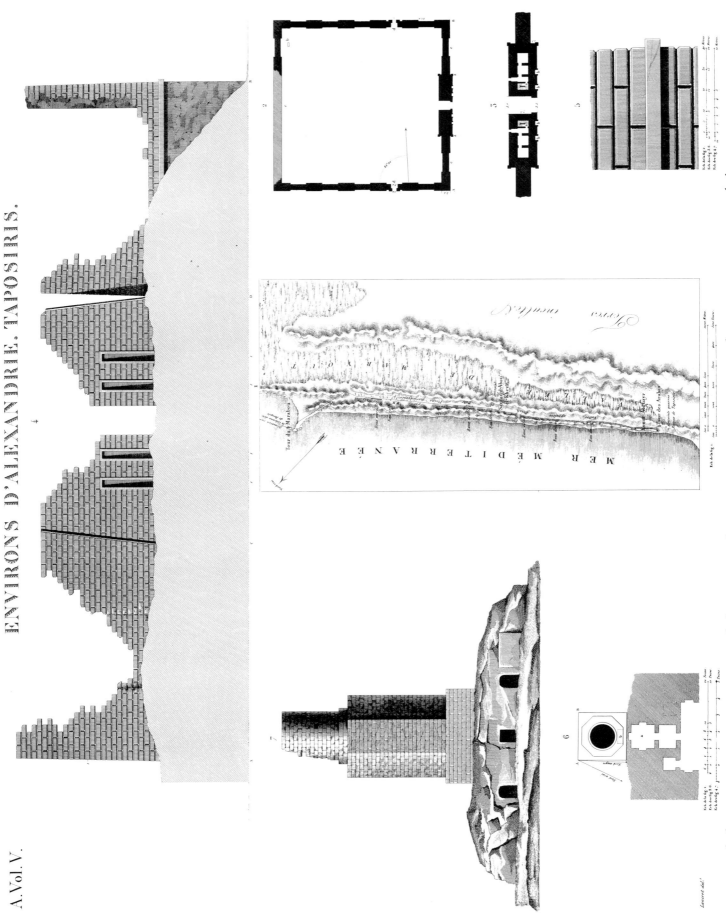

Lancret del.¹

1. Thuillier et J.J. Dupont sc.¹

1. PLAN GÉNÉRAL DE TAPOSIRIS. 2.3.4.5 PLAN, ÉLÉVATION ET DÉTAIL D'UNE ENCEINTE ANTIQUE À TAPOSIRIS. 6.7 PLAN ET ÉLÉVATION DE LA TOUR DITE DES ARABES.

PAPYRUS, HIÉROGLYPHES, INSCRIPTIONS ET MÉDAILLES.

MANUSCRIT SUR PAPYRUS.

PAPYRUS, HIÉROGLYPHES, INSCRIPTIONS ET MÉDAILLES.

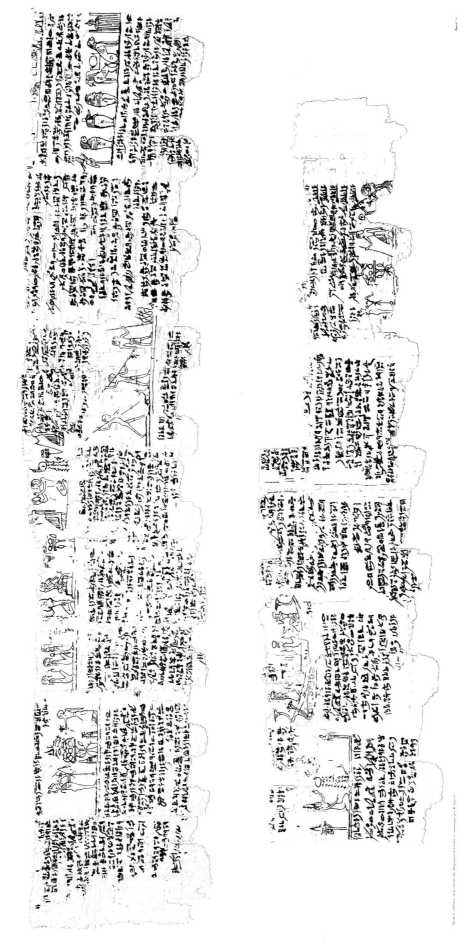

MANUSCRIT SUR PAPYRUS.

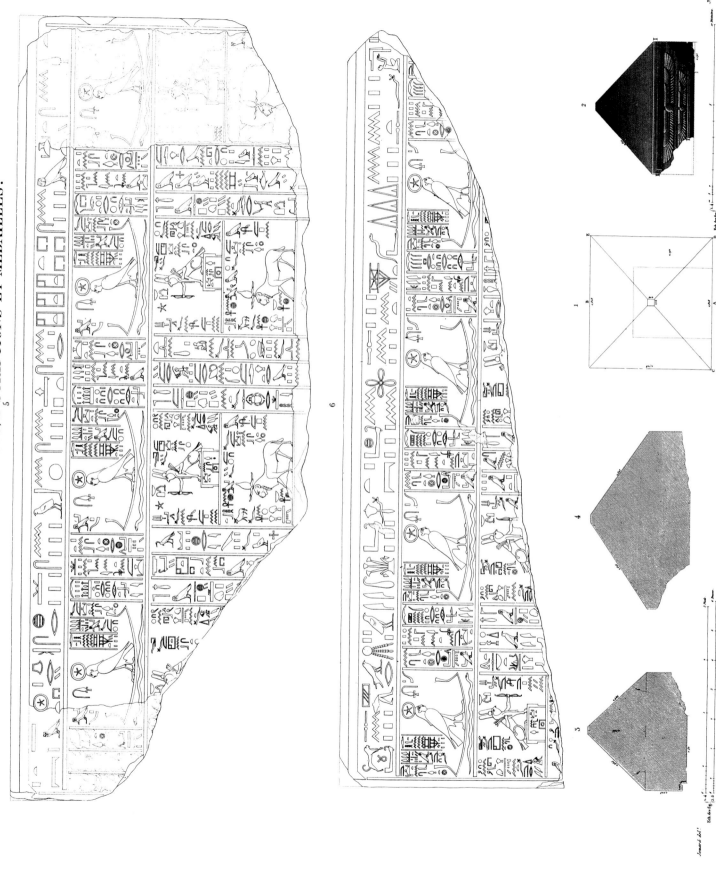

PLAN, COUPES ET DÉTAILS HIÉROGLYPHIQUES D'UN MONOLITHE ÉGYPTIEN, TROUVÉ À DAMIETTE.

Dessiné par M.Jomard d'après une empreinte en plâtre prise par lui sur le monument et d'après le moule rapporté d'Egypte par M.Raffeneau Delile.

PIERRE TROUVÉE À ROSETTE, (PARTI

ΒΑΣΙΛΕΥΟΝΤΟΣΤΟΥΝΕΟΥΚΑΙΠΑΡΑΛΑΒΟΝΤΟΣΤΗΝΒΑΣΙΛΕΙΑΝΠΑΡΑΤΟΥΠΑΤΡΟΣΚΥ

Raffeneau Delile del.'

PIERRE TROUVÉE A ROSETTE, (PARTIE INTE

ΛΕΙΩ.Ν ΜΕΓΑΛΟΔΟΞΟΥ ΤΟΥ ΤΗΝΑΙΓΥΠΤΟΝΚΑΤΑΣ ΤΗΣΑΜΕΝΟΥ ΚΑΙ ΤΑ ΠΡΟΣ ΤΟΥΣ

(EN LANGUE ÉGYPTIENNE VULGAIRE)

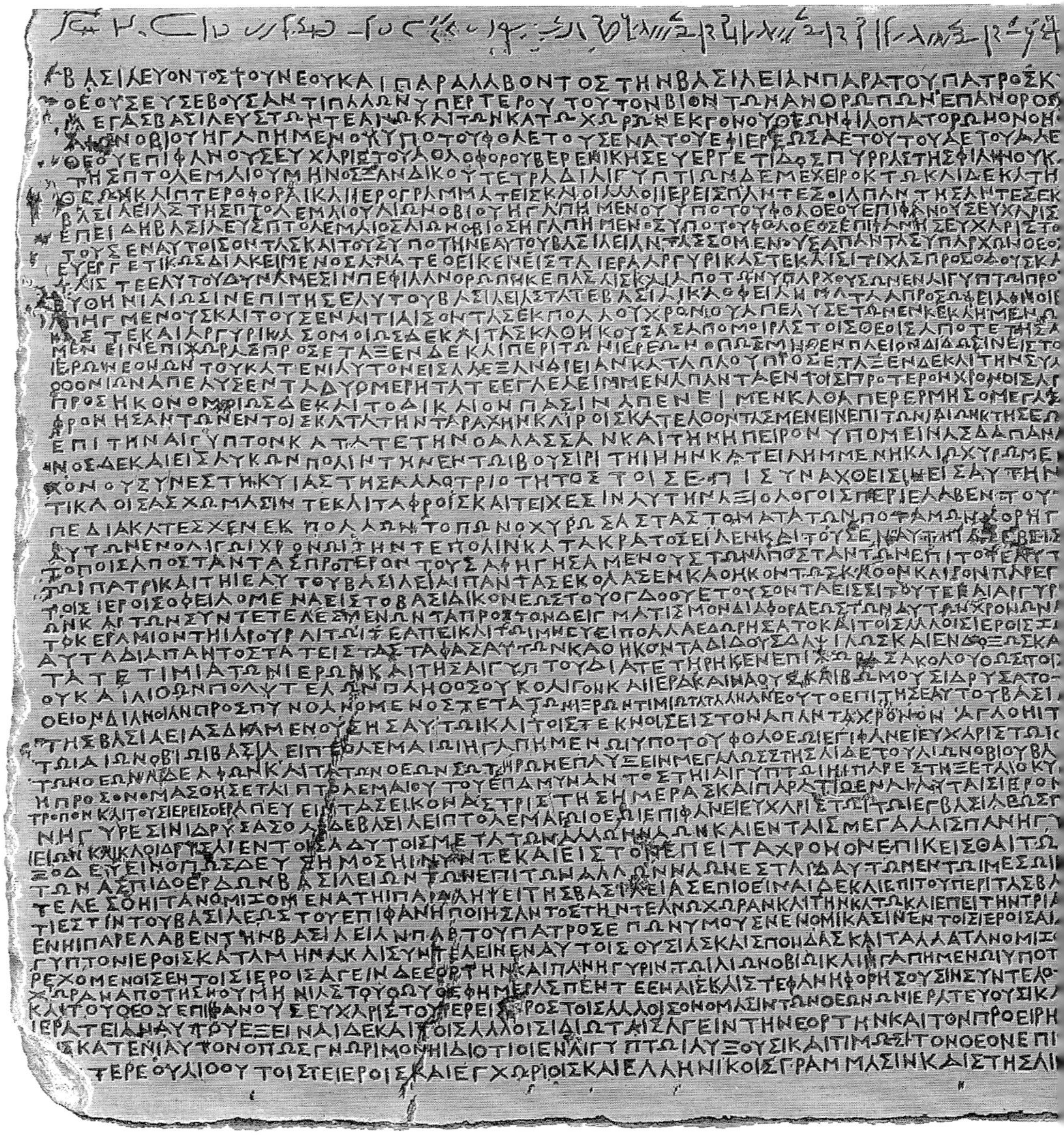

Raffeneau Delile del.t

PIERRE TROUVÉE À ROSETTE.(

ΣΙΛΕΙΩΝΜΕΓΑΛΟΔΟΞΟΥΤΟΥΤΗΝΑΙΓΥΠΤΟΝΚΑΤΑΣΤΗΣΑΜΕΝΟΥΚΑΙΤΑΠΡΟΣΤΟΥΣ
ΚΥΡΙΟΥΤΡΙΑΚΟΝΤΑΕΤΗΡΙΔΩΝΚΑΘΑΠΕΡΟΗΦΑΙΣΤΟΣΟΜΕΓΑΣΒΑΣΙΛΕΩΣΚΑΘΑΠΕΡΟΗΛΙΟΣ
ΕΔΟΚΙΜΑΣΕΝΩΙΟΚΑΙΟΣΕΔΩΚΕΝΤΗΝΝΙΚΗΝΕΙΚΟΝΟΣΤΟΠΣΠΥΔΙΟΣΥΙΟΥΠΤΟΛΥΛΙΟΥΠΤΟΛΕΜΛΙΟΥ
ΥΚΑΙΘΕΩΝΣΩΤΗΡΩΝΚΑΙΘΕΩΝΑΔΕΛΦΩΝΚΑΙΟΕΩΝΕΥΕΡΓΕΤΩΝΚΑΙΘΕΩΝΦΙΛΟΠΑΤΟΡΩΝΚΑΙ
ΥΑΡΣΙΝΟΗΣΦΙΛΑΔΕΛΦΟΥΑΡΕΙΑΣΤΗΣΔΙΟΓΕΝΟΥΣΙΕΡΕΙΑΣΑΡΣΙΝΟΗΣΦΙΛΟΠΛΑΤΟΡΟΣΕΙΡΗΝΗΣ
ΑΘΗΡΧΙΕΡΕΙΣΚΑΙΠΡΟΦΗΤΑΙΚΑΙΟΙΕΙΣΤΟΑΔΥΤΟΝΕΙΣΠΟΡΕΥΟΜΕΝΟΙΠΡΟΣΤΟΝΣΤΟΛΙΣΜΟΝΤΩΝ
ΤΑΣΤΗΝΧΩΡΑΝΙΕΡΩΝΔΕΙΣΜΕΜΦΙΝΤΩΙΒΑΣΙΛΕΙΠΡΟΣΤΗΝΠΑΝΗΓΥΡΙΝΤΗΣΠΑΡΑΛΗΨΕΩΣΤΗΣ
ΡΕΛΑΒΕΝΠΑΡΑΤΟΥΠΑΤΡΟΣΤΟΥΣΥΝΑΧΘΕΝΤΕΣΕΝΤΩΙΕΝΤΙΕΜΦΕΝΕΡΩΙΤΗΙΗΜΕΡΑΙΤΑΥΤΗΙΕΙΠΑΝ
ΛΕΡΣΠΤΟΛΕΜΑΙΟΣΚΑΙΒΑΣΙΛΙΣΣΗΣΑΡΣΙΝΟΗΣΟΕΩΝΦΙΛΟΠΑΤΟΡΩΝΚΑΤΑΠΛΑΝΕΥΕΡΓΕΤΗΚΕΝΤΑΙΕΡΑΚΑΙ
ΛΙΘΕΑΔΕΚΑΟΛΠΕΡΩΡΟΣΟΤΗΣΙΣΟΣΚΑΙΟΣΙΡΙΟΣΥΙΟΣΟΕΠΑΜΥΝΑΣΤΩΙΠΑΤΡΙΛΥΤΟΥΟΣΙΡΕΙΤΑΠΡΟΣΘΕΟΥΣ
ΛΣΠΟΛΛΑΣΥΠΟΜΕΜΕΝΗΚΕΝΕΚΑΤΟΥΤΗΝΑΙΓΥΠΤΟΝΕΙΣΕΥΔΙΑΝΑΓΑΓΕΙΝΚΑΙΤΑΙΕΡΑΚΑΤΑΣΤΗΣΑΣΘΑΙ
ΦΟΡΟΛΟΓΙΩΝΤΙΝΑΣΜΕΝΕΙΣΤΕΛΟΣΑΦΗΚΕΝΑΛΛΑΣΔΕΚΕΚΟΥΦΙΚΕΝΟΠΩΣΟΤΕΛΛΟΣΚΑΙΟΙΑΛΛΟΙΠΑΝΤΕΣΕΝ
ΔΙΚΑΙΟΤΗΤΗΙΛΟΙΠΙΕΒΑΣΙΑΛΥΤΟΝΤΑΠΟΛΛΑΤΩΙΠΑΘΟΕΙΛΑΦΗΚΕΝΚΑΙΤΟΥΣΕΝΤΑΙΣΦΥΛΑΚΑΙΣ
ΑΞΕΔΕΚΑΙΤΑΣΠΡΟΣΟΔΟΥΣΤΩΝΙΕΡΩΝΚΑΙΤΑΣΔΙΔΟΜΕΝΑΣΕΙΣΑΥΤΑΚΑΤΕΝΙΑΥΤΟΝΣΥΝΤΑΞΕΙΣΕΙΣΤΙ
ΙΚΟΝΟΥΕΤΑΣΣΟΝΤΩΝΕΙΣΤΟΠΡΩΤΟΥΕΤΟΥΣΕΠΙΤΟΥΠΑΤΡΟΣΑΥΤΟΥΑΠΕΛΥΣΕΝΔΕΚΑΙΤΟΥΣΕΚΤΩΝ
ΛΗΕΙΣΤΗΝΝΑΥΤΕΙΑΝΜΗΠΟΙΗΣΕΣΑΙΤΩΝΤΕΙΣΤΟΒΑΣΙΛΙΚΟΝΣΥΝΤΕΛΟΥΜΕΝΩΝΕΝΤΟΙΣΙΕΡΟΙΣΒΥΕΣΣΙΝΩΝ
ΤΗΣΕΝΕΙΣΤΗΝΚΛΟΗΚΟΥΣΑΝΤΑΞΙΝΦΡΟΝΤΙΖΩΝΟΠΩΣΤΑΕΙΟΙΜΕΝΑΣΥΝΤΕΑΝΤΑΤΑΤΟΙΣΘΕΟΙΣΚΑΤΑΤΟ
ΣΗΡΣΕΤΑΞΕΝΔΕΚΑΙΤΟΥΣΚΑΤΑΠΟΡΕΥΟΜΕΝΟΥΣΕΚΤΕΤΑΝΜΑΧΙΜΩΝΚΑΙΤΩΝΑΛΛΩΝΤΩΝΑΛΛΟΤΡΙΑ
ΩΗΟΗΔΕΚΑΙΟΠΩΣΕΞΑΠΟΣΤΑΛΩΣΙΝΔΥΝΑΜΕΙΣΙΠΠΙΚΑΙΤΕΚΑΛΠΕΖΙΚΑΙΚΑΙΝΗΕΣΕΠΙΤΟΥΣΕΠΕΛΘΟΝΤΑΣ
ΚΑΣΤΕΚΛΙΒΙΤΙΚΑΣΕΜΕΓΑΛΛΑΣΟΠΩΣΤΛΟΙΕΡΑΚΑΙΟΙΕΝΑΥΤΗΙΠΑΝΤΑΣΕΝΑΣΑΛΕΙΑΙΩΣΙΝΠΑΡΑΓΙΝΟΜΕ
ΠΟΛΙΟΦΚΙΑΝΟΜΑΡΝΤΕΠΑΡΑΘΕΣΕΡΑΔΦΙΛΕΣΤΕΡΑΙΚΑΙΤΗΙΑΛΛΗΙΧΩΡΗΠΑΙΠΑΣΗΚΛΑΝΕΚΠΟΛΛΟΥ
ΝΟΙΗΣΑΝΕΙΣΤΕΤΑΙΕΡΑΚΑΙΤΩΣΕΝΑΙΓΥΠΤΩΙΚΑΤΟΙΚΟΥΝΤΑΣΠΟΛΛΑΚΑΘΑΣΥΝΤΕΤΕΛΕΣΜΕΝΟΙΚΑΙΑΝ
ΤΗΝΑΝΑΒΑΣΙΝΜΕΓΑΛΗΝΠΟΙΗΣΑΜΕΝΟΥΕΝΤΩΙΟΓΔΟΩΙΕΤΕΙΚΛΙΕΙΔΙΣΜΕΝΟΥΚΑΤΑΚΑΥΣΕΙΝΤΑ
ΛΥΤΑΧΡΗΜΑΤΩΝΟΛΙΓΟΝΚΑΙΚΑΤΑΣΤΗΣΑΣΙΠΠΕΙΣΤΕΚΛΙΠΕΙΣΟΥΣΠΡΟΣΤΗΙΦΥΛΑΚΗΙ
ΕΦΘΕΙΡΕΝΚΑΘΑΣΚΑΛΟΣΟΤΗΕΙΞΙΟΣΚΑΙΟΣΙΡΙΟΣΥΙΟΣΕΧΕΙΡΩΣΑΝΤΟΤΟΥΣΕΝΤΟΙΣΑΥΤΟΙΣ
ΑΣΚΛΙΤΗΝΧΩΡΛΝΕΝΤΑΣΚΑΙΤΑΙΕΡΑΑΔΙΚΗΣΑΝΤΑΣΠΑΡΑΓΕΝΟΜΕΝΟΣΕΙΣΜΕΜΦΙΝΕΠΑΜΥΝΩΝ
ΩΣΤΟΥΤΗΤΕΛΕΣΟΧΛΟΥΛΕΠΟΝΤΑΣΤΙΜΑΣΤΩΝΜΗΣΥΝΤΕΤΕΛΕΣΜΕΝΩΝΕΙΣΤΟΒΑΣΙΛΙΚΟΝΕΩΣΕΙΜΗΝΟΘ
ΣΟΥΚΟΛΙΓΟΜΣΕΛΛΟΝΠΑΣΤΑΣΤΙΜΑΣΤΩΝΜΗΣΥΝΤΕΤΕΛΕΣΜΕΝΩΝΕΙΣΤΟΒΛΣΙΛΙΚΟΝΕΩΣΕΙΜΗΝΟΘ
ΔΕΤΑΙΕΡΑΚΛΙΤΗΣΑΔΑΜΕΝΗΣΑΡΤΑΣΗΣΙΙΙΑΡΟΥΡΑΙΤΗΣΙΕΡΑΣΓΗΣΚΑΙΤΗΣΑΜΠΕΛΙΤΙΔΟΣΟΜΟΙ
ΕΝΑΙΓΥΠΤΛΙΠΟΛΥΤΑΣΤΑΕΣΕΝΤΙΠΛΗΥΠΕΡΤΩΝΑΝΗΚΩΝ
ΚΟΜΕΝΑΕΙΣΤΑΙΕΡΑΙΑΛΤΕΤΑΟΥΣΕΙΝΚΑΙΠΑΝΗΓΥΡΕΙΣΚΑΙΤΩΝΑΛΑΩΝΤΩΝΝΟΜΙΤ
ΑΙΤΟΛΠΙΕΙΟΝΕΡΓΟΙΣΠΟΛΥΤΕΛΕΣΙΝΚΑΤΕΣΚΕΥΑΣΕΝΧΟΡΗΓΗΣΑΣΕΙΑΥΤΟΧΡΥΣΙΟΥΤΕΚ
ΒΔΕΟΜΕΝΑΕΠΙΣΚΕΥΗΣΠΡΟΣΔΙΩΡΟΡΘΩΣΑΤΟΕΧΩΝΘΕΟΥΕΥΕΡΓΕΤΙΚΟΥΕΝΤΟΙΣΑΝΗΚΟ
ΚΑΟΗΚΕΙΑΝΟΜΟΝΔΕΔΩΚΑΙΝΑΥΤΩΙΟΙΟΕΟΙΤΓΙΕΙΑΝΝΙΚΗΝΚΡΑΤΟΣΚΑΙΤΑΛΛΑΛΑ
ΞΕΝΤΟΙΣΙΕΡΕΥΣΙΤΩΝΚΑΤΑΤΗΝΧΩΡΑΝΙΕΡΩΝΠΑΝΤΩΝΤΑΥΠΑΡΧΟΝΤΑ
ΚΑΙΤΑΤΩΝΓΟΝΕΩΝΑΥΤΟΥΘΕΩΝΦΙΛΟΠΑΤΟΡΩΝΚΑΙΤΑΤΩΝΤΙΡΟΓΟΝΩΝΘΕΩΝΕΥΕΡΤ
ΤΟΜΛΙΟΥΘΕΟΥΕΠΙΦΑΝΟΥΣΕΥΧΑΡΙΣΤΟΥΕΙΚΟΝΑΕΝΕΚΑΣΤΩΙΙΕΡΩΙΕΝΤΩΙΕΠΙΦ
ΞΕΟΣΤΟΥΙΕΡΟΥΘΙΔΟΥΣΑΥΤΩΙΟΠΛΟΝΝΙΚΗΣΤΙΜΟΝΔΕΣΤΑΙΚΑΤΕΣΚΕΥΑΣΜΕΝ
ΚΑΙΤΑΛΛΑΤΑΝΟΜΙΖΟΜΕΝΑΣΥΝΤΕΛΕΙΚΟΔΑΚΑΙΤΟΙΣΑΛΛΟΙΣΘΕΟΙΣΙΝ
ΟΥΚΑΙΒΑΣΙΛΙΣΣΗΣΑΡΣΙΝΟΗΣΟΕΩΝΦΙΛΟΠΑΤΟΡΩΝΣΞΟΛΑΝΟΝΤΕΚΛΙΝΑΟΝΧΡΥ
ΝΑΙΣΕΞΟΔΕΙΛΙΤΩΝΗΛΑΩΝΙΗΟΝΤΑΙΚΑΙΤΟΝΤΟΥΘΕΟΥΕΠΙΦΑΝΟΥΣΕΥ
ΛΣΤΟΥΒΑΣΙΛΕΩΣΚΑΙΥΣΑΣΒΑΣΙΛΕΙΑΣΔΕΚΑΛΙΣΠΡΟΣΚΕΝΤΑΕΤΑΙΕ
ΜΕΝΗΒΑΣΙΛΕΙΑΥΣΧΕΝΤΗΝΠΕΡΙΟΘΕΜΕΝΟΣΕΙΣΗΛΘΕΝΕΙΣΤΟΕΝΜΕΜΦ
ΤΕΤΡΑΓΩΝΟΥΚΑΤΑΤΟΠΡΟΕΙΡΗΜΕΝΟΝΒΑΣΙΛΕΙΟΝΦΥΛΑΚΤΗΡΙΑΧΡ
ΤΟΥΜΕΣΟΡΗΕΝΗΙΤΑΓΕΝΕΘΛΙΑΤΟΥΒΑΣΙΛΕΩΣΕΣΤΙΝΟΜΟΙΩΣΔΕΚΑΙ
ΝΑΓΛΩΜΑΡΧΗΓΟΙΙΑΣΙΝΕΙΣΙΝΛΓΓΕΙΝΤΑΣΗΜΕΡΑΣΤΑΥΤΑΣΕΟΡΤ
ΑΚΑΙΕΝΤΑΙΣΑΛΛΑΙΣΠΑΝΗΓΥΡΕΣΙΝΤΑΣΤΕΓΙΝΟΜΕΝΑΣΠΡΟΣΘ
ΕΙΛΕΙΠΤΟΝΕΜΑΙΟΙΟΕΩΙΕΠΙΦΑΝΕΙΕΥΧΑΡΙΣΤΩΙΚΑΤΕΝΙ
ΕΙΛΣΚΑΙΣΠΟΝΔΑΣΚΑΙΤΑΛΛΑΤΑΚΑΟΗΚΟΝΤΑΠΡΟΣΑΓΟΡΕ
ΡΙΣΑΙΕΙΣΠΑΝΤΑΣΤΟΥΣΧΡΗΜΑΤΙΣΜΟΥΣΚΑΙΕΙΣΤΟΥΣ
ΟΝΙΔΡΥΕΣΟΛΙΚΑΙΕΧΕΙΝΠΑΡΑΥΤΟΙΣΣΥΝΤΕΛΟ
ΑΡΙΣΤΟΝΒΑΣΙΛΕΑΚΑΟΑΠΕΡΝΟΜΙΜΟΝΕΣΤ
ΑΩΙΤΩΝΤΕΠΡΩΤΩΚΝΙΣΕΥΤΕΡΩΝ

PAPYRUS, HIÉROGLYPHES, INSCRIPTIONS ET MÉDAILLES.

TABLEAU MÉTHODIQUE DES HIÉROGLYPHES, PREMIÈRE PARTIE.

Pl. 51.

PAPYRUS, HIÉROGLYPHES, INSCRIPTIONS ET MÉDAILLES.

TABLEAU MÉTHODIQUE DES HIÉROGLYPHES, SECONDE PARTIE.

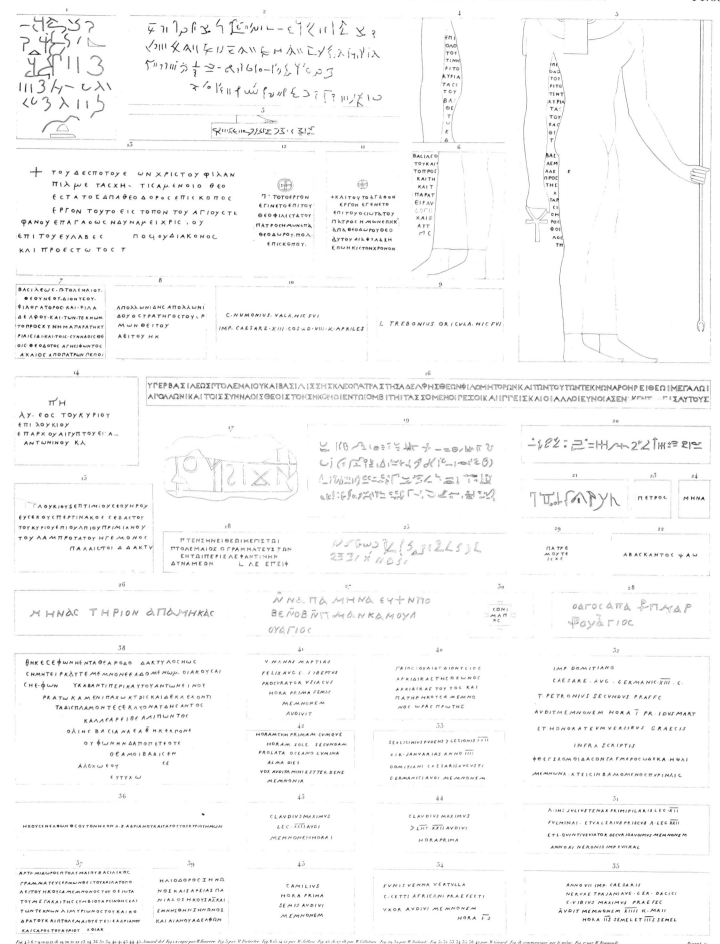

9

6

8

4

MNHCΘHACKΛHΠIAΔHCIATPOCΛEΓEωBTPAS
ICXYPAC LLANTωNINOYMEXEPΔ

5

ΔIOKΛHC OPTHC

KΛEOΠATP

POCOCKE ANGLUS VIDIT ANNO

1

CωTHPIXOCKAIHPAKΛEIΔHC HKAMENωΔE
ΔΙ KΛAYΔIOYΦAMEN ω Σ

3

ΛAMΠωNHKAIMETACTATIOYΠHMOY

2

EYCTAΘIOCAΠOΛΛωNIOY

7

JANVARIVS VIDI ET MIRAVI LOCOM

10

ΘΑΣΙΛΙΣΣΑΚΛΕΟΠΑΤΡΑΚΑΙΒΑΣΙΛΕΥΣΠΤΟΛΕΜΑΙΟΣΘΕΟΙΜΕΓΑΛΟΙΦΙΛΟΜΗΤΟΡΕΣ
...ΜΕΓΙΣΤωΙΚΑΙΤΟΙΣΣΥΝΝΑΟΙΣΘΕΟΙΣ

18

ΑΓΑΘΗΙ ΤΥΧΗΙ

ΑΥΤΟΚΡΑΤΟΡΙΚΑΙΣΑΡΙΜΑΡΚωΙΑΥΡΗΛΙωΙ
ΣΕΟΥΗΡωΙΑΛΕΞΑΝΔΡΙΕΥΣΕΒΕΙΕΥΤΥΧΗΙ
ΣΕΒΑΣΤ   ΣΕ. Σ
ΜΗΤΡΙΑΥΤΟΥ   ΙΛΙΙΤ ΤΗΤΩΝ
ΣΤΡΑΤΟΠΕ...Ν   ΣΚΑΙΑΙωΝΙΟΥ
ΔΙΑΜΟΝΗΣΑΥΤΩΝ ΠΑΝΤΟΣΑΥΤΩΝΟΙΚΟΥ
ΕΠΙΜΗΘΥΙΟΙΟΝ... ΠΑΡΧΟΥΑΙΓΥΠΤΟΥ
...ΙΑ...ΟΙΝΙ...
ΑΝΤΙΝΟΕΩΝΝΕΩΝΕΛΛΗΝΩΝΙ
ΠΡΥΤΑΝΕΥΟΝΤΟΣΑΥΡΗΛΙΟΥΩΡΙΓΕΝ
ΥΚΑΙΑΠΟΛΛΩΝΙΟΥΒΟΥΛΕΥΤΟΥΓΥΜΝ
ΕΠΙΤΩΝΣΤΕΜΜΑΤΩΝΚΑΙΕΣΧΡΗΜΑ
ΟΥΛΗΣΑΘΗΙΝΑΙΟΣ LIΛ//Τ

11

ΥΠΕΡΑ...ΟΚ...ΤΟΤΟΣΚΑΙΣΑΡΟΣΘΕΟΥ...Ο...ΛΑΕΙΘΕΙΙΟΥΣΕΒΑΣΙΟΥ
ΚΑΙΜΑΡΚΟΥΚΛΩΔΙΟΥΠΟ...ΟΜΟΥΕΠΙΣΤΡΑΤΗΓΟΥΤΡΥΦΩΝΟΣΣ
ΚΑΙΤΟΥΝΟΜΟΥΤΟΠΡΟΣ...ΣΙΔΙΘΕΑΙΜΕΓΙΣΤΗΙΚΑΙΤΟ

12

ΥΠΕΡΑΥΤΟΚΡΑΤΟΡ ΣΚΑΙΣΑΡΟΣΘΕΟΥΥΙΟΥΔΙΟΣΕΛΕ...ΣΕΒΑΣΤΟ..ΠΙ ΥΠΛΙΟΥΟΚΤΑΙΟΥΗΓΕΜΟΝΟΣΚΑΙ
.ΜΑΡΚΟΥΚΛΩΔΙΟΥΠΟΣΤΟΜΟΥΕΠΙΣΤΡΑΤΗΓΟΥΤΡΥΦΩΝΟΣΣΤΡΑΤΗΓΟ ΥΝΤΟΣΟΙΑΠΟΤΗΣΜΗΤΡΟΠΟΛΕΩΣ
.ΥΝΟΜΟΥΤΟΠΡΟΠΥΛΩΝΙΣΙΔΙΘΕΑΙΜΕΓΙΣΤΗΙΚΑΙΤΟΙΣ ΣΥΝΝΑΟΙΣΘΕΟΙΣΙ ΤΟΥΣΛΑΚΑΙΣΑΡΟΣΘΛΥΘΥΣΕΒΑΣΤΗΙ

13

...ΓΟΣΚΑΙ...   ΛCΙΟ...ΣΕΒΑΣΤΗ...ΕΜΑΝΙΧΗΑ...
ΚΑΙΤΟΥΠΑΝΤΟΣ... ΠΑΝΙΟ...ΤΕ...ΠΟΣΕΕ
ΤΙΒΕΡΙΟΣΚΛΑΥΔΙΟΣΤΙΒΕΡΙΟΥΚ... ΣΝΟΣΥ...ΑΠΟ
ΤΣΣΝΚΣΧΣΓΛΓΑΡΧΗΚΟΤΣΣ... ΙΣΤΡΙΣ
...ΓΥΝΣΤΟΛ...ΟΙΙ...
...ΑΠΡΟΣ ΚΑΙΣΑΡΟΣΤΙΟΥ ΤΡΑΙΑ... ΟΥΣΣΕΒΑΣΤΟΥΓΕΡΜΑΝΙΚΟΥ

14

ΣΠΤΟΛΕΜΑ
ΙΛΙΣΣΑΚΛ
ΛΟΝΑΝΤΑΙω ΑΙΤΟΙΣΣΙΝΝΑΣ
ΣΣΕΡ.ΣΤΟ...ΕΝΕΩΣΑΝΤ

...ΟΠΑΤΡΑΣΘΕω ΝΕΠΙΦΑΝΩΝΚ· ΕΥΧΑΙ ΙΣ ΤΩΝ
..ΕωΣΑΔΕΛΦΘΕΟΙΦΙΛ ΜΗΤΟΡΕΣ
..ΚΙΤΟ ΣΚ ΣΑΡΕΣΛ.ΡΗ ΟΙΑΝΤΩΝΙΟΣ
ΔΑ Ο Ε ΝΙΘ

19

ΑΓΑΘΗΙ ΤΥΧΗΙ

ΑΥΤΟΚΡΑΤΟΡΙΚΑΙΣΑΡΙΜΑΡΚωΙΑΥΡΗΛΙωΙ
ΣΕΟΥΗΡωΙΑΛΕΞΑΝΔΡ ΙΕΥΣΕΒΕΙΕΥΤΥΧΕΙ
ΣΕΒΑΣΤ...   ΣΕΒΛΣΤΗ
ΜΗΤΡΙΑΥΤΟΥΚΑΙ   ΑΠΤ ΤΗΤΩΝ
Σ ΤΡΑΤΟΠΕ...ΩΝ ΗΣΚΑΙΑΙΩΝΙΟΥ
ΔΙΑΜΟΝΗΣ ΑΥΤΩΝ ΙΠΑΝΤΟΣΑΥΤΩΝΟΙ
ΕΓΙΜΗΘΥΙΟΥΟΝ Π Ρ ΕΠΑΡΧΟΥΑΙΓΥΠΤΟΥ
ΑΝΤΙΝΟΕΩΝ ΝΕΩΝΕΛΛΕΝ ΩΝ·
Π ΡΥΤΑΝΕΥ ΟΝΤΟΣΑΥΡΗΛΙΟΥ ΩΡΙΓΕΝ
Υ ΚΑΙΑΠΟΛΛ ΩΝΙΟΥ ΒΟΥΛΕΥ ΤΟΥ ΓΥΜ
ΕΠΙΤΩΝ ΣΤΕΜΜΑΤΩΝΚΑΙΕΣΧ ΡΗΜΑΤ
ΟΥΛΗΣΑΘΗΝΟΙΔΟΣ LIΛ//Τ

17

ΑΓΑΘΗΙ ΤΥΧΗΙ
ΥΠΕΡΑΥΤΟΚΡΑΤΟΡωΝΚΑΙCΑΡωΝ
ΜΑΡΚΟΥΑΥΡΗΛΙΟΥΑΝΤωΝΙΝΟΥ

15

ΑΣΠΙΔΛΣ ΗΡΑΚΛΗΟΥ
ΤΟΝ ΚΥΡΙΟΝ ΠΛΛ΄ Ν

20

ΓΡΑΜ Μ ΜΑΤΑ ΑΧΡΗΜΑΤΙCΤΟCΕCCΗ

16

ΑΒΡΑΙΑΜ ΙC ΔΚ ΙΔΚωΕ ΠΑΝΟΥ ΠΑΥΛΟC
ΔΝΤΡΕC ΠΕΤΡΟC ΠΦΙΛΕΠΠΟC ΑΠΟΛΛω
ΙωCΗΦ

21

Ι ΙL ΙC ΝΙ ΜΟΥΘΙ Α

22

ΒΑΣΙΛΕΑΠΤΟΛΕΜΑΙΟΝΘΕΟΝΕΥΕΡΓΕΤΗΝ
ΘΕΩΝΕΠΙΦΑΝωΝΑΠΟΛΛΟΔωΡΟΣΑΕΤΟΥ
ΤωΝΠΡΟΤωΝΦΙΛωΝΟΓΕΙΣΤΑΤΗΣΚΑΙ
ΓΡΑΜΜΑΤΕΥΣΤωΝΚΑΤΟΙΚωΝΙΠΠΕωΝ

25

ΓΕΥ ΕΙΝΟC
ΑΝΕΘΗΚΕΝ
ΥΠΕ ΙΧ

28

23

ΜΗΤΡΙΘΕΩΝΣΩΤΕΙΡΑΙ
ΕΓΗΚΟΩΙΓΟΛΥΚ ΡΑΤΗΣ
ΚΑΙΕΡΜΙΟΝΗΥΓΕΡΑΥΤΩΝ
ΚΑΙΤΩΝΤΕΚΝΩΝΕΥΧΗΝ

27

ΗΒΟΥΛΗΚΑΙΟΔΗΜοC
ΛΟΥΚΙοΝ ΠοΠΙΛΛΙοΝΒΑΛΒοΝ
ΠΡΕCΒΕΥΤΗΝΤΙΒΕΡΙοΥ
ΚΛΑΥΔΙοΥ ΚΑΙCΑΡοC
CΕΒΑCΤοΥΓΕΡΜΑΝΙΚοΥ
ΤοΝΠΑΤΡΩΝΑΤΗC ΠοΛΕΩC

26

LICINIAE·L·F SECVNDAE
DOMITI CATVLLI

30

24

ΤΟ ωΤΑΤΟΝΑΥΤΟΚΡΑΤΟΡΑ
ΤΟΝΠΟΛΙΟΥΧΟΝΑΛΕΞΑΝΔΡΕΙΑC
ΔΙΟΚ Η ΙΑΝΟΝΤΟΝΑ ΤΟΝ
ΠΟ ΕΠΑΡΧΟΣΑΙΓΥΠΤΟΥ

29

ΗΗCΘΙΙ F H
ΚΕΕΝ FΡΑC
ΤΟΝCΟΝΔ&ΛΟΝ
ΤC ωΓΟΝ

1. 9. u. 22 25 Jomard del. 23 copié par M Le Gentil 26.27 par M. H Le Gentil et Fevre. 28 29 par M Fevre 5o par M Duterte. 30 par M Jollois.

1.9.15.16 DES TOMBEAUX DES ROIS ET AUTRES HYPOGÉES. 10 D'APOLLINOPOLIS PARVA. 11.12. DE TENTYRIS. 13 DE PANOPOLIS. 14 D'ANT.EOPOLIS. 17 D'HERMOPOLIS
MAGNA. 18.19 D'ANTINOË. 20 D'ACORIS. 21 DE FAYOUM. 22 DU KAIRE. 23 DE CANOPE. 24.25 D'ALEXANDRIE. 26...29 DE DAMIETTE.

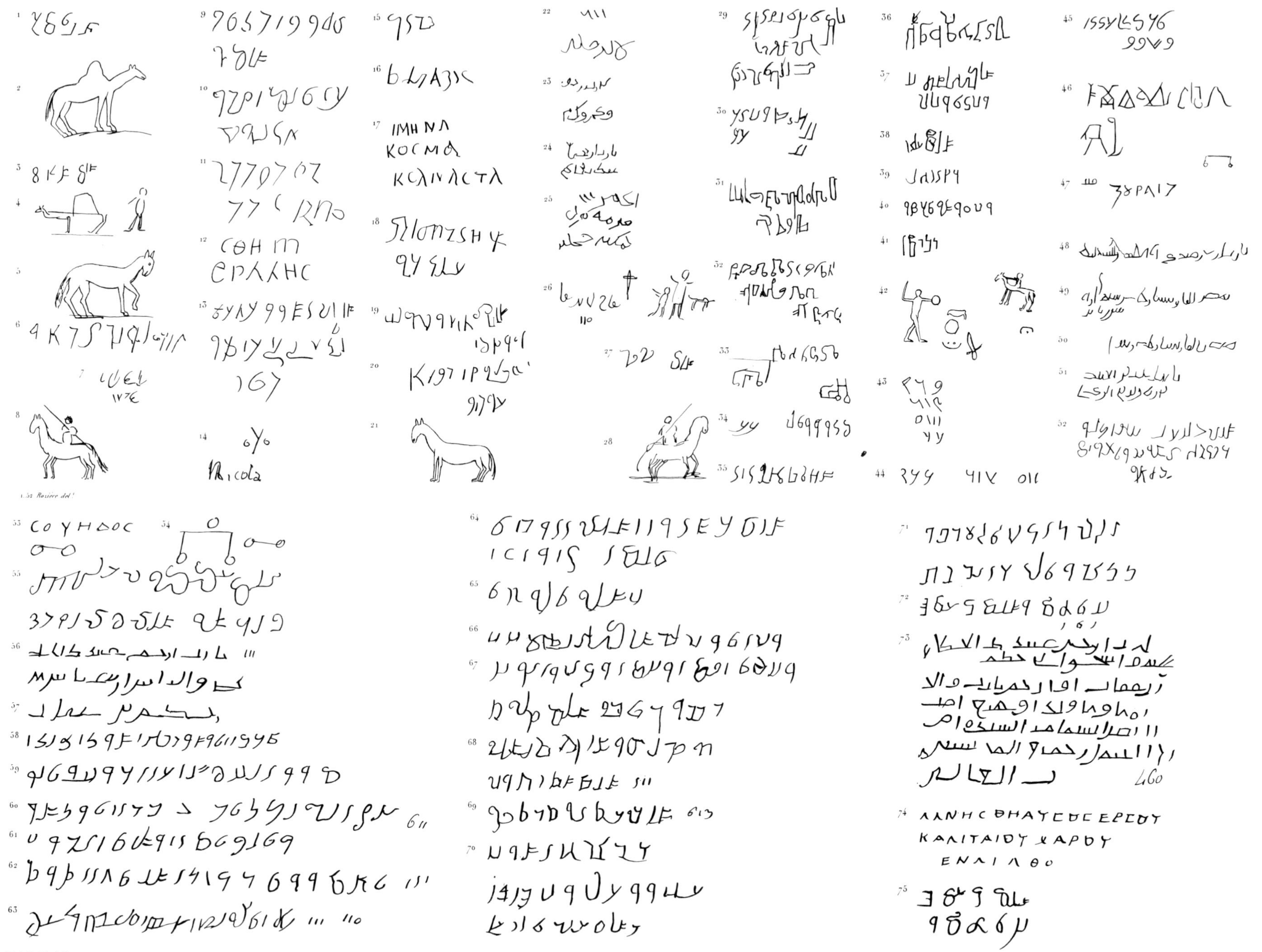

Pl. 57.

PAPYRUS, HIÉROGLYPHES, INSCRIPTIONS ET MÉDAILLES.

DIFFÉRENTES INSCRIPTIONS RECUEILLIES SUR LA ROUTE DU MONT-SINAÏ.

Willemin &c.

PAPYRUS, HIÉROGLYPHES, INSCRIPTIONS ET MÉDAILLES.

Pl. 58.

NOMES DE LA HAUTE ÉGYPTE ET DE L'HEPTANOMIDE.

NOMES DE LA BASSE ÉGYPTE.

MÉDAILLES DES NOMES D'ÉGYPTE.

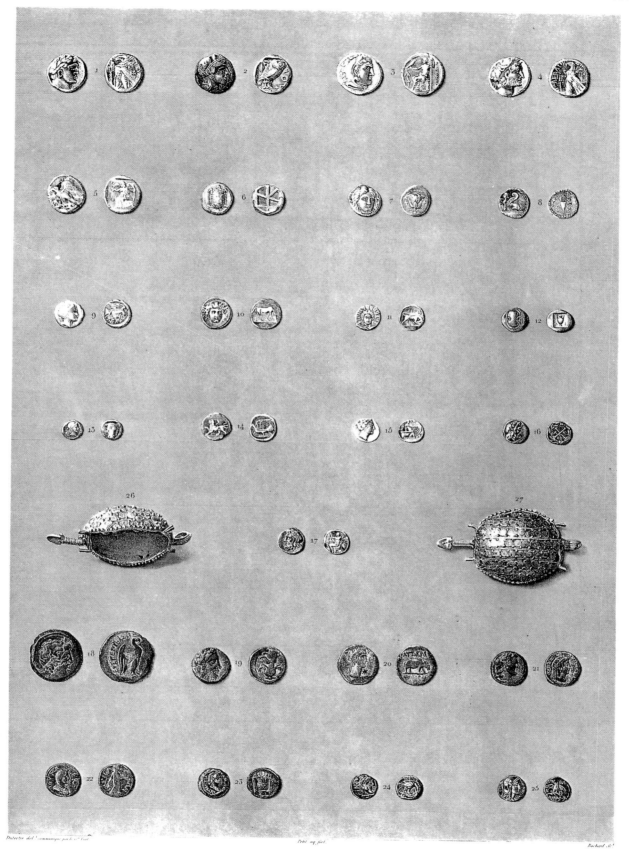

MÉD. TROUVÉE À TYR. 5 M. D'ALEXANDRE. 4 18 21 DES PTOLÉMÉES. 19 DE CYRÈNE. 23 1 24 25 M. GRECQUES. 20 22 25 M. ROMAINES. 26 2 TORTUE EN OR.

1..4. FIGURE EN GRANIT NOIR. 5.6.7. FRAGMENS EN ALBÂTRE.

1...5. **BUSTES EN BASALTE NOIR.** 6.7. **TÊTE EN ALBÂTRE.** 8. **BUSTE EN STÉATITE.**

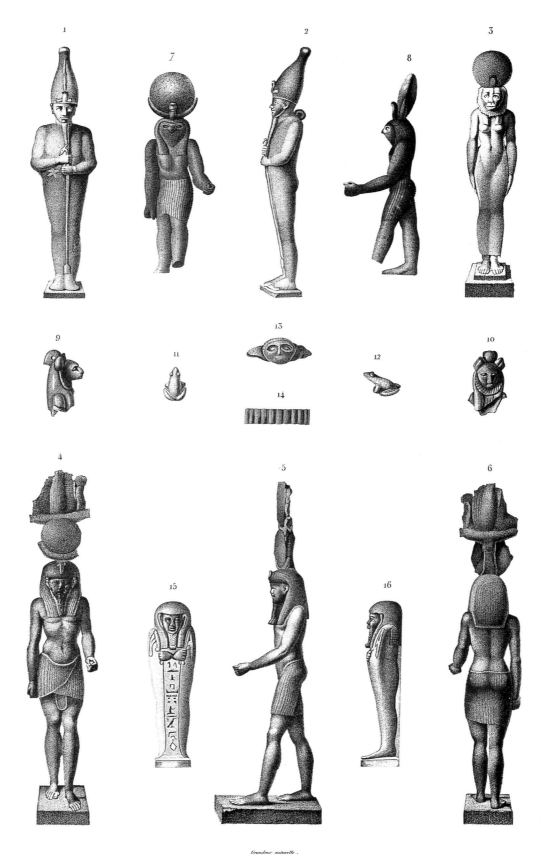

1...8 FIGURES EN BRONZE. 9...16 FIGURES ET FRAGMENS EN TERRE CUITE ÉMAILLÉE.

COLLECTION D'ANTIQUES.

Pl. 63.

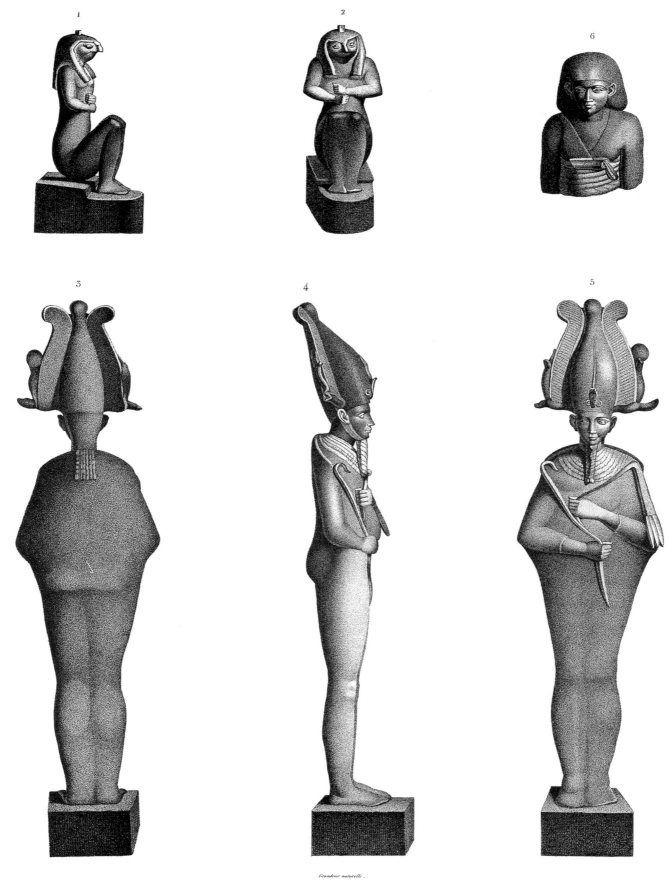

Castex del.

Grandeur naturelle.

Gauthier ainé. Sc.

1...5 FIGURES EN BRONZE. 6 BUSTE EN BASALTE GRIS.

1

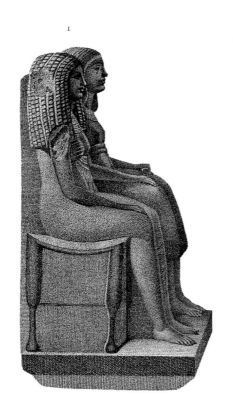

2

3

4

Grandeur naturelle.

GROUPE EN BASALTE.

1. 2. 3 **FIGURES EN BRONZE. 4.5 FIGURE EN BASALTE. 6 FIGURE EN TERRE CUITE ÉMAILLÉE.**

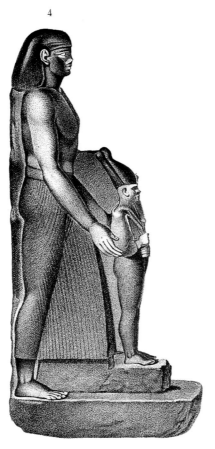

Castex del.t   Gabriel sc.t

1.2.3. FIGURE EN BRONZE. 4.5.6. FIGURE EN SERPENTINE.

1....12 Castaz del. 13.....30 H. J. Redouté del.

Tassaert Sc.

1. 2. 3. 12. 13...30 FIGURES ET AMULETTES EN TERRE CUITE. 4...9 EN BRONZE. 10.11 EN SERPENTINE. 21 EN VERRE.

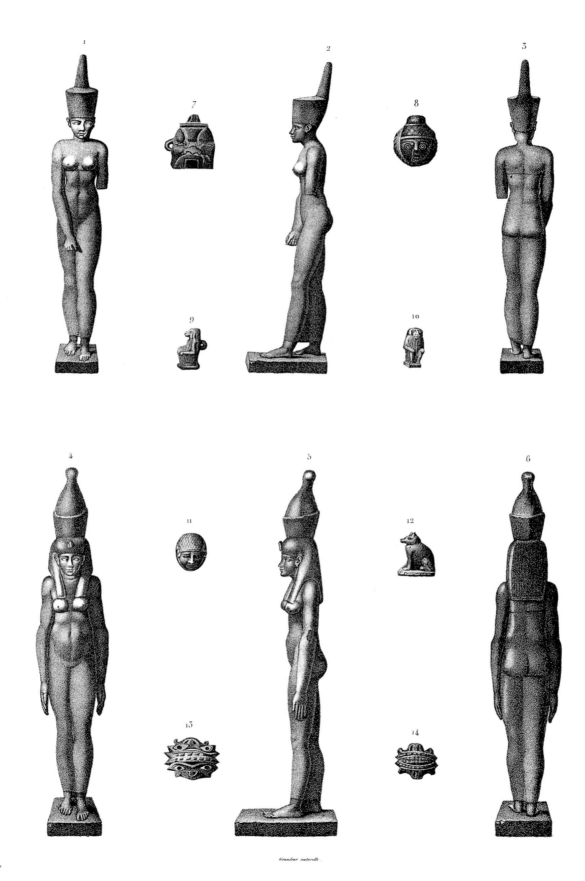

1...6 **FIGURES EN BRONZE.** 7.8 **EN SERPENTINE.** 9...14 **EN TERRE CUITE.**

1.2 FIGURE EN PÂTE DE PORCELAINE. 3..6.9.10.21.22 EN BOIS PEINT. 7.8.12.13 EN BASALTE. 11 BAS-RELIEF EN PIERRE. 16.17.20.23 MASQUES EN TERRE. 18.19 EN BRONZE.

1..6 GROUPE EN BASALTE APPORTÉ DES OASIS. 7..11 EN PIERRE OLLAIRE. 12..15 MASQUES EN BOIS. 16..18 ENVELOPPES DE MOMIES.

Pl. 71.

COLLECTION D'ANTIQUES.

Grandeur naturelle.

1...10.12.13.20...24 FIGURES EN BRONZE. 11 FRAGMENT DE BAS RELIEF EN PIERRE. 14.15.16 EN MARBRE. 17.18 EN HÉMATITE. 19 EN PLOMB.

Tiré de la Collection de M.ʳ Marcel.   1.2.3.8.9.10.12.13.15 grandeur naturelle. 6.7. n.14 doublé.   Monsaldy Sc.ᵗ

1.2.3.7.8.12.15 FIGURES EN BRONZE. 4.5.9.10 FIGURES EN PIERRE SCHISTEUSE ET EN SERPENTINE. 6.11.13.14 FIGURES EN TERRE CUITE.

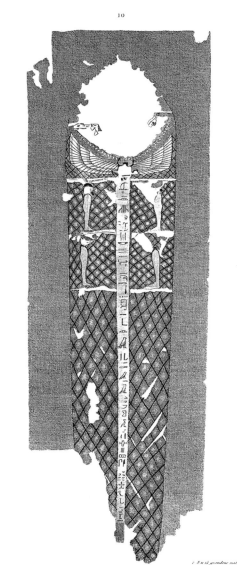

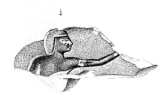

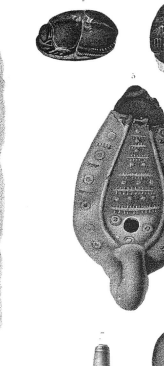

COLLECTION D'ANTIQUES.

Pl. 74.

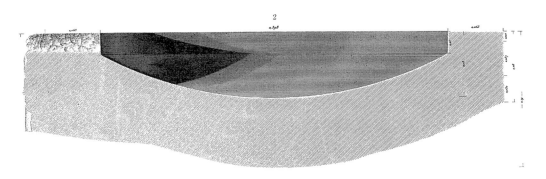

Jomard et Chabrol del.

Allais Sc.

VASE EN GRANIT NOIR, TROUVE PRES DE DAMANHOUR, HERMOPOLIS PARVA.

H. J. Redouté del.   Rrara sc.

VASES EN TERRE CUITE, TROUVÉS À THÈBES, ÉLÉPHANTINE, ALEXANDRIE, DENDERAH, SAQQÂRAH, ANTINOË ET AUTRES ENDROITS.

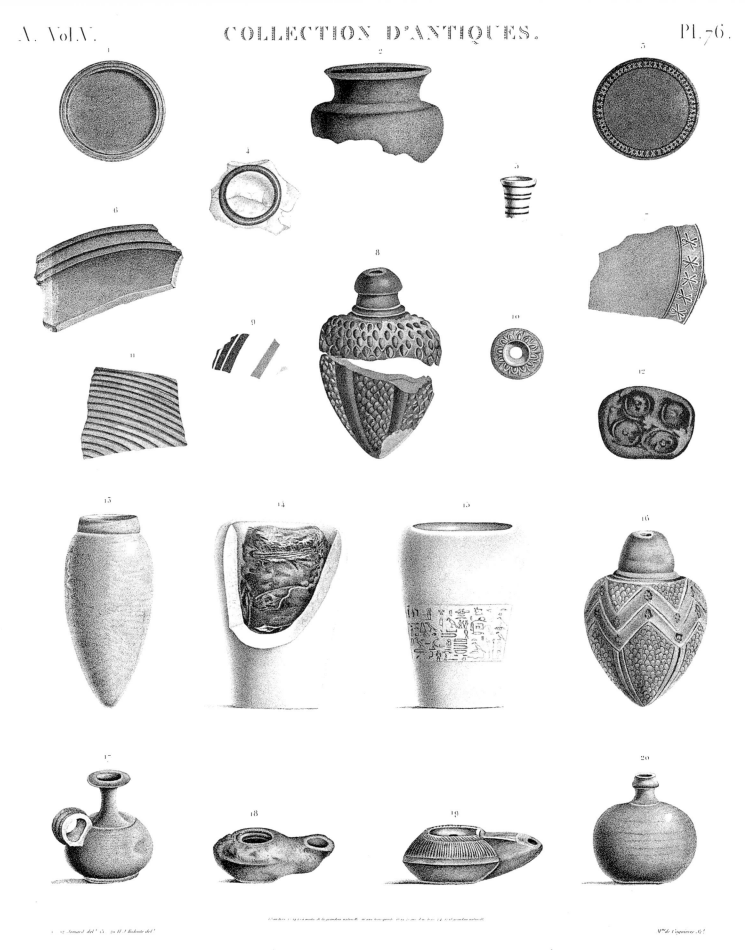

12 Jomard del.t 5. 20 H.J Redouté del.t   M.me de Cinquieres Sc.t

1.2.3.6.7.10.11.17.20 VASES ANTIQUES DE LA HAUTE ÉGYPTE, 8.16 AUTRES VASES, 4.5.9.12 VERRES COLORÉS ET PORCELAINE ANTIQUES.

13.14.15.18.19 POTS DE MOMIE ET LAMPES TROUVÉS A SAQQARAH, THÈBES ET DENDERAH.

Pl. 77.

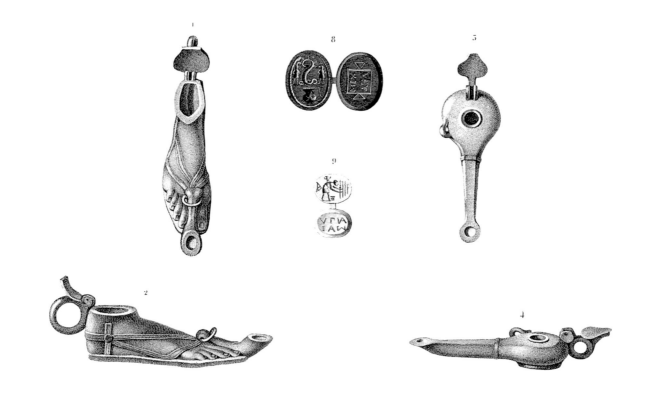

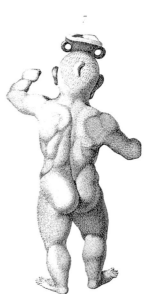

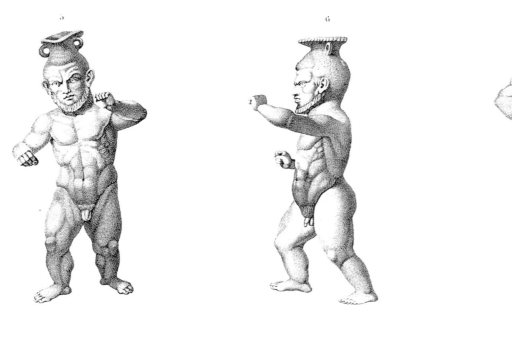

Grandeur naturelle.

Castes del. 8.9 H.J. Redouté del.

Hulk. Sc.

LAMPES EN BRONZE, 8.9 PIERRES GRAVÉES.

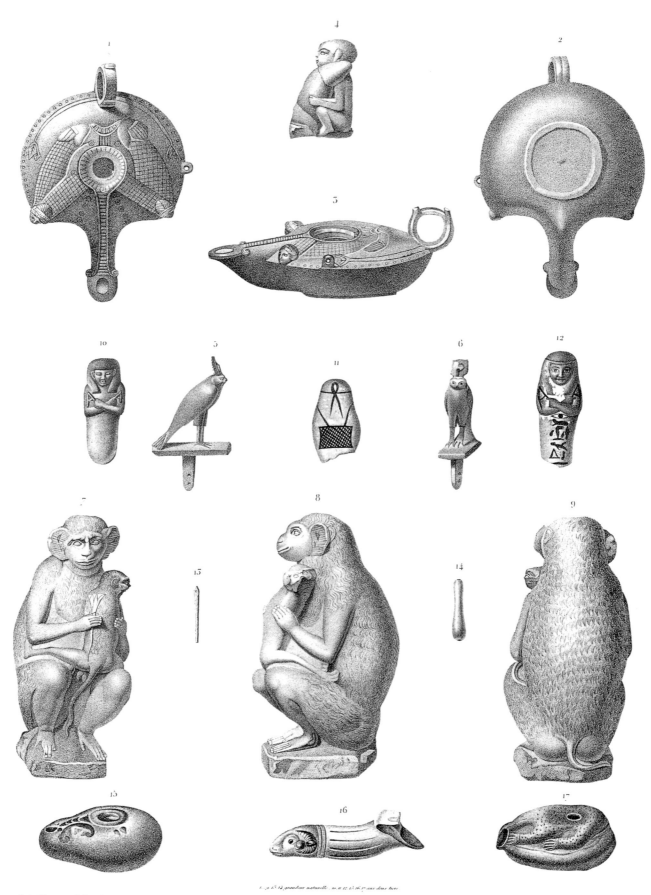

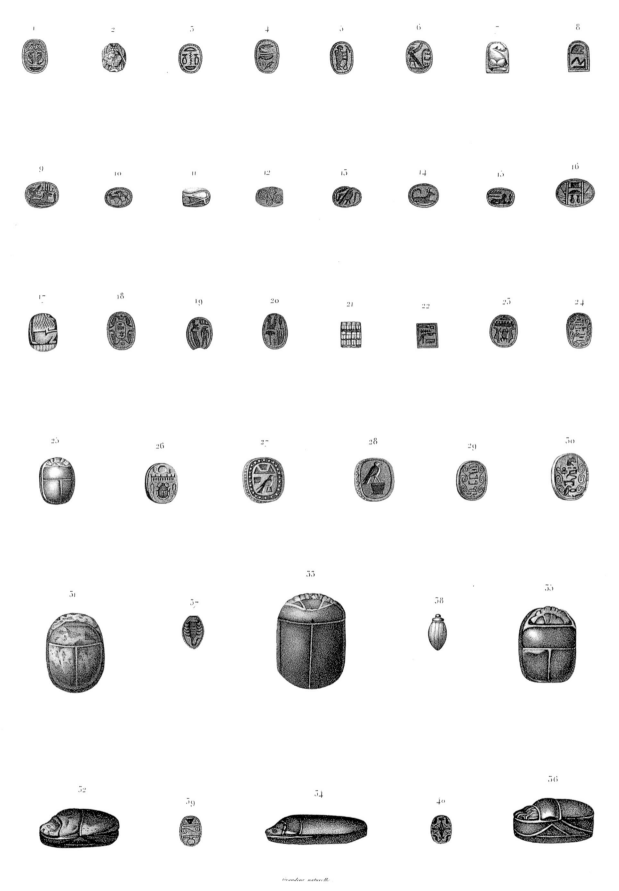

AMULETTES EN FORME DE SCARABÉES, EN TERRE CUITE, EN JADE ET AUTRES PIERRES DURES.

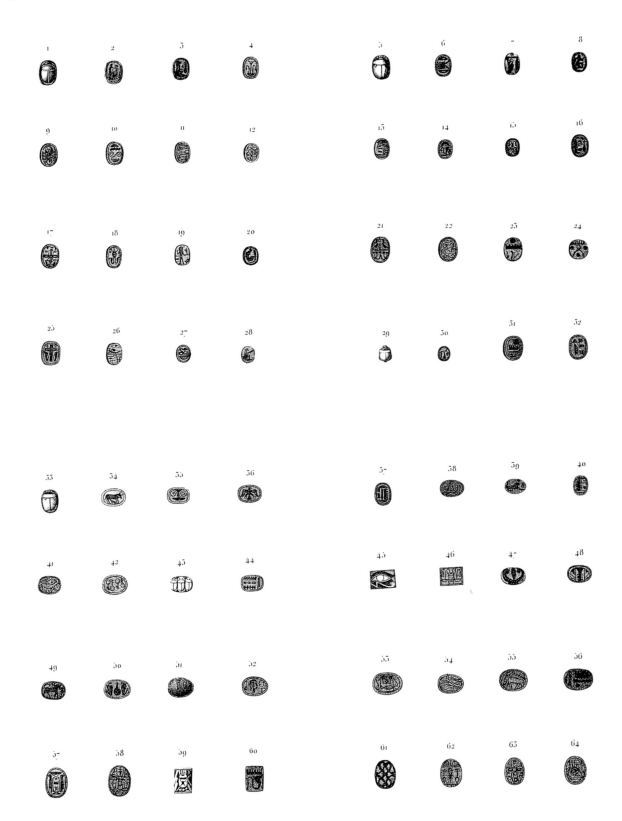

AMULETTES EN FORME DE SCARABÉES, EN TERRE CUITE, EN JASPE ET AUTRES PIERRES DURES.

Grandeur naturelle.

Castex del.

Tassaert Sc.

AMULETTES EN FORME DE SCARABÉES ET DIVERSES FIGURES EN TERRE CUITE, EN ARGENT, EN HÉMATITE ET AUTRES PIERRES DURES.

1.3...18 PIERRES GRAVÉES EN AMÉTHYSTE, JASPE, AGATHE, CORNALINE, LAPIS-LAZULI ET GRENAT. 2 EN VERRE. 19.20.23...36 AMULETTES

EN SCARABÉE ET AUTRES. 21.22.37...46 FIGURES EN TERRE CUITE, EN BOIS ET EN BRONZE.

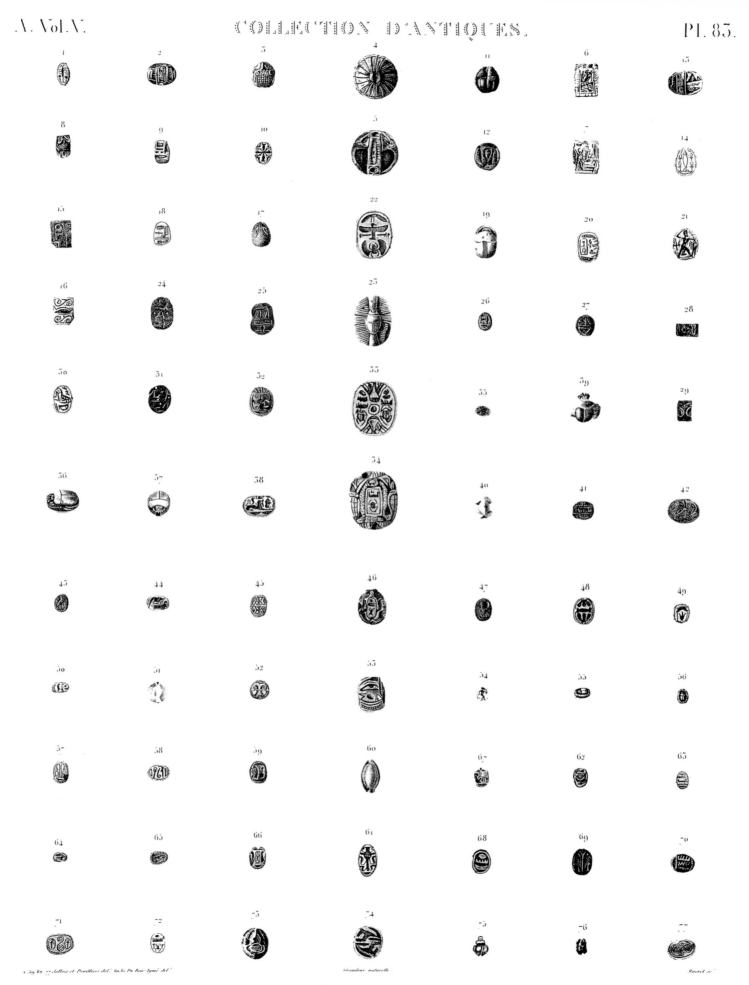

1.39.62. 77. *Sallier et Devilliers del.* 6.6.12. *Du Bois-Aymé del.* *Grandeur naturelle.* *Marcel sc.*

1.2.3.10..14.17..27.29..34.36..39.41..50.55..39.62..77. AMULETTES EN FORME DE SCARABÉE, EN TERRE CUITE ET EN PORCELAINE. 4..9.13.16.28..33.40.51.52.60.61. AUTRES AMULETTES.

1. 16. 14. 20. 25. 26. 51. 32. 42. 43. 49. 55. 57. 616. 72. 76. 78. FIGURES, AMULETTES EN SCARABÉE ET AUTRES, EN TERRE CUITE. 5. 56. FRAGMENS DE SCULPTURE. 15. 16. 18. 19. 24. 56. 65. 66. VASES EN TERRE CUITE.

7. EN BASALTE. 22. 38. 59. 76. EN VERRE. 23. EN ALBÂTRE. 33. 35. PIERRE GRAVÉE EN CORNALINE. 45. EN BRONZE. 46. 47. MÉDAILLE EN OR. 48. EN PIERRE DE TOUCHE.

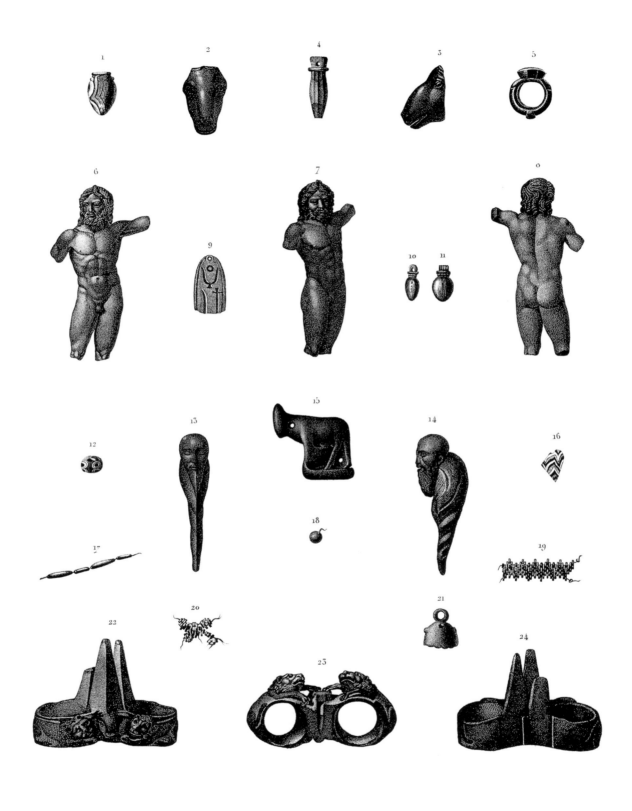

COLLECTION D'ANTIQUES.

Pl. 86.

Adam et Devilliers del.

grandeur naturelle.

Dubois et Chailly sc.

1. 19. 21. 27. 29. 30. 32...34. 36. 38..41. 43. 46. 48. 49..51. 62. 64. 65. FIGURES EN TERRE CUITE. 20. EN MARBRE. 26. 28. 35. 52..54. 11. 15. AMULETTES. 42. 4°. EN PIERRE. 19. EN SERPENTINE. 50. 63. VASE ET LAMPE EN TERRE CUITE.

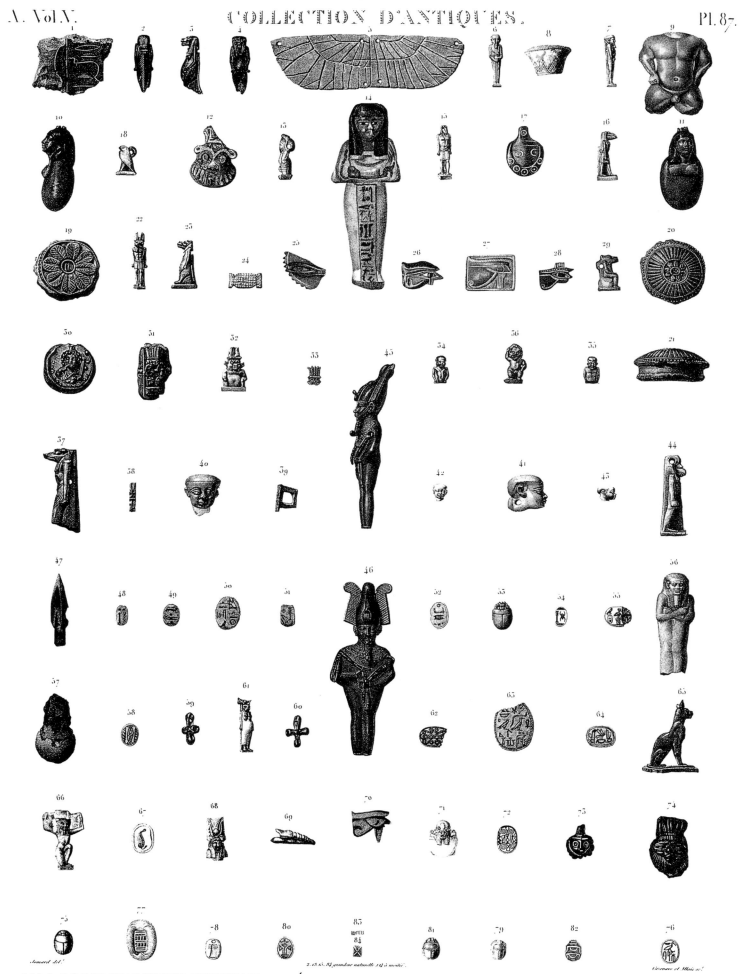

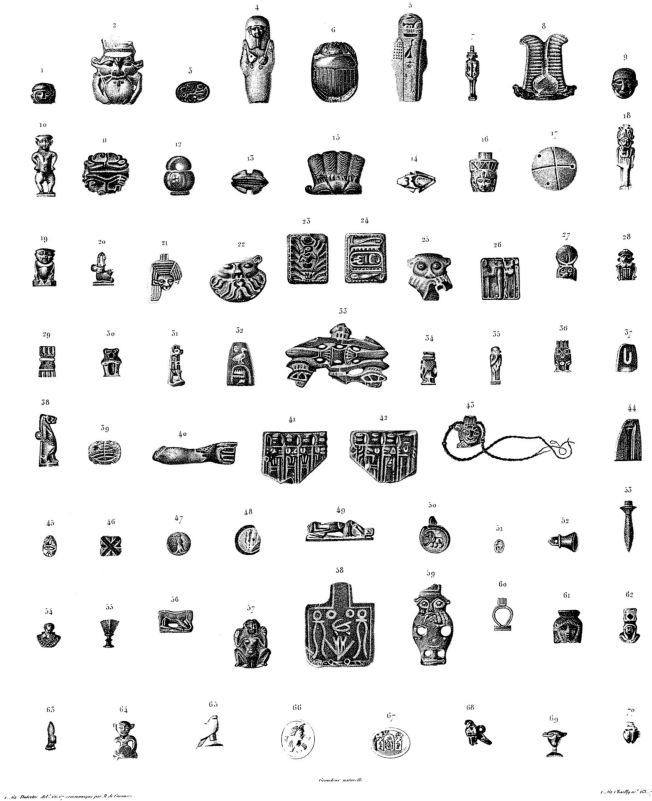

1.2.7..51.55...36.58.59.41...44.46.4..49.52...65.68...70 AMULETTES EN TERRE CUITE. 5.6.45.51 AMULETTES EN FORME DE SCARABÉE. 4.5 FIGURE EN TERRE CUITE.

52.5-.48.50 FRAGMENS À FOND DE COULEUR ÉMAILLÉ, ET VERRES COLORÉS AVEC HIÉROGLYPHES EN BLANC. 40 EN BRONZE.

66.6- PIERRES GRAVÉES, TROUVÉES EN SYRIE.

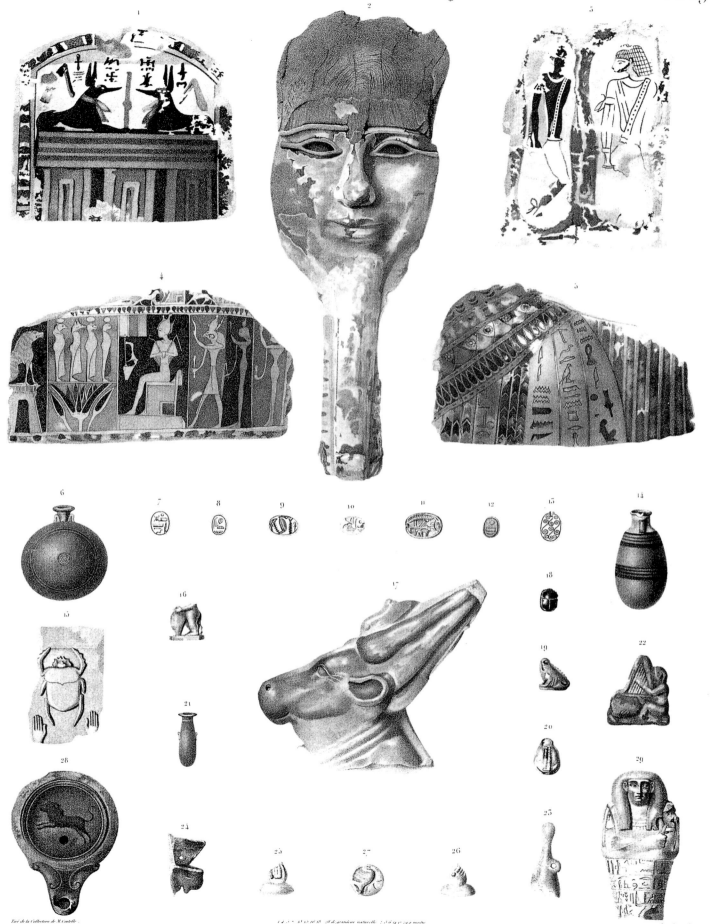

1.3.4.5 TOILES PEINTES. 2 MASQUE EN BOIS. 6.14.28 OBJETS EN TERRE CUITE.-.15.16.18..2-29 DIVERSES FIGURES ET AMULETTES EN FORME
DE SCARABÉES. 15 FRAGMENT DE BAS RELIEF. 17 TÊTE DE BŒUF EN PIERRE.